Springer Series in Supply Chain Management

Volume 10

More information about this series at http://www.springer.com/series/13081

Jayashankar M. Swaminathan • Vinayak Deshpande
Editors

Responsible Business Operations

Challenges and Opportunities

Springer

Editors
Jayashankar M. Swaminathan
Kenan-Flagler Business School
UNC Chapel Hill
Chapel Hill, NC, USA

Vinayak Deshpande
Kenan-Flagler Bussiness School
UNC Chapel Hill
Chapel Hill, NC, USA

ISSN 2365-6395 ISSN 2365-6409 (electronic)
Springer Series in Supply Chain Management
ISBN 978-3-030-51959-9 ISBN 978-3-030-51957-5 (eBook)
https://doi.org/10.1007/978-3-030-51957-5

This Springer imprint is published by the registered company Springer Nature Switzerland AG
The registered company address is: Gewerbestrasse 11, 6330 Cham, Switzerland

Introduction

With the increase in climate emergency, global social inequalities, and a need to develop rural agricultural systems, there is an increased focus on developing responsible business models. Operations plays an integral role in delivering value to any business model; therefore, at present, there is an increased emphasis on responsible operations. The Brundtland commission defines "sustainable development" as development that meets the needs of the present without compromising the ability of future generations to meet their own needs. There are many dimensions of sustainability which are often captured through triads such as the "three Es" (Economics, Environment, and Equity) or the "three P's" (Profit, Planet, and People). Responsible operations includes workforce, environmental, as well as social impact. For example, Goodyear Corporation states responsible operations "includes our day to day efforts to produce high quality products in an efficient manner supported by a culture of health and safety. It also includes managing our environmental impacts. Operating in a responsible manner worldwide leads to protecting our people, our customers/consumers and the planet."

Operations management is defined as the design, operation, and improvement of the systems that create and deliver a firm's primary products and services. The operations function of a firm focuses on adding value through the transformation process of converting inputs to outputs. Since operations has an effect on the value delivery process, from design to procurement to production to delivery, there is tremendous opportunity for firms to make progress on their responsibility mandate through their operations. While firm level corporate responsibility is important, there is also a great need for governments and international agencies to innovate their models of execution to promote development, growth, and inclusion across the world. This book presents a collection of recent innovative research and ideas around responsible operations from leading researchers of the world. In particular, it focusses on two important themes: (1) development of emerging economies and addressing the needs of the bottom of the pyramid and (2) developing responsible practices both within and outside the firm.

Along the first theme, the chapter titled "Value Chain Innovations to Foster Development" by Hau Lee discusses five effective ways to develop innovation strategies for emerging economies. These include—mobilizing ecosystems, product and process innovation, designing the right value chain, leveraging geopolitical lubricants, and servicization. This is followed by the chapter titled "The Impact of Crop Minimum Support Prices (MSP)" by Tang and Chintapalli, which presents alternative models of support prices. By examining the dynamic interactions among farmers for the case when there are two (complementary or substitutable) crops for each farmer to select and grow, it is revealed that regardless of the values of the MSP, price disparity between the crops worsens as complementarity between them increases. Another finding is that offering MSP is not always beneficial to farmers. In fact, offering MSP for a crop can hurt the profit of those farmers who grow that crop especially when the proportion of strategic farmers is sufficiently small. This followed by the chapter titled "Improving Crop Yield: A Model for Plant Growth and Optimal Seeding" by Swaminathan and Zhang, the authors present an innovative model of plant growth and embed that in an optimization framework to study a farmer's planting schedule problem under rainfall uncertainty and planting capacity constraint. They establish the optimal planting schedule given the soil water content, planting capacity, and future rainfall uncertainty. In their computational study, they use field weather data from Southern Africa in a real-size large-scale problem and demonstrate significant relative crop production advantage of the optimal planting schedule over commonly used heuristics in practice. Following this chapter, in the one titled "The Role of Donors in Global Health Supply Chains," Rashkova and Berringer discuss the important role of funding in enabling development and capacity building in emerging countries of the world. They use the global health supply chains to provide the context and utilize that to highlight the shortcomings and potential opportunities. Finally, in the chapter titled "Prepositioning Inventories at UNCEF," Swaminathan et al. describe the benefits of utilizing inventory prepositioning and postponement strategies in the Horn of Africa for PlumpyNut supply chain. They describe the costs, benefits, as well as challenges in implementing such an approach.

The second part of the book deals with development of sustainable practices both within and outside the firm. In the chapter titled "Abilities First Approach to Workforce Inclusion in Organizations," Narayanan et al. describe how Pekham Inc. has developed a robust strategy around inclusion of disabled workers in their firm and the changes they have made to make it a successful endeavor. In the next chapter titled "Socially Responsible Co-Product Design," Lin et al. examine coproduction technologies that manufacture products of different qualities from a common source of raw material to reduce natural resource consumption. Specifically, coproduction technology allows a manufacturer to introduce a new coproduct using raw material that would otherwise be discarded because of its inferior quality relative to conventional quality standards. They examine whether and how a manufacturer should leverage coproduction technology to design its product offerings. In the following chapter titled "Vertical Integration for Corporate Social and Environmental Responsibilities," Deshpande et al. study how Taylor Guitars implemented a series of sustainability efforts related to ebony sourcing. The authors create an analytical model to study the implications of horizontal sourcing and vertical sustainable integration and provide managerial insights about when vertical sustainable sourcing strategy may be beneficial. The next chapter titled "Environmental Sustainability Tradeoffs in a Product Supply Chain" by Olsen et al. compares a product's life cycle perspective to environmental sustainability and highlight the opportunities therein. In the next chapter titled "Renewable Energy Sourcing," Yucel and Agarwal discuss the growing phenomenon related to solar power generation by corporations and consumers. In this chapter, they survey the extant academic literature on sourcing of renewable energy by utility firms and consumers and shed light on the advantages and disadvantages of different mechanisms used by corporations to source renewable energy. Another important aspect of responsibility relates to supply chain transparency. In the next chapter titled "Supply Chain Transparency at Goodio Chocholate," Hamallen et al. examine the topic of supply chain transparency from both practice and academic perspectives. They use the Goodio Chocolate as a case example and discuss how discloser of supply chain practices to consumers can impact their choice. They also present examples of innovative methods that companies are using to provide visibility into their supply chains. In the final chapter titled "Auditing, Inspection and Testing for Social Responsibility in Supply Networks," Dawande and Qi discuss research studies that analyze auditing of suppliers for non-compliance of socially responsible practices such as child labor as well as those papers that analyze inspection and testing of social responsibilities violations such as adulteration of milk.

As a collection, these pioneering chapters uniquely and significantly advance our knowledge of responsible operations and present a path forward for future researchers to explore this important topic in greater depth.

Contents

Value Chain Innovations to Foster Development

Hau L. Lee

Keywords Value chain innovations · Economic development · Supply chain reengineering · Supply chain design · Servicization

Despite the rapid economic development of countries like China and India, there are still many parts of the world where people live in poverty. The World Bank has used income to group countries. Sometimes, we refer to parts of the world with very low per-capita income as "developing world" or "developing economies." Of course, such terms have been criticized as the focus was on categorization instead of the people (Khokhar and Serajuddin 2015). Shifting to people, the low-income economies are plagued with people living in poverty. The World Bank (Global Monitoring Report 2016) has reclassified global extreme poverty as those living on $1.90 or less a day. In 2015, 9.6% of the world's population lived under such a definition of extreme poverty. So our focus should be on how to address the needs and also help improve the welfare of the people in these economies.

Statistics, however, still requires some form of categorization. In the following figure, we can see the prevalence of extreme poverty in different parts of the world. The statistics was based on countries, which perhaps was the basis of the reference to "developing countries" (Fig. 1).

In the remaining of this chapter, we will simply refer to as "developing economies" for regions that have significant population living under extreme poverty. Such economies can be in low-, middle-, or high-income countries.

Value chains are crucial in supporting innovations so that economic development can be supported (Lee and Schmidt 2017). There are many ways in which we can make use of the value chains to accelerate or foster such innovations. I like to share five, illustrated with business cases, in this chapter. These five ways are as follows:

- Mobilize ecosystem to orchestrate the three flows

H. L. Lee (✉)
Stanford Graduate School of Business, Stanford University, Stanford, CA, USA
e-mail: haulee@stanford.edu

J. M. Swaminathan, V. Deshpande (eds.), *Responsible Business Operations*, Springer Series in Supply Chain Management 10,
https://doi.org/10.1007/978-3-030-51957-5_1

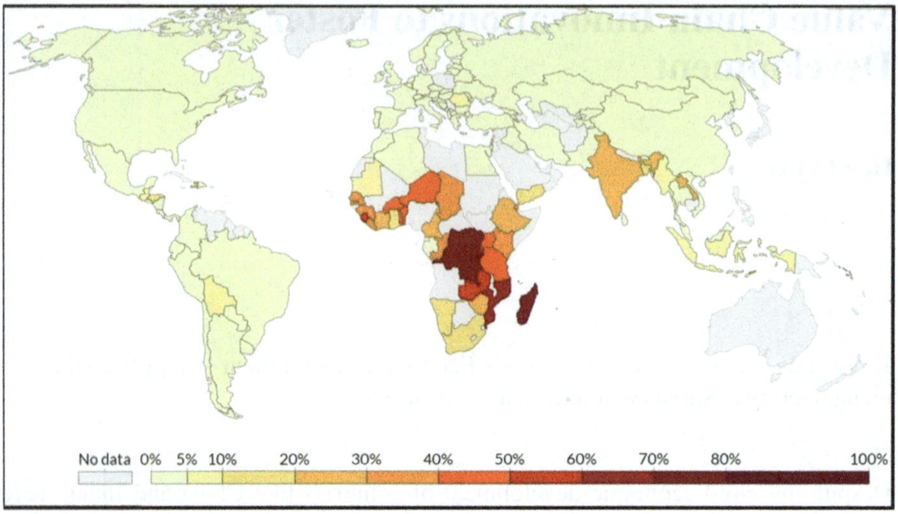

Fig. 1 Prevalence of worldwide extreme poverty. (Source: World Bank 2014)

- Product and process innovation
- Designing the right value chain
- Leveraging geo-political-economic lubricants
- Servicization

1 Mobilize Eco-system to Orchestrate the Three Flows

It is well known that the management of a supply chain or a value chain requires sound coordination of the information, material or service, and financial flows, which can span multiple organizations of the value chain. To help create values and stimulate development in developing economies, we must find ways to re-engineer these three flows under the often challenging environments of developing economies. In this section, we present two case examples to illustrate how the orchestration of the three flows can make a difference.

In Africa, it was estimated that at least 150,000 tons of shea kernels are consumed annually for cooking, as a skin pomade, for medicinal applications, in soap, for lanterns, and for cultural purposes at ceremonies (Rammohan 2010). On the other hand, 90% of shea nuts internationally were used for the food and confectionary industry and for cosmetics. Ghana is a major shea butter-producing country. Per-capita gross domestic product (GDP) in Ghana was $2201 in 2018 (Countryeconomic.com 2018), placing the country 141st out of 196 countries in terms of GDP. Agriculture constituted a major industry of the country. Shea butter trees grew wild in the country, allowing women farmers, many of whom illiterates, to easily pick the fruits from the ground. Loads of nuts were heavy, and it was common that the farmer had to walk down long dirt roads for several kilometers to the village market, where she became a price taker as it would be difficult for her to bring the crops back even if the price was not satisfactory.

Shea butter often had to go through multiple intermediaries before it reached the real buyer. As a result, the prices paid to the women farmers were just a fraction of the final price offered by the buyers. Farmers were also cash-strapped. Hence, when a farmer had unexpected financial needs such as a child getting sick needing hospitalization, she might have to sell her crop prematurely to a middleman who might take advantage of the situation by offering an extremely low price. A farmer therefore was often in extreme poverty position with little hope of recovery.

To alleviate this poverty cycle, SAP, PlaNet Finance, Maata-N-Tudu (MTA), and Grameen Ghana (GG) joined forces in 2009 to create a program to help the women farmers. The program required the orchestration of the three flows in butter production.

To begin, PlaNet Finance, MTA, and GG enlisted women into an organized group called the Star Shea Network (SSN). Such organizations had both physical and financial flow implications. The association gained scale for the farmers, so that they could have better negotiation power with buyers. This scale also affords more efficient trainings using videos on how to produce quality nuts and butter, management of finances, and even group dynamics. One major buyer, Olam International, was also enlisted to be part of the value chain as the market for the outputs of SSN. Olam also provided women with protective gear such as boots and gloves to safeguard against hazards such as snake bites when harvesting shea fruits. This should enable them to collect higher quantities over time.

To improve information flow, SAP developed a website (www.starshea.com) to help market the products to buyers all over the world. A specialized order fulfillment and management software was offered to the farmers to manage orders from buyers. Women are sent SMS text messages regarding logistics information, and market prices from Esoko, a market information exchange. SAP also developed the Microloan Management software to enable field credit officers to monitor their loan portfolios and calculate portfolio aging at a glance.

PlaNet Finance conducted research to understand the credit needs of shea women and key service providers, and with funding from MTA and Grameen Ghana, microloans were provided for purchasing processing equipment, transporters and grinders, for hiring extra labor, or to help cover general expenses during the cash-strapped summer months before nuts were sold (Fig. 2).

Since the launch of the program, the following positive developments were noticed:

- The number of women trained on quality nut and butter processing had grown to 22,000 in 2016; 40 shea companies have become buyers now.
- Farmers received prices at 0.40 cedi (premium) and 0.35 cedi (standard) per kg, which were 82% and 59% increase over prices of distressed sales in the summer.
- 50% reduction of distressed sales by farmers.

Fig. 2 Innovating with the three flows for Ghana shea butter farmers

Going forward, proper growing method, sanitized product, processing capabilities could lead to shea butter to be used as special products with higher values, for example, 100% natural handcrafted shea butter, shea body balm, and shea butter oil in cosmetics. This would further increase the incomes of the farmers.

The second case is based on hazelnut plantation in Bhutan. The GDP per capita in Bhutan was $3160 in 2018 (Plecher 2019), ranked 161st in the world. Among the total population, 69 percent lived in rural areas as farming was their main source of income. Out of this, 40 percent lived at subsistence level, with income at less than $1 a day (Hoyt and Lee 2011). To make ends meet, many young men had to leave the country to serve as migrant workers in neighboring countries, destroying the harmony and happiness of family life with their wives and children. Farmers had also deforested to make room to grow crops, resulting in severe soil erosion. Mountain Hazelnut (MH) was created as a social enterprise that would provide farming jobs with stable income, while at the same time improve environmental sustainability in rural Bhutan.

The co-founders of MH identified hazelnut as a crop that could be introduced in Bhutan, since the weather and soil conditions there were suitable. Hazelnut was a high-value crop with increasing demand worldwide. Yet, there was a constraint in supply, as not too many countries besides Turkey, Italy, and the United States could be fit for the cultivation of such a crop.

Farmers in Bhutan were initially skeptical, as they had never grown such a crop before, and it was known that much knowhow was needed to get good yield in growing hazelnut. MH has to innovate in new ways to orchestrate the three flows.

First is the physical flow. It might be too much to ask for the farmers in Bhutan to grow hazelnuts from seed to tree. Instead, MH found it more effective to cultivate hazelnuts tissues in in laboratories in Yunnan, China. Then, the tissues were flown to nurseries in the eastern part of Bhutan, where the tissues were grown to become baby trees. The farmers would then grow the baby trees to maturity. When the crops were ripe for harvest, the collection and transportation flows needed to be developed as well. Since Bhutan is a land-locked country, MH had to invest in logistics processes for the collection of the nuts, processing and warehousing them, then transporting them to cross the border to ports in India or Bangladesh possibly by trucks and rails, and then using ocean freight to get the products to the markets in Europe and China.

Moreover, MH innovated with the hillside conservation methods so that the trees could be planted on degraded slopes, in fallow land, or land otherwise unusable for food crops. The hazelnut roots could stabilize erosion-prone soil. This showed that MH was actually making a positive contribution to the environment, including stabilizing slopes, reducing erosion, protecting watersheds, reducing the amount of forest cut to obtain fuelwood, and sequestering firewood. It was a way to gain acceptance of the local communities to the introduction of the crop there.

One major challenge was that the physical road infrastructure in Bhutan was not well established; hence, it would be very difficult for the MH experts to travel to the farmers to give them advice from time to time on the proper ways to grow the crop, make appropriate irrigation and trimming work as weather changed, monitor their progress, diagnose potential problems, and help make treatment plans. Doing so would require innovations in the information flow. MH instituted a comprehensive system to track all its trees starting at the stage of tissue culture. The pictures of the tree and the farmer, his ID number, his field, and the GPS location were taken and tracked. MH built 25 solar-powered standalone weather stations across Bhutan to monitor weather conditions and climate change. Then, they used technologies such as mobile phones to make use of the weather information to provide farmers with advanced information on growing conditions, advice on orchard management, and adapt farming techniques to climate change. The phones could also be used to monitor the growth of the trees; to give instructions to farmers; and to provide right information to help farmers to irrigate, fertilize, and take care of the trees. It was possible for farmers to take pictures of the trees and send them to MH to diagnose problems or monitor progress. The information flow was supplemented by MH "field monitors" who would visit each field approximately once a month, depending on the season. They carried GPS devices and digital cameras, photographed the fields, filled out forms, and geotagged their photographs.

Besides the information and physical flows, MH also had to align the financial flows. First, MH could not sell the baby trees from their nurseries to farmers, even at a low price like $1 per tree. This was because even $1 was considered to be too high to the farmers, and many farmers also did not have the confidence that they could grow hazelnuts well to justify the investment. As a result, MH chose to give to the baby trees to farmers for free, on the condition that, when nuts were collected, MH would purchase them from the farmers according to preagreed upon prices. In addition, a new business model was created to gain the trust and acceptance of the local government and communities—MH would give 20% of the revenue back to the local communities.

MH's target was to plant 10 million trees over a 5-year period, and eventually had 15% of Bhutan's population engaged in hazelnut farming, reducing the number of migrant workers, restoring complete families, and lifting many out of poverty along the way (Fig. 3).

Orchestrating the three flows in value chains has always been of great interest to operations management researchers. The challenge is to study how the three flows

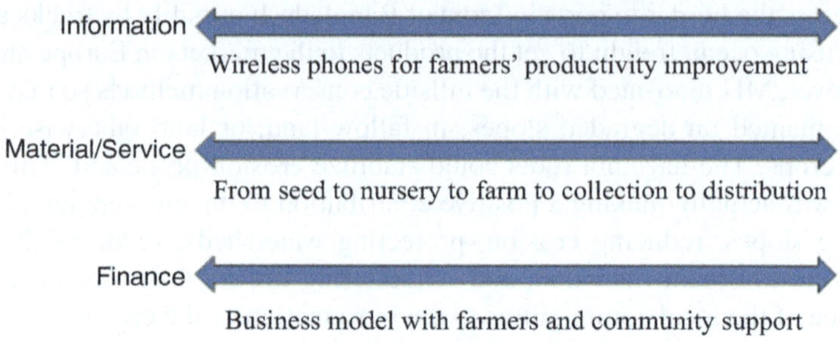

Fig. 3 Innovating with the three flows at mountain hazelnuts

interact: in some cases, one may substitute another; in another, one can change the timing of another; and finally, we can use one flow to re-engineer the other flows. In developing economies, we have to understand the obstacles faced by having efficient, accurate, and timely flows, due to the lack of infrastructure in information, logistics, and finance.

2 Product and Process Innovations

For enterprises in developing economies to prosper and grow, or to add value to the overall value chain, innovations in products or processes may help or accelerate the development. Often times, such innovations may have to be initiated or resulted from investments by global enterprises. This is because global companies have the financial means and the engineering resources for such innovations, and that they have the necessary network of other companies to participate in making the innovations scalable. With the innovations, enterprises in developing economies can participate in the value chain, adding values and gaining from such participation. Global companies, of course, benefit from such developments, since the innovations can bring forth better products or improved processes to begin with, and they also gain valuable partners from these economies in the overall value chain. Partners can contribute as supply sources, as additional innovation collaborators, or as channels of markets.

The McDonald's India case (Rammohan 2015) is one that I like to use to illustrate this point. McDonald's entered the Indian market in the early 1990s. French fries were very popular with Indian customers, and the supply of MacFries was critical to the company's success in India. In the beginning, McDonald's joint venture partner McCain, itself the largest producer of frozen French fries and potato specialties, invested in French fry processing plant and machinery, and storage facilities. The resulting fries, however, were oily and limp, since the locally sourced potatoes did not contain the ideal amount of solids and the desired size. As a result, McDonald's had to resort to imports from the United States, which was tricky, since the Indian government had many restrictions with high customs duties of 56% for potatoes, in order to protect the domestic industry. The lead time for imports was also long, at around 60 days. The alternative was to import frozen fries from New Zealand, the United States and Europe, again with steep import duties. As the market grew, it was clear that imports would not be a long-term solution to satisfy the demand for MacFries.

Recognizing that innovating in developing the right potato using the right growing method locally was the way to go, McCain's began to work on potato agronomy—a branch of agriculture dealing with field crop production and soil management. This way, they could develop the right variety of potato so that potatoes could be grown and produced into French fries within India.

The first big focus would have to be cultivating the appropriate variety of potato where current suppliers had failed. McCain learned that cultivating potato seeds in high elevations was ideal, because seeds grown at high altitude had high vigor, enabling a commercial crop planted with those seeds to have higher yield and larger-sized potatoes. So, it instituted a Shepody potato seed multiplication program in the 13,000-foot high part of the Himalayan mountain range in Northern India. Seeds were sown in May, and harvested and brought back by donkeys in September.

Second, farmers would need to grow the full potatoes in a suitable, more accessible location than the Himalayas. Here, McCain conducted regional trials to locate the ideal growing area, and experimented with 13 types of potatoes to pinpoint the right variety. They also conducted management trials to identify the best combination of growing practices, and storage trials to figure out the best protocol for storing potatoes. From this experimentation, McCain zeroed in on the central Indian state Gujarat as the prime growing area. Three varieties were identified that could work. McCain established a one-acre demonstration farm to show farmers how to improve yields through better sowing, drip irrigation, and better harvesting techniques. The company transformed storage practices by applying a potato sprout suppressant in combination with using controlled temperature storage. This helped to avoid deterioration in potato quality during storage.

With seeds planted in September and October, the potatoes were harvested in February and March. Once they were processed into fries, the fries were frozen and sent to third-party logistics storage facilities or to McDonald's distribution centers. From here, they were shipped to restaurants.

In 2007, after many years of refinements to agronomy and developing farmer partnerships, McCain was finally able to produce fries that met McCain and McDonald's specifications. By 2008, 30 percent of McDonald's India's supply was being manufactured locally. By 2010, that number had grown to 75 percent. In 2012, imports had become necessary only on rare occasions (Fig. 4).

The benefits to McDonald's from using local fries were a 30 percent lower cost structure and no exposure to the fluctuating exchange rate. With local fries, inventory levels were reduced from an average holding of 15 days for imported fries to 6 days for local fries. The reduction in shipping time (60 days from the United States to less than a day for getting local product) also had a significant benefit for risk management and contingency planning.

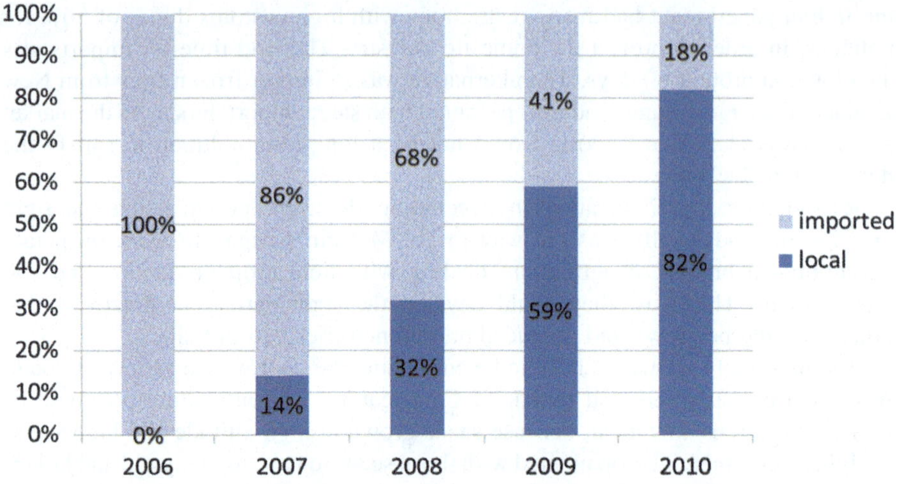

Fig. 4 McDonald's potato supply. (Source: McDonald's India with permission)

There were benefits to farmers as well. Traditionally, farmers sold produce at the local "mandi," or village market. Mandi sales and prices could fluctuate dramatically. The benefits to farmers of doing business with McCain were guaranteed sales of farm output, an increase in yields of 30–40 percent compared with "regular" potatoes, reduction in operating costs, increased and predictable farm income, and reduction in consumption of natural resources like water.

This case illustrated how local farmers could participate in the global value chain and increase their economic value capture, as a result of innovations created by a global enterprise. The innovations include experimentations to find the right potato types (product innovation) and the right farming and growing method (process innovation). The original objective of the global enterprise could be a selfish one, which in this case was about getting local supply to avoid the headache of having to import potatoes and fries with complex restrictions, heavy customs duties, and the risk associated with long lead time and fluctuating exchange rates. But the innovations have resulted in value-creation for the local farmers.

As discussed, product and process innovations often have to be initiated by a large-scale global enterprise that has the financial means and R&D capability to pursue such innovations. The beneficiaries are the small- and median-sized enterprises in developing economies, as well as the global enterprise itself. But how can one safeguard that such innovations might not spill over to competitors of the global enterprise, or does it matter? In addition, to convince and induce the players in the developing economies, such as the farmers in the case of McDonald's, to be willing to take part in this undertaking, which was not without risks, what kind of incentive systems are necessary? These are all interesting research questions.

3 Designing the Right Value Chain

Besides the product and process innovations of the last section, innovations can be in the form of the value chain design, that is, the right configuration of what part to own and what part to outsource, and what part to be offshored and what part to be done on-shore. In developing economies, with uncertain environment and challenging infrastructure, figuring out the right configuration, or the right value chain, is important for successful ventures.

I will use the Mekelle poultry case to illustrate the importance of designing the right value chain (Elist and Kennedy 2014). The case was based on Ethiopia, a country in which chicken price was higher than that of beef due to chronic supply shortage, and had been rising over 100 percent in merely 5 years from 2005 to 2010. Despite the rising chicken price, many poultry farms had gone out of business in Ethiopia because of the steep cost of animal feed, contributing to the undersupply problem.

Mekelle Poultry Farms was formed in 2010 by two young entrepreneurs, after intensive negotiations with the regional government. To launch the company, the pair gave minority equity stake to the regional government, which enabled Mekelle be granted a 10-year lease on the poultry farm. Their deal with the government also came with some difficult stipulations: the pair could not legally sell any part of the farm; the chickens had to be sold at a certain size; and chicken sales were capped at $2.25 for month-old chickens. Mekelle planned to import live day-old chicks (DOCs), raise them, and then sell them to the government 1 month later for distribution to local markets. Their initial calculations suggested that they could achieve gross margins of 20 percent under this model. Thus, the initial value chain design was to procure DOC from abroad, and focus on raising the DOC to one-month old chicken. Thereafter, distribution was provided by the government. Mekelle felt that this would minimize its risks, as egg hatching to raise DOC required more substantial investment, and was risky, while with the government taking control of logistics distribution and sales, there was a level of stability and reliability that reduced risks.

However, Mekelle soon found that their design did not work well. First, their costs were much higher than they had anticipated. Each DOC would cost them $0.45, and the cost to transport them from India (a global leader in exporting DOCs) was $0.55 per DOC. Moreover, working with the government turned out to be not easy. While the government had guaranteed sales, distribution, and the cost of transportation, there was no stipulation on repercussions or remedies for Mekelle Farms should the government be late in picking up the chickens. In the initial months of operation, the government was picking up chickens closer to the 60-day mark than the 30-day mark, adding significant costs to feeding, vaccinating, and raising the chickens. They were also late in distributing the chickens to the local farmers after they had been picked up.

More damaging was the fact that it was unclear whether or not the government's price cap included sales taxes, which ran up to 15 percent of the retail price. The government insisted that the $2.25 cap included taxes, which Mekelle Farms had not accounted for in their financial projections.

Faced with mounting losses, Mekelle had to revamp their value chain. Instead of importing live DOCs, Mekelle Farms decided to import eggs, which cost about $0.60 each, including transportation to the farm. The variable costs for hatching the eggs were minimal, and Mekelle Farms had to acquire the necessary equipment. The key is to ensure that the hatching process was sanitized to allow for healthy hatching of the eggs at a 60 percent rate to break even, and continue improving the rate so as to get some decent margin. This turned out to be a very difficult task, since it was not possible to control the quality of the imported eggs. Plus, there was the unexpected delay incurred at customs in Dubai, so that the inventory of imported eggs was stuck for days.

To succeed, Mekelle needed to gain greater control over the eggs, that is, they had to continue the vertical integration of the egg and DOC production stages. They decided to build a parent stock by importing 3450 chickens to produce eggs on-site. Eggs produced by the parent stock were incubated and hatched. With well-controlled process and sanitary conditions, they finally achieved an averaged hatch rate of 76 percent.

With egg-production brought in-house, input costs were now under control. But there were still significant costs related to raising the chickens for 30 full days. Mekelle Farms redesigned the outbound part of their value chain by selling DOCs to local farmers who would then raise the DCO to maturity, thereby capturing the highest margin segment of the value chain and offloading the riskiest portion of the operation.

The biggest question facing Mekelle Farms management was whether they could establish a network of local poultry farmers who could effectively and efficiently raise DOCs into month-old chickens. It was important to enlist model farmers who would be trained to do a good job, and who would then serve as their stable outlets as well as recruiters of other farmers. To support these farmers with high success rate, Mekelle Farms provided vaccinations for the chickens, sold feed to the farmers at cost, provided equipment to raise the chickens, offered marketing assistance, provided mortality coverage for any chickens that died in transit, and offered free delivery of the DOCs to the model farmers (Fig. 5).

In order to achieve this brand equity and establish greater trust with model farmers and end users, the team looked to leverage their relationship with the regional government, given the fact that the government was held in such high esteem among residents of the region. The partners realized that, as in most frontier markets, it was not a question of whether to work with the government, but rather a question of how. Their initial value chain design was built on the assumption that the government would be efficient, formal, and timely in logistics—assumptions that ultimately proved naive. Nevertheless, the government was adept at farmer mobilization, communication, and messaging, and proved to be a successful platform for building brand recognition and trust with farmers. The partners worked to incorporate the government's strengths into their business model. Since taking

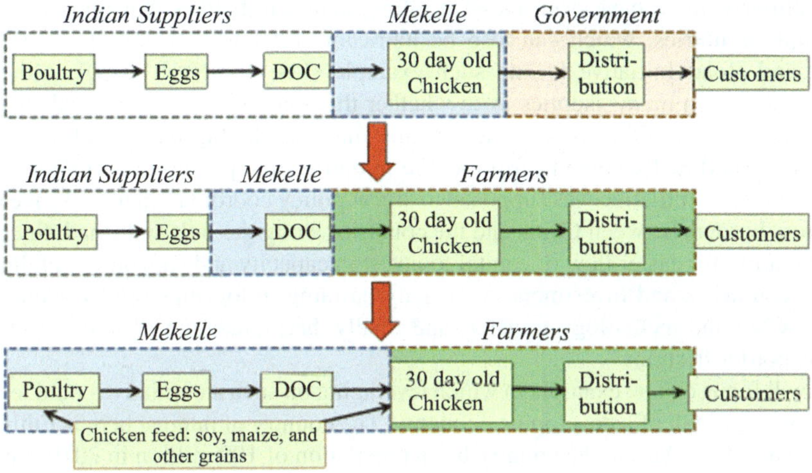

Fig. 5 Evolution of Mekelle Farms' value chain design

over the poultry farm, Mekelle Farms had increased production from 15,000 chicks per year under government ownership to over 360,000 DOCs per year.

Value chain design requires answering the question of what to outsource and what to do in-house, as well as whether to do the task locally or remotely. In standard operations management problems, such design decisions have been the subject of research. In developing economies, the added complexities of the significant role of regional governments in either being help or obstacles must be factored into such decisions. Often, incentive alignment under special institutional and cultural settings is also necessary to make the right design decisions.

4 Leverage Geo-Political-Economic Lubricants

While economic values are often created in the private sector, we should not forget about the nonmarket forces that could either be lubricants or deterrents to business success. Deterrents could be in the form of taxes and customs, government regulations, corruptions and bureaucracy, and potential interventions by groups of vested interests such as NGOs. But there are lubricants, in the form of favorable trade treaties and agreements, local support in subsidies, and existing infrastructure investments by governments.

In Cohen and Lee (2020), the exponential growth of regional trade agreements indicated that there were opportunities in understanding the implications of the often complicated agreements. These agreements may serve as lubricants provided that they covered the right products and regions that could impact a company.

Similarly, there have been massive infrastructure initiatives that often involved multiple countries, which can also be lubricants for business opportunities. The Belt and Road Initiative is one such example (Lee and Shen 2020). Although there have been many skeptics as to whether this initiative was a political strategy for China's expansion agenda, and whether many of the big-budget infrastructure projects could really come to fruition, the initiative did open up opportunities. The Belt and Road Initiative was supposed to aim at policy coordination to make it easier to cross borders between China and the countries along the Belt and Road; financial cooperation for easier flow of capital to invest in capacity and capability building in these countries; and investment in capacity building in logistics infrastructure and knowledge and technology transfer; and finally, harmonization of trade to reduce cross-border frictions.

I will focus on one example in which leveraging on such an initiative could lead to economic growth of a developing economy. The country of interest here is Ethiopia. Located in East Africa, the country has a population of 109 million in 2019 (ranked 12th in the world), 60% of which were below the age of 25. The country was among the poorest in the world, with per capita GDP of $790 in 2018 (The World Bank 2019). Yet the country had potentials, as the working population was relatively well educated, with English being a common foreign language. Their working wage was among the lowest in Africa, only 1/10 of that in China (Lee and Shen 2020). How could such potentials be developed?

The first lubricant was internal government support. The Ethiopian Government had identified the textile and apparel industry as a focal industry as part of its ambitious target to steer the country to be the leading manufacturing hub in Africa. Industry associations had been set up to provide training and skill improvements of workers. While the Belt and Road Initiative was being developed, major apparel companies started to explore and build up Ethiopia as part of their value chain. For example, H&M and PVH had started to source from the country. The moves by such major companies signaled that this could be a promising country to source from. Chinese manufacturers such as Huajian has also started manufacturing shoes in Ethiopia.

The second lubricant was external trade treatments. Ethiopian apparel and shoe exporters enjoyed duty-free access to the US market, thanks to the African Growth and Opportunity Act, which was renewed by the American government in 2015 for another decade. In addition, the country also enjoyed duty-free access to EU as well as preferential treatment to Japan.

Some lubricants were natural resources that required proper investments and developments to turn them to be of value. Ethiopia had great potential of cotton supply as inputs to textile and garment manufacturing. It was also one of the largest untapped livestock resources in the world. Working with the tanning industry, cattle, sheep, and goat hides could be turned into a variety of leather, thereby providing material sources for the shoe industry. Ethiopia also enjoyed low electricity cost, due to the country having one of the largest hydroelectric power dam in the continent.

Finally, the biggest break came in as logistics infrastructure support. Ethiopia is a landlocked country without a sea port. The only way to get products out through ocean freight is to get the products trucked to the nearest seaport in Djibouti, a neighboring country. The road to Djibouti was highly congested, and the port capacity of Djibouti in handling cargoes had already maxed out. Lead time delays would have deterred expansion of the manufacturing sector in Ethiopia. Under the Belt and Road Initiative, Chinese firms have invested heavily in a new national road network as well as an electrified railway line that connect Ethiopia to the port in Djibouti. Chinese firms had also invested in capacity-building in Ethiopia. The Hawassa Industrial Park was built by a Chinese contractor at an unprecedented speed of 9 months. The park was devoted solely to apparel and textile. The Chinese firms also brought in know-hows for the Ethiopian factories to improve their sustainability performances. For example, the Hawassa Industrial Park boasted zero-emission water treatment plant. The initial positive results had lured global brands, such as Calvin Klein and Tommy Hilfiger, to manufacture in Ethiopia.

In the "Vision and Actions on Jointly Building Silk Road Economic Belt and 21st-Century Maritime Silk Road" in 2015 (NDRC et al. 2015), the Chinese government has declared that "The Belt and Road Initiative aims to ..., and establish entrepreneurial and investment cooperation mechanisms." Hence, it was part of its game plan to foster entrepreneurial development in developing economies, so that there could be more new supply sources as well as demand points, leading to economic growth along the Belt and Road.

Besides government-led efforts, lubricants could exist through investments by global enterprises. In March 2017, Alibaba launched its first global digital free trade zone in Malaysia, as part of the electronic world trade platform (eWTP) that Alibaba founder Jack Ma wanted to champion. The vision of eWTP was to lower trade barriers and provide more equitable access to markets for small- and medium-sized enterprises (SMEs) around the world. The digital free trade zone consisted of a regional logistics center near Kuala Lumpur International Airport, with speedy storage, fulfilment, customs clearance, and warehousing operations. A one-stop solution platform had been set up to provide export facilitation support to local SMEs, with services ranging from marketing and customs clearance, to streamlined permit application procedures and tax declaration, etc. Such a platform would help stimulate developments of SMEs, enabling them to participate in the global value chains. In turn, such developments would bring forth economic benefits to the communities where such SMEs reside.

In 2018, a US$600 million Technology and the Innovation Fund was launched by eWTP (Daily Times 2018). "The fund's mission is to drive strategic investments that helps companies accelerate their international expansion and support ideas that drive life-changing technological innovations around the world, including initiatives closely related to the "One Belt, One Road" push." Lubricants therefore included direct financial support.

Lubricants are helpful to foster development, provided that your products or service and the geographies match up with the lubricants. However, these lubricants are not risk-free. For example, favorable trade agreements are subject to renewals, and changes in the terms of the trade agreements are common. They are often the result of political negotiations between countries that is beyond economic rationales. In addition, we have to recognize that a lubricant to you may also be a lubricant to your competitor. When multiple companies move in the same direction, it changes the economics of the original initiative. For example, as more and more companies are manufacturing in Ethiopia, even the new highways connecting the manufacturing hubs to Djibouti will become congested, and the logistics bottlenecks may make it no longer attractive to manufacture there. This calls for research that incorporates new dimensions in risk management and modeling the effects of externalities and network effects.

5 Servicization

Developing economies face challenges that the local workers might not have the education and skill level for the particular business needs for growth, and the poor logistics infrastructure would also inhibit easy access and movements to provide support in such situations. The result is that, even if there were powerful equipment that could enhance productivity in the developing economies, the full potential of such equipment could not be realized. Here, one can innovate in the form of providing the usage of the equipment as a service, that is, "servicization." Orsdemir et al. (2018) defined servicization as "Servicization is a business strategy to sell the functionality of a product rather than the product itself." It is a way to enable workers and small businesses in developing economies to make use of productivity enhancement tools and equipment, so as to improve their business performances.

I will use the Netafim case (Michlin 2006) to illustrate this. Agriculture had traditionally been a low-tech industry. However, innovative technologies have been introduced into the agricultural industry that could improve the productivity of the farm, enhanced logistics and distribution, and allow the farmers to capture greater values of their farm produce (see Lee et al. 2017). Irrigation was one part of the farming production process, which has seen significant technological advancements.

Water shortage has been a major challenge faced by many parts of the world, and it was estimated that, by 2050, two-thirds of the population will be faced with water scarcity (Mancosu et al. 2015). Agriculture required fresh water and so it has been the industry that had been hit hard with the water shortage problem. Farm irrigation consumed significant amount of water and, hence, innovative methods to reduce water usage in irrigation have been a major focus.

The irrigation market was generally divided into two segments: low-pressure irrigation and high-pressure irrigation. Low-pressure irrigation was almost synonymous with flood or furrow irrigation, a method that was based on flooding all or part of a field. Though flood irrigation wasted water and caused soil erosion, it was still widely used around the globe, especially in underdeveloped countries due to its low cost. Drip irrigation was a method of controlled, high-pressure irrigation in which water was either dripped onto the precise part of the soil surface, or delivered to the root system of plants. Drip irrigation saved water usage significantly, and it prevented leaf diseases and improve crop yields. The main barriers to adoption were its relatively high price and that it required the farmer to be skilled in installing and operating the equipment to achieve maximum benefit from the system.

Netafim was one of the world leaders in drip irrigation. Its irrigation system consisted of networks of drip-points that were armed with microprocessors, which allowed direct control of the timing, speed, and duration of the drips. Such controls could be customized based on weather conditions, the soil environment, and the kinds of crops that the farmers were growing. By 2017, Netafim's annual revenue had reached almost $1 billion with earnings of $133 million (Arnold 2018).

While Netafim had been successful in selling their powerful drip irrigation systems to farmers in the United States, Italy, and Australia, etc., the company's global expansion in developing economies faced roadblocks. Agriculture was the most important industry sector for many developing economies, and so the potential of Netafim's system for such economies was great. But the challenges in these economies were many. First, farmers were often uneducated and so requiring them to operate such a sophisticated system was almost impossible. Second, farmers lacked financial means to purchase such a system, and financial institutions like the IFC, which usually would be the source for such applications, were reluctant to give out loans to farmers as it was difficult to expect that the farmers would be able to use the system well, improve crop yields, and increase their incomes, thereby being able to pay the loan back. Third, even if Netafim was willing to invest in having their engineers to travel to the farms to help tune the controls of the system periodically, the logistics to reach the farmers could be equally challenging, as many of the farms were in rural areas without access to paved roads.

To penetrate to the markets in developing economies, Netafim initiated the development of a system called Crop Management Technologies (CMT). The first models included a collection of sensors, some of which were soil-installed, while others worked in the air. These sensors received regular input on levels of soil water content, salinity, fertilizer, and meteorological data. Also included was an irrigation computer that controlled irrigation and fertilization frequency, as well as scheduling. The input received was radio-transmitted to a central control system, with figures/graphs made visible on the computer screen, thus enabling a controller to review the results and make any required modifications. CMT's latest generation device allowed Netafim agronomists stationed in Israel to monitor data over the Internet and guide farmers by phone, mail, or online communications. Netafim's narrow plastic pipes, which revolutionized the field of drip irrigation a half-century ago, also contained sensors and software that allowed farmers to monitor and control their fields via mobile phone (Fig. 6).

The value of CMT was that a farmer, who did not have much knowledge or skill in operating such an advanced system, could enjoy the productivity benefits of having such a system. The Netafim controller would be doing the job of what a sophisticated farmer in developed economy in monitoring and controlling the system. Indeed, with the advanced data analytics inside Netafim, the drips were even more precise and optimal than what most farmers would be able to do. The CMT setup could also be used to help farmers apply fertilizers and manage energy in more optimal manner. This is like servicization of the irrigation task of the farmers.

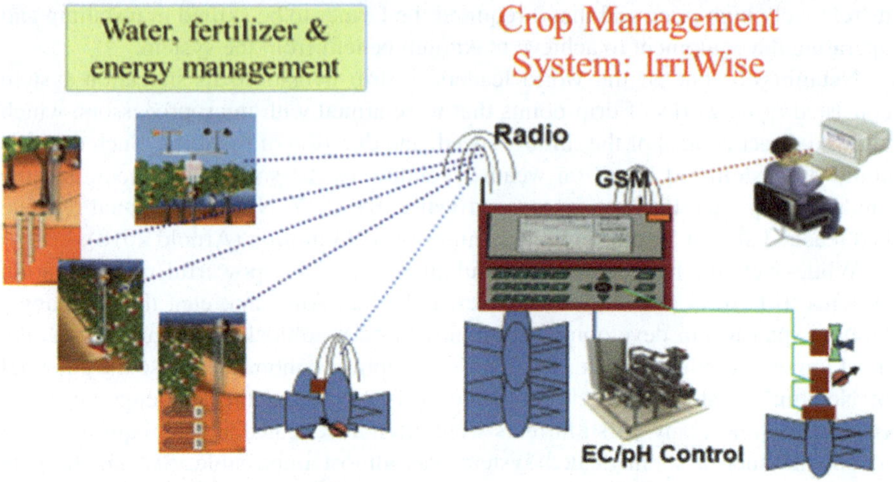

Fig. 6 Netafim's crop management system

As an added benefit, the collection of Web-based version of the CMT would enable Netafim to receive direct streams of information from hundreds of thousands of fields around the world. Netafim's agronomists would then use this data for research and would serve as online consultants and as facilitators of information-sharing between farmers. For example, farmers, growing similar crops in similar growing conditions in different countries around the world, would be able to share best practices through the portal and help each other with fertilization formulas, pesticide fumigation, irrigation plans, etc.

It is interesting to note that, in the past, Netafim aspired to be the "Best drip irrigation equipment company." Today, they viewed themselves as a solution provider, and the motto of the company now read "Grow More with Less".

Servicization is a useful way to help farmers and business people in developing economies to make use of advanced technological tools available in developed economies. Servicization often resulted in new business models, and so is a key part of the emerging field of operations management research on business model innovations. As part of servicization launch, a company is selling service instead of a product. Service can be paid based on fixed fees, or on performance. The latter showed that the research on performance-based contracts would be important. Finally, although farmers in developed economies might be limited to the servicization model, some of the more sophisticated farmers there, or farmers in developed economies as strategic customers, could potentially have the choice of owning the equipment versus buying the service. In pricing their equipment and service, Netafim needs to consider some of their customers as strategic, and make the proper pricing decisions in light of such strategic customers.

6 Summary

Poverty alleviation requires economic growth in the developing economies. The best way to foster economic growth is through entrepreneurship as well as increasing engagement of those economies into the global value chains. There are inherent challenges faced, due to underdeveloped infrastructures and skill gaps. But innovations in the value chain could help to overcome these challenges, unleashing potential economic and social values. Hence, value chain innovations can be a significant enabler or accelerator for value creation in such economies.

Finally, this topic can also be a great opportunity for creative, impactful, and rewarding research ground for supply chain and logistics professionals.

References

Arnold M (2018) Mexichem says Netafim deal puts it at forefront of global trends. Bloomberg 21 Mar 2018

Cohen MA, Lee HL (2020) Designing the right global supply chain network. Manuf Serv Oper Manag 22(1):15–24

Countryeconomy.com, Ghana GDP 2018. Accessed 30 Oct 2019. https://countryeconomy.com/gdp/ghana

Daily Times (2018) eWTP ecosystem $600m fund established to focus on 'one belt, one road' countries. 24 May 2018

Elist J, Kennedy M (2014) Mekelle poultry farms: succeeding in East Africa as an entrepreneur. *Graduate School of Business,* Case IDE-5, Stanford University

Global Monitoring Report (2015/2016) Development goals in an era of demographic change. World Bank Group. Washington, DC

Hoyt D, Lee H (2011) Mountain hazelnuts: social entrepreneurship in Bhutan. *Graduate School of Business,* Case GS-78, Stanford University

Khokhar R, Serajuddin U (2015) Should we continue to use the term "developing world". *World Bank Blogs*, 16 Nov 16, 2015. https://blogs.worldbank.org/opendata/should-we-continue-use-term-developing-world. Accessed 30 Oct 2019

Lee H, Mendelson H, Rammohan S, Srivastava A (2017) Technology in agribusiness: opportunities to drive value. *Stanford Value Chain Innovation Initiative White Paper*

Lee HL, Schmidt G (2017) Using value chains to enhance innovation. Prod Oper Manag 26(4):617–632

Lee HL, Shen MZ (2020) Supply chain and logistics innovations with the belt and road initiative. J of Management Science and Engineering 5:77–86

Mancosu N, Snyder RL, Kyriakakis G, Spano D (2015) Water scarcity and future challenges for food production. Water 7:975–992

Michlin G (2006) Netafim: micrgating from products to solutions. Stanford Graduate School of Business Case, GS-46

National Development and Reform Commission, Ministry of Foreign Affairs and Ministry of Commerce (2015) *Vision and actions on jointly building silk road economic belt and 21st-century Maritime Silk Road, People's Republic of China*, with State Council Authorization

Orsdemir A, Deshpande V, Parlakturk AK (2018) Is servicization a win-win strategy? Profitability and environmental implications of servicization. *Manufacturing & Service Operations Management*, forthcoming, 2018, 21, 3

Plecher H (2019) GDP per capita Bhutan, 2024. https://www.statista.com/statistics/527245/gross-domestic-product-gdp-per-capita-in-bhutan/. Accessed 30 Oct 2019

Rammohan S (2010) The shea value chain reinforcement initiative in Ghana. *Stanford Global Supply Chain Management Forum Case Study*

Rammohan S (2015) McDonald's India: optimizing the French fries supply chain. *Graduate School of Business,* Case GS-79, Stanford University

The World Bank (2019) The World Bank in Ethiopia, 26 Sept 2019. https://www.worldbank.org/en/country/ethiopia/overview. Accessed 31 Oct 2019

The Impact of Crop Minimum Support Prices on Crop Selection and Farmer Welfare in the Presence of Strategic Farmers

Prashant Chintapalli and Christopher S. Tang

Abstract In many developing countries, governments often use *minimum support prices* (MSPs) as interventions to (i) safeguard farmers' income against crop price falls and (ii) ensure sufficient and balanced production of different crops. In this chapter, we examine two questions: (1) What is the impact of MSPs on the farmers' crop selection and production decisions, future crop availabilities, and farmers' expected profits? (2) What is the impact of strategic farmers on crop selection and production decisions, future crop availabilities, and farmers' expected profits? To explore these questions, we present a model in which the market consists of two types of farmers (with heterogeneous production costs): myopic farmers (who make their crop selection and production decisions based on recent market prices) and strategic farmers (who make their decisions by taking all other farmers' decisions into consideration). By examining the dynamic interactions among these farmers for the case when there are two (complementary or substitutable) crops for each farmer to select to grow, we obtain the following results. First, we show that, regardless of the values of the MSPs offered to the crops, the price disparity between the crops worsens as the complementarity between the crops increases. Second, we find that offering MSP is not always beneficial to the farmers. In fact, offering MSP for a crop can hurt the profit of those farmers who grow that crop especially when the proportion of strategic farmers is sufficiently small. Third, offering a wrong choice of MSPs can cause the expected quantity disparity between crops to worsen. By taking these two drawbacks of MSPs into consideration, we discuss ways to select effective MSPs that can improve farmers' expected profit and reduce quantity disparity between crops.

P. Chintapalli
Indian Institute of Management, Bangalore, India

C. S. Tang (✉)
UCLA Anderson School of Management, University of California, Los Angeles, CA, USA
e-mail: chris.tang@anderson.ucla.edu

J. M. Swaminathan, V. Deshpande (eds.), *Responsible Business Operations*, Springer Series in Supply Chain Management 10,
https://doi.org/10.1007/978-3-030-51957-5_2

Keywords Minimum support prices · Subsidies · Agricultural supply chains · Government and public policy

1 Introduction

In many developing countries, the agricultural sector is important because (1) it offers a source of income to a large number of small rural households and (2) it provides a stable food supply for the country. As such, developing efficient and effective agro-policies to improve farmers' earnings and to stabilize crop availabilities and prices is critical (Thorbecke 1982). While governments in developing countries design and develop a wide variety of agro-policies ranging from input subsidies (for seeds and fertilizers, power, etc.) to output subsidies (for storage and transportation), we shall focus on a particular type of output subsidies that is called the *credit-based minimum support price* (credit-based MSPs) in this chapter. MSPs can be classified into two types: (a) procurement-based MSPs and (b) credit-based MSPs. While a procurement-based MSP requires government to procure crop from farmers, credit-based MSP does not entail such a procurement and transfer of crop inventory from farmers to government. In credit-based MSP, a government compensates the difference between the pre-announced MSP and the realized market price, should the latter be lower, for a crop. Thus, by guaranteeing minimum prices for crops, governments intend to provide incentives for farmers to protect their income and to entice them to grow a more balanced mixture of crops.

A form of credit-based MSP has been launched in the state of Madhya Pradesh in India that is known as the *Price Deficit Financing Scheme* (named as *Bhavantar Bhugtan Yojana*) for eight crops. Motivated by this emerging credit-based MSP scheme, we develop a parsimonious model to analyze the impact of credit-based MSPs on farmers' earnings, crop availabilities, and crop prices in this chapter. We consider a setting in which there are two (complementary or substitutable) crops available for each farmer to cultivate. In addition to heterogeneous production costs for each crop, we also consider the case when the market is comprised of myopic farmers (who make their crop selection and production decisions based on recent market prices) and strategic farmers (who make their decisions by taking all other farmers' decisions into consideration). By examining the dynamic interactions among myopic and strategic farmers, we aim to examine two research questions:

1. What is the impact of MSPs on the farmers' crop selection and production decisions, future crop availabilities, and farmers' expected revenues?
2. What is the impact of strategic farmers on crop selection and production decisions, future crop availabilities, and farmers' expected revenues?

Our equilibrium analysis enables us to obtain the following results. First, we show that, regardless of the values of MSPs for crops, the price disparity between the crops worsens as the complementarity between the crops increases. Second, we find that offering moderately low MSP for a crop will degrade the expected profits of the farmers growing the crop if the number of strategic farmers is very small. Third, we find that offering a wrong choice of MSPs can cause the production quantity disparity between crops to worsen. Hence, to reduce quantity disparity between crops, a carefully designed MSP policy is critical.

2 Literature Review

Our research pertains to agro-policies that affect both crop selection and crop production by myopic and strategic farmers. The literature on MSPs is vast in the agricultural economics discipline, and the reader is referred to Tripathi et al. (2013) and the references therein for a good synopsis on MSPs in developing countries. Without accounting for the price interactions between crops with MSP support and those crops without MSP support, Fox (1956) develops macro-economics analysis to evaluate the impact of MSPs and finds that MSPs can mitigate the fall in GNP during a recession. Dantwala (1967) finds that in spite of the increasing MSPs, the crop market prices continue to rise. More recently, Subbarao et al. (2011) show evidence that the increase in market price is caused by the increase in MSPs. In the same vein, Chand (2003) presents qualitative assessment of the ill effects of the wheat- and-rice-centric MSPs on the Indian economy. Chhatre et al. (2016) point out that many farmers in India moved to cultivating high-yield varieties of rice and wheat due to the wheat- and-rice-centric MSPs offered by the Indian government. The authors also identify the various socioeconomic and environmental problems associated with an improper choice of MSPs. Besides the Indian context, Spitze (1978) analyzes the impact of federal policy (The Food and Agriculture Act of 1977) on agriculture in the United States. The author states that continuous improvement in gathering and analyzing information is a prerequisite for the design of effective MSPs. Finally, Guda et al. (2016) examine the role of MSPs in emerging economies, but there are two fundamental differences. We consider heterogeneity in farmers' production costs (instead of homogeneous costs), and we examine the impact of the MSPs of two crops (instead of one crop).

Recent papers on agricultural operations in OM literature can be classified into four groups: (i) Tang et al. (2015), Chen and Tang (2015), Parker et al. (2016), and Liao et al. (2019) focus on the economic value of disseminating agricultural information to the farmers; (ii) Kazaz and Webster (2011), Dawande et al. (2013), and Huh and Lall (2013) examine the issue of resource and inventory management; (iii) Huh et al. (2012), Federgruen et al. (2015), and An et al. (2015) focus on contract farming and farmer aggregation; and (iv) Hu et al. (2016), Alizamir et al. (2015), and Guda et al. (2016) examine social responsibility and public policy issues arising from the agricultural sector.

While our paper is related to group (iv), it differs from the these papers in the following manner. First, Hu et al. (2016) focus on the value of strategic farmers in the context of a single crop with a deterministic demand function. They show that a tiny fraction of strategic farmers can stabilize the steady-state prices. They also extend their analysis to two crops with independent market prices. In contrast, our goal is to evaluate the impact of MSPs on farmers' crop selection and production decisions and on the market prices of two crops with dependent and yet stochastic market price.

3 Model Preliminaries

We consider two crops (A and B) to be produced by heterogeneous farmers whose production costs are uniformly distributed over the interval $[-0.5, 0.5]$ as in the Hotelling model. These two crops can be substitutes (e.g., cereals like rice, wheat and the others) or complements (e.g., cereals and pulses/lentils). For a farmer located at $x \in [-0.5, 0.5]$, his costs of producing crops A and B are given by $c_A(x) = 0.5 + x$ and $c_B(x) = 0.5 - x$, respectively. We assume that the farmers are infinitesimally small so that each farmer is a price taker. We scale the production capacity of each farmer to 1.

In our model, the market price of a crop depends on the available quantity of both crops. Let q^{kT} denote the "total" availability of crop $k \in \{A, B\}$, and let p^k denote the market price of crop $k \in \{A, B\}$. For ease of exposition, we normalize the size of markets to 1 so that $q^{kT} \leqslant 1$ for $k \in \{A, B\}$. Throughout this paper, we assume that the market price p^k for crop $k \in \{A, B\}$ satisfies:

$$
\begin{aligned}
p^A &= a - \rho q^{AT} - \alpha q^{BT} + \epsilon^A = \mathbb{E}[p^A] + \epsilon^A, \text{ and} \\
p^B &= a - \alpha q^{AT} - \rho q^{BT} + \epsilon^B = \mathbb{E}[p^B] + \epsilon^B,
\end{aligned} \tag{1}
$$

where ρ (>0) is the price sensitivity and α is a measure of substitutability (if $\alpha > 0$) or complementarity (if $\alpha < 0$) between the two crops. As commonly assumed in the literature for substitutable/complementary products, we shall assume that $\alpha < \rho$. The random variables ϵ^k denote the market uncertainty for crop $k \in \{A, B\}$. We assume $\epsilon^k, k \in \{A, B\}$ are iid with mean 0, variance σ^2, and distribution and density functions $F(\cdot)$ and $f(\cdot)$, respectively.[1] We also assume that the distribution $F(\cdot)$ has support over a range of value so that the market price p^k is non-negative. The expected profit of a farmer at location x who grows crop $k \in \{A, B\}$ is given by:

$$
\Pi^k(x) = \mathbb{E}[p^k] - c_k(x) = a - \rho q^{kT} - \alpha q^{jT} - c_k(x), \; j \neq k. \tag{2}
$$

For ease of exposition, we define $r \equiv \rho - \alpha$ (> 0), so that r measures the "dissimilarity" between the two crops, and $\phi \equiv a - \frac{\rho+\alpha}{2}$, which corresponds to the expected market price when half of the market grows A (grows B) (i.e., when

[1] To keep the notation simple, we assume that ϵ^A and ϵ^B follow the same distribution. However, our analysis can be extended to the case when ϵ^A and ϵ^B have non-identical distributions.

$q^{AT} = q^{BT} = 0.5$). Finally, wherever applicable, we denote the price vector by $\mathbf{P} = [p^A, p^B]^T$ and the recent market prices by $\mathbf{P}_0 = [p_0^A, p_0^B]^T$. To simplify our exposition and our analysis (e.g., by ruling out the boundary equilibrium solution), we shall make the following assumptions:

ASSUMPTION 1 *In each period, no farmer chooses not cultivate a crop.*

The non-idling assumption is reasonable especially when the farmer's production cost is lower than the market price p^k in general.

Next, let Δp be the price disparity between crops A and B. By applying (1) and the fact that $r = \rho - \alpha$, we obtain:

$$\Delta p = p^A - p^B = -r(q^{AT} - q^{BT}) + \xi, \ \forall t,$$

where $\xi = \epsilon^A - \epsilon^B$. To ensure that the price disparity Δp is stable over time so that we can rule out boundary equilibrium solution, we shall make the following assumption.

ASSUMPTION 2 *The dissimilarity between two crops r satisfies $0 < r \equiv (\rho - \alpha) < 1$. Also, the variance of the market uncertainty is sufficiently less than 1, which is the range of the farmers' (scaled) production costs (i.e., $\sigma^2 \ll 1$).*

Since, r measures the "dissimilarity" between two crops, we can treat the crops to be substitutes if r is small and to be complements if r is large. Furthermore, because $0 < r < 1$, $|q^A - q^B| \leqslant 1$, and $\mathbb{E}[\xi] = 0$, it is easy to check that $|\mathbb{E}[\Delta p]| \leqslant r < 1$, for all t. Also, when $|\mathbb{E}[\Delta p]| \leqslant 1$ and $\sigma^2 \ll 1$, we can ascertain that $|\Delta p| < 1$ nearly always holds so that we can effectively assume $\mathbb{P}(|\Delta p| < 1) \approxeq 1$. The assumption that $\sigma^2 \ll 1$ is not a very restrictive assumption because we have scaled the range of farmer production costs to 1, and this assumption indicates that the variance in the market prices is relatively lower than the variance in the farmers' production costs.

ASSUMPTION 3 *There are two types of farmers in the market: myopic and strategic. Also, the proportion of strategic farmers is $\theta \in [0, 1]$.*

In our model, we assume that myopic farmers are those who make their crop selection and production decisions purely based on recent market prices. However, strategic farmers are forward looking, and they make their decisions by taking all other farmers' decisions into consideration. For the convenience of notation, we define $z^+ = \max\{z, 0\}$.

4 Model Analysis: In the Absence of MSPs

To explicate the analysis that involves crop selection and crop production by myopic and strategic farmers with heterogeneous production costs, we first examine the case when MSPs are absent, and we deal with the case when MSPs are present in Sect. 5. By considering different decision-making mechanisms adopted by different types of farmers, we now determine their crop selection and production decisions in period t for any recently realized market prices p_0^k for $k \in \{A, B\}$.

4.1 Myopic Farmers' Crop Selection and Production Decisions in Period t

Let q^{km} denote the quantity of crop $k \in \{A, B\}$ to be produced by the myopic farmers in period t, and let p^{km} denote the price of crop k as "anticipated" by the myopic farmers. In our model, each myopic farmer anticipates that $p^{km} = p_0^k$, $k \in \{A, B\}$. Hence, a myopic farmer at $x \in [-0.5, 0.5]$ will grow crop A if $p^{Am} - c_A(x) \geqslant p^{Bm} - c_B(x)$ and will grow crop B, otherwise. Observe that the myopic farmer located in τ^m is indifferent between the two crops, where $\tau^m = \{x : p^{Am} - c_A(x) = p^{Bm} - c_B(x)\}$. Because $p^{km} = p_0^k$ for $k \in \{A, B\}$, $\tau^m = \frac{p_0^A - p_0^B}{2}$. By applying Assumption 2, we can conclude that $\tau^m \in (-0.5, 0.5)$. Given the threshold τ^m, the segment $\{x : -0.5 \leqslant x < \tau^m\}$ of myopic farmers will grow only crop A, while the segment $\{x : \tau^m < x \leqslant 0.5\}$ of myopic farmers will grow only crop B.

4.2 Strategic Farmers' Crop Selection and Production Decisions

Let q^{ks} denote the quantity of crop $k \in \{A, B\}$ to be produced by the strategic farmers, and let p^{ks} denote the price of crop k as "anticipated" by the strategic farmers. By taking all other farmers' decisions into consideration, we shall show that strategic farmers can actually anticipate the expected market price in equilibrium so that $p^{ks} = \mathbb{E}[p^k]$. Also, we shall show later that, among the strategic farmers, the segment $\{x : -0.5 \leqslant x < \tau^s\}$ will grow only A and the segment $\{x : \tau^s < x \leqslant 0.5\}$ will grow only B, where $\tau^s \equiv \tau^s(p^{As}, p^{Bs}) = \{x : p^{As} - c_A(x) = p^{Bs} - c_B(x)\}$. (The value of threshold τ^s is given in Proposition 1).

We illustrate the equilibrium decisions of the two types of farmers in Fig. 1. Without loss of generality, we consider the case when $p_0^A > p_0^B$. Next, by noting that the market consists of θ strategic and $(1-\theta)$ myopic farmers, the figure depicts the overall crop production. Since τ^s and τ^m are the threshold values associated with the myopic and the strategic farmers, respectively, the total quantities of crop A produced by the myopic and the strategic farmers are $q^{Am} = (1-\theta)(\tau^m + 0.5)$ and $q^{As} = \theta(\tau^s + 0.5)$, respectively. Thus, the total availability of crop A is given by $q^{AT} = q^{Am} + q^{As} = \theta(\tau^s + 0.5) + (1-\theta)(\tau^m + 0.5) = \tau + 0.5$, where $\tau = \theta\tau^s + (1-\theta)\tau^m$. (Regarding the availability of crop B, it is easy to see that the total availability of crop B is $q^{BT} = \theta(0.5 - \tau^s) + (1-\theta)(0.5 - \tau^m) = 0.5 - \tau$.)

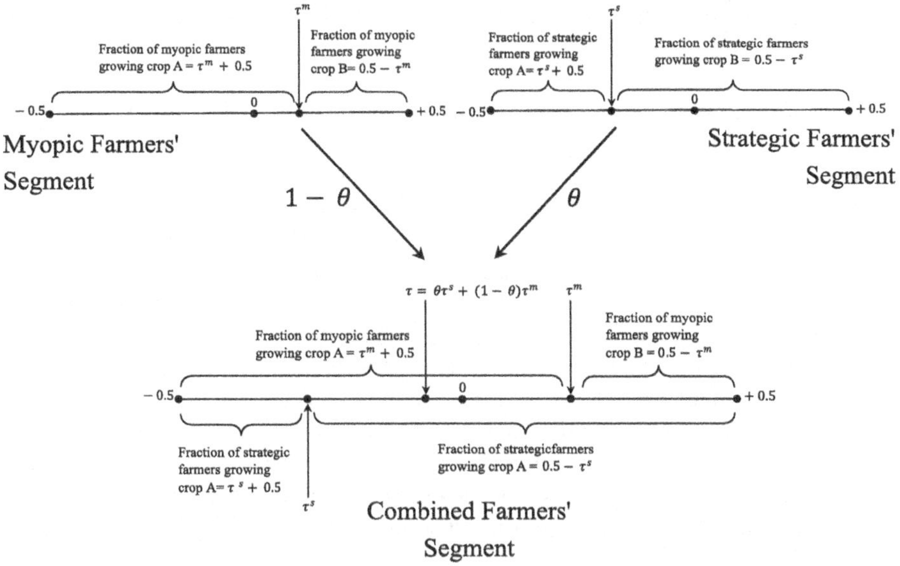

Fig. 1 Total product availability when $\theta \in [0, 1]$ farmers are strategic and $p_0^A > p_0^B$

4.3 Farmers' Crop Selection and Production Decisions in Equilibrium

While the threshold τ^m has been established earlier, the determination of the threshold τ^s is more involved because each strategic farmer takes the sowing decisions of all other farmers into consideration. In Proposition 1 we describe the farmers' sowing decisions that are illustrated in Fig. 1. For exposition, let:

$$\hat{r} = \frac{(1-\theta)r}{1+r\theta}, \tag{3}$$

where $r \equiv (\rho - \alpha) > 0$ measures the "dissimilarity" between the two crops. Notice that $\hat{r}$ is increasing in r.

Proposition 1 (Crop selection and production decisions for any realized $\mathbf{P}_0$) *For any realized prices $\mathbf{P}_0$, the equilibrium crop selection and production decisions of the farmers can be described as follows:*

1. ***Myopic farmers' decisions:*** *The amount of crop A produced by myopic farmers is given by $q^{Am} = (1-\theta)(\tau^m + 0.5)$, where $\tau^m = \frac{p_0^A - p_0^B}{2} = \frac{\Delta p_0}{2} \in [-0.5, 0.5]$.*
2. ***Strategic farmers' decisions:*** *The amount of crop A produced by strategic farmers is given by $q^{As} = \theta(\tau^s + 0.5)$, where $\tau^s = -\hat{r}\tau^m \in [-0.5, 0.5]$.*

3. ***Total production:*** *The total production of crop A is given by* $q^{AT} = \tau + 0.5$, *where* $\tau = \theta\tau^s + (1-\theta)\tau^m = \left(\frac{\hat{r}}{r}\right)\tau^m \in [-0.5, 0.5]$.

(All proofs are provided in Chintapalli and Tang 2017.) Even though we focus on crop A in the above proposition, the quantity of crop B produced by myopic and strategic farmers can be obtained through symmetry as $q^{Bm} = 0.5 - \tau^m$ and $q^{Bs} = 0.5 - \tau^s$, respectively. Also, the total production of crop B is $q^{BT} = 0.5 - \tau$.

For any given proportion of strategic farmers θ in the market, the first and the second statements of Proposition 1 describe the equilibrium production decisions of the myopic and strategic farmers through the threshold values τ^m and τ^s, respectively. By combining the corresponding production decisions of these two types of farmers, the third statement gives the total availability of each crop in equilibrium. It is interesting to note that, when $\theta = 1$ (i.e., all the farmers are strategic), $\tau = \tau^s = 0$ so that $q^{As} = q^{Bs} = 0.5$, which indicates that equal number of farmers grow the two crops. Also, the recent market prices p_0^A and p_0^B have no bearing on the strategic farmers' sowing decisions. Next, by using the third statement of Proposition 1 and (1), the equilibrium expected crop prices are given by:

$$\mathbb{E}[p^A] = \phi - r\tau = \phi - \hat{r}\tau^m = \phi - \frac{\hat{r}}{2}\left(p_0^A - p_0^B\right) = \phi - \frac{\hat{r}}{2}\Delta p_0, \text{ and}$$

$$\mathbb{E}[p^B] = \phi + r\tau = \phi + \hat{r}\tau^m = \phi + \frac{\hat{r}}{2}\left(p_0^A - p_0^B\right) = \phi + \frac{\hat{r}}{2}\Delta p_0. \quad (4)$$

Let $\pi^m(x)$ and $\pi^s(x)$ denote the equilibrium profits of a myopic and a strategic farmer who is located at $x \in [-0.5, 0.5]$, respectively. By using (2) and Proposition 1 that a farmer of type $v \in \{m, s\}$ will grow crop A if $x \leqslant \tau^v$ and will grow crop B, otherwise, we can apply (4) and the production costs $c_A(x) = 0.5 + x$ and $c_B(x) = 0.5 - x$ to show that the profit of a farmer of type $v \in \{m, s\}$ located at x is given as:

$$\pi^v(x) = \begin{cases} \Pi^A(x) = \mathbb{E}[p^A] - c_A(x) = \phi - \frac{\hat{r}}{2}\Delta p_0 - (x + 0.5) & \text{if} x \leqslant \tau^v, \\ \Pi^B(x) = \mathbb{E}[p^B] - c_B(x) = \phi + \frac{\hat{r}}{2}\Delta p_0 - (0.5 - x) & \text{if} x > \tau^v. \end{cases} \quad (5)$$

5 Minimum Support Prices

We now extend our analysis presented in the last section to incorporate crop MSPs. To begin, let m^k denote the MSP associated with crop $k \in \{A, B\}$ in period t.[2] Also, let $\hat{p}^{km}$ and $\hat{p}^{ks}$ denote the *effective* market prices of crop $k \in \{A, B\}$ as

[2]In general, the MSPs are announced before the crop sowing season; the farmers make their sowing decisions with the complete knowledge of the MSPs and the price history of the crops.

"anticipated" by myopic and strategic farmers, respectively.[3] Because each myopic farmer anticipates that the future selling price is equal to the most recently observed market price p_0^k, myopic farmers will anticipate that $\hat{p}^{km} = \max\{p_0^k, m^k\}$ for crop k. However, because each strategic farmer accounts for the actions of all other farmers, each strategic farmer can anticipate the *effective* market price in equilibrium based on its expected value so that $\hat{p}^{ks} = \mathbb{E}_{\epsilon^k} \max\{p^k, m^k\}$ for crop k, where p^k is the actual market price as given in (1).

The decision-making process employed by the farmers remains the same as explained in Sect. 4, except that the anticipated prices p^{km} and p^{ks} are now replaced by $\hat{p}^{km}$ and $\hat{p}^{ks}$ for $k \in \{A, B\}$. To ease our exposition and to identify the conditions under which increasing MSPs could hurt farmers, we shall assume throughout this section that the difference between the MSPs of two crops is bounded by 1 (i.e., $|m^A - m^B| < 1$). (However, except Propositions 4 and 5 that discuss possible disadvantages of MSPs, all other results described in this section can be extended to MSPs such that $|m^A - m^B| > 1$, with additional notation.) We first characterize the unique equilibrium in the presence of MSPs in Proposition 2, which is analogous to Proposition 1.

Proposition 2 (Equilibrium under MSPs) *For any realized prices $\mathbf{P}_0$ and for any given MSPs (m^A, m^B), the equilibrium crop selection and production decisions of the farmers can be described as follows:*

1. ***Myopic farmers' decisions:*** *The amount of crop A produced by myopic farmers is given by $\hat{q}^{Am} = (1-\theta)(\hat{\tau}^m + 0.5)$, where*

$$\hat{\tau}^m = \frac{\hat{p}^{Am} - \hat{p}^{Bm}}{2} \in [-0.5, 0.5], \tag{6}$$

   $\hat{p}^{km} = \max\{p_0^k, m^k\}$, $k \in \{A, B\}$.
2. ***Strategic farmers' decisions:*** *The amount of crop A produced by strategic farmers is given by $\hat{q}^{As} = \theta(\hat{\tau}^s + 0.5)$, where*

$$\hat{\tau}^s = -\hat{r}\hat{\tau}^m - \left[\frac{1}{2(1+r\theta)} \int_{m^A-\phi+r\hat{\tau}}^{m^B-\phi-r\hat{\tau}} F(\epsilon)\, d\epsilon\right] \in [-0.5, 0.5], \tag{7}$$

   $\hat{r} = \frac{(1-\theta)r}{1+r\theta}$ *and* $\hat{\tau} = \theta\hat{\tau}^s + (1-\theta)\hat{\tau}^m$.[4]
3. ***Total production:*** *The total production of crop A is given by $\hat{q}^{AT} = \hat{\tau} + 0.5$ where $\hat{\tau} = \theta\hat{\tau}^s + (1-\theta)\hat{\tau}^m \in [-0.5, 0.5]$.*

---

[3] To differentiate between the base case and the case when positive MSPs are offered, we use ˆ over the variables of interest in the latter case.

[4] Note that (7) can be alternatively written as $\hat{\tau}^s = -r\hat{\tau} - \frac{1}{2}\int_{m^A-\phi+r\hat{\tau}}^{m^B-\phi-r\hat{\tau}} F(\epsilon)\, d\epsilon \in [-0.5, 0.5]$. We will use either of these two definitions of $\hat{\tau}^s$ in our analysis, based on convenience.

By using $\hat{\tau}^m$ from (6) and the fact that $\hat{\tau} = \theta\hat{\tau}^s + (1-\theta)\hat{\tau}^m$, we can convert (7) into an equation in $\hat{\tau}^s$ alone and solve it to obtain $\hat{\tau}^s$, using which we can retrieve $\hat{\tau}$ accordingly.

Next, consider a special case when all farmers are strategic so that $\theta = 1$. In this case, statement 2 reveals that, when $\theta = 1$, $\hat{r} = 0$, $\hat{\tau} = \hat{\tau}^s$, $\hat{q}^{AT} = (0.5 + \hat{\tau}^s)$, $\hat{q}^{BT} = (0.5 - \hat{\tau}^s)$, and (7) can be simplified as $\hat{\tau}^s = -\frac{1}{2(1+r)} \int_{m^A-\phi+r\hat{\tau}^s}^{m^B-\phi-r\hat{\tau}^s} F(\epsilon)\, d\epsilon$, which is independent of the recent market prices, thereby indicating that when all farmers are strategic, past prices do not affect farmers' decisions.

Finally, the equilibrium described in Proposition 2 possesses the same characteristics as the results stated in Proposition 1. First, observe that the threshold associated with the strategic farmers given in (7) involves two components: (i) the response to the actions of myopic farmers (which is the first term in the RHS of (7), i.e., $-\hat{r}\hat{\tau}^m$, which is analogous to the expression of τ^s given in the second statement of Proposition 1) and (ii) the response to the crop MSPs announced (which is the second term in the RHS of (7)). Thus, MSPs influence the decisions of the strategic farmers in two ways. First, they influence the decisions of strategic farmers via the decisions of the myopic farmers as explained in (i), and we term this effect as the *indirect* effect. Second, the MSPs influence the decisions of strategic farmers directly as explained in (ii), and we term this effect as the *direct* effect. Their two effects play an important role in our analysis of the impact of MSPs.

It can be shown that the threshold $\hat{\tau}^s$ for strategic farmers is decreasing and the total product availability threshold $\hat{\tau}$ is increasing in the threshold $\hat{\tau}^m$ for myopic farmers. Specifically, it is easy to observe from Proposition 2 that $\frac{\partial \hat{\tau}^s}{\partial \hat{\tau}^m} < 0$ and $\frac{\partial \hat{\tau}}{\partial \hat{\tau}^m} > 0$. The same characteristics of the thresholds can be observed from Proposition 1 as well. Essentially, these two characteristics of $\hat{\tau}^s$ and $\hat{\tau}$ imply that strategic farmers "counteract" the actions of myopic farmers; however, strategic farmers' counteractions cannot fully nullify the impact of myopic farmers even when MSPs are offered. Also, for any given MSPs of the crops, we found that the impact of crop dissimilarity r, recent prices $\mathbf{P}_0$, and the proportion of strategic farmers θ are on equilibrium; we refer the readers to Chintapalli and Tang (2017).

Next, for a farmer located at $x \in [-0.5, 0.5]$, we compute his profits in equilibrium as:

$$\begin{aligned}
\hat{\Pi}^k(x) &= \mathbb{E}_{\epsilon^k}\left[\max\{p^k, m^k\}\right] - c_k(x) \\
&= \mathbb{E}[p^k] + \mathbb{E}_{\epsilon^k}\left[\max\{\epsilon, m^k - \mathbb{E}[p^k]\}\right] - c_k(x) \\
&= \mathbb{E}[p^k] + \left(m^k - \mathbb{E}[p^k]\right) F\left(m^k - \mathbb{E}[p^k]\right) + \int_{m^k-\mathbb{E}[p^k]}^{\infty} \epsilon f(\epsilon)\, d\epsilon - c_k(x).
\end{aligned} \tag{8}$$

By using the thresholds $\hat{\tau}^m$, $\hat{\tau}^s$, and $\hat{\tau}$ stated in Proposition 2 along with the production cost $c_A(x) = 0.5 + x$ and $c_B(x) = 0.5 - x$ to determine the expected profit in equilibrium for a farmer of type $v \in \{m, s\}$ and who is located at $x \in [-0.5, 0.5]$, we obtain:

$$\hat{\pi}^v(x) = \begin{cases} \hat{\Pi}^A(x) = \mathbb{E}[p^A] + \left(m^A - \mathbb{E}[p^A]\right) F\left(m^A - \mathbb{E}[p^A]\right) + \int_{m^A - \mathbb{E}[p^A]}^{\infty} \epsilon f(\epsilon)\, d\epsilon - (0.5 + x) \text{if} x \leqslant \hat{\tau}^v, \\ \hat{\Pi}^B(x) = \mathbb{E}[p^B] + \left(m^B - \mathbb{E}[p^B]\right) F\left(m^B - \mathbb{E}[p^B]\right) + \int_{m^B - \mathbb{E}[p^B]}^{\infty} \epsilon f(\epsilon)\, d\epsilon - (0.5 - x) \text{if} x > \hat{\tau}^v. \end{cases} \tag{9}$$

Also, by using statement 3 of Proposition 2 stating that $\hat{q}^{AT} = 0.5 + \hat{\tau}$ and $\hat{q}^{BT} = 0.5 - \hat{\tau}$, we can apply (1) to determine the expected market price $\mathbb{E}[p^A]$ and $\mathbb{E}[p^B]$ in equilibrium as a function of $\hat{\tau}$, which in turn depends on the MSPs via (7).

5.1 *Impact of MSPs*

We now examine the impact of MSPs on the farmer's crop selection and production decisions (again, we focus on crop A alone). In preparation, let us define the following two bounds on the MSP of crop A.

$$\underline{m}^A \equiv \underline{m}^A(\mathbf{P}_0, m^B) = \max\{p_0^A, \max\{m^B, p_0^B\} - 1\} \text{ and}$$

$$\overline{m}^A \equiv \overline{m}^A(\mathbf{P}_0, m^B) = \max\{p_0^A, \max\{m^B, p_0^B\} + 1\}.$$

With these two bounds, MSP m^A is considered to be *low* when $m^A < \underline{m}^A$, *moderate* when $\underline{m}^A \leqslant m^A \leqslant \overline{m}^A$, and *high* when $m^A > \overline{m}^A$. By using the two bounds $\underline{m}^A$ and $\overline{m}^A$, along with the results as stated in Proposition 2, we obtain the following results:

Proposition 3 (Impact of MSPs on Equilibrium) *For any given MSP m^B of crop B, the MSP of crop A, m^A, affects the production decisions of myopic and strategic farmers as follows:*

1. ***Total production:*** *The total availability of crop A is always increasing in the MSP of A so that* $\frac{\partial \hat{q}^{AT}}{\partial m^A} = \frac{\partial \hat{\tau}}{\partial m^A} \geqslant 0$.
2. ***Low MSP:*** *When $m^A \leqslant \underline{m}^A$, then (a)* $\hat{q}^{Am} = (1-\theta)\left[\frac{p_0^A - \max\{m^B, p_0^B\}}{2} + \frac{1}{2}\right]^+$ *so that* $\frac{\partial \hat{q}^{Am}}{\partial m^A} = 0$, *and (b)* $\frac{\partial \hat{q}^{As}}{\partial m^A} \geqslant 0$.
3. ***High MSP:*** *When $m^A \geqslant \overline{m}^A$, then (a) $\hat{q}^{Am} = (1-\theta)$ so that* $\frac{\partial \hat{q}^{Am}}{\partial m^A} = 0$, *and (b)* $\frac{\partial \hat{q}^{As}}{\partial m^A} \geqslant 0$.
4. ***Moderate MSP:*** *When $\underline{m}^A < m^A < \overline{m}^A$, then (a) $\hat{q}^{Am} \in (0, (1-\theta))$, and (b)* $\frac{\partial \hat{q}^{Am}}{\partial m^A} = \frac{(1-\theta)}{2} \geqslant 0$.

The first statement of Proposition 3 shows that the availability of a crop is always increasing in the MSP. Due to this increase in crop's availability, its market price drops as its MSP increases. Hence, the equilibrium expected market price of crop A is decreasing in m^A (and increasing in m^B with details omitted). Therefore, to achieve a better balance of different crops, a policy-maker has to account for the MSP cross-effect (i.e., the effect of a crop's MSP on the production of other crops). Furthermore, it is always possible to obtain a desired production mix of the crops using MSPs.

We shall focus on statement 4 when MSP m^A is *moderate* (i.e., $\underline{m}^A < m^A < \overline{m}^A$), while statements 2 and 3 can be interpreted easily. For statement 4, it can be shown that the production of crop A by the myopic farmers is strictly increasing in m^A (and decreasing in m^B with details omitted). As shown in the fourth statement, when the MSP is moderate so that $\underline{m}^A < m^A < \overline{m}^A$, more myopic farmers will grow crop A as m^A increases (i.e., $\hat{\tau}^m$ is increasing so that $\hat{q}^{Am}$ is increasing in m^A). Hence, by anticipating myopic farmers' behavior, strategic farmers make decisions in a more intricate manner, when the MSP m^A is *moderate*. However, as it turns out, the amount of crop A produced by strategic farmers q^{As} (or equivalently $\hat{\tau}^s$) is not necessarily monotonic in the MSP m^A: a marginal increase of MSP for a crop can cause strategic farmers to produce less of the crop, if the crop's MSP is moderate. We shall explore this seemingly counter-intuitive result in more detail.

Due to the complexity of the analysis, we shall consider a special case when the market uncertainty $\epsilon^k \sim U[-\delta, \delta]$, $k \in \{A, B\}$, instead of a general probability distribution $F(\cdot)$.[5] For exposition, we let:

$$\widetilde{m} = \phi - \delta\left(\frac{1-r}{1+r}\right) < \phi = a - \frac{\rho + \alpha}{2}.$$

Notice that $\widetilde{m} > 0$ when a is sufficiently large and δ is sufficiently small. By considering $\widetilde{m}$, we obtain the following result:

Proposition 4 (Impact of MSPs on strategic farmers) *Suppose the given MSP m^B of crop B is such that $m^B \geqslant p_0^B$. Then, for any moderately low MSP of A such that $m^A \in \left(\underline{m}^A, \min\{m^B + 1, \widetilde{m}\}\right)$, there exists a threshold $\theta_0 \equiv \theta_0(m^A, m^B) > 0$ such that $\frac{\partial \hat{\tau}^s}{\partial m^A} < 0$ if and only if $0 \leqslant \theta < \theta_0$.*

Proposition 4 shows that when m^A, the MSP for crop A, is *moderately low* (i.e., $\underline{m}^A < m^A < \widetilde{m}$), the proportion of strategic farmers producing crop A (i.e., $\hat{\tau}^s$) can be decreasing in m^A. Intuitively, one expects more farmers to grow crop A as m_A increases. While this is always true in the case of myopic farmers, as shown in Proposition 3 when the MSP is moderately low, it is not true for strategic farmers when $\theta < \theta_0$, as shown in Proposition 4.

[5]Our results continue to hold broadly for general distribution. We refer the readers to Chintapalli and Tang (2017) for details.

The rationale for this counter-intuitive result as stated in Proposition 4 is as follows. Strategic farmers know that, when m_A is moderate, more myopic farmers will grow crop A as m^A increases. The resulting increase in production of crop A is substantial when θ is small because, by Proposition 2 (i.e., $\hat{q}^{Am} = (1-\theta)(\hat{\tau}^m + 0.5)$), it is easy to see that $\frac{\partial \hat{q}^{Am}}{\partial m^A} = (1-\theta)\frac{\partial \hat{\tau}^m}{\partial m^A} = \frac{(1-\theta)}{2}$ when $m^A > p_0^A$. This substantial increase in the total production quantity q^{AT} causes a significant drop in the price of crop A (and causes a steep increase in the price of crop B). By anticipating myopic farmers' behavior, strategic farmers are better off by producing less of crop A and more of crop B. This explains the seemingly counter-intuitive result that is stated in Proposition 4.

This seemingly counter-intuitive finding offers a hint regarding the condition(s) under which offering MSP for a crop can hurt the earnings of farmers who grow that crop. We shall explore this next.

5.2 *Impact of MSPs on Farmers' Profits*

We now examine the impact of the MSP of crop A on the ex ante expected profits of farmers of each type $v \in \{m, s\}$ as given by (9). By differentiating (9) with respect to m^A and by using the fact that the expected market price $\mathbb{E}[p^A]$ and $\mathbb{E}[p^B]$ in equilibrium depend on the MSPs via $\hat{\tau}$, we obtain:

$$\frac{\partial \hat{\pi}^v(x)}{\partial m^A} = \begin{cases} F\left(m^A - \mathbb{E}[p^A]\right) + \left[1 - F\left(m^A - \mathbb{E}[p^A]\right)\right] \cdot \frac{\partial \mathbb{E}[p^A]}{\partial m^A} & \text{if} x \leqslant \hat{\tau}^v \\ \left[1 - F\left(m^B - \mathbb{E}[p^B]\right)\right] \cdot \frac{\partial \mathbb{E}[p^B]}{\partial m^A} & \text{if} x > \hat{\tau}^v \end{cases} \tag{10}$$

where $\frac{\partial \mathbb{E}[p^A]}{\partial m^A} = -r\frac{\partial \hat{\tau}}{\partial m^A} \leqslant 0$ and $\frac{\partial \mathbb{E}[p^B]}{\partial m^A} = r\frac{\partial \hat{\tau}}{\partial m^A} \geqslant 0$. As before, we focus on the impact of m_A on the expected profits of the farmers, while m_B is fixed. We give the following lemma.

Lemma 1 (Impact of MSPs on farmers' profits) *Consider a farmer of type $v \in \{m, s\}$ who is located at $x \in [-0.5, 0.5]$.*

1. ***Farmers growing crop B:*** *If $x > \hat{\tau}^v$, then $\frac{\partial \hat{\pi}^v(x)}{\partial m^A} \geqslant 0$.*
2. ***Low or high m^A on farmers growing crop A:*** *If $x \leqslant \hat{\tau}^v$ and m^A is either low or high (i.e., $m^A < \underline{m}^A$ or $m^A > \overline{m}^A$), then $\frac{\partial \hat{\pi}^v(x)}{\partial m^A} \geqslant 0$.*

The lemma explains the *indirect* benefit that m^A offers to the farmers growing crop B (i.e., farmers who are located at $x > \hat{\tau}^v$) in equilibrium. When m^A is increased, the total availability of crop A (B) increases (decreases) according to Proposition 3. Hence, the expected market price of crop B increases, which will increase the expected profit of the farmers who grow crop B in equilibrium. Furthermore, the lemma proves that, as long as the decisions of the myopic farmers are not "affected" by m^A (i.e., $m^A \leqslant \underline{m}^A$ or $m^A \geqslant \overline{m}^A$), an increase in m^A will always make strategic farmers take sowing decisions in such a way that the expected profit of farmers of crop A is increased.

Finally, to analyze the impact of moderate MSP of crop A (i.e., $\underline{m}^A < m^A < \overline{m}^A$) on farmers' expected profits, we consider a special case when ϵ^A and ϵ^B are independent random variables that follow $U[-\delta, \delta]$ (see Chintapalli and Tang (2017) for results pertaining to generic distribution). Further, assume $m^k \geqslant p_0^k$, $k \in \{A, B\}$, so that both the MSPs are effective, and let:

$$\widetilde{m}^A(m^B) = \left(\frac{r}{r+2}\right) m^B + \frac{2}{r+2}\left[\phi - \delta\left(\frac{2-r}{2+r}\right)\right],$$

to facilitate exposition. We have the following proposition:

Proposition 5 (Impact of moderate m^A on farmers' profits) *For any given MSP m^B of crop B, suppose that MSP for crop A is moderately low (i.e., $m^A \in (\underline{m}^A, \widetilde{m}^A)$). Then there exists a threshold $\theta_1 \equiv \theta_1(m^A, m^B)$ such that $\frac{\partial \hat{\pi}^v(x)}{\partial m^A} < 0$ for all $\theta < \theta_1$, for each farmer of type $v \in \{m, s\}$ at $x \leqslant \hat{\tau}^v$. Furthermore, if θ is sufficiently high, then $\frac{\partial \hat{\pi}^v(x)}{\partial m^A} \geqslant 0$.*

In Proposition 5, we indicate that marginally increase in MSP of a crop can decrease the expected profits of the farmers who grow the crop. According to the proposition, when $m^A \in (\underline{m}^A, \widetilde{m}^A)$ and when there are very few strategic farmers (i.e., $\theta < \theta_1$), then marginally increasing m^A will hurt the expected profits of the farmers who grow crop A. This is because, even with a small increase in m^A, there is a substantial increase in the production of crop A by the myopic farmers (because the proportion of myopic farmers $(1 - \theta)$ is large when θ is small). Consequently, there is a drop in the price of crop A, which, coupled with the moderately low value of m^A, will reduce the expected profits of farmers of crop A.

We can conclude that, when θ is sufficiently small, there exists a threshold, say, m^{A*} (as shown in Fig. 2), such that offering MSP of A in $(\underline{m}^A, m^{A*})$ is disadvantageous to the farmers who grow crop A. By choosing m^A in the interval $(\underline{m}^A, m^{A*})$, the policy-maker creates an undesirable frenzy among the myopic

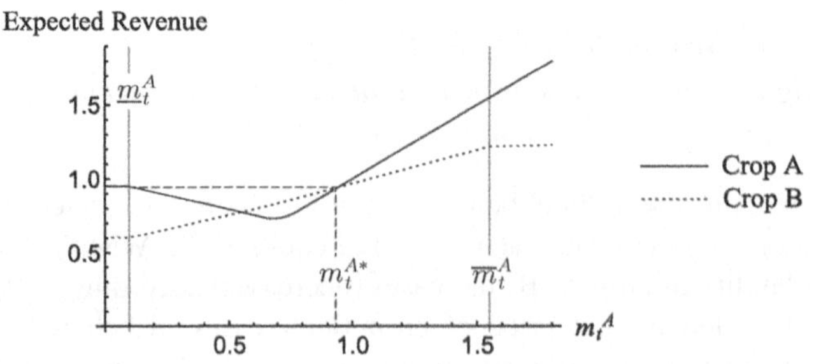

Fig. 2 Expected revenue from crop A and crop B as a function of MSP m^A

farmers who switch to crop A, thereby substantially increasing the production of crop A that causes a significant drop in the price of the crop, which overrides the benefit accrued by the marginal increase in m^A, thereby hurting the expected profits of all farmers growing crop A in equilibrium. Figure 2 provides an illustration of how equilibrium revenue of farmers of crop A can decrease with an increase in m^A.

6 Conclusions

In this chapter, we analyzed the role of *credit-based* MSP, which is a government intervention to safeguard farmers' incomes against crop price falls and, at the same time, to ensure sufficient and balanced production of different crops. By examining the interactions among a mixed population of myopic and strategic farmers for the case when there are two (complementary or substitutable) crops, we made the following findings. First, we showed that, regardless of the MSPs offered to the crops, the price disparity between the crops always worsens as the complementarity between the crops increases. Second, we found that MSPs may not always be beneficial to farmers. We proved that when there are very few strategic farmers, an improper choice of MSP of a crop can negatively impact the profits of the farmers, both myopic and strategic, who grow that crop. This defeats the actual goal of MSP for a crop, which is to benefit the farmers who grow that crop. Third, we showed that the total production of a crop is increasing in the MSP offered for the crop and decreasing in the MSP offered for the other crop. Therefore, a carefully chosen MSPs can always be used to balance crop productions. Hence, to reduce quantity disparity between crops, a carefully designed MSP policy is critical. While it is omitted in this chapter, we formulate an optimization problem so that a policy-maker (eg., government) can use to set optimal MSPs in Chintapalli and Tang (2017).

References

Alizamir S, Iravani F, Mamani H (2015) Price vs. revenue protection: an analysis of government subsidies in the agriculture industry. Technical report, Working paper

An J, Cho SH, Tang CS (2015) Aggregating smallholder farmers in emerging economies. Prod Oper Manag 24(9):1414–1429

Chand R (2003) Minimum support price in agriculture: changing requirements. Econ Polit Weekly 38(29): 3027–3028

Chen YJ, Tang CS (2015) The economic value of market information for farmers in developing economies. Prod Oper Manag 24(9):1441–1452

Chhatre A, Devalkar S, Seshadri S, Ramaswami B (2016) Crop diversification = profit and risk: the role of intermediaries (Presented at the 4th ISB – POMS workshop, Indian School of Business, Hyderabad)

Chintapalli P, Tang CS (2017) The impact of crop minimum support prices on crop selection and farmer welfare in the presence of strategic farmers. Technical report, Unpublished manuscript, UCLA Anderson School, available at SSRN 3024583

Dantwala M (1967) Incentives and disincentives in Indian agriculture. Indian J Agric Econ 22(2):1
Dawande M, Gavirneni S, Mehrotra M, Mookerjee V (2013) Efficient distribution of water between head-reach and tail-end farms in developing countries. Manuf Serv Oper Manag 15(2):221–238
Federgruen A, Lall U, Simsek AS (2015) Supply chain analysis of contract farming. Technical report, Working paper
Fox KA (1956) The contribution of farm price support programs to general economic stability. Policies to Combat Depression, pp. 295–356 (NBER)
Guda H, Rajapakshe T, Dawande M, Janakiraman G (2016) Agricultural support prices in developing economies: operational analysis and its use in policy making. Technical report, Working paper
Hu M, Liu Y, Wang W (2016) Altruistic rationality: the value of strategic farmers, social entrepreneurs and for-profit firms in crop planting decisions
Huh WT, Lall U (2013) Optimal crop choice, irrigation allocation, and the impact of contract farming. Prod Oper Manag 22(5):1126–1143
Huh WT, Athanassoglou S, Lall U (2012) Contract farming with possible reneging in a developing country: can it work? IIMB Manag Rev 24(4):187–202
Kazaz B, Webster S (2011) The impact of yield-dependent trading costs on pricing and production planning under supply uncertainty. Manuf Serv Oper Manag 13(3):404–417
Liao CN, Chen YJ, Tang CS (2019) Information provision policies for improving farmer welfare in developing countries: heterogeneous farmers and market selection. Manuf Serv Oper Manag 21(2): 254–270
Parker C, Ramdas K, Savva N (2016) Is it enough? Evidence from a natural experiment in India's agriculture markets. Manag Sci 62(9):2481–2503
Spitze R (1978) The food and agriculture act of 1977: issues and decisions. Am J Agric Econ 60(2):225–235
Subbarao D et al (2011) The challenge of food inflation. Technical report
Tang CS, Wang Y, Zhao M (2015) The implications of utilizing market information and adopting agricultural advice for farmers in developing economies. Prod Oper Manag 24(8):1197–1215
Thorbecke E (1982) Agricultural sector analysis and models in developing countries. Number 5 (Food & Agriculture Org.)
Tripathi AK et al (2013) Agricultural price policy, output, and farm profitability—examining linkages during post-reform period in India. Asian J Agric Dev 10(1):91–111

Improving Crop Yields Through Better Planting Schedules

Jayashankar M. Swaminathan and Ying Zhang

Abstract Improvement of agricultural productivity is often regarded as a solution to the impending food shortage problem in the world. In this paper we develop a novel model for seed growth using plant physiology literature and embed that in an optimal seed planting problem for a farmer facing rainfall uncertainty and planting capacity constraints. We establish the optimal planting schedule given the soil water content, planting capacity, and future rainfall uncertainty. In our computational study, we use field weather data from Southern Africa in a real size large-scale problem and demonstrate significant relative crop production advantage of the optimal planting schedule over commonly used heuristics in practice.

Keywords Optimal seeding schedules · Rainfall uncertainty · Plant physiology

1 Introduction

With the growing population of the globe, there appears an increasing food gap between current food supply capability and the amount of food to feed everyone in the near future. Driven by this demand from population growth, we must double the food production to support nearly ten million people on Earth by 2050 (United Nations 2009). Africa appears to be a critical player to feed the world with around 60% of the world's uncultivated arable land and vast room of agriculture productivity improvement. However, as irrigation infrastructure is rarely available for resource-poor farmers in this area and many countries such as South Africa have

J. M. Swaminathan (✉)
Kenan-Flagler Business School, University of North Carolina at Chapel Hill, Chapel Hill, NC, USA
e-mail: msj@unc.edu

Y. Zhang
Department of Management, College of Business, Clemson University, Clemson, SC, USA
e-mail: ying6@clemson.edu

J. M. Swaminathan, V. Deshpande (eds.), *Responsible Business Operations*, Springer Series in Supply Chain Management 10,
https://doi.org/10.1007/978-3-030-51957-5_3

minimal surplus water to extract, over 80% of Africa's agriculture is dependent on rainfall rather than irrigation (Obasanjo 2012). Besides, due to outdated farming technologies and techniques and rare application of farming machines coupled with unpredictable rainfall, the crop yields of African countries are far below the average of other developing countries. Africa provides barely 10% of the global agricultural production, and as a result about 240 million Africans already suffer from hunger (Lopes 2014). If the current situation persists, African can satisfy only 13% of the food needs by 2050 (Munang and Andrews 2014). Furthermore, this semiarid area is characterized by low precipitation and highly variable rainfall occurrence, and the ongoing climate change would lead to increased droughts, worsen farmers' access to water, and shorten the planting time window. Therefore ensuring to complete planting within the best time window has become extremely crucial to increase crop yield (Kings 2019). Scientific agriculture such as effective planting, fertilizing, irrigation, pest control, and mechanization could potentially help farmers improve crop yields and proceed to sustainable economy and societal growth.

Many international firms in the agriculture industry are endeavoring to develop innovative solutions to help small- and medium-scale farmers improve agriculture productivity in developing countries. Our motivation for this work comes from our interactions with AGCO, the third largest manufacturer of farm equipment in the world, that is, introducing modern farming practices in Africa. In its efforts to promote the application of farming mechanization, AGCO needs to quantify the benefits of scientific farming for funding agencies and governments that could finance these efforts and provide supporting policies and initiatives. In order to do that, it is important to understand the optimal approach of seed planting under limited planting speed and uncertain rainfall in the rain-fed agriculture and the associated crop production advantage compared to commonly used heuristics in farmers' practice.

In this paper, we study a farmer's seeding schedule throughout a planting season for a single crop under rainfall uncertainty. We use the cumulative biomass production to measure the crop yield and estimate the daily biomass production as the minimum of the values by two methods each day, one limited by water transpiration and the other limited by solar radiation. Utilizing earlier work in plant physiology related to biomass production, we further assume that the daily biomass production is zero during rainy days and proportional to water transpiration during sunny days and that in turn is dependent on the soil water content (Patteron 2018). We consider a planting schedule problem with planting capacity constraint and show that the optimal planting schedule is a time-dependent threshold-type policy where the threshold is dependent on soil water content, planting capacity, and remaining time in the horizon.

In our computational study, we use field weather data from Southern Africa to evaluate the advantage of the optimal seeding policy over commonly used heuristics in practice. The relative biomass production advantage of the optimal schedule is related to the initial soil water content and could be as high as 16.81%. Even when the initial soil water content is very low, the relative biomass production advantage of the optimal schedule is 8.88%.

The rest of the paper is organized as follows. Section 2 discusses the related literature. Section 3 studies the basic (manual) planting model, and Sect. 4 analyzes the mechanized planting model. In Sect. 5 we conduct an extensive computational study and explore the relative biomass production advantage of the optimal planting schedule over commonly used heuristics in practice. We conclude in Sect. 6.

2 Related Literature

Our work is in the area of agricultural operations. Lowe and Preckel (2004) review applications of planting models and decision technology to agriculture problems related to operations management. Recent papers in agricultural operations study capacity and production planning with random yield and demand (Kazaz 2004; Kazaz and Webster 2011; Tan and Çömden 2012; Boyabatlı et al. 2017; Hu et al. 2019), crop planning (Maatman et al. 2002; Boyabatlı et al. 2019), irrigation resource allocation (Dawande et al. 2013; Huh and Lall 2013), harvest risk (Allen and Schuster 2004; Lejeune and Kettunen 2017), food gleaning operations (Ata et al. 2019), contracting (Boyabatli et al. 2011; Ferreira et al. 2017; Federgruen et al. 2019), government policy (Gupta et al. 2017; Alizamir et al. 2019), agriculture market in developing economies (An et al. 2015; Tang et al. 2015; Liao et al. 2017), farmers' adulteration behavior (Levi et al. 2020), and data-driven agriculture operations (Devalkar et al. 2018). Among these, Tan and Çömden (2012) study the optimization of farm area and seeding time of multiple farms under uncertain demand. For a specific farm, the unit crop yield is purely dependent on the seeding time. Kazaz (2004) and Kazaz and Webster (2011) study pricing and production planning in a two-stage stochastic programming framework where the crop yield is dependent on the seeded amount. These papers do not study planting schedule and ignore the impact of uncertain rainfall on crop yield. In contrast, we model the schedule of seeding in a finite-horizon stochastic dynamic program framework and incorporate the impact of uncertain rainfall on biomass production and dynamics of soil water content. Maatman et al. (2002) model farmers' strategies of production, consumption, selling, purchasing, and storage in a two-stage stochastic programming framework with the objective to minimize deficits of various nutrients over multiple farming seasons. The production decision is dependent on observed rainfall that determines the number of days available for sowing. In our model, however, the objective is to maximize the expected crop production throughout a single planting season. The seeding decision is dependent on the soil water content, which in turn determines the growth of planted seeds and survival rate of seeds after planting. Ata et al. (2019) study the dynamic staffing policy in gleaning operations under uncertain food and labor supply and show that the optimal policy is a nested threshold policy. In the context of farming operations, we study the optimal seeding policy under uncertain rainfall (water supply) with the objective to maximize the crop yield and show that the optimal policy is a threshold policy.

Production scheduling in manufacturing industry has been extensively studied in operations management literature (Graves 1981). Most of the production scheduling models focus on minimizing total inventory cost during the planning horizon. In each period, inventory cost is incurred due to leftover inventory or unsatisfied demand, and the inventory (or backlog) carries over to the next period. The optimal production schedule minimizes the total expected cost. For the planting problem, however, seeds can only be planted in sunny periods. The survival of a newly planted seed and the biomass production of a seed living in the ground are dependent on the soil water content, the evolution of which is driven by uncertain rainfall and nonstationary precipitation. The optimal planting schedule maximizes the cumulative crop production at the end of the planting horizon.

In agriculture literature, searching for the optimal planting dates for a single crop in rain-fed agriculture in Africa has been studied (Laux et al. 2010; Wolf et al. 2015; Srivastava et al. 2016). Using simulation methods on historical or simulated rainfall data, these studies search for the start of the rainy season and hence the onset date of planting. However, these papers ignore the uncertainty of rainfall as well as planting capacity constraints faced by farmers. Our work, on the other hand, models a farmer's planting decisions using a finite-horizon stochastic dynamic program framework. In addition we model the dynamics of soil water content and seed growth. Our model incorporates the impact of rainfall uncertainty and limited planting capacity on farming operations and crop production and assumes that farmers only plant when it does not rain. Therefore in pursuing the highest expected crop production with a certain number of seeds and limited planting capacity, in our model, the optimal planting schedule is characterized by a series of planting operations rather than a one-shot planting decision.

3 Single Crop Planting Model

In this section we present a planting model for a single crop in a finite planting horizon. A planting horizon consists of N periods with reverse time indexing. For period t in the planting horizon, we define the probability of rainfall occurrence p_t^r to describe the uncertain weather: rainy or sunny. We assume that the weather is sunny when it does not rain because the average daily sunshine time is long and the intensity of solar radiation is high in Africa (SOLA 2013). Let $prec_t$ denote the conditional precipitation in period t given it is rainy. Since the local weather forecast information is available to most farmers nowadays, we assume that the farmer knows the weather of a given period (rainy or sunny) and the corresponding conditional precipitation at the beginning of that period. For future periods, however, she only knows the probability of rainfall occurrence and the conditional precipitation if it rains. Because farmers cannot plant when it rains, the farmer's decision is whether to plant in each sunny period throughout the planting horizon. Besides, for small-scale farmers in Africa, the majority of seeds come from farm-save seeds or other fellow farmers (McGuire 2016; GRAIN and AFSA 2018), and they rely largely on the government support to obtain seeds and other resources for farming (Olingo 2016). Therefore we assume that the farmer cannot obtain additional seeds or higher planting capacity once the planting season starts. Recent evidence has shown that in sub-Saharan Africa the low planting speed of farmers results in only a proportion of arable land to be optimally cultivated and the planting time window would shrink under the ongoing climate change, which explains why farmers encounter significant loss of crop production under severe climate conditions (Kings 2019). To model planting capacity, we assume that only one seed can be planted in one period in this section. In Sect. 4, we generalize this model to the case where multiple seeds can be planted in a given period, up to the planting capacity. Note that for simplicity we assume that each period represents one day. However, one could assume that one period represents half a day or smaller intervals as well.

We assume that subsequent applications of fertilizers and insecticides (if possible) and harvesting operations are automatically optimized by the farmer given the planting schedule and do not explicitly model these decisions. The effectiveness of fertilizing crops is highly dependent on the planting date and growth stage of crops, because fertilizers are often used to strengthen the root and leaf growth, blossom formation, and fruit production (Grant 2018). In sub-Saharan Africa, however, due to the price issue, the fertilizer use is significantly less than the world average (Gilbert 2014). Similarly the schedule of applying insecticides is dependent on the planting date because treatments are required to target specific growth stages and a time window shortly before or after the planting date (Allen et al. 2017). Besides, as the time gap between planting and harvesting is determined by the crop species and geographical characteristics, harvesting is largely dependent on the planting date (NASS and USDA 1997). Therefore scheduling any of these operations is dependent on and needs to be coordinated with the planting schedule.

After a seed is planted, it begins to germinate and establish the seedling under favorable conditions. When the seed imbibes water, it consumes the stored food reserve for metabolism and embryo growth and breaks the seed coat to develop a seedling (George and Rice 2016). Therefore whether a seed survives after planting and successfully establishes the seedling is significantly dependent on the soil water content in a short period after planting, about 6 days for maize in Africa (du Plessis 2003; George and Rice 2016). As this is a small proportion of the growing cycle, say 100 or 120 days for maize in Africa, we ignore the time of seedling emergence and thus assume that the survival probability of a seed after planting is a function of soil water content of the planting period ($sv(sw_t)$, where sw_t is the soil water content at the beginning of period t). We assume that once a seed survives the planting period, it will survive the rest of the planting horizon. We discuss the generalization where multiple seeds could be planted in Sect. 4.

Once a seedling is established, its growth relies on photosynthesis and transpiration. Photosynthesis is the bonding of carbon dioxide (CO_2) with water (H_2O) to make sugar ($C_6H_{12}O_6$) and oxygen (O_2), using the sun's energy (George and Rice 2016). The formation of sugars, starches, carbohydrates, and proteins in the plant is dependent on photosynthesis. The sugar stores energy and supports the metabolic process of the plant (respiration), including growth, reproduction, and

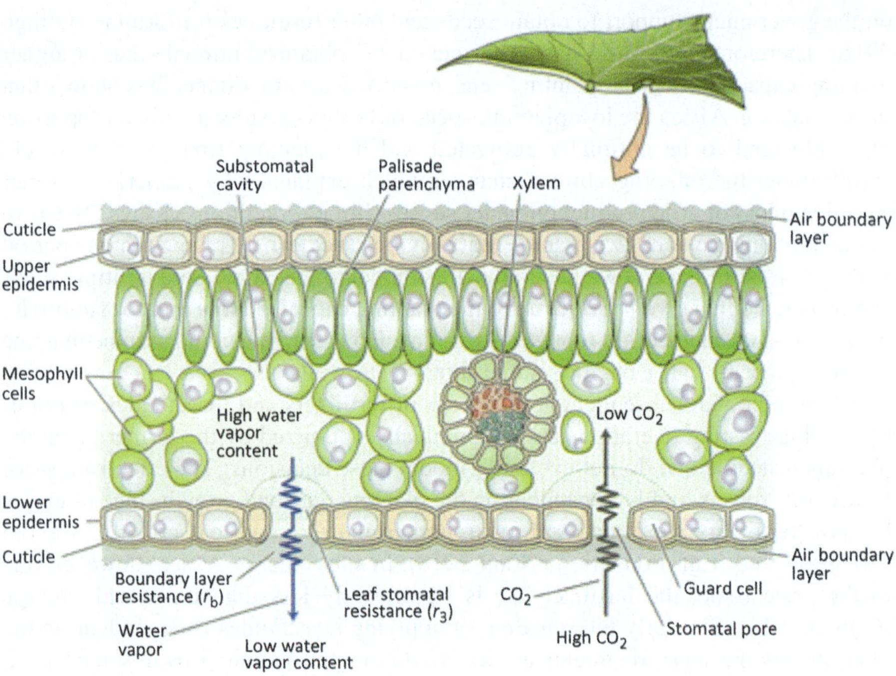

Fig. 1 Illustration of CO_2 input and water pathway. (Source: Taiz and Zeiger 2010)

other life processes. Transpiration refers to the movement of liquid water into, through, and out of the plant. Water in the soil enters the plant through the root to support photosynthesis and cell growth and gets evaporated through the stomata of the leaves. Transpiration is closely related to photosynthesis as both processes are controlled by the stomata. Stomata are the pores in leaves through which the atmospheric CO_2 required for photosynthesis enters the plant and the O_2 generated during photosynthesis gets released. Meanwhile water is transpired through the stomata when they are open. When the plant reduces the width of stomata opening to reduce water lost during the drought, it also reduces the photosynthesis output as less CO_2 could enter the leaves (Holding and Streich 2013). Figure 1 illustrates the movement of CO_2 and water through the stomata.

Crop yield is considered as the product of biomass production (also referred as total dry matter or aboveground biomass) and harvest index, where the latter often varies with crop species and genotypes (Atwell et al. 1999). As we consider the planting schedule for a single crop, we use the cumulative biomass production to measure the crop yield. To estimate daily biomass production, we use the same method as in Agricultural Production Systems Simulator (APSIM, a modular modeling framework developed by the Agricultural Production Systems Research Unit in Australia to simulate biophysical process in farming systems, Keating et al. 2003). The biomass production is the minimum of the values by two methods each day, one limited by water transpiration and the other limited by solar radiation interception, biomass production = min{transpiration × transpiration efficiency, radiation interception × radiation use efficiency} (APSIM 1996; Vijaya Kumar 2011).

The biomass production estimation method (transpiration or radiation interception) that limits the biomass production is dependent on the weather, rainy or sunny. During rainy days, the relative humidity of the air is high, and this results in low driving force of water movement through the leaves and even stomata closure with the leaves and roots hydrated. Thus the transpiration level is minimal (Taiz and Zeiger 2010), and we assume that the water transpiration is zero during a rainy period. Therefore the biomass production in a rainy period is zero. During sunny days, the plant could intercept abundant radiation as Africa receives more hours of bright sunshine than the rest of the world and has high intensity of solar radiation (SOLA 2013). However, to avoid wilting in dry air and high temperature, the plant would reduce the opening width of the stomata to reduce water loss through transpiration (Taiz and Zeiger 2010). Furthermore, for the rain-fed agriculture in Africa, water supply is regarded as the limiting factor for crop yield. Hence during a sunny day, the biomass production is dependent on water transpiration.

Atwell et al. (1999) summarizes the relationship that the daily biomass production is proportional to daily transpiration, and other studies in the agronomy literature show that biomass production is linear in cumulative transpiration (de Wit 1958; Bierhuizen and Slatyer 1965; Kemanian et al. 2005). Since previous work measures the cumulative transpiration for biomass production, we consider stationary transpiration efficiency and thus keep track of the cumulative transpiration of a seed throughout the seedling growth. Further, the agronomy literature shows that daily transpiration is a piece-wise linear function of soil water content (Gardner and Ehlig 1963). Therefore we model the daily biomass production expressed as a stationary function of soil water content. We use $bm(sw_t)$ to denote the daily biomass production of a living seed in the ground in a sunny period t. We assume that if a seed survives the planting period, it contributes the biomass production in that period as any other seed living in the ground does. We can show that our results still hold when a seed that survives the planting period only starts to contribute the biomass production from the next period.

For each period t, we keep track of the system state that includes the number of seeds living in the ground (gsd_t), the number of seeds available on hand for future planting (asd_t), and the soil water content (sw_t) at the beginning of that period. We use a function of soil water content and precipitation amount (zero if sunny) to describe the dynamics of soil water content, $sw_{t-1} = \omega_t(sw_t, prec_t)$. If period t is rainy, the farmer cannot plant and no decision needs to be made. The numbers of seeds living in the ground and available on hand remain the same till the beginning of the next period. If it is sunny, the farmer needs to decide whether to plant a seed. If the decision is not to plant, the numbers of seeds living in the ground and available on hand remain the same till the beginning of the next period. The seeds living in the ground contribute to the biomass production of $gsd_t \times bm(sw_t)$. If the decision is to plant, the number of seeds available on hand decreases by one. If this seed survives, the number of seeds living in the ground increases by one, and the newly planted seed and the seeds already living in the ground contribute to biomass production of $(gsd_t + 1) \times bm(sw_t)$ in total. If the seed does not survive after planting, the number of seeds living in the ground does not change, and only seeds living in the ground contribute to biomass production of $gsd_t \times bm(sw_t)$.

Our objective is to find a seeding schedule that maximizes the expected cumulative biomass production at the end of the planting horizon. We use a stochastic dynamic programming framework to model this problem. Our results show that for any period, seeds that are already living in the ground and seeds available on hand for future planting independently contribute to cumulative biomass production. That is to say, the expected biomass production contributed by a seed that is already living in the ground is not dependent on the future planting decisions of the farmer. Hence for a sunny period, it is sufficient to focus on the soil water content and amount of seeds available on hand to explore the optimal planting decision. Let $U_t(asd_t, sw_t)$ denote the maximum expected biomass production of all seeds available on hand (asd_t) and $Q_t(sw_t)$ denote the expected future biomass production of one seed living in the ground with t periods to go given that the soil water content at the beginning of period t is sw_t. Then,

$$\begin{aligned} U_t(asd_t, sw_t) &= p_t^r U_{t-1}(asd_t, \omega_t(sw_t, prec_t)) + (1 - p_t^r) \max \{U_{t-1}(asd_t, \omega_t(sw_t, 0)), \\ &\quad sv(sw_t)(bm(sw_t) + Q_{t-1}(\omega_t(sw_t, 0))) + U_{t-1}(asd_t - 1, \omega_t(sw_t, 0))\}, \\ Q_t(sw_t) &= p_t^r Q_{t-1}(\omega_t(sw_t, prec_t)) + (1 - p_t^r)(bm(sw_t) + Q_{t-1}(\omega_t(sw_t, 0))), \\ U_0(asd_0, sw_0) &= 0, \quad Q_0(sw_0) = 0. \end{aligned}$$

Theorem 1 *Given the number of seeds in the ground* (gsd_t)*, the number of seeds available on hand* (asd_t)*, and the soil water content* (sw_t) *in a sunny period* t*,*

1. *The optimal planting decision is dependent on the amount of seeds available on hand* (asd_t) *and soil water content* (sw_t)*.*
2. *There exists a planting threshold* $SD_t(sw_t)$ *that the optimal decision is to plant if the number of seeds available on hand is higher than the threshold* $(asd_t > SD_t(sw_t))$ *and not to plant otherwise.*

We show that the optimal planting decision is characterized by a planting threshold where the farmer should plant if the seed amount on hand is higher than the threshold and not plant otherwise. Planting early allows seeds to contribute to biomass production for a long time. However the soil water content at planting may be low, and this results in low seed survival after planting. On the other hand, seeds can only contribute to biomass production for a short period if they are planted late. But seeds would survive with a high chance as the soil water content tends to become higher at the late stage of the planting horizon. For a sunny period, the farmer should plant if planting one seed in this period contributes to higher biomass production than reserving this seed to the next period. The optimal planting decision can be characterized by the optimal planting threshold $SD_t(sw_t)$. This is because the expected biomass production by planting one seed in the current period remains constant regardless of the seed amount on hand, while the marginal biomass production by reserving this seed to the next period becomes lower when the farmer has more seeds available on hand; she should plant if she has enough seeds on hand. We further explore conditions under which the farmer is more willing to plant with higher soil water content.

4 Mechanized Planting Model

Mechanization can increase the planting speed. In this section, we study a mechanized planting problem where the farmer can plant up to m ($m > 1, m \in \mathcal{N}$) seeds in each period with m denoting the planting capacity. Note that the mechanized planting problem can be regarded as a generalized case of the planting problem in Sect. 3. For a sunny period t, the farmer's decision is the number of seeds to plant (i_t). We assume that for a given period, the survival probability and growth rate of seeds are identical and independent of each other. If i_t seeds are planted in period t, the probability that k seeds would survive after planting is $(sv(sw_t))^k(1 - sv(sw_t))^{i_t-k}$, and the corresponding biomass production brought by the newly planted seeds in period t is $k \times bm(sw_t)$. Similar to the model in Sect. 3, we can show that the expected biomass production of seeds available on hand is independent of the biomass production of seeds already living in the ground. Let $U_t^m(asd_t, sw_t)$ denote the maximum expected biomass production of all seeds available on hand (asd_t) with t periods to go given that the soil water content at the beginning of period t is sw_t and planting capacity is m. Then,

$$
\begin{aligned}
U_t^m(asd_t, sw_t) =& p_t^r U_{t-1}^m(asd_t, \omega_t(sw_t, prec_t)) \\
&+ (1 - p_t^r) \max_{i_t=0,1,\ldots,\min\{asd_t,m\}} \Big\{ \sum_{k=0}^{i_t} \tbinom{k}{i_t} (sv(sw_t))^k \times \\
&(1 - sv(sw_t))^{i_t-k}(k \times (bm(sw_t) + Q_{t-1}(\omega_t(sw_t, 0))) \\
&+ U_{t-1}^m(asd_t - i_t, \omega_t(sw_t, 0)))\Big\}, \\
U_0^m(asd_0, sw_0) =& 0.
\end{aligned}
$$

Theorem 2 *Given the number of seeds in the gound (gsd_t), the number of seeds available on hand (asd_t), the soil water content (sw_t), and the planting capacity (m) in a sunny period t,*

1. *The optimal planting decision is dependent on the amount of seeds available on hand (asd_t), soil water content (sw_t), and planting capacity (m).*
2. *There exists a planting threshold $SD_t^m(sw_t)$ that the optimal decision $a_t^m(asd_t, sw_t)$ satisfies:*

$$asd_t^m(asd_t, sw_t) = \begin{cases} \min\{m, asd_t - SD_t^m(sw_t)\} & \textit{if } asd_t > SD_t^m(sw_t) \\ 0 & \textit{otherwise} \end{cases}.$$

The optimal planting decision can be characterized by a time-dependent planting threshold $SD_t^m(sw_t)$. In a sunny period, if the seed amount on hand is higher than the threshold, the farmer should keep planting till the seed amount on hand reaches the planting threshold, unless the planting capacity does not allow. As a result, given the current optimal decision is to plant, if the available seed amount on hand increases by one unit, the optimal planting amount also increases by one unit, as long as the planting capacity allows. This result is similar to the modified base stock policy for the inventory problem under capacity constraint (Federgruen and Zipkin 1986).

Proposition 1 *$SD_t^m(sw_t)$ is non-decreasing in m. Furthermore, $SD_t^m(sw_t) + 1 \leq SD_t^{m+1}(sw_t)$ when $SD_t^m(sw_t) > 0$.*

The optimal planting threshold is non-decreasing in the planting capacity m. Under unlimited capacity, the optimal planting behavior is to plant all seeds in one period. However, with planting capacity constraint, the optimal planting behavior is a series of planting operations. As lower planting capacity allows fewer seeds to be planted under favorable planting conditions, it hurts the expected biomass production. In order to mitigate the loss due to low planting capacity, the optimal planting amount tends to be larger under less favorable planting conditions, resulting in low optimal planting thresholds. This result is consistent with the literature of capacitated inventory system where the order-up-to level is non-increasing in the production capacity (Federgruen and Zipkin 1986).

5 Computational Study

In the computational study, we aim to investigate the benefit of using an optimal seeding policy in comparison to commonly used heuristics in practice.

Seed Survival After Planting We characterize the seed survival probability after planting with a logit model of soil water content. This is consistent with the generalized linear mixed model (GLMM) that is commonly used to analyze the impact of soil water content on seed survival and seedling emergence in agriculture literature (Bolker et al. 2009).

Biomass Production As the crop physiology literature indicates, we assume that the daily biomass production is proportional to the soil water content (de Wit 1958; Gardner and Ehlig 1963). Because $bm(sw_t)$ is proportional to sw_t, we can show that when comparing two planting policies, the relative crop production difference of the two policies is irrelevant to the coefficient. Without loss of generality, we set the coefficient to be one.

Dynamics of Soil Water Content We apply a widely used Antecedent Precipitation Index (API) model to describe the dynamics of soil water content as a function of rainfall precipitation (Kohler and Linsley 1951). Since the model parameter differs minimally among different geographical areas (Kohler and Linsley 1951), we use the same parameter as the study on soil water content in West Africa (Pellarin et al. 2009).

5.1 *Weather Data*

We use daily weather data from 124 weather stations that span nine countries in Southern Africa (Zambia, Malawi, Zimbabwe, Botswana, Mozambique, Namibia, South Africa, Lesotho, and Swaziland) from www.wunderground.com. The data coverage is from September 2010 to May 2017, and we consider weather stations that have at least 1 full year of records. The data records indicate whether a given day was rainy or not at a given station as well as the amount of rain. We use this data set to calculate the probability of rainfall occurrence for a specific date (month, day) and the conditional rainfall precipitation amount for a specific date given that day is rainy.

5.2 *The Real Size Problem*

In the real problem that motivated this work, the rainy season typically spans 6 months from November to April. As crops need time to grow to maturity, we consider the maize planting window from November to February (long season 120-day type). This is consistent with the practice in Southern Africa that farmers start to plant cereal crops in early November and stop planting around the beginning of March (FEWS NET 2017). The planting window spans from November 1st to February 28th, thereby having 120 periods (days) in which the planting thresholds (functions of soil water content) need to be searched out. In order to handle such a large-scale problem and find the optimal solution, we develop an approximation algorithm based on IPA (Infinitesimal Perturbation Analysis) to search for the optimal planting schedules. IPA guarantees that the expectation of sample-path gradient we obtain converges to the gradient of the expected biomass production value.

5.3 *Relative Advantage of Optimal Planting Schedule Using Approximation*

We study the cases with the planting capacity $m = \{1, 2, 3, 4\}$ and investigate the relative biomass production advantage of the optimal planting schedule over commonly used myopic heuristics in practice. In Africa, planting normally starts after several consecutive days of rain or enough cumulative precipitation. For the staple product, maize, one of the rules of thumb in Southern Africa is to start planting after observing 25 mm of cumulative precipitation in a 10-day period starting from November 1st and then keep planting at full capacity until all seeds are depleted (Tadross et al. 2009). Based on this convention, we adopt the commonly used heuristics in practice using the rainfall data in Southern Africa and compare the final biomass production values to those generated by the optimal planting schedule. We use the relative advantage of the optimal planting schedule over commonly used heuristics in biomass production to measure the performance of the optimal planting schedule:

$$\begin{aligned}&\textit{Performance of Optimal Planting Schedule}\\&=\frac{\textit{Biomass Prodction of Optimal Planting Schedule}-\textit{Biomass Production of Commonly Used Heuristics}}{\textit{Biomass Production of Commonly Used Heuristics}}.\end{aligned}$$

Note that under commonly used heuristics, the amount of seeds planted is set to be the planting capacity value (the maximum number of seeds that the farmer can plant in one period) whenever planting occurs.

We consider three levels of initial soil water content from the field weather data: the average soil water content (10.39 mm), the minimum soil water content (2.26 mm), and the maximum soil water content (24.53 mm). For each of the seven rainy seasons from November 2010 to April 2017, we calculate the soil water content on November 1st using the rainfall data in September and October before the start of that rainy season (November 1st), assuming that the soil water content at the beginning of September 1st is zero. The average (minimum, maximum) level is the average (minimum, maximum) soil water content on November 1st over the seven rainy seasons.

Table 1 demonstrates the relative biomass production advantage of the optimal planting schedule over commonly used myopic heuristics when the planting capacity under both planting policies is the same. With low level of initial soil water content, the final biomass production under the optimal schedule gets hurt since it takes a long time for the soil water content to reach the optimal threshold for planting. In spite of that, adopting the optimal schedule leads to improvement in the final biomass production even under minimum initial soil water content. The relative biomass production improvement of the optimal policy under manual planting (planting capacity = 1) is 12.75% under average initial soil water content, 8.88% under minimum initial soil water content, and 15.04% under maximum initial

Table 1 Relative biomass production improvement of the optimal policy

Planting capacity	1	2	3	4
Avg. soil water content	12.75%	15.05%	15.05%	15.10%
Min. soil water content	8.88%	14.02%	13.95%	13.96%
Max. soil water content	15.04%	16.81%	16.78%	16.81%

Table 2 Relative biomass production improvement of the optimal policy and mechanization

Planting capacity	1	2	3	4
Avg. soil water content	12.75%	125.64%	245.49%	360.89%
Min. soil water content	8.88%	116.68%	242.04%	356.05%
Max. soil water content	15.04%	129.96%	250.26%	367.26%

soil water content. Under mechanized planting, the relative biomass production improvement of the optimal policy minimally changes as the planting capacity changes. The relative improvement is about 15% under average initial soil water content, 14% under minimal soil water content, and 17% under maximum soil water content. We also conduct out-of-sample testing where the optimal thresholds are searched out using the first 3 years' data, and the advantage of the optimal policy over the myopic policy is evaluated based on the remaining years' data. The relative improvement of the optimal policy is close to but lower than the corresponding full information case in Table 1.

Table 2 shows the relative biomass production advantage of mechanized or manual planting under the optimal policy over manual planting under commonly used myopic heuristics. When moving from manual planting to mechanized planting, the number of seeds available at the beginning of the planting window is increased proportional to the increased planting speed. By adopting mechanization (planting capacity $= 3$) under the optimal policy, the final biomass production can be improved by nearly 250% regardless of the initial soil water content. This improvement by adopting both the optimal policy and mechanization is consistent with the observations made in the pilot study in Zambia by AGCO (Swaminathan 2018).

6 Concluding Remarks

Food needs with increasing population of the world have brought a lot of pressure to agricultural productivity in African countries. With the crop production significantly less than the average of the developing world, farmers in Africa need to adopt advanced planting techniques to improve crop yields.

In this paper we study the planting schedule problem of a single crop under rainfall uncertainty and planting capacity constraint. Planting early may allow more seeds to be planted, but higher soil water content later on could lead to a higher chance of seed survival. We show that the optimal planting schedule is a time-dependent threshold-type policy where the threshold is dependent on the soil water content and planting capacity. In practice, farmers start to plant each year after observing enough cumulative rainfall. Utilizing field weather data collected from Southern Africa, we show that adopting the optimal schedule could significantly improve crop production.

In this work we only focus on the seeding schedule and assume that other decisions such as fertilizer addition and pest control are done optimally. In this process, we developed a new model on seed growth based on plant physiology literature. In a follow-up study (Zhang and Swaminathan 2020), we develop a more robust model of plant growth using the DSSAT simulation tool used by FAO. Using that model, we establish the optimal seeding policy and test the benefits of optimal planting policy over heuristics used in practice and provide computational insights on climate conditions. In many real situations, other agricultural operations such as fertilizer addition, pest control and irrigation are critical but difficult to optimize. In Africa, farmers start to obtain access to advanced technology in farming such as soil and solar sensors, satellite data, and plant growth monitors. Application of these technologies would influence the optimal seeding policy. Further, we only consider a single crop in this work. Sometimes, crop rotation has an important impact on crop production, and in such cases that needs to be integrated. Finally, we do not consider any budget constraints that a farmer might face for seed procurement, automation, fertilizers, or pest control, and we do not consider fixed cost associated with planting in any given day (hiring labor or machinery). All the above issues are ripe for future studies in this area.

Acknowledgments The authors thank Dr. Bob Patterson from NC State University for his valuable input.

Appendix: Proof of Optimal Planting Policy

Proof of Theorem 1 The first part of Theorem 1 is a direct application of the result that seeds that are living in the ground and seeds available on hand for future planting independently contribute to the cumulative biomass production. To show the second part, it is sufficient to show that $U_t(asd_t, sw_t)$ is concave in asd_t, i.e., the incremental difference of $U_t(asd_t, sw_t)$ with respect to asd_t is non-increasing. We show this result by induction. Let $\Delta U_t(asd_t, sw_t) = U_t(asd_t + 1, sw_t) - U_t(asd_t, sw_t)$ denote the incremental indifference of $U_t(asd_t, sw_t)$ with respect to asd_t, and we need to show that $\Delta U_t(asd_t, sw_t) \geq \Delta U_t(asd_t + 1, sw_t)$. For $t = 0$, obviously this result holds based on Sect. 3. Assume that $\Delta U_{t-1}(asd_{t-1}, sw_{t-1}) \geq \Delta U_{t-1}(asd_{t-1} + 1, sw_{t-1})$. Note that $SD_t(sw_t)$ is the largest integer value of asd_t that satisfies

$$\Delta U_{t-1}(asd_t - 1, \omega_t(sw_t, 0)) \geq sv(sw_t) \times (bm(sw_t) + Q_{t-1}(\omega_t(sw_t, 0))).$$

Then

$$\Delta U_t(asd_t, sw_t) = p_t^r \Delta U_{t-1}(asd_t, \omega_t(sw_t, prec_t)) + (1 - p_t^r)*$$

$$\begin{cases} \Delta U_{t-1}(asd_t - 1, \omega_t(sw_t, 0)), & asd_t > SD_t(sw_t) \\ \Delta U_{t-1}(asd_t, \omega_t(sw_t, 0)), & asd_t < SD_t(sw_t) \\ sv(sw_t) \times (bm(sw_t) + Q_{t-1}(\omega_t(sw_t, 0))), & asd_t = SD_t(sw_t) \end{cases},$$

$$\Delta U_t(asd_t + 1, sw_t) =$$

$$p_t^r \Delta U_{t-1}(asd_t + 1, \omega_t(sw_t, prec_t)) + (1 - p_t^r)\times$$

$$\begin{cases} \Delta U_{t-1}(asd_t, \omega_t(sw_t, 0)), & asd_t > SD_t(sw_t) - 1 \\ \Delta U_{t-1}(asd_t + 1, \omega_t(sw_t, 0)), & asd_t < SD_t(sw_t) - 1 \\ sv(sw_t) \times (bm(sw_t) + Q_{t-1}(\omega_t(sw_t, 0))), & asd_t = SD_t(sw_t) - 1 \end{cases}.$$

If $asd_t \geq SD_t(sw_t) + 1$, $\Delta U_t(asd_t + 1, sw_t) \leq \Delta U_t(asd_t, sw_t)$ is non-positive by assumption; if $asd_t \leq SD_t(sw_t) - 2$, $\Delta U_t(asd_t + 1, sw_t) \leq \Delta U_t(asd_t, sw_t)$ is non-positive by assumption; if $asd_t = SD_t(sw_t) - 1$, $\Delta U_t(asd_t + 1, sw_t) - \Delta U_t(asd_t, sw_t)$ is

$$p_t^r(\Delta U_{t-1}(asd_t + 1, \omega_t(sw_t, prec_t) - \Delta U_{t-1}(asd_t, \omega_t(sw_t, prec_t))))+$$
$$(1 - p_t^r)(sv(sw_t)(bm(sw_t) + Q_{t-1}(\omega_t(sw_t, 0))) - \Delta U_{t-1}(asd_t, \omega_t(sw_t, 0))),$$

which is non-positive because the optimal decision is not to plant when the seed amount $asd_t + 1$ equals to $SD_t(sw_t)$; if $asd_t = SD_t(sw_t)$, $\Delta U_t(asd_t + 1, sw_t) - \Delta U_t(asd_t, sw_t)$ is

$$p_t^r(\Delta U_{t-1}(asd_t + 1, \omega_t(sw_t, prec_t) - \Delta U_{t-1}(asd_t, \omega_t(sw_t, prec_t))))+$$
$$(1 - p_t^r)(\Delta U_{t-1}(asd_t, \omega_t(sw_t, 0)) - sv(sw_t)(bm(sw_t) + Q_{t-1}(\omega_t(sw_t, 0)))),$$

which is non-positive because the optimal planting decision is to plant when the seed amount $asd_t + 1$ equals to $SD_t(sw_t) + 1$.

Proof of Theorem 2 Similar to the proof of Theorem 1, the first part of Theorem 2 is the direct application of the result that seeds living in the ground and seeds available on hand independently contribute to the cumulative biomass production. Note that the meaning of $Q_t(.)$ in the mechanized planting model is the same as in the manual planting model in Sect. 3, which is the expected future biomass production of a seed living in the ground with t periods to go, and it is independent of the planting capacity m. To show the optimality of the threshold policy, it is sufficient to show that $\Delta U_t^m(asd_t, sw_t) = U_t^m(asd_t + 1, sw_t) - U_t^m(asd_t, sw_t)$ is non-increasing in asd_t. For $t = 0$, obviously $\Delta U_t^m(asd_t, sw_t)$ is non-increasing in asd_t. Assume that $\Delta U_{t-1}^m(asd_{t-1}, sw_{t-1})$ is non-increasing in asd_{t-1}. Then

$$
\begin{aligned}
&\Delta U_t^m(asd_t, sw_t)\\
=&p_t^r \Delta U_{t-1}^m(asd_t, \omega_t(sw_t, prec_t)) + (1-p_t^r)\times\\
&\begin{cases}
\Delta U_{t-1}^m(asd_t - m, \omega_t(sw_t, 0)), & asd_t \geq SD_t^m(sw_t) + m\\
\Delta U_{t-1}^m(asd_t, \omega_t(sw_t, 0)), & asd_t < SD_t^m(sw_t)\\
sv(sw_t) \times (bm(sw_t) + Q_{t-1}(\omega_t(sw_t, 0))), & o.w.
\end{cases},
\end{aligned}
$$

$$
\Delta U_t^m(asd_t+1, sw_t) = p_t^r \Delta U_{t-1}^m(asd_t+1, \omega_t(sw_t, prec_t)) + (1-p_t^r)\times
\begin{cases}
\Delta U_{t-1}^m(asd_t + 1 - m, \omega_t(sw_t, 0)), & asd_t \geq SD_t^m(sw_t) + m - 1\\
\Delta U_{t-1}^m(asd_t + 1, \omega_t(sw_t, 0)), & asd_t < SD_t^m(sw_t) - 1\\
sv(sw_t) \times (bm(sw_t) + Q_{t-1}(\omega_t(sw_t, 0))), & o.w.
\end{cases}.
$$

If $asd_t \geq SD_t^m(sw_t)+m$, $\Delta U_t^m(asd_t+1, sw_t) \leq \Delta U_t^m(asd_t, sw_t)$ by assumption; if $asd_t \leq SD_t^m(sw_t)-2$, $\Delta U_t^m(asd_t+1, sw_t) \leq \Delta U_t^m(asd_t, sw_t)$ by assumption; if $asd_t = SD_t^m(sw_t)-1$, $\Delta U_t^m(asd_t+1, sw_t) - \Delta U_t^m(asd_t, sw_t)$ is

$$
\begin{aligned}
&p_t^r(\Delta U_{t-1}^m(asd_t+1, \omega_t(sw_t, prec_t) - \Delta U_{t-1}^m(asd_t, \omega_t(sw_t, prec_t))))+\\
&(1-p_t^r)(sv(sw_t)(bm(sw_t) + Q_{t-1}(\omega_t(sw_t, 0))) - \Delta U_{t-1}^m(asd_t, \omega_t(sw_t, 0))),
\end{aligned}
$$

which is non-positive because the optimal decision is not to plant when the seed amount asd_t+1 is $SD_t^m(sw_t)$; if $asd_t = SD_t^m(sw_t)+m-1$, $\Delta U_t^m(asd_t+1, sw_t) - \Delta U_t^m(asd_t, sw_t)$ is

$$
\begin{aligned}
&p_t^r(\Delta U_{t-1}^m(asd_t+1, \omega_t(sw_t, prec_t) - \Delta U_{t-1}^m(asd_t, \omega_t(sw_t, prec_t))))+\\
&(1-p_t^r)(\Delta U_{t-1}^m(asd_t+1-m, \omega_t(sw_t, 0))\\
&- sv(sw_t)(bm(sw_t) + Q_{t-1}(\omega_t(sw_t, 0)))),
\end{aligned}
$$

which is non-positive because the optimal planting decision is to plant when the seed amount asd_t+1 is $SD_t^m(sw_t)+m$. If $SD_t^m(sw_t) \leq asd_t \leq SD_t^m(sw_t)+m-2$, $\Delta U_t^m(asd_t+1, sw_t) - \Delta U_t^m(asd_t, sw_t)$ is zero, and it is obviously non-positive.

Proof of Proposition 1 To show that $SD_t^m(sw_t) \leq SD_t^{m+1}(sw_t)$, it is sufficient to show that $\forall \beta > 0$, $\Delta U_{t-1}^m(asd_t, \omega_t(sw_t, \beta))$ is non-decreasing in m,

$$
\begin{aligned}
&U_{t-1}^m(asd_t+1, \omega_t(sw_t, \beta)) - U_{t-1}^m(asd_t, \omega_t(sw_t, \beta)) \leq U_{t-1}^{m+1}(asd_t+1, \omega_t(sw_t, \beta))\\
&\quad - U_{t-1}^{m+1}(asd_t, \omega_t(sw_t, \beta)).
\end{aligned}
$$

We show this result by induction. For $t = 1$, it is easy to show that the above inequality holds. We assume that $\Delta U_{t-1}^m(asd_t, \omega_t(sw_t, \beta))$ is non-decreasing in m. Note that $asd_t = SD_t^m(sw_t)$ is the largest integer that satisfies

$$
\Delta U_{t-1}^m(asd_t - 1, \omega_t(sw_t, 0)) \geq sv(sw_t)(bm(sw_t) + Q_{t-1}(\omega_t(sw_t, 0)))
$$

and $\Delta U_{t-1}^m(asd_t - 1, \omega_t(sw_t, 0))$ is non-decreasing in m by assumption. Therefore at $asd_t = SD_t^m(sw_t)$, we have $\Delta U_{t-1}^{m+1}(asd_t - 1, \omega_t(sw_t, 0)) \geq sv(sw_t)(bm(sw_t) + Q_{t-1}(\omega_t(sw_t, 0)))$. Since $SD_t^{m+1}(sw_t)$ is the largest integer that satisfies

$$\Delta U_{t-1}^{m+1}(asd_t - 1, \omega_t(sw_t, 0)) \geq sv(sw_t)(bm(sw_t) + Q_{t-1}(\omega_t(sw_t, 0))),$$

and $asd_t = SD_t^m(sw_t)$ satisfies the above inequality, $SD_t^{m+1}(sw_t) \geq SD_t^m(sw_t)$. When $SD_t^m(sw_t) = 0$, obviously $SD_t^{m+1}(sw_t) \geq SD_t^m(sw_t)$ holds.

We then show that $\Delta U_t^m(asd_{t+1}, \omega_{t+1}(sw_{t+1}, \beta))$ is non-decreasing in m. For a t-period problem with capacity m, we have

$$\Delta U_t^m(asd_{t+1}, \omega_{t+1}(sw_{t+1}, \beta)) = p_t^r \Delta U_{t-1}^m(asd_{t+1}, \omega_t(\omega_{t+1}(sw_{t+1}, \beta), prec_t)) + (1 - p_t^r)\times$$

$$\begin{cases} \Delta U_{t-1}^m(asd_{t+1} - m, \omega_t(\omega_{t+1}(sw_{t+1}, \beta), 0)), & asd_{t+1} \geq SD_t^m(\omega_{t+1}(sw_{t+1}, \beta)) + m \\ \Delta U_{t-1}^m(asd_{t+1}, \omega_t(\omega_{t+1}(sw_{t+1}, \beta), 0)), & asd_{t+1} < SD_t^m(\omega_{t+1}(sw_{t+1}, \beta)) \\ sv(\omega_{t+1}(sw_{t+1}, \beta)) \times (bm(\omega_{t+1}(sw_{t+1}, \beta)) & \\ +Q_{t-1}(\omega_t(\omega_{t+1}(sw_{t+1}, \beta), 0))), & o.w. \end{cases}.$$

For a t-period problem with capacity $m + 1$, we have

$$\Delta U_t^{m+1}(asd_{t+1}, \omega_{t+1}(sw_{t+1}, \beta)) = p_t^r \Delta U_{t-1}^{m+1}(asd_{t+1}, \omega_t(\omega_{t+1}(sw_{t+1}, \beta), prec_t)) + (1 - p_t^r)\times$$

$$\begin{cases} \Delta U_{t-1}^{m+1}(asd_{t+1} - m - 1, \omega_t(\omega_{t+1}(sw_{t+1}, \beta), 0)), & asd_{t+1} \geq SD_t^{m+1}(\omega_{t+1}(sw_{t+1}, \beta)) + m + 1 \\ \Delta U_{t-1}^{m+1}(asd_{t+1}, \omega_t(\omega_{t+1}(sw_{t+1}, \beta), 0)), & asd_{t+1} < SD_t^{m+1}(\omega_{t+1}(sw_{t+1}, \beta)) \\ sv(\omega_{t+1}(sw_{t+1}, \beta)) \times (bm(\omega_{t+1}(sw_{t+1}, \beta)) & \\ +Q_{t-1}(\omega_t(\omega_{t+1}(sw_{t+1}, \beta), 0))), & o.w. \end{cases}.$$

We define

$$\Lambda_{t-1}^m(asd_{t+1}, \omega_t(\omega_{t+1}(sw_{t+1}, \beta), 0)) = \frac{\Delta U_t^m - p_t^r \Delta U_{t-1}^m(asd_{t+1}, \omega_t(\omega_{t+1}(sw_{t+1}, \beta), prec_t))}{1 - p_t^r}.$$

By assumption, $\Delta U_{t-1}^m(asd_{t+1}, \omega_t(\omega_{t+1}(sw_{t+1}, \beta), prec_t))$ is non-decreasing in m. It remains to show that $\Lambda_{t-1}^m(asd_{t+1}, \omega_t(\omega_{t+1}(sw_{t+1}, \beta), 0))$ is non-decreasing in m. We consider the following three cases of $SD_t^m(sw_t)$ as in the proof of Theorem 2.

1. $SD_t^m(\omega_{t+1}(sw_{t+1}, \beta)) \leq \max\{0, asd_{t+1} - m\}$,

$$\Lambda_{t-1}^{m}(asd_{t+1},\omega_t(\omega_{t+1}(sw_{t+1},\beta),0)) =$$

$$\begin{cases} \Delta U_{t-1}^{m}(asd_{t+1}-m,\omega_t(\omega_{t+1}(sw_{t+1},\beta),0)), & asd_{t+1}\geq m \\ sv(\omega_{t+1}(sw_{t+1},\beta))(bm(\omega_{t+1}(sw_{t+1},\beta))+Q_{t-1}(\omega_t(\omega_{t+1}(sw_{t+1},\beta),0))), & asd_{t+1}<m \end{cases},$$

$$if\, SD_t^{m+1}(\omega_{t+1}(sw_{t+1},\beta)) \leq \max\{0, asd_{t+1}-m-1\},$$

$$\Lambda_{t-1}^{m+1}(asd_{t+1},\omega_t(\omega_{t+1}(sw_{t+1},\beta),0)) =$$

$$\begin{cases} \Delta U_{t-1}^{m+1}(asd_{t+1}-m-1,\omega_t(\omega_{t+1}(sw_{t+1},\beta),0)), & asd_{t+1}\geq m+1 \\ sv(\omega_{t+1}(sw_{t+1},\beta))(bm(\omega_{t+1}(sw_{t+1},\beta))+Q_{t-1}(\omega_t(\omega_{t+1}(sw_{t+1},\beta),0))), & asd_{t+1}<m+1 \end{cases},$$

$$if\, \max\{0, asd_{t+1}-m\} \leq SD_t^{m+1}(\omega_{t+1}(sw_{t+1},\beta)) \leq asd_{t+1},$$

$$\Lambda_{t-1}^{m+1}(asd_{t+1},\omega_t(\omega_{t+1}(sw_{t+1},\beta),0)) =$$

$$sv(\omega_{t+1}(sw_{t+1},\beta))(bm(\omega_{t+1}(sw_{t+1},\beta))+Q_{t-1}(\omega_t(\omega_{t+1}(sw_{t+1},\beta),0))),$$

$$if\, SD_t^{m+1}(\omega_{t+1}(sw_{t+1},\beta)) \geq asd_{t+1}+1,$$

$$\Lambda_{t-1}^{m+1}(asd_{t+1},\omega_t(\omega_{t+1}(sw_{t+1},\beta),0)) = \Delta U_{t-1}^{m+1}(asd_{t+1},\omega_t(\omega_{t+1}(sw_{t+1},\beta),0));$$

2. $\max\{0, asd_{t+1}+1-m\} \leq SD_t^m(\omega_{t+1}(sw_{t+1},\beta)) \leq asd_{t+1},$

$$\Lambda_{t-1}^{m}(asd_{t+1},\omega_t(\omega_{t+1}(sw_{t+1},\beta),0)) =$$

$$sv(\omega_{t+1}(sw_{t+1},\beta))(bm(\omega_{t+1}(sw_{t+1},\beta))+Q_{t-1}(\omega_t(\omega_{t+1}(sw_{t+1},\beta),0))),$$

$$if\, SD_t^{m+1}(\omega_{t+1}(sw_{t+1},\beta)) \geq asd_{t+1}+1,$$

$$\Lambda_{t-1}^{m+1}(asd_{t+1},\omega_t(\omega_{t+1}(sw_{t+1},\beta),0)) = \Delta U_{t-1}^{m+1}(asd_{t+1},\omega_t(\omega_{t+1}(sw_{t+1},\beta),0)),$$

$$if\, SD_t^{m+1}(\omega_{t+1}(sw_{t+1},\beta)) \leq asd_{t+1}, \Lambda_{t-1}^{m+1}(asd_{t+1},\omega_t(\omega_{t+1}(sw_{t+1},\beta),0)) =$$

$$sv(\omega_{t+1}(sw_{t+1},\beta))(bm(\omega_{t+1}(sw_{t+1},\beta))+Q_{t-1}(\omega_t(\omega_{t+1}(sw_{t+1},\beta),0)));$$

3. $SD_t^m(\omega_{t+1}(sw_{t+1},\beta)) \geq asd_{t+1}+1,$

$$\Lambda_{t-1}^{m}(asd_{t+1},\omega_t(\omega_{t+1}(sw_{t+1},\beta),0))=\Delta U_{t-1}^{m}(asd_{t+1},\omega_t(\omega_{t+1}(sw_{t+1},\beta),0)),$$

$$\Lambda_{t-1}^{m+1}(asd_{t+1},\omega_t(\omega_{t+1}(sw_{t+1},\beta),0))=\Delta U_{t-1}^{m+1}(asd_{t+1},\omega_t(\omega_{t+1}(sw_{t+1},\beta),0)).$$

For case 1, if $SD_t^m(\omega_{t+1}(sw_{t+1},\beta)) \leq \max\{0, asd_{t+1}-m\}$, $\Delta U_{t-1}^{m}(asd_{t+1}-m,\omega_t(\omega_{t+1}(sw_{t+1},\beta),0)) \leq \Delta U_{t-1}^{m+1}(asd_{t+1}-m,\omega_t(\omega_{t+1}(sw_{t+1},\beta),0))$ by assumption and $\Delta U_{t-1}^{m+1}(asd_{t+1}-m,\omega_t(\omega_{t+1}(sw_{t+1},\beta),0)) \leq \Delta U_{t-1}^{m+1}(asd_{t+1}-m-1,\omega_t(\omega_{t+1}(sw_{t+1},\beta),0))$ as $\Delta U_{t-1}^{m+1}(asd_{t+1})$ is non-increasing in asd_{t+1}. For $asd_{t+1}=m$, as

$$\Delta U_{t-1}^{m}(asd_{t+1}-m,\omega_t(\omega_{t+1}(sw_{t+1},\beta),0))$$

$$\leq sv(\omega_{t+1}(sw_{t+1},\beta))(bm(\omega_{t+1}(sw_{t+1},\beta))+Q_{t-1}(\omega_t(\omega_{t+1}(sw_{t+1},\beta),0)))$$

when $SD_t^m(\omega_{t+1}(sw_{t+1}, \beta)) \le \max\{0, asd_{t+1} - m\}$, we have

$$\Lambda_{t-1}^m(asd_{t+1}, \omega_t(\omega_{t+1}(sw_{t+1}, \beta), 0)) \le \Lambda_{t-1}^{m+1}(asd_{t+1}, \omega_t(\omega_{t+1}(sw_{t+1}, \beta), 0)).$$

If $\max\{0, asd_{t+1} - m\} \le SD_t^{m+1}(\omega_{t+1}(sw_{t+1}, \beta)) \le asd_{t+1}$,

$$\Lambda_{t-1}^m(asd_{t+1}, \omega_t(\omega_{t+1}(sw_{t+1}, \beta), 0)) \le \Lambda_{t-1}^{m+1}(asd_{t+1}, \omega_t(\omega_{t+1}(sw_{t+1}, \beta), 0))$$

as

$$\Delta U_{t-1}^m(asd_{t+1} - m, \omega_t(\omega_{t+1}(sw_{t+1}, \beta), 0)) -$$
$$sv(\omega_{t+1}(sw_{t+1}, \beta))(bm(\omega_{t+1}(sw_{t+1}, \beta)) + Q_{t-1}(\omega_t(\omega_{t+1}(sw_{t+1}, \beta), 0))) < 0$$

when $asd_{t+1} \ge m$. If $SD_t^{m+1}(\omega_{t+1}(sw_{t+1}, \beta)) \ge asd_{t+1} + 1$,

$$\Lambda_{t-1}^m(asd_{t+1}, \omega_t(\omega_{t+1}(sw_{t+1}, \beta), 0)) \le \Lambda_{t-1}^{m+1}(asd_{t+1}, \omega_t(\omega_{t+1}(sw_{t+1}, \beta), 0))$$

as

$$\Delta U_{t-1}^{m+1}(asd_{t+1}, \omega_t(\omega_{t+1}(sw_{t+1}, \beta), 0)) -$$
$$sv(\omega_{t+1}(sw_{t+1}, \beta))(bm(\omega_{t+1}(sw_{t+1}, \beta)) + Q_{t-1}(\omega_t(\omega_{t+1}(sw_{t+1}, \beta), 0))) > 0.$$

Hence for case 1, $\Lambda_{t-1}^m(asd_{t+1}, \omega_t(\omega_{t+1}(sw_{t+1}, \beta), 0)) \le \Lambda_{t-1}^{m+1}(asd_{t+1}, \omega_t(\omega_{t+1}(sw_{t+1}, \beta), 0))$. For case 2, as

$$\Delta U_{t-1}^{m+1}(asd_{t+1}, \omega_t(\omega_{t+1}(sw_{t+1}, \beta), 0)) -$$
$$sv(\omega_{t+1}(sw_{t+1}, \beta))(bm(\omega_{t+1}(sw_{t+1}, \beta)) + Q_{t-1}(\omega_t(\omega_{t+1}(sw_{t+1}, \beta), 0))) > 0$$

if $SD_t^{m+1}(\omega_{t+1}(sw_{t+1}, \beta)) \ge asd_{t+1} + 1$, we have

$$\Lambda_{t-1}^m(asd_{t+1}, \omega_t(\omega_{t+1}(sw_{t+1}, \beta), 0)) \le \Lambda_{t-1}^{m+1}(asd_{t+1}, \omega_t(\omega_{t+1}(sw_{t+1}, \beta), 0)).$$

For case 3, by assumption $\Delta U_{t-1}^m(asd_{t+1}, \omega_t(\omega_{t+1}(sw_{t+1}, \beta), 0)) \le \Delta U_{t-1}^{m+1}(asd_{t+1}, \omega_t(\omega_{t+1}(sw_{t+1}, \beta), 0))$. Hence $\Lambda_{t-1}^m(asd_{t+1}, \omega_t(\omega_{t+1}(sw_{t+1}, \beta), 0)) \le \Lambda_{t-1}^{m+1}(asd_{t+1}, \omega_t(\omega_{t+1}(sw_{t+1}, \beta), 0))$. Therefore we show that $\Delta U_t^m(asd_{t+1}, \omega_{t+1}(sw_{t+1}, \beta))$ is non-decreasing in m, i.e., $U_t^m(asd_{t+1}, \omega_{t+1}(sw_{t+1}, \beta))$ is supermodular in (asd_{t+1}, m).

Finally to show that $SD_t^m(sw_t) + 1 \le SD_t^{m+1}(sw_t)$ when $SD_t^m(sw_t) > 0$, we only need to consider the case where $asd_t = SD_t^m(sw_t)$ is the largest positive integer that satisfies $\Delta U_{t-1}^m(asd_t - 1, \omega_t(sw_t, 0)) \ge sv(sw_t)(bm(sw_t) + Q_{t-1}(\omega_t(sw_t, 0)))$ and $asd_t = SD_t^{m+1}(sw_t)$ is the largest positive integer that satisfies $\Delta U_{t-1}^{m+1}(asd_t - 1, \omega_t(sw_t, 0)) \ge sv(sw_t)(bm(sw_t) + Q_{t-1}(\omega_t(sw_t, 0)))$.

If we can show that $\Delta U_{t-1}^{m+1}(SD_t^m(sw_t), \omega_t(sw_t, 0)) \geq sv(sw_t)(bm(sw_t) + Q_{t-1}(\omega_t(sw_t, 0)))$, then we show that $SD_t^m(sw_t)+1 \leq SD_t^{m+1}(sw_t)$. It is sufficient to show that $\Delta U_{t-1}^m(asd_t, sw_t) \leq \Delta U_{t-1}^{m+1}(asd_t + 1, sw_t)$ for all $asd_t \in \mathcal{N}$. We show this by induction. For $t = 1$, it is obvious that $\Delta U_{t-1}^m(asd_t, sw_t) \leq \Delta U_{t-1}^{m+1}(asd_t + 1, sw_t)$. Assume that $\Delta U_{t-1}^m(asd_t, sw_t) \leq \Delta U_{t-1}^{m+1}(asd_t + 1, sw_t)$. For period t,

$$\Delta U_t^m(asd_{t+1}, sw_t) = p_t^r \Delta U_{t-1}^m(asd_{t+1}, \omega_t(sw_t, prec_t)) + (1 - p_t^r) \times$$

$$\begin{cases} \Delta U_{t-1}^m(asd_{t+1} - m, \omega_t(sw_t, 0)), & asd_{t+1} \geq SD_t^m(sw_t) + m \\ \Delta U_{t-1}^m(asd_{t+1}, \omega_t(sw_t, 0)), & asd_{t+1} < SD_t^m(sw_t) \\ sv(sw_t) \times (bm(sw_t) + Q_{t-1}(\omega_t(sw_t, 0))), & o.w. \end{cases}.$$

By assumption $\Delta U_{t-1}^m(asd_{t+1}, \omega_t(sw_t, prec_t)) \leq \Delta U_{t-1}^{m+1}(asd_{t+1} + 1, \omega_t(sw_t, prec_t))$. Then we need to show that $\Lambda_{t-1}^m(asd_{t+1}, sw_t) \leq \Lambda_{t-1}^{m+1}(asd_{t+1} + 1, sw_t)$. We consider the following three cases. Note that $SD_t^m(sw_t) \leq SD_t^{m+1}(sw_t)$.

1. $SD_t^m(sw_t) \leq \max\{0, asd_{t+1} - m\}$,

$$\Lambda_{t-1}^m(asd_{t+1}, sw_t) = \begin{cases} \Delta U_{t-1}^m(asd_{t+1} - m, \omega_t(sw_t, 0)), & asd_{t+1} \geq m \\ sv(sw_t) \times (bm(sw_t) + Q_{t-1}(\omega_t(sw_t, 0))), & asd_{t+1} < m \end{cases},$$

if $SD_t^{m+1}(sw_t) \leq \max\{0, asd_{t+1} - m\}$,

$$\Lambda_{t-1}^{m+1}(asd_{t+1}+1, sw_t) = \begin{cases} \Delta U_{t-1}^{m+1}(asd_{t+1}+1 - m, \omega_t(sw_t, 0)), & asd_{t+1} \geq m \\ sv(sw_t) \times (bm(sw_t) + Q_{t-1}(\omega_t(sw_t, 0))), & asd_{t+1} < m \end{cases},$$

if $\max\{0, asd_{t+1} - m + 1\} \leq SD_t^{m+1}(sw_t) \leq asd_{t+1} + 1$,

$\Lambda_{t-1}^{m+1}(asd_{t+1} + 1, sw_t) = sv(sw_t) \times (bm(sw_t) + Q_{t-1}(\omega_t(sw_t, 0)))$,

if $SD_t^{m+1}(sw_t) \geq asd_{t+1} + 2$, $\Lambda_{t-1}^{m+1}(asd_{t+1} + 1, sw_t)$

$= \Delta U_{t-1}^{m+1}(asd_{t+1} + 1, \omega_t(sw_t, 0))$;

2. $\max\{0, asd_{t+1} + 1 - m\} \leq SD_t^m(sw_t) \leq asd_{t+1}$,

$\Lambda_{t-1}^m(asd_{t+1}, sw_t) = sv(sw_t) \times (bm(sw_t) + Q_{t-1}(\omega_t(sw_t, 0)))$,

if $SD_t^{m+1}(sw_t) \geq asd_{t+1}+2$, $\Lambda_{t-1}^{m+1}(asd_{t+1}+1, sw_t) + \Delta U_{t-1}^{m+1}(asd_{t+1}+1, \omega_t(sw_t, 0))$,

if $SD_t^{m+1}(sw_t) \leq asd_{t+1}+1$, $\Lambda_{t-1}^{m+1}(asd_{t+1}+1, sw_t) = sv(sw_t) \times (bm(sw_t) + Q_{t-1}(\omega_t(sw_t, 0)))$;

3. $SD_t^m(sw_t) \geq asd_{t+1} + 1$,

$$\Lambda_{t-1}^m(asd_{t+1}, sw_t) = \Delta U_{t-1}^m(asd_{t+1}, \omega_t(sw_t, 0)),$$

$$\Lambda_{t-1}^{m+1}(asd_{t+1} + 1, sw_t) = \Delta U_{t-1}^{m+1}(asd_{t+1} + 1, \omega_t(sw_t, 0)).$$

For case 1, when $asd_{t+1} \leq m-1$, it is obvious that $\Lambda_{t-1}^{m}(asd_{t+1}, sw_t) \leq \Lambda_{t-1}^{m+1}(asd_{t+1}+1, sw_t)$ as $\Delta U_{t-1}^{m+1}(asd_{t+1}+1, sw_t) \geq sv(sw_t) \times (bm(sw_t) + Q_{t-1}(\omega_t(sw_t, 0)))$ when $SD_t^{m+1}(sw_t) \geq asd_{t+1}+2$. When $asd_{t+1} \geq m$, as $\Delta U_{t-1}^{m}(asd_{t+1}-m, \omega_t(sw_t, 0)) \leq sv(sw_t) \times (bm(sw_t) + Q_{t-1}(\omega_t(sw_t, 0)))$ when $SD_t^{m}(sw_t) \leq \max\{0, asd_{t+1}-m\}$ and by assumption $\Delta U_{t-1}^{m}(asd_{t+1}-m, \omega_t(sw_t, 0)) \leq \Delta U_{t-1}^{m+1}(asd_{t+1}-m, \omega_t(sw_t, 0))$, $\Lambda_{t-1}^{m}(asd_{t+1}, sw_t) \leq \Lambda_{t-1}^{m+1}(asd_{t+1}+1, sw_t)$. For case 2, as $\Delta U_{t-1}^{m+1}(asd_{t+1}+1, \omega_t(sw_t, 0)) - sv(sw_t) \times (bm(sw_t) + Q_{t-1}(\omega_t(sw_t, 0))) \geq 0$ when $SD_t^{m+1}(sw_t) \geq asd_{t+1}+2$, $\Lambda_{t-1}^{m}(asd_{t+1}, sw_t) \leq \Lambda_{t-1}^{m+1}(asd_{t+1}+1, sw_t)$. For case 3, $\Delta U_{t-1}^{m}(asd_{t+1}, \omega_t(sw_t, 0)) \leq \Delta U_{t-1}^{m+1}(asd_{t+1}+1, \omega_t(sw_t, 0))$ by assumption. Thus we show that $\Lambda_{t-1}^{m}(asd_{t+1}, sw_t) \leq \Lambda_{t-1}^{m+1}(asd_{t+1}+1, sw_t)$.

References

Alizamir S, Iravani F, Mamani H (2019) An analysis of price vs. revenue protection: government subsidies in the agriculture industry. Manag Sci 65(1):32–49

Allen SJ, Schuster EW (2004) Controlling the risk for an agricultural harvest. Manuf Serv Oper Manag 6(3):225–236

Allen C, Bibb J, Catchot D, Cook D, Crow W, Dean J, Gore J, Layton B, Little N, MacGown J, Musser F (2017) 2018 insect control guide for agronomic crops. Technical report, Mississippi State University

An J, Cho S, Tang CS (2015) Aggregating smallholder farmers in emerging economies. Prod Oper Manag 24(9):1414–1429

APSIM (1996) Maize module. https://www.apsim.info/Documentation/Model,CropandSoil/CropModuleDocumentation/Maize.aspx. Accessed on 28 Mar 2018

Ata B, Lee D, Sönmez E (2019) Dynamic volunteer staffing in multicrop gleaning operations. Oper Res 67(2):295–314

Atwell BJ, Kriedemann PE, Turnbull CGN (1999) Plants in action: adaptation in nature, performance in cultivation. MacMillan Education Australia, South Yarra, Australia

Bierhuizen JF, Slatyer RO (1965) Effect of atmospheric concentration of water vapour and CO2 in determining transpiration-photosynthesis relationships of cotton leaves. Agric Meteorol 2(4):259–270

Bolker BM, Brooks ME, Clark CJ, Geange SW, Poulsen JR, Stevens MHH, White JS (2009) Generalized linear mixed models: a practical guide for ecology and evolution. Trends Ecol Evolut 24(3):127–135

Boyabatli O, Kleindorfer PR, Koontz SR (2011) Integrating long-term and short-term contracting in beef supply chains. Manag Sci 57(10):1771–1787

Boyabatlı O, Nguyen J, Wang T (2017) Capacity management in agricultural commodity processing and application in the palm industry. Manuf Serv Oper Manag 19(4):551–567

Boyabatlı O, Nasiry J, Zhou Y (2019) Crop planning in sustainable agriculture: dynamic farmland allocation in the presence of crop rotation benefits. Manag Sci 65(5):2060–2076

Dawande M, Gavirneni S, Mehrotra M, Mookerjee V (2013) Efficient distribution of water between head-reach and tail-end farms in developing countries. Manuf Serv Oper Manag 15(2):221–238

Devalkar SK, Seshadri S, Ghosh C, Mathias A (2018) Data science applications in indian agriculture. Prod Oper Manag

de Wit CT (1958) Transpiration and crop yields. Technical report, Unknown Publisher

du Plessis J (2003) Maize production. Accessed on 29 Feb 2020

Federgruen A, Zipkin P (1986) An inventory model with limited production capacity and uncertain demands II. The discounted-cost criterion. Math Oper Res 11(2):208–215

Federgruen A, Lall U, Şimşek AS (2019) Supply chain analysis of contract farming. Manuf Serv Oper Manag 21(2):361–378

Ferreira K, Goh J, Valav E (2017) Intermediation in the supply of agricultural products in developing economies. Available at SSRN

FEWS NET (2017) ZAMBIA Food Security Outlook. http://www.fews.net/southern-africa/zambia/food-security-outlook/february-2017. Accessed on 29 Feb 2020

Gardner WR, Ehlig CF (1963) The influence of soil water on transpiration by plants. J Geophys Res 68(20):5719–5724

George MR, Rice K (2016) Plant growth and development. In: George MR (ed) Ecology and management of annual rangelands, Department of Plant Science, Davis, CA, pp 73–95

Gilbert N (2014) Costly fertiliser holds back a green revolution in Africa. https://www.theguardian.com/global-development/2014/dec/05/costly-fertiliser-holds-back-a-green-revolution-in-africa. Accessed on 29 Feb 2020

GRAIN, AFSA (2018) The real seeds producers: small-scale farmers save, use, share and enhance the seed diversity of the crops that feed africa. https://www.grain.org/en/article/6035-the-real-seeds-producers-small-scale-farmers-save-use-share-and-enhance-the-seed-diversity-of-the-crops-that-feed-africa. Accessed on 29 Feb 2020

Grant BL (2018) When to fertilize plants: best times for application of fertilizer. https://www.gardeningknowhow.com/garden-how-to/soil-fertilizers/best-times-to-apply-fertilizer.htm. Accessed on 29 Feb 2020

Graves SC (1981) A review of production scheduling. Oper Res 29(4):646–675

Gupta S, Dawande M, Janakiraman G, Sarkar A (2017) Distressed selling by farmers: model, analysis, and use in policy-making. Prod Oper Manag 26(10):1803–1818

Holding DR, Streich AM (2013) Plant growth processes: transpiration, photosynthesis, and respiration. The Board of Reagents of the University of Nebraska, University of Nebraska, Nebraska pp. 1–10

Hu M, Liu Y, Wang W (2019) Socially beneficial rationality: the value of strategic farmers, social entrepreneurs, and for-profit firms in crop planting decisions. Manag Sci 65(8):3654–3672

Huh WT, Lall U (2013) Optimal crop choice, irrigation allocation, and the impact of contract farming. Prod Oper Manag 22(5):1126–1143

Kazaz B (2004) Production planning under yield and demand uncertainty with yield-dependent cost and price. Manuf Serv Oper Manag 6(3):209–224

Kazaz B, Webster S (2011) The impact of yield-dependent trading costs on pricing and production planning under supply uncertainty. Manuf Serv Oper Manag 13(3):404–417

Keating BA, Carberry PS, Hammer GL, Probert ME, Robertson MJ, Holzworth D, Huth NI, Hargreaves JN, Meinke H, Hochman Z et al (2003) An overview of apsim, a model designed for farming systems simulation. Eur J Agron 18(3–4):267–288

Kemanian AR, Stöckle CO, Huggins DR (2005) Transpiration-use efficiency of barley. Agric For Meteorol 130(1–2):1–11

Kings S (2019) Maize vs time: the race to feed sa. https://mg.co.za/article/2019-01-25-00-maize-vs-time-the-race-to-feed-sa. Accessed on 29 Feb 2020

Kohler MA, Linsley RK (1951) Predicting the runoff from storm rainfall, vol. 30. US Department of Commerce, Weather Bureau

Laux P, Jäckel G, Tingem RM, Kunstmann H (2010) Impact of climate change on agricultural productivity under rainfed conditions in cameroon—a method to improve attainable crop yields by planting date adaptations. Agric For Meteorol 150(9):1258–1271

Lejeune MA, Kettunen J (2017) Managing reliability and stability risks in forest harvesting. Manuf Serv Oper Manag 19(4):620–638

Levi R, Singhvi S, Zheng Y (2020) Economically motivated adulteration in farming supply chains. Manag Sci 66(1):209–226

Liao C, Chen Y, Tang CS (2017) Information provision policies for improving farmer welfare in developing countries: heterogeneous farmers and market selection. Manuf Serv Oper Manag 21(2):254–270

Lopes C (2014) We need more agribusiness in Africa. http://www.un.org/africarenewal/magazine/special-edition-agriculture-2014/we-need-more-agribusiness-africa. Accessed on 29 Feb 2020

Lowe TJ, Preckel PV (2004) Decision technologies for agribusiness problems: a brief review of selected literature and a call for research. Manuf Serv Oper Manag 6(3):201–208

Maatman A, Schweigman C, Ruijs A, van Der Vlerk MH (2002) Modeling farmers' response to uncertain rainfall in burkina faso: a stochastic programming approach. Oper Res 50(3):399–414

McGuire S (2016) Africa's informal seed system needs to be brought in from the cold. https://theconversation.com/africas-informal-seed-system-needs-to-be-brought-in-from-the-cold-54609. Accessed on 29 Feb 2020

Munang R, Andrews J (2014) Despite climate change, Africa can feed Africa. http://www.un.org/africarenewal/magazine/special-edition-agriculture-2014/despite-climate-change-africa-can-feed-africa. Accessed on 29 Feb 2020

NASS, USDA (1997) Usual planting and harvesting dates for u.s. field crops. Technical report, United States Department of Agriculture

Obasanjo O (2012) How Africa could feed the world. http://globalpublicsquare.blogs.cnn.com/2012/11/06/how-africa-could-feed-the-world/. Accessed on 29 Feb 2020

Olingo A (2016) Farmers use seed, storage and market in fighting grain loss. https://www.theeastafrican.co.ke/scienceandhealth/Farmers-use-seed-storage-and-market-in-fighting-grain-loss-/3073694-3350740-dhpnc6z/index.html. Accessed on 29 Feb 2020

Patteron B (2018) Personal Communication with Dr. Bob Patterson, Alumni Distinguished Professor of Crop Science in NC State University

Pellarin T, Tran T, Cohard J-M, Galle S, Laurent J-P, De Rosnay P, Théo Vischel (2009) Soil moisture mapping over west africa with a 30-min temporal resolution using amsr-e observations and a satellite-based rainfall product. Hydrol Earth Syst Sci Discuss 13(10):1887–1896

SOLA (2013) South Africa's solar resource compared to the rest of the world. https://sola.africa/news/south-africas-solar-resource-compared-to-the-rest-of-the-world/. Accessed on 29 Feb 2020

Srivastava AK, Mboh CM, Gaiser T, Webber H, Ewert F (2016) Effect of sowing date distributions on simulation of maize yields at regional scale–a case study in central ghana, West Africa. Agric Syst 147:10–23

Swaminathan JM (2018) Agco: innovating the agricultural value chain in Africa, case study. Technical report, Kenan-Flagler Business School, UNC – Chapel Hill

Tadross M, Suarez P, Lotsch A, Hachigonta S, Mdoka M, Unganai L, Lucio F, Kamdonyo D, Muchinda M (2009) Growing-season rainfall and scenarios of future change in Southeast Africa: implications for cultivating maize. Clim Res 40(2–3):147–161

Taiz, L, Zeiger E (2010) Plant physiology, 5th edn. Sinauer Associates, Sunderland

Tan B, Çömden N (2012) Agricultural planning of annual plants under demand, maturation, harvest, and yield risk. Eur J Oper Res 220(2):539–549

Tang CS, Wang Y, Zhao M (2015) The implications of utilizing market information and adopting agricultural advice for farmers in developing economies. Prod Oper Manag 24(8):1197–1215

United Nations (2009) Food production must double by 2050 to meet demand from world's growing population, innovative strategies needed to combat hunger, experts tell second committee. http://www.un.org/press/en/2009/gaef3242.doc.htm. Accessed on 29 Feb 2020

Vijaya Kumar P(2011) Lecture notes in crop weather modeling: phenology, biomass and its partitioning in crops. Available at http://www.crida.in/Training%20material/CWM/index.html. Central Research Institute for Dryland Agriculture

Wolf J, Ouattara K, Supit I (2015) Sowing rules for estimating rainfed yield potential of sorghum and maize in burkina faso. Agric For Meteorol 214:208–218

Zhang Y, Swaminathan JM (2020) Manufacturing & Service Operations Management. In: Improved crop productivity through optimized planting schedules

Role of Donors in Global Health Supply Chains

Gemma Berenguer and Iva Rashkova

Abstract This chapter describes the donors' role in global health supply chain, an area within the broader field of Responsible Operations. We start by defining global health and describing the major donors in this domain. Historically, these donors have had a paternalistic role of managing the procurement and other major supply chain management activities. More recently, their role closely resembles a financier, leaving the operational execution to its grant recipients (e.g., ministry of health) in low- and middle-income countries (LMICs). We discuss emerging innovative financial mechanisms including performance-based funding and bridge-financing. These various roles and activities make evaluating value for money and preventing stockouts particularly challenging. Finally, we discuss opportunities for improvement of donor's impact, specifically through knowledge transfer support to grant recipients.

Keywords Global health supply chains · Donors · Financial mechanisms · Procurement · Knowledge transfer

1 Introduction to Global Health Supply Chains

Global health is an area of health care with the goal of providing essential medicines to the population of low- and middle-income countries (LMICs), where essential medicines are cataloged by the World Health Organization (WHO) as those that

G. Berenguer (✉)
Department of Business Administration, Universidad Carlos III de Madrid, Getafe, Spain
e-mail: gemma.berenguer@uc3m.es

I. Rashkova
Olin Business School, Washington University, St Louis, MO, USA

J. M. Swaminathan, V. Deshpande (eds.), *Responsible Business Operations*, Springer Series in Supply Chain Management 10,
https://doi.org/10.1007/978-3-030-51957-5_4

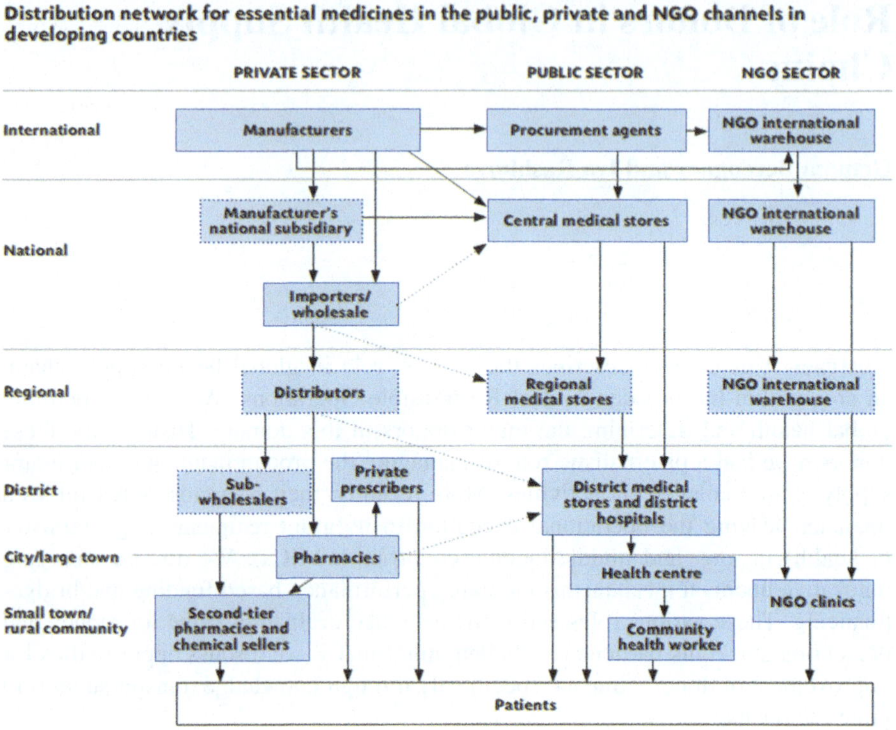

Fig. 1 Distribution network for essential medicines in the public, private, and NGO channels in developing countries (Yadav et al. 2011)

satisfy the priority health-care needs of the population.[1] Global health supply chains consist of a composite of global or international operations that are run by a large number of actors from different countries starting at the suppliers' site and finishing at the final patients' closest pharmacy or clinic. Consequently, multiple supply chain tiers of storage and distribution are needed. Yadav et al. (2011) note that while in high-income countries, medicines are distributed largely by the private sector, in low- and middle-income countries, organizations from the three sectors (private, public, and nonprofit) coexist and might connect in some parts of the supply chain (Fig. 1). Specifically, in a large number of low-income countries, the majority of essential medicines is distributed by the local government, which uses a central medical store (CMS) to distribute to regional and/or district-level stores.

The main actors in global health supply chains can be identified while reviewing the financial and physical flows. The major agents that compose the financial flow are the international donors, local governments, and manufacturers. The physical flow starts at the manufacturer site (i.e., the pharma companies), and the next step

[1] https://www.who.int/topics/essential_medicines/en/

is represented by the procurement agent, which can be the same international donor that funded the drugs, the local government, or a different separate entity. Next, when the public sector runs the supply chain, drugs are placed in the CMS and subsequent regional stores; otherwise, drugs are distributed by nonprofit or mission entities or the private sector (Fig. 1).

Global supply chains are complex networks due to the large number of participant agents at each different tier for each different essential medicine. Kraiselburd and Yadav (2013) claim that the main inefficiencies of global supply chains result from the following issues:

1. Coordination problems across multiple agents with different objectives
2. Lack of considering context-specific factors while designing the supply chain
3. Taking a myopic financial approach compromising efficiencies in physical and informational flows

A large number of scholars concur with the issue of lack of coordination as one of the major factors that affect efficiencies in global health supply chains (e.g., Buse and Walt 1996, Privett and Gonsalvez 2014). In relation to the direct implication of the donors to this issue, it has been observed that the efficiency of country-level supply chains for essential medicines is negatively correlated with the number of donors involved in the supply chain (Berenguer et al. 2016, Knack and Rahman 2007). Berenguer et al. (2016) empirically test this negative correlation for reproductive health products in 44 different Sub-Saharan countries. In this study, besides using the number of donors as the measure, an alternative measure of funding concentration based on the Herfindahl-Hirschman Index (HHI) is employed.[2] In addition, Knack and Rahman (2007) show empirical evidence that suggests that when there are many small donors and no dominant donor, administrative capacity in recipient country governments is eroded.

The issue related to context-specific factors is often overlooked, but these factors can significantly affect supply chain performance. Dowling (2011) states that confounding factors affecting medicine availability in low- and middle-income countries are difficult to identify. This report refers to the adequate health workforce as one of the bottlenecks to improve health systems in many developing countries. In the previously cited empirical study by Berenguer et al. (2016) it is found that socioeconomic factors have a significant impact on the efficiency of reproductive health programs. In particular, the logistics capabilities of a country and the public health expenditure are found to be the most significant factors influencing logistics efficiency. In this study, the country's female literacy rate and, again, the public health expenditure are the most significant factors that affect a country's uptake of modern contraceptives.

The third factor relates to the dominance of design decisions based on the financial flow (donors), causing inefficiencies in the information and physical flows. Information flows should be fundamental inputs in the decision-making process;

[2]This measure is defined as the sum of squares of each donor's fund share.

however, often times, in global health supply chains, data is not available due to the extremely stringent budgets that do not prioritize data-gathering activities or data-based analytics. For example, Levine et al. (2008) claim that demand forecasting is often overlooked in global health, but accurate demand forecasting is critical in improving health outcomes. There are many other data-based analytic tools, which use can be extremely beneficial in global health. Natarajan and Swaminathan (2018) offer a survey of literature that study analytical models and best practices to allocate resources to advance global health outcomes.

This chapter is centered on the role of donors in improving global supply chain efficiencies. The next section provides a general description of the major donors in global health. Section 3 reports the most interesting financing mechanisms offered by donors. Section 4 describes the donors' procurement and supply chain management roles. Section 5 discusses challenges and opportunities for donors in their different roles. Section 6 briefly summarizes and concludes this chapter.

2 The Donor Landscape

Since 2009, the Institute for Health Metrics and Evaluation (IHME) has been providing data related to global health expenditure in the form of Development Assistance for Health (DAH) (IHME 2019). To be precise, DAH accounts for all "*financial and in-kind resources that are transferred through major international development agencies to low- and middle-income countries with the primary purpose of maintaining or improving health.*" In 2018, DAH totaled $38.9 billion, down 3.3% from 2017, and it corresponds to around 24.5% of all health spending in low-income countries. Global health funding has remained stagnant since 2013, where over the last 5 years, the annualized growth rate of DAH has been −0.3% (IHME 2019).

According to the 2018 HICME report, the largest single contributing funders of 2018 have been the following: the US government ($13.2 billion in DAH, down 8.8% from 2017), followed by the UK government ($3.3 billion), and the Bill & Melinda Gates Foundation ($3.2 billion). The largest multilateral and public-private partnerships that disbursed DAH in 2018 included the following: the Global Fund ($3.2 billion), WHO ($2.6 billion), and UNICEF ($1.9 billion) (Chang et al. 2019). Next, we describe the major distinctive characteristics of each one of the big global health donors. Each donor has historically taken a different approach and specialization in the global health field that is important to emphasize. In accordance with the DHA list of major single and multilateral donors provided above, we develop the following descriptions that are also summarized in Table 1. Major attention is focused on showing the major funding and procurement mechanisms

Table 1 Summary of major global health donors

Donor	Origin of funds	Health focus	Financial mechanisms (Sect. 3)	Procurement service (Sect. 4)
USAID	US government	Child and maternal health, HIV/AIDS, and infectious diseases	Grant provider	Contracted to private global health organizations (e.g., JSI International, Chemonics)
PEPFAR	US government	HIV/AIDS, TB and malaria	Grant provider	Products procured by supply chain management system project (SCMS)
Bill & Melinda Gates Foundation	Private	Multiple (special focus on maternal and child health care)	Grant provider	
The Global Fund	Multilateral public-private donors (USA, UK, Gates Foundation, France, etc.)	AIDS, tuberculosis and, malaria	Performance-based financing (PBF) of donor pledges	Volunteered pooled procurement (VPP) service Procurement of capacity-building services (CBS) Supply chain management assistance (SCMA) service
WHO	Multilateral	Multiple	Focuses on fundraising and funding WHO programs	WHO/Contracting and Procurement Service (WHO/CPS)
UNICEF	Multilateral public-private donors	Children and mothers' health	Focuses on raising funds to invest on UNICEF's own programs	Vaccine pooled procurement service
GAVI	Multilateral public-private donors (UK, Gates Foundation, USA, Norway, etc.)	Vaccines	International Finance Facility for Immunization (IFFIm) (Dickens 2011)	UNICEF designated as procurement agent for specific vaccines (Dickens 2011)

used by each donor. The most innovative mechanisms are described in the following sections of this chapter.

USAID It is the United States Agency for International Development and it is the largest bilateral agency funded by the US government. Its main goal is to administer civilian foreign aid and development assistance. The USAID global health branch focuses on three specific areas: preventing child and maternal deaths, controlling the HIV/AIDS epidemic, and combating infectious diseases.[3]USAID supply chain procurement assistance to recipient countries has been contracted out to third-party organizations such as John Snow International and Chemonics International. In 2015, USAID awarded to Chemonics its largest single contract of $9.5 billion (Pisa and McCurdy 2019).

PEPFAR It is the President's Emergency Plan for AIDS Relief, which manages all the funds from the US government related to managing the global HIV/AIDS epidemic. Thus, PEPFAR is the USAID's HIV and AIDS program. Related to working with in-country supply chains, PEPFAR has worked closely with local staff (Pisa and McCurdy 2019). For example, PEPFAR operated its own supply chain owning regional distribution centers and provided technical support and medicines to national government supply chains via PEPFAR's Supply Chain Management System project (SCMS) (Sullivan et al. 2012).

Bill & Melinda Gates Foundation It is considered the largest private foundation in the world, and it is controlled by three trustees Bill Gates, Melinda Gates, and Warren Buffet. The Gates foundation has a specific global health division that grants money to a diversity of institutions. In 2018, the Gates Foundation gave $371.0 million of DAH funds to UN agencies, $310.4 million was directed to GAVI, and $269.0 million went to the Global Fund (IHME 2019).

The Global Fund to Fights AIDS, Tuberculosis, and Malaria It is an international financing organization founded in 2002. Its major focus is on accelerating the end of AIDS, tuberculosis, and malaria. Related to working with in-country supply chains, during its initial 10 years, the Global Fund took a hands-off approach and was serving mainly as a financier. However, since an internal report that revealed large risks and vulnerability, the organization started to focus on supporting the last mile distribution and storage activities (Pisa and McCurdy 2019). In this direction, in June 2009, the Global Fund launched the Volunteered Pooled Procurement (VPP) service, procurement capacity-building services (CBS), and the Supply Chain Management Assistance (SCMA) service.

WHO The World Food Organization is a United Nations (UN) agency concerned with international public health. The WHO's core functions are the following[4]:

[3]https://www.usaid.gov/global-health

[4]https://www.who.int/about/role/en/

- Providing leadership on matters critical to health and engaging in partnerships where joint action is needed
- Shaping the research agenda and stimulating the generation, translation, and dissemination of valuable knowledge
- Setting norms and standards and promoting and monitoring their implementation
- Articulating ethical and evidence-based policy options
- Providing technical support, catalyzing change, and building sustainable institutional capacity
- Monitoring the health situation and assessing health trends

WHO funds several health program throughout the world in partnership with other entities and countries. WHO does not act as a major financier as other major donor organizations do.

UNICEF The United Nations Children's Fund is another UN agency that is devoted to provide long-term humanitarian and development assistance to children and mothers. It specializes on nutrition, immunization, HIV/AIDS, and basic sanitation and emergency assistance. UNICEF receives funding from multiple sources and mainly runs programs based on the funds obtained. Thus, UNICEF's major role is not that of a grant provider or financier.

GAVI, the Vaccine Alliance Founded in 2000, it is a multilaterally private-public organization committed to improve immunization rates in low-income countries. The major role of GAVI is to procure and distribute large volumes of vaccines. In order to purchase such large volumes, innovative financial mechanisms involving several donor countries have been created and implemented. In the next section, we describe one of them, the *International Finance Facility for Immunization* (IFFIm) mechanism.

3 The Donors' Financial Role

The large multilateral donors described above are major players in the global health space and their positive impact on health programs throughout the world is unambiguous. In this section, we first position the donor's financial role broadly and then move to discuss the predominant performance-based financing (PBF) mechanisms (Sect. 3.1) as well as other financial initiatives (Sect. 3.2).

In the environment of financial austerity, donors are under increasing pressure from their stakeholders (e.g., governments in high-income countries; private organizations) to adhere to strict transparency and accountability standards. In fact, multiple donors have been involved in corruption scandals and criticized for political dependence. As a result, a common theme in the discussion of the financial role of donors in global health revolves around the value for money they create. Related discussions span the tactical level – the cost-effectiveness trade-off in a donor's operation – as well as the strategic overall value proposition. A definition of value for money applicable to most donors refers to the "goal of maximizing health impact, given disease-control goals and a health funder's resource constraint" (Glassman et al. 2013). The two seemingly conflicting pillars in this definition are *disease-control goals* and *resource constraint*.

Disease-Control Goals Donors strive to achieve these goals directly from the eight Millennium Development Goals (agreed in September 2000 to try to achieve by 2015), later broadened to the seventeen Sustainable Development Goals (SDG, agreed in September 2015 to try to achieve by 2030) agreed by all 191 UN member states. The SDGs are interdependent goals related directly or indirectly to global health. For example, SDG #6: Clean Water and Sanitation helps to prevent the transmission of infectious diseases. Furthermore, SDG #3: Good Health and Well-being refers specifically to health and emphasizes improving child and maternal health, as well as combatting the deadliest infectious diseases, namely, HIV, malaria, and tuberculosis. These goals are very ambitious and progress is tracked through well-defined quantitative targets. Financial austerity measures and population growth rates, particularly in countries lagging behind the SDGs targets, present a challenge in keeping up the progress toward these targets.

Resource Constraints Reliance on financial pledges from governments and private organizations poses a resource constraint to donors. Naturally, these stakeholders expect donors to adhere to the best transparency and accountability practices, especially after the 2010 World Health Report estimated that 20–40% of potential health gains from health spending are lost through inefficiencies, including availability of substandard and falsified medical products, losses due to waste, corruption, and fraud (Cohen-Kohler 2006, Vian 2008). Aligning the incentives of donors and fund recipients had already led to the idea of performance-based global financing (PBF). The PBF basic principle of linking future donor financing to measured output of health providers resonated well with the pay-for-performance practices observed in high-income countries. Yet, over time, implementation challenges led to criticism of PBF mechanisms (Paul et al. 2018). Next, we turn to the detailed discussion of performance-based financing mechanisms for global health.

3.1 Performance-Based Financing (PBF) Models

The Global Fund to Fight AIDS, Tuberculosis and Malaria (The Global Fund), mentioned earlier, was the pioneer global health organization financing grant recipients (ministries of health, NGOs, or local private institutions), which in turn are responsible for all health program implementation in the field. To justify to its stakeholders the funds disbursed, the Global Fund adopted at its inception a specific performance-based financing model: future disbursements to grant recipients are conditional on meeting fund usage transparency standards and achieving predefined result targets, such as number of patients treated, or number of health facilities opened (Glassman et al. 2013). The Global Fund model was met with great optimism (Brugha et al. 2004).

In the Global Fund's legacy model, financing of a grant recipient's health program is typically initiated through the Global Fund approval of a disease-specific program. The approval consists of setting a total program budget and a disbursement schedule of successive reporting periods for the awarded grant, each typically 90 or 180 days. Each reporting period carries a planned disbursement amount and represents how frequently the grant recipient is scheduled to submit a progress report. Local fund agents (academic institutions, or private management consulting firms) audit the report before the Global Fund issues a grant evaluation score from A (meeting or exceeding expectations) to C (unacceptably poor performance). Based on these scores, the Global Fund responds to disbursement requests for the following period, where a C score could lead to the discontinuation of the grant altogether.

With close to $45 billion USD committed to date since its inception in 2002, the Global Fund's operations attracted various quantitative studies. Radalet and Siddiqi (2007) uses an ordered probit multivariate model to examine the correlation between grant evaluation scores and characteristics of the health program. They analyze 134 grants evaluated in 2006 and find features of the grant recipient, disease and auditor correlated with lower scores. The authors do not argue for performance-based disbursement adjustments for grants exhibiting such features, but rather for the Global Fund's explicit allocation for oversight and risk management of such grants. Grant implementation risks include overspending, improper accounting procedures, lack of documentation for spending, inadequate storage and distribution of pharmaceuticals, vague subcontractor selection criteria, and data quality issues. Subsequently, Fan et al. (2013) uses regression analysis on 508 Global Fund grants from 2003 to 2012 to show that Global Fund evaluation scores are not replicable by external observers. They appear subjective and discretionary or the underlying data is not available. The authors therefore conclude that evaluation scores are not adequate incentive mechanisms for grant recipients and recommend explicitly linking disbursement funds to an independently measurable and robust performance measure.

Since 2015, the Global Fund has been revising its performance-based financing model to improve its transparency to grant recipients. While the implementation is ongoing and systematic studies on the resulting health effects is lacking, other organizations have adopted similar principles. For example, the World Bank assigns ratings to its projects, which are taken into account during the approval of subsequent projects in the same country/sector. USAID also uses PBF elements in some of its programs such as in Rwanda, where the following program payment is determined by:

$$\text{Total award payment to a facility} = (\text{Volume} * \text{Unit Fee}) * \%\text{Quarterly Quality Score}.$$

The quality score is based on the facility's performance against a checklist of quality indicators, performed quarterly (Management Sciences for Health 2011).

GAVI also uses a PBF approach to link funding to immunization outcomes. Their support consists of two types of disbursements: a fixed amount, based on satisfactory implementation progress, and a performance amount, based on actual immunization outcomes. In the first year of the program, countries can budget for up to 100% of the funding ceiling approved by GAVI. In subsequent years, however, the fixed amount is 80% of this ceiling, with the remaining 20% serving as a performance bonus.

While these implementations of PBF across donors vary, the common theme of linking funding to performance remains. The challenge is to define and evaluate performance in a timely manner, thus supporting program progress. One approach does not fit all situations, and the PBF principles need to be carefully calibrated for each disease and location. The PBF Handbook (Management Sciences for Health 2011) lays the roadmap to designing and implementing PBF mechanisms for global health.

3.2 Other Financial Initiatives

Financial initiatives exist as either alternatives or supplements to PBF. Here we discuss the details of the most popular and highest monetary volume ones:

The *International Finance Facility for Immunization* (IFFIm) is an innovative financing mechanism in which the GAVI Alliance borrows on capital markets against donor countries' pledges raising funds to finance the loans used for vaccine procurement through issuing "vaccine bonds" (Dickens 2011). This mechanism allows to obtain large, secure, and fast funds for GAVI, which has allowed the organization to pay large up-front cash payments to obtain large volumes of vaccine dosages. The World Bank is the IFFIm's treasury manager and there are ten sponsoring countries: United Kingdom, France, Italy, Spain, the Netherlands, Sweden, Norway, Australia, South Africa, and Brazil.

The Affordable Medicines Facility - Malaria (AMFm) is a Global Fund initiative to improve artemisinin combination therapy (ACT) availability in countries, which rely primarily on the private sector for antimalarial drugs. The three key elements of the initiative are as follows: (i) price reductions through negotiations with ACT manufacturers, (ii) a per-unit purchase subsidy through a "copayment" from the Global Fund, (iii) interventions to promote appropriate use of ACTs, such as training and outreach. The initiative was piloted in seven countries: in all but two of them (Nigeria and Zanzibar), large increases in availability (25–50%) and market share (15–40%) were observed (Tougher et al. 2012).

Pledge Guarantee for Health (PGH) is an innovative bridge-financing mechanism designed to reduce the delays of funding from international donors for health commodities. PGH leverages short-term credit from commercial banks extended to grant recipients as follows[5]:

[5]http://www.aidspan.org/gfo_article/global-fund-joins-pledge-guarantee-health

1. A donor has an existing commitment to a recipient for certain health commodities.
2. A bank extends a line of credit to purchase the commodities and sends a letter of credit to the supplier.
3. The supplier ships the commodities to the recipient.
4. The bank pays for the commodities after receiving an invoice from the supplier.
5. The donor sends money to the bank to cover the amount of the purchase.

PGH allows grant recipients to use committed donor funding in advance of actual disbursement, resulting in increased buying power and earlier procurement and delivery. Nevertheless, Gallien et al. (2017) warn that the PGH, as a bridge financing mechanism, does not address the structural problem of consistently long disbursement interarrival times of 90-day reporting Global Fund grants. Furthermore, it often involves additional financial costs (e.g., interest). Instead, they propose a synchronized financing mechanism whereby each disbursement amount includes a cash buffer designed to cover the recipient's needs during the *expected actual* time until the next disbursement, rather than the planned period length. While this is the only intervention they consider, which consistently decreases stockout risks for 90-day reporting Global Fund grants, its implementation requires increased donor's financial exposure and is fundamentally opposing the performance-based funding principles.

World Bank has financed more than 1500 Health Projects around the globe through the International Development Association (IDA), International Bank for Reconstruction and Development (IBRD), and others. The World Bank's approach is more hands-on, relies on local employees' presence, and goes beyond financing. Adjustment of financial disbursements is possible on as-needed basis, thus alleviating the requirements for auditing and monitoring. The scope and range of projects is defined on per-project basis. For example, a recent 226 million USD project in the Democratic Republic of Congo focuses on Health System Strengthening for better maternal and child health results. The projects utilize the World Bank's global network and often require longer time frames than the operations of other donors.

4 The Donors' Procurement and Supply Chain Management Role

Over the years, the role of the donors in global health supply chains has changed. In general, there has been a shift from donors actively participating in procurement and supply chain management activities to taking a more hands-off approach by recognizing the need to strengthen the local governments' medicine procurement systems. Nowadays, donor organizations' primary goal is to finance the operation, but donors also provide procurement advice and assessment, as well as help with capacity building if needed. Toward this goal, a new UN agency was created in 2008 named UN Procurement Capacity Development Centre (UNPCDC). Also, private companies providing support to local governments for procurement and distribution activities have been created: examples are JSI Research & Training Institute, Inc. (JSI), Crown Agents, and Charles Kendall.

Challenges, weaknesses, and constraints are observed during these transitions from international donors financing and procuring drugs to developing countries self-financing and self-procuring health products. The Center for Global Development (CGD) working group on global health procurement has recently identified the following challenges for public purchasers (Silverman et al. 2019):

1. Procurement managers at the local country often face high and highly variable prices.
2. Unknown and poor-quality drugs are being sold.
3. Lower-middle-income countries get about 80% of medicines from the private sector, implying that patients have to purchase these medicines at high prices out-of-pocket.
4. Disproportionally high purchase of expensive branded generics, while unbranded generics is a tiny part of the market.
5. Little competition in the supply of essential medicines, which affects the prices.

When thinking about ways to address these issues, there are two strategies to secure bulk prices in global health supply chains that are being implemented at the moment. One is pooled procurement and the second one is long-term contracts, also called "framework contract" (Sullivan et al. 2012). Furthermore, Silverman et al. (2019) suggest recommendations that complement the above two. For example, to support in-country procurement policy reform via ensuring leadership and commitment at the national level. Also, this would entail the start of country-based reforms to certain procurement constraints related to limited competition, inappropriate quality assessments, and legal restrictions to more effective purchasing modalities (e.g., current market entry barriers for quality-assured generics manufacturers). Another recommended reform is at the WHO level, where it is recommended to facilitate and expedite drug registration at the country level. To finish, Silverman et al. (2019) also recommend to professionalize procurement by building capacity and driving strategic practice.

Next, we further develop on the role of the donors in addressing these challenges by describing some specific initiatives.

PEPFAR'S Supply Chain Management System Project (SCMS)

SCMS was a project that ran from 2005 to 2017 funded by PEPFAR through USAID led by the Partnership of Supply Chain Management (PFSCM), which was a partnership of 16 organizations led by JSI and MSH[6] (Sullivan et al. 2012). SCMS

[6]Affordable Medicines for Africa; AMFA Foundation; Booz Allen Hamilton, Crown Agents Consultancy, Inc.; The Fuel Logistics Group; IDA Solutions; John Snow Inc. Research & Training Institute, Inc. (JSI); Management Sciences for Health (MSH); The Manoff Group; MAP International; North-West University; Northrop Grumman; PATH; UPS Supply Chain Solutions; Voxiva; and 3i Infotech.

achieved significant improvements in PEPFAR-supported countries' supply chains, such as virtually eliminating central-level stock out of HIV commodities, averaging 80% on-time deliveries for all products, reducing the rates of expiry in SCMS's regional distribution centers to 0.73% (developed world standards are between 3% to 7%).[7] As this project came to an end, USAID Global Health Supply Chain Program (GHSC) can offer support and PFSCM is also providing SCM services as a nonprofit organization.

The Global Fund Volunteered Pooled Procurement (VPP) Service
The Global Fund offers voluntary pooled procurement (VPP) services since 2009. VPP services are offered to principal recipients of Global Fund grants and consist of aggregating order volumes on behalf of grant participants, establishment of long-term supplier contracts, and negotiation of direct payments to obtain favorable delivery conditions and pricing (Dickens 2011). In addition to VPP, the Global Fund also provides voluntary services that are centered toward addressing supply chain management challenges. These are called Procurement capacity-building services (CBS), and supply chain management assistance (SCMA) service. CBS/SCMA services are related to the provision of technical support, training, and development of tools on aspects related to forecasting, procurement planning, inventory, distribution, and logistics management.

UNICEF Vaccine Procurement Pooled Mechanism
Access and distribution of vaccines is a challenging task due to supplier shortages and production costs and the need to distribute and store vaccines supplies at the proper temperature and at the right time. Due to these specific challenges, vaccines supply chains have been distributed separately from other drugs and specific pooled procurement programs have been created to respond to these needs (Zaffran et al. 2013). The UNICEF Supply Division is running the oldest pooled procurement system in the purchase of vaccines, procuring immunization supplies on behalf of around 100 countries annually and providing 2.79 billion doses in 2013.[8] Countries eligible for support from GAVI procure vaccines through UNICEF, but non-GAVI-eligible countries, may also use UNICEF procurement services for a fee of between 3% and 5% depending on the income of the country.[9]

We have described some particular initiatives that mainly focus on pooled or bulk procurement, but we want to highlight that most of these initiatives are also accompanied by long-term agreements (LTAs) with the manufacturers. For example, UNICEF engages its suppliers in single- and multiple-supplier LTAs following a competitive tendering process to ensure greater supply security (Arney et al. 2014). The United Nations Population Fund (UNFPA), which is the largest procurer of

---

[7]https://www.jsi.com/JSIInternet/IntlHealth/project/display.cfm?ctid=na&cid=na&tid=40&id=293

[8]https://www.unicef.org/supply/files/3._Overview_of_UNICEF_vaccine_procurement.pdf

[9]https://www.who.int/immunization/programmes_systems/procurement/mechanisms_systems/pooled_procurement/en/index2.html

reproductive health (RH) commodities, has engaged in LTAs with a large number of manufacturers. These contracts benefit any public organization that purchases these RH products, because they can access them at the competitive prices negotiated by UNFPA via its procurement and information service online system.[10]

As mentioned above, international donors are gradually reducing in-kind donations and offering more direct financial support. As a result, LMICs are becoming increasingly responsible for their procurement of essential drugs and national framework agreements between a country's ministry of health and a manufacturer are occurring. Arney et al. (2014) describe and analyze several cases of countries engaging with LCAs for the direct procurement of essential medicines.

5 Further Challenges and Opportunities for Donors

Next, we discuss three broad categories of challenges and improvement opportunities for donors. These are related to the three supply chain inefficiencies presented in the Introduction: coordination problems across multiple agents (including donors), the differences in product availability and affordability, and the different context-specific factors. All these inefficiencies present a challenge in evaluating the value for money of health programs (Sect. 5.1). Similarly, taking a myopic financial approach to budget allocation decisions and ignoring disease, drug, and location factors contribute to stockout risks (Sect. 5.2). Knowledge transfer donor support could lead the way in alleviating these inefficiencies (Sect. 5.3).

5.1 Evaluating Value for Money

The donor- and disease-specific definition of value for money presents challenges in evaluating cumulative results on affected populations.

Firstly, evaluating the value for money at the individual donor level ignores the complementarity between donors. For example, the Bill and Melinda Gates foundation serves as a donor itself as well as pledges contributions to the Global Fund, thus making the value for money generated by the two organizations dependent. The same applies to the various organizations utilizing pledges by the US government. As a result, countries' dependence on funding from each individual donor varies significantly across countries. A comprehensive interconnected map of the various funding streams, human populations, and diseases would provide a better representation of the critical role of each donor to each population. Compiling such a map is challenging due to the dynamic nature of global health programs, donor pledges, and disbursements. Yet, such a comprehensive view would not only

[10]https://www.unfpaprocurement.org/rhi-home

Fig. 2 Efficient frontier representation

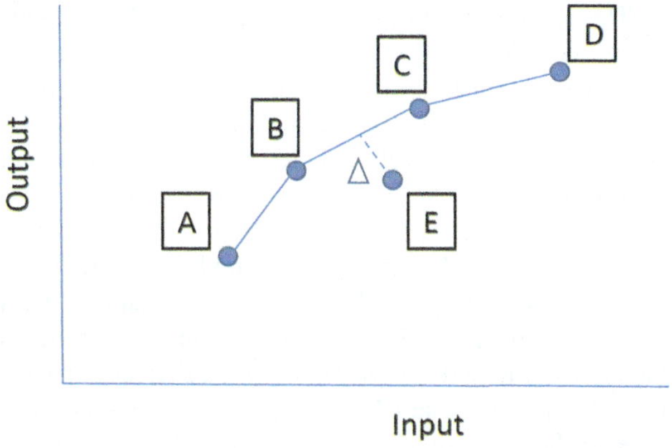

inform the vulnerability of the affected populations, but also present an opportunity to coordinate the various funding streams and hedge the risk of gaps in program coverage.

Secondly, for health products, a donor's value for money should include both the availability and affordability of these products. The traditional funding model of the large donors mentioned involves public, not-for-profit providers distributing highly affordable products. More recently, the population in many countries relies heavily on the private, for-profit sector for access to malaria medicines, making the preferred artemisinin combination therapies (ACTs) treatment unaffordable to a fraction of the population (Taylor and Xiao, 2014). Careful design of financial incentives through subsidies to the private sector is crucial for maximizing the consumption of the preferred treatment by managing both its availability and affordability. The traditional grants to the public providers are still important in managing affordability to the poorest patients. Rashkova (2019) analyzes the current levels of combined Global Health funding to private and public providers of malaria-related health products and concludes that synergies between them would benefit patients in most African countries rather than a dominating provider type (public or private), which is the case currently.

At a broader level, performance evaluation and benchmarking are critical analysis for donors and recipient country organizations in global health supply chains. Donors are interested in measuring value for money or efficiency to decide their next round of funding assignments. In turn, recipient organizations are interested in learning about their performance given their current conditions. Benchmarking can be done when the efficiency frontier is estimated. Then, recipient organizations on the frontier represent those that are running their operations at the maximum feasible efficiency (points A, B, C, D in Fig. 2), while inefficient organizations (E in Fig. 2) can quantitatively learn how far away are they from achieving efficiency (distance Δ in Fig. 2) and what they should do to get on the frontier by learning from their closest peer-efficient organizations (points B and C in Fig. 2).

The technical definition of efficiency is the ratio between output generated and input needed. When operations are complex, such as the ones in global health, specific relationships and multiple input and output measures might be needed to accurately represent efficiency. The research field of Operations Research has studied methods that are capable of estimating the efficiency frontier and efficiency scores of a pool of different organizations or units in complex environments. In particular, Data Envelopment Analysis (DEA) is a nonparametric linear programming method that is well suited for evaluating efficiency in global health supply chains (Iyer et al. 2015). For example, Masiye (2007) provides a DEA analysis of hospitals in Zambia. Similarly, stochastic frontier analysis (SFA) is a parametric method for estimating the efficiency frontier via regression techniques. For example, Greene (2004) uses SFA to estimate the efficiency of 191 different national health-care systems using WHO panel data. The author claims that cross-country heterogeneity is a relevant factor that can be masqueraded as inefficiency in previous WHO benchmarking studies. Following this discussion, Berenguer et al. (2016) suggest a three-stage DEA/SFA technique that takes into account the benefits of SFA in terms of identifying random shocks and environmental heterogeneity and the benefits of DEA, that permits the creation of efficiency scores and reference sets for benchmarking. The reference sets should allow the creation of knowledge transfer from efficient to inefficient organizations. This study also defines the notion of extended reference set, which includes in the reference set organizations that could serve as reference to an inefficient organization, because they shared similar environmental features. More of these benchmarking studies can contribute to improve efficiency of global health supply chains.

5.2 Preventing Stockouts of Essential Medicines

A broader supply chain problem can be observed at the national level (see Fig. 1), where drug stockouts are common for grant recipients in Africa. Despite the large Global Fund budgets, such stockouts have been the norm, rather than the exception (Yu et al. 2008, PloS Medicines Editors, 2009). In the short term, such stockouts increase the morbidity and mortality of affected patients (Hawkes 2011). In the long run, they increase drug resistance and negatively affect provider's performance and patient perception. The proposed drivers of such stockouts include procurement delays, fund disbursement delays (Lane and Glassman 2008), and insufficient visibility of stock levels in peripheral health facilities (Shretta and Yadav 2012).

Gallien et al. (2017) build a discrete-event simulation model predicting the joint impact of procurement and grant disbursement processes on national drug availability for the Global Fund's recipient countries in Africa. Their model uses nonparametric estimation of procurement lead-times, disbursement lead-times (time between successive disbursements), and grant rating transitions based on 3027 procurement orders and 2068 grant disbursements. They validate the predicted quantitative link between these lead-times and the risks of national drug stockouts using out-of-sample grant information. The validated model shows not only significant and wide stockouts risks in Africa (ranging from 1% to 55% of projected demand) but also a strong effect of higher grant reporting frequency (90-day instead of 180-day reporting frequency) on increasing stockout risks by 17% to 50% of projected demand. This points to an effective trade-off between higher performance monitoring and the effectiveness of the disbursed procurement funds. This more generally shows the importance of properly accounting for the resource and time requirements of performance-monitoring activities when planning for the execution of performance-based funding grants.

Another challenge for many grant recipients is the budget allocation decision of what to procure from each fund disbursement. Budget allocations are often common for both prevention (e.g., bed nets) and treatment (e.g., ACTs) products, when the implications of a stockout (unavailability or unaffordability of the product) are quite different. Table 2 compares prevention and treatment drugs based on a few dimensions, exemplifying the difficulty in allocating common budgets across them. Stockouts of treatment health products pose higher short-term health impact than prevention products due to the associated morbidity and mortality. For the same reason, however, they impose lower requirements on future inventory levels. Random disease outbreaks also generate more demand uncertainty for treatment products, leading to structurally different demand patters for the two types of products.

Grant recipients often lack technical support in accounting for the differences just mentioned and in making budget allocation decisions. Rashkova and Gallien (2019) utilize the Global Fund procurement and disbursement data from 2002 to 2013 and find that surprisingly, many grant recipients order the same quantities of each health product – constant ordering policy – despite highly unpredictable disbursements, interarrival times, and seasonal demand patterns. They propose a heuristic index policy, based on the Gittins index in the context of the multiarmed bandit problem (Gittins et al. 2011). It evaluates the attractiveness of each additional unit of each health product in the current demand period (myopic) and for the future state of the health system (lookahead). Even though the heuristic results from a weakly coupled dynamic programming approximation, it has attractive theoretical properties, is computationally quick, and easy to implement in a resource-constrained environment. The proposed heuristic also leads to up to 120% increase in consumption

Table 2 Comparative characteristics of prevention and treatment health product

Type of product and impact of stockouts	Prevention health products	Treatment health products
Health impact	Long term: Future susceptibility risk	Short term: High morbidity and mortality
Demand pattern	Predictable based on population and seasonality	Unpredictable due to random outbreaks
Inventory dynamics	Patients wait: Higher future demand	Patients potentially lost: Lower future demand

relative to constant order quantities and up to 40% relative to other budget allocation policies that do not consider health impact, demand and inventory dynamics, as outlined in Table 2.

5.3 Knowledge Transfer

The global and multifaceted role of donors generates a large body of knowledge and data about the global health supply chains. While such data is often publicly available, for example, the Global Fund's Price and Quality Reporting (PQR) dataset, it is rarely in a form that is easily accessible for analysis and interpretation by health-care providers, who often lack the technical and labor requirements for data analysis. A worthwhile role of the donor is to invest in data analysis and disseminate knowledge and insights from such analysis to its partners in the field and further improve value for money.

Donors typically gather data on procurement prices paid, logistic costs and spending. For example, the limited PQR data available suggests consistent variability across prices paid for core health commodities. For instance, West Bank and Gaza paid almost 18 times more than South Africa (around the same time) for Ritonavir 100 milligrams (a second-line ARV) (Glassman et al. 2013). Disclosure of such information would help drive price reductions and improve transparency and standardization, ultimately reducing stockouts. A deeper analysis into the drivers of such variability would be even more beneficial, but it is unfortunately lacking.

A similar picture emerges beyond commodity prices when considering service delivery. PEPFAR aimed at providing data on which interventions provide the highest epidemic impact. In Mozambique, a cost reduction of up to 45% resulted from PEPFAR's analysis on variation in unit expenditures on facility-based care (Glassman et al. 2013), although the analysis failed to provide causality in reducing spending.

Such knowledge transfer efforts remain scarce in the global health domain, partly because of the high variability of procurement and service delivery both across and within a single country. It is often difficult, if not impossible, to disentangle intrinsic and systematic drivers of observed variability. Nevertheless, the technical skills required for such analyses are much more accessible to donors than to healthcare providers in low- and medium-income countries, necessitating a more consistent and systematic approach. The first step is for donors to improve the completeness and timeliness of available data, follow through with a strategy for the use and dissemination of such data, and finally allocate resources for technical support.

6 Conclusion

Donors play a significant role in global health not only because they financially sustain the projects but because they can also act as procurement agents and can sometimes even coordinate the projects' operations (Kraiselburd and Yadav 2013). The donor is a very powerful force in global health supply chains and, by extension, any supply chain that depends on donations (Berenguer and Shen 2020). In this chapter, we describe the donors' role in global health supply chain, an area within the broader field of Responsible Operations. We start by defining global health and describing the major donors in this domain. Historically, these donors have had a paternalistic role of managing the procurement and other major supply chain management activities. More recently, their role closely resembles a financier, leaving the operational execution to its grant recipients (e.g. ministry of health) in low- and middle-income countries (LMICs). We discuss emerging innovative financial mechanisms including performance-based funding and bridge-financing. These various roles and activities make evaluating value for money and preventing stockouts particularly challenging. Finally, we discuss opportunities for improvement of donor's impact, specifically through knowledge transfer support to grant recipients.

References

Arney L, Yadav P, Miller R, Wilkerson T (2014) Strategic contracting practices to improve procurement of health commodities. Global Health: Science and Practice 2(3):295–306

Berenguer G, Iyer A, Yadav P (2016) Disentangling the efficiency drivers in country-level global health programs: an empirical study. J Oper Manag 45:30–43

Berenguer G, Shen ZJM (2020) Challenges and strategies in managing nonprofit operations: an operations management perspective. Manuf. Serv Oper Manag 22(5):888–905

Buse K, Walt G (1996) Aid coordination for health sector reform: a conceptual framework for analysis and assessment. Health Policy 38(3):173–187

Brugha R, Donoghue M, Starling M, Ndubani P, Ssengooba F, Fernandes B, Walt G (2004) The global fund: managing great expectations. Lancet 364:95–100

Chang AY, Cowling K, Micah AE, Chapin A, Chen CS, Ikilezi G, Sadat N, Tsakalos G, Wu J, Younker T and others (2019) Past, present, and future of global health financing: a review of development assistance, government, out-of-pocket, and other private spending on health for 195 countries, 1995–2050. The Lancet 393(10187):2233–2260

Cohen-Kohler J (2006) Pharmaceuticals and corruption: a risk assessment. In: Kotalik J, Rodriguez D (eds) Global corruption report 2006. Transparency international. Pluto Press, London, pp 77–85. Available from: http://www1.worldbank.org/publicsector/anticorrupt/corecourse2007/Pharmaceuticals.pdf. Accessed 18 Jun 2019

Dickens T (2011) Procurement of medicines. In: World medicines situation report 2011. World Health Organization, Geneva

Dowling P (2011) Healthcare supply chains in developing countries: situational analysis, people that deliver, Arlington

Fan Y, Duran D, Silverman R, Glassman A (2013) Performance-based financing at the Global Fund to fight AIDS, tuberculosis and malaria: an analysis of funding practice, 2002. Lancet Global Health 1:e161–e168

Gallien J, Rashkova I, Atun R, Yadav P (2017) National drug stockout risks and the global fund disbursement process for procurement. Prod Oper Manag 26:997–1014

Gittins J, Glazebrook K, Weber R (2011) Multi-armed Bandit Allocation Indices. John Wiley & Sons.

Glassman A, Fan V, Over M, Silverman R, McQueston K, Duran D (2013) More health for the money: putting incentives to work for the global fund and its partners. Center for Global Development. Consultation Draft.

Greene W (2004) Distinguishing between heterogeneity and inefficiency: stochastic frontier analysis of the world health organization's panel data on national health care systems. Health Econ 13(10):959–980

Hawkes N (2011) Gains in malaria control will be lost if funding stalls. Br Med J 343:d5970

Institute for Health Metrics and Evaluation (IHME) (2019) Financing global health 2018: countries and programs in transition. IHME, Seattle, WA

Iyer A, Berenguer G, Yadav P, Glassman A (2015) Benchmarking supply chains for better performance, center for global development, Policy Paper 057

Knack S, Rahman A (2007) Donor fragmentation and bureaucratic quality in aid recipients. J Dev Eco 83(1):176–197

Kraiselburd S, Yadav P (2013) Supply chains and global health: an imperative for bringing operations management scholarship into action. Prod Oper Manag 22(2):377–381

Lane C, Glassman A (2008) Smooth and predictable aid for health: A role for innovative financing? Brookings Institution Global Health Financing Initiative working paper

Levine R, Pickett J, Sekhri N, Yadav P (2008) Demand forecasting for essential medical technologies. Am J Law Med 34:269–297

Management Sciences for Health (2011) The PBF handbook: designing and implementing effective performance-based financing programs, Cambridge, MA

Masiye F (2007) Investigating health system performance: an application of data envelopment analysis to zambian hospitals. BMC Health Serv Res 7(1):1–11

Natarajan K, Swaminathan J (2018) Global health. In: Handbook of healthcare analytics: theoretical minimum for conducting 21st century research on healthcare operations, pp 137–158

Pisa M, McCurdy D (2019) Improving global health supply chains through traceability. Center for Global Development Policy Paper 139. Washington, DC

Privett N, Gonsalvez D (2014) The top ten global health supply chain issues: perspectives from the field. Oper Res Health Care 3:226–230

Paul E, Albert L, Bisala BN et al (2018) Performance-based financing in low-income and middle-income countries: isn't it time for a rethink? BMJ Glob Health 3:e000664

Radalet S, Siddiqi B (2007) Global Fund grant programmes: an analysis of evaluation scores. Lancet 369:1807–1813

Rashkova I (2019) Donor funding for drug availability. Working paper

Rashkova I, Gallien J (2016) Public procurement of multiple health products: the dynamic inventory budget allocation problem. Manufacturing and Service Operations Management Conference Presentation, Auckland, New Zealand

Shretta R, Yadav P (2012) Stabilizing supply of artemisinin and artemisinin-based combination therapies in an era of widespread scale-up. Malar J 11:399

Silverman R, Keller JM, Glassman A, Chalkidou K (2019) Tackling the triple transition in global health procurement. Final Report of CGD's Working Group on the Future of Global Health Procurement

Sullivan E, Goentzel J, Weintraub R (2012) The global health supply chain. Concept note GHD-C01. Harvard Business School Publishing, Boston

Taylor TA, Xiao W (2014) Subsidizing the distribution channel: donor funding to improve the availability of malaria drugs. Manag Sci 60(10):2461–2477

The PLoS Medicine Editors (2009) Time for a "third wave" of malaria activism to tackle the drug stock-out crisis. PLoS Med 6(11):e1000188

Tougher S, Ye Y, Amuasi J, Kourgueni IA, Thomson R, Goodman C, Mann AG, Ren R, Willey BA, Adegoke CA, Amin A, Ansong D, Bruxvoort K, Diallo DA, Diap G, Festo C, Johanes B, Juma E, Kalolella A, Malam O, Mberu B, Ndiaye S, Nguah SB, Seydou M, Taylor M, Rueda ST, Wamukoya M, Arnold F, Hanson K (2012) Effect of the affordable medicines facility–malaria (AMFm) on the availability, price, and market share of quality-assured artemisin-based combination therapies in seven countries: a before-and-after analysis of outlet survey data. Lancet 380:1916–1926

Vian T (2008) Review of corruption in the health sector: theory, methods and interventions. Health Policy Plan 23(2):83–94

Yadav P, Tata HL, Babaley M (2011) Storage and supply chain management. In: World medicines situation report 2011. World Health Organization, Geneva

Yu D, Souteyrand Y, Banda M, Kaufman J, Perriens J (2008) Investment in HIV/AIDS programs: does it help strengthen health systems in developing countries? Glob Health 4:8. https://doi.org/10.1186/1744-8603-4-8

Zaffran M, Vandelaer J, Kristensen D, Melgaard B, Yadav P, Antwi-Agyei KO, Lasher H (2013) The imperative for stronger vaccine supply and logistics systems. Vaccine 31(Suppl. 2):B73–B80

[illegible]

Inventory Prepositioning for UNICEF Plumpy Nut Supply Chain

Jayashankar M. Swaminathan, Wendell Gilland, Vidya Mani, Anthony So, and Corrina Moucheraud Vickery

Abstract In recent years, natural and man-made disasters have led to nutritional emergencies in many countries around the world, and especially in the Horn of Africa. UNICEF, along with other humanitarian agencies, has adopted the use of ready-to-use therapeutic food (RUTF) to alleviate the rapidly deteriorating situation of children in some of the most adversely affected countries in this region, including Kenya, Somalia, and Ethiopia. The supply chain for RUTF spans across the globe and is fraught with frequent delays, limited production capacity, highly variable ordering patterns, and rapidly increasing costs of delivery. In this chapter, we present a decision support tool that helped analyze the current supply chain for RUTF and explored a prepositioning strategy as an approach that would make the supply chain more efficient and responsive. We utilized real data to conduct simulations that help provide insights and recommendations on such a strategy.

Keywords Global health supply chains · Postponement · Inventory · Humanitarian operations · Simulation

J. M. Swaminathan (✉) · W. Gilland
Kenan-Flagler Business School, University of North Carolina at Chapel Hill, Chapel Hill, NC, USA
e-mail: msj@unc.edu

V. Mani
Darden School of Business, University of Virginia, Charlottesville, VA, USA

A. So
Bloomberg School of Public Health, Johns Hopkins University, Baltimore, MD, USA

C. M. Vickery
Fielding School of Public Health, UCLA, Los Angeles, CA, USA

J. M. Swaminathan, V. Deshpande (eds.), *Responsible Business Operations*,
Springer Series in Supply Chain Management 10,
https://doi.org/10.1007/978-3-030-51957-5_5

1 Introduction

In 2000, all members of the United Nations committed to achieving the eight Millennium Development Goals (MDGs) for the year 2015. Goal 1 aimed to eradicate extreme poverty and hunger and set a target to reduce, by half, the proportion of people who suffer from hunger by the year 2015. The effects of poverty and hunger can be catastrophic on children as it affects all aspects of their development. In response to this call, the United Nations Children's Fund (UNICEF) introduced a program to provide nutrition supplies to children in need. This need is especially acute in regions that are subject to natural or man-made disasters. Post disaster, a nutritional emergency arises in these regions due to lack of basic amenities for sustenance like food, water, and sanitation. This leaves many children in a state of severe acute malnutrition and susceptible to a host of fatal illnesses. UNICEF, along with other humanitarian organizations, helps in disbursing necessary food and medical supplies to such children in need.

At UNICEF, the upstream activities (assessment, procurement, and shipping) as well as the downstream activities (customs, storage, and distribution) for these products are managed by its central organization, UNICEF Supply Division (headquartered in Copenhagen, Denmark), along with 158 country and regional offices. In most countries, UNICEF works in partnership with local communities, numerous national and international NGOs, multilateral organizations, funding agencies, local administrations, civil society and the private sector, as well as in close coordination with the UN Country and Regional Teams. In countries that experience continual internal conflicts, the emergency is further exacerbated by the absence of adequate infrastructure that facilitates rapid response.[1]

The global nutrition community is currently participating in a shift to a community-based therapeutic care model for the treatment of children with severe acute malnutrition (http://www.who.int/nutrition/topics/statement_commbased_malnutrition/en/), an approach that relies heavily on the availability of ready-to-use therapeutic foods (RUTFs). Coupled with the rise in need due to an increase in natural and man-made disasters, there is also an increase in demand for RUTF as more programs transition to the community therapeutic care model for treatment of severe acute malnutrition. UNICEF first purchased RUTF in 2001, and continued, dramatic increase in demand resulted in a Compound Annual Growth Rate of 130% between 2004 and 2008 (Fig. 1). Countries experiencing large-scale, ongoing nutrition emergencies (including Malawi, Niger, Ethiopia, DR Congo, and Somalia) are consistently among those with the largest RUTF orders. Just over half of orders placed within UNICEF each year come from their offices in the eastern and southern Africa region (ESARO). The type of RUTF that has been purchased most often by UNICEF is called Plumpy'Nut®. At the time of this research, Plumpy'Nut® was

[1] For example, UNICEF's Somalia Country Office reported widespread malnutrition rates above the 15% emergency threshold—with some regions over 20%—and estimated that 180,000 children were acutely malnourished in 2008 (UNICEF Somalia, 2008).

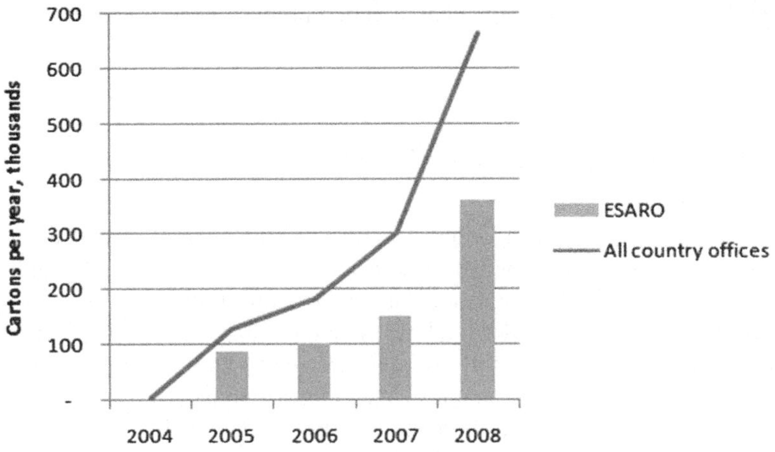

Fig. 1 Cartons of RUTF ordered by UNICEF, 2004–2008

primarily manufactured by Nutriset in Malaunay, France. It has a shelf life of 2 years. To provide focus to the study, UNICEF requested that the analysis be restricted to demand for RUTF from UNICEF country offices in the Horn of Africa (Kenya, Somalia, and Ethiopia). This was done for two reasons. First, UNICEF considered malnutrition to be a persistent concern in these areas and second, UNICEF had observed a rapid rise in supply chain costs, delivery lead time, and emergency orders from these three countries. Even though these were just three of many countries that had come to depend on RUTF as treatment for severe acute malnutrition, they represented 45–50% of UNICEF's RUTF demand during 2005–2008 and were felt to be representative of the challenges facing all locales.

Several factors make the management of a humanitarian supply chain, such as for RUTF, particularly challenging. Due to the nature of the product, the underlying demand can vary by orders of magnitude in specific regions as nutritional disasters, such as drought, as well as political instability or violence, have a major impact on the incidence of childhood malnutrition. Many of these underlying causes arise with little or no warning. Once the need arises, most purchasing organizations (such as UNICEF) must raise money from outside funding organizations to purchase humanitarian products, adding additional variability to the demand placed upon RUTF manufacturers. Finally, the lack of political stability combined with the underdeveloped infrastructure in many of the regions with greatest need for nutritional products makes the physical distribution of products in these areas especially difficult.

In the context of these supply chain challenges, UNICEF sought assistance in analyzing their current supply chain's performance and making recommendations for improvements in how their RUTF supply chain was managed. The study examined many facets of the RUTF supply chain. In this chapter, we focus on the development of a decision support tool and the opportunities to improve supply chain performance through implementation of a prepositioned buffer inventory that the decision support tool helped identify.

2 Current Supply Chain for RUTF

UNICEF places two types of orders for RUTF: Nonemergency and emergency. Nonemergency orders are planned in advance. These comprise nearly half of all orders placed by Kenya, Somalia, and Ethiopia Country Offices. Often these orders are entered into UNICEF's order-tracking system months in advance of actual need. Nonemergency orders are typically shipped via sea freight. Emergency orders are expedited orders placed due to an unexpected increase in the need for RUTF arising out of a disaster situation. Many emergency orders are shipped via airfreight, to any location in the world within a few days. Most of the demand from Ethiopia in 2008 and 2009 was transported via airfreight.

UNICEF and its partners maintain estimates of RUTF need in their communities, based on demographic information combined with partners' knowledge of their projects and catchment areas, which is relayed either directly to the UNICEF country office (as in Somalia) or to the Ministry of Health and then UNICEF (as in Kenya). Once sufficient funds are available, the country office submits a purchase requisition to UNICEF Supply Division (SD) in Copenhagen; funds are transferred from Country Office to Supply Division (to cover purchase and transport of RUTF to port of entry) and Supply Division then releases the purchase order to the RUTF producer. Supply Division is responsible for payment of global transportation—from point of production to the point of entry (port if by sea or airport if by air). In most cases, in-country transportation is paid for by Ministries of Health and implementing partners in the respective countries, and at times supplemented by funds from UNICEF. Once the product is ready for shipment, a third-party logistics provider (primarily Kuehne+Nagel) manages the transportation of RUTF to the country of destination. Sea freight goes out of Le Havre (France), and airfreight is handled out of Paris. Kenyan and Somali orders of RUTF have largely been shipped via sea (due to lower cost), so they travel via a transshipment port to Mombasa from France. Upon arrival at Mombasa, the containers bound for Kenya clear customs and are then transported by truck to the UNICEF warehouse in Nairobi. The RUTF that is provided to partners in Somalia is held at a bonded in-transit warehouse in Mombasa until a local freight forwarder can move it to Somalia. This usually happens by sea, from Mombasa to Mogadishu, at which point, it is either stored at a UNICEF warehouse in Mogadishu or is moved by truck to warehouses in districts throughout Somalia. Product Flow and Funds Flow in the current supply chain configuration for Kenya and Somalia are as depicted in Figs. 2a and b respectively. Delivery of RUTF to Ethiopia follows a similar process as for Kenya, with Kuehne+Nagel shipping RUTF from Le-Havre to Addis Ababa and from thereon, it is distributed to the required districts. Ethiopia also has a small-scale local production facility that satisfies a small percentage of its RUTF needs.

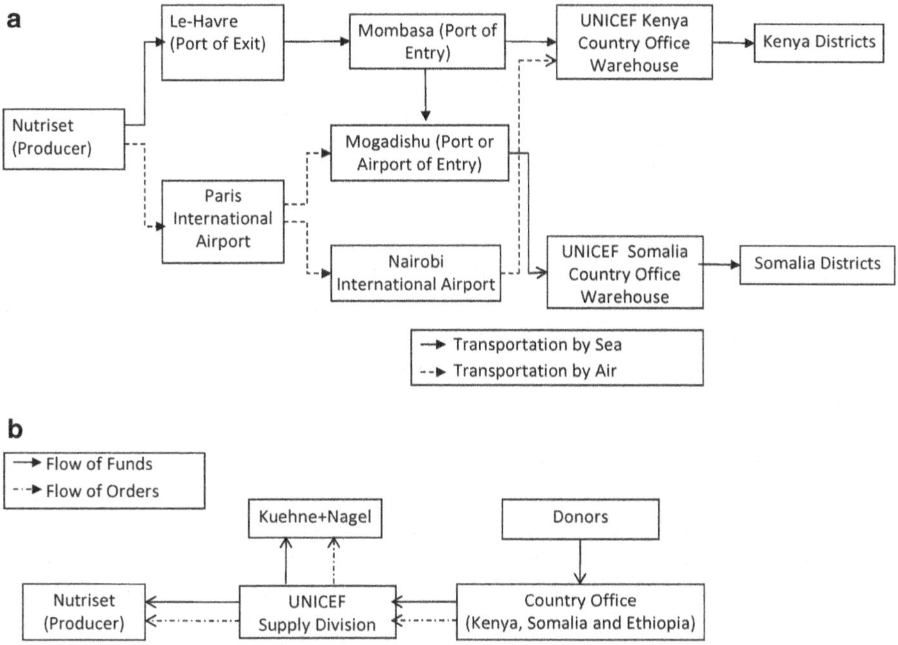

Fig. 2 (**a**) Existing product flow to Kenya and Somalia. (**b**) Existing order and funds flow for Horn of Africa

3 Literature Review

The primary objective of many humanitarian organizations, like UNICEF, is to provide aid in a timely and cost-effective manner to victims of natural and man-made disasters. Supply chain logistics plays a key role in these disaster relief operations. Early literature on humanitarian relief logistics was restricted to handbooks developed by individual relief organizations and training documents prepared by the United Nations (Beamon and Kotleba 2006b, UNICEF Supply Division).[2] These handbooks explain the nature of logistics operations in a relief environment and describe the general procedures followed in various relief sectors. In wake of the growing number of disasters across various parts of the globe, many humanitarian relief organizations have begun to understand the criticality and importance of relief chain management on the success of disaster relief operations. An excellent review of the unique characteristics of the disaster relief environment and comparison of humanitarian relief chains with commercial supply chains is available in Thomas and Kopczak (2005), Van Wassenhove (2006), Oloruntoba and Gray (2006), and Thomas (2007). The fundamental differences between commercial

[2]http://www.supply.unicef.dk/catalogue/

supply chains and humanitarian relief chains, as summarized in the above papers, come from differences in their strategic goals, in their demand characteristics, and in the complex geopolitical environment that surrounds these supply chains.

Common challenges faced by humanitarian relief chains include unpredictability of demand in terms of timing, location, type, and size; demand shocks that occur in very large amounts and short lead times for a wide variety of supplies; high stakes associated with adequate and timely delivery, and lack of resources (supply, people, technology, transportation capacity, and money) as well as lack of coordination among multiple stakeholders. Also, in contrast to research in traditional supply chains, meaningful analytical models for humanitarian relief chains need to have an intimate knowledge of government organizations, their operations, and politics involved (Green and Kolesar, 2004). A broad overview of different analytical models that have been leveraged for research in humanitarian logistics is available in Apte (2009).

One of the strategic initiatives recently proposed for improving supply chain efficiency in humanitarian operations is the prepositioning of inventory instead of procurement after the fact. Drawing from the concept of prepositioning in the traditional operations management literature, prepositioning of emergency supplies allows for not only faster response, but also better procurement planning and an improvement on distribution costs. Examples of mitigating adverse impacts of natural disasters through prepositioning emergency supplies are available in Balcik and Beamon (2008), Duran et al. (2011). Balcik and Beamon (2008) find the optimal warehouse locations and capacities when demand for relief supplies can be met from suppliers and warehouses. The authors use historical information to create scenarios for disaster location and impact (demand) for a single event and minimize the expected response time over all scenarios. Duran et al. (2011) find the optimal number and location of prepositioning warehouses given that demand for relief supplies can be met from both prepositioned warehouses and suppliers. The authors allow multiple events to occur within a replenishment period, thus capturing the adverse effect of warehouse replenishment lead time, but assume that a maximum amount of inventory is maintained throughout the prepositioning network and that suppliers are available to ship all relief items to any demand point within 2 weeks. Sodhi and Tang (2014) show that prepositioning inventory in temporarily leased earmarked places before an anticipated flood can help get essential goods faster to flood-affected individuals faster as compared to traditional methods.

While the above literature shows that prepositioning increases the ability of relief organizations to mobilize relief supplies and deliver aid quickly, the majority of NGOs avoid the use of stockpiles and consider them prohibitively complicated and expensive. Hence, it is imperative that the improvements in supply chain also incorporate a cost-benefit analysis on the investment and return from adopting a prepositioning strategy. In order to accomplish this, it is necessary to map the supply chain and understand the major stakeholders and their objectives, incorporate practical constraints in the solution approach, and show how this approach would complement other initiatives on improving supply chain efficiency.

This challenge is very much a part of the RUTF distribution problem. In what follows, we first map out the key challenges in the supply chain and discuss their root causes and interdependencies. While it is difficult to incorporate these challenges in a mathematical model, the decision support tool developed in this chapter provides the flexibility of choosing between alternative scenarios under these constraints.

4 Supply Chain Complexities

The key challenges in the current supply chain are (1) demand uncertainty, (2) funding variability, (3) difficulties in physical distribution, and (4) limited production capacity.

4.1 Demand Uncertainty

The current RUTF supply chain has been struggling to cope with the rapid increases in demand for the product, leading to poor performance in terms of cost and lead time. Demand for RUTF has increased annually but at a variable rate, which makes it difficult to predict future patterns of demand for the product. This is especially so with much of the annual supply of RUTF consumed in areas hit by emergencies. Additionally, orders can be placed only when funds are available; hence, annual order volume could depend not only on need but also on funding availability. As the debate on sustainability of a large-scale treatment program continues, the demand for RUTF products will continue to remain uncertain. For example, Medecins Sans Frontieres (MSF) actively advocates using RUTF to prevent severe acute malnourishment in addition to treatment, while other organizations like WHO (World Health Organization) express reservations in doing so (Enserink, 2008). Continuing variation in demand for RUTF is also seen from different regions of Eastern and Southern Africa.

4.2 Funding Variability

For UNICEF, the funding process begins with the Country and Regional Offices. Donors examine proposals, assess needs on the ground, and decide which proposals to fund and how much funding to provide. Once Country Offices have the funds lined up, they can submit purchase requisitions for RUTF. The staggered distribution of funds from donors often led to uneven ordering from Country Offices, which in turn made it difficult for Nutriset to plan its production ahead of time. For example, nonemergency orders from the Country Offices, though planned well ahead in time, could remain in the system at Supply Division for up to 80 days before being

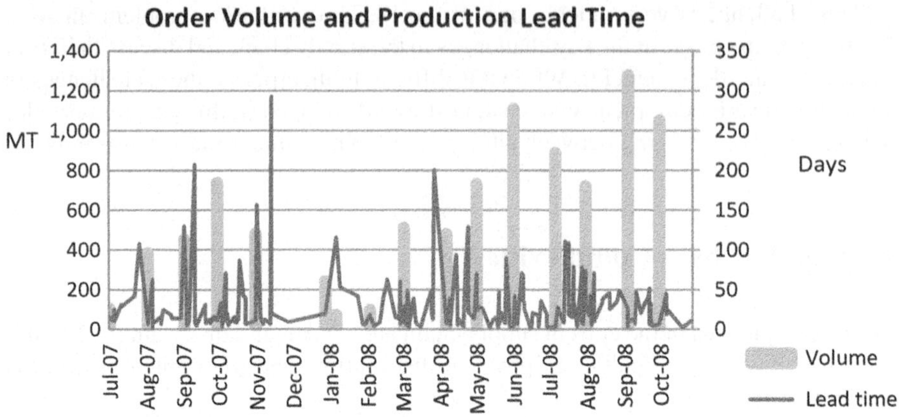

Fig. 3 Spike in order volume stresses production lead time

forwarded to Nutriset for production. As shown in Fig. 3, this frequently led to long lead times when the production was close to capacity.

4.3 Difficulties in Physical Distribution

Transportation of RUTF from Le Havre/Paris to Mombasa is one of the longest and most variable steps in the supply chain, regardless of whether the shipment is classified as an emergency or nonemergency order. Figure 4 shows the minimum, average, and maximum lead time experienced at each of the stages in the physical distribution for emergency and nonemergency orders. Each horizontal bar represents the lead time and the variation around it for that particular stage. The dark-shaded part of the bar indicates the minimum to average time, while the light-shaded part of the bar indicates the average to maximum lead time as observed from the data. For example, while pure sailing time from Le Havre to Mombasa, without interruptions, is 25 to 27 days, nonemergency orders sent by sea to Mombasa since 2005 have experienced on average transportation lead times of 34 days (with a range of 25 to 45). Congestion at the port of arrival in Mombasa and issues with regulatory paperwork are cited as some of the frequent problems when bringing goods through the port of Mombasa. Even though the UNICEF Kenya Country Office works closely with Ministry of Health (MOH), Kenya, to obtain speedy clearances, this process could take up to 16 days. Additionally, there is usually a 30% backlog of orders at the customs office in Nairobi. Orders bound for Somalia frequently face a number of potential disruptions during transport from Mombasa to Mogadishu, and then to UNICEF warehouses and beyond. Other disruptions include recent port strike at Le Havre and the postelection violence in Kenya. As a result of variable lead times, the average cost of transporting RUTF from France to eastern Africa

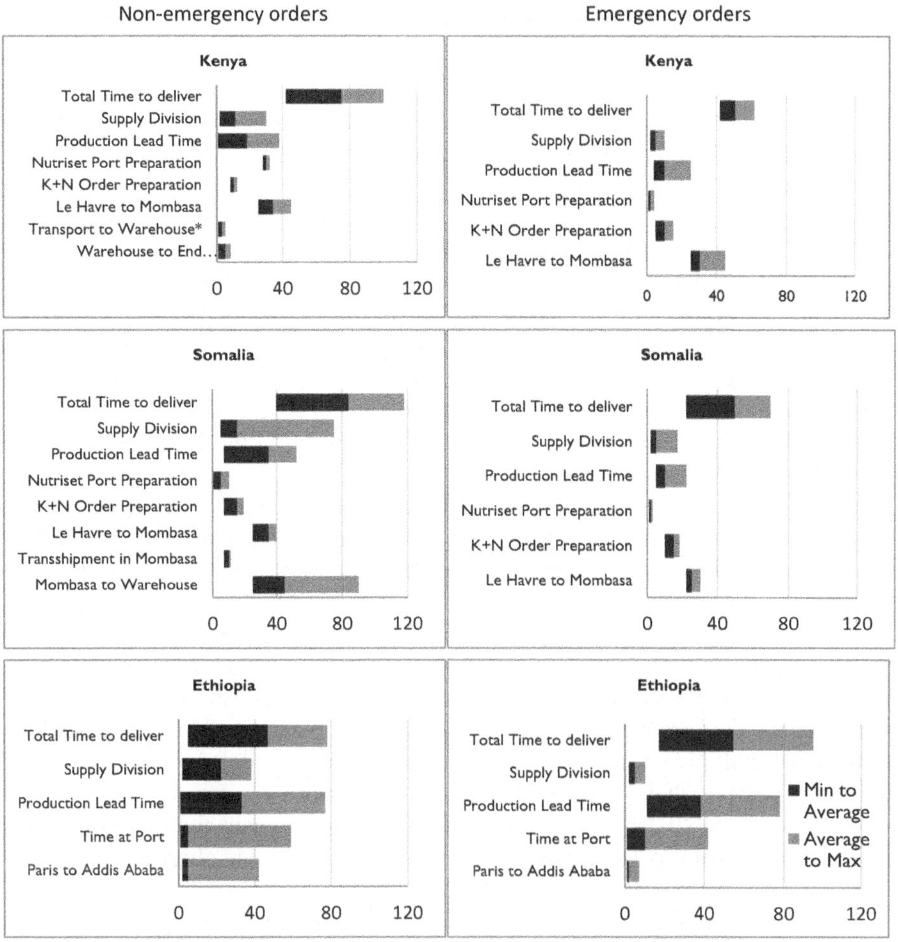

*Includes time for custom clearance, anecdotal evidence

Fig. 4 Average lead times for order delivery to Ethiopia, Kenya, and Somalia (2007–2008)

has significantly increased as a larger number of orders are shipped via air freight. For instance, between May to September 2008, airfreight was used for 33% of emergency orders and 21% of nonemergency orders to Kenya and Somalia, and all orders to Ethiopia. Between January of 2007 and October of 2008, airfreight to the Horn of Africa cost, on average, $2.40 per kilogram; by contrast, sea freight cost an average of only $0.17 per kilogram. Even if RUTF is available in one Horn of Africa country, air shipments become necessary, because complex geopolitical issues prevent transshipment among Ethiopia, Kenya, and Somalia.

4.4 Limited Production Capacity

The production capacity for RUTF has not kept pace with the increases in demand. While the amount of RUTF sold has nearly doubled every year since 2005, the manufacturing capacity during the same period has increased only by approximately 30%. Nutriset currently holds a worldwide patent over Plumpy'Nut. The company operates in the delicate balance of being a for-profit firm that focuses on the production of products to meet the nutritional needs of the world's most impoverished people. UNICEF has a long-term agreement with Nutriset that specifies the cost of Plumpy'Nut they purchase. Although Nutriset has provided license agreements to franchises in several countries and UNICEF is actively seeking new sources of RUTF, these new manufacturers may face some challenges as they come on line, including a reliance on international sourcing of inputs (which may be more costly in future), the potential role of patent protection on the RUTF product and production process, and logistical difficulties in scaling up production including raising capital funds, procuring equipment, and securing contracts. In the current supply chain configuration, orders are typically handled on a first-come, first-served basis within each class (e.g., emergency orders filled first, then regular orders), so any demand that exceeds capacity is backlogged for fulfillment in later periods.

The performance of the supply chain had become a bottleneck to the UNICEF nutritional emergency operations as it was inflexible to changing requirements. UNICEF was interested in exploring the impact of alternative supply chain configurations on the performance of their RUTF supply process for the Horn of Africa. The presence of multiple stakeholders (and decision makers), and the evolving nature of the RUTF supply chain, necessitated the development of a decision support tool that would help UNICEF easily evaluate alternate supply chain configurations. This included the possibility of prepositioning inventory and having alternate production sites.

Due to the long lead time of sea shipment and the high cost of air shipment, in this portion of the project, we looked at the efficacy of utilizing an inventory prepositioning strategy that would decouple demand and supply through establishment of a buffer stock at a convenient location. Such a strategy could potentially provide quicker response, reduce the cost of transportation, and facilitate storage of pooled buffer inventory that could help the supply chain during times of insufficient production capacity. Possible locations for prepositioning buffer stock included existing Country Office Warehouses, the UNICEF warehouse at port of entry in Mombasa, and the existing warehouse hub at Jebel Ali (Dubai) that already housed other emergency supplies for UNICEF. The decision support tool allowed comparison of different scenarios of holding buffer stock at the different locations with the existing scenario and quantification of the potential improvement in supply chain performance.

5 RUTF Distribution Problem

Given UNICEF's problems and goals, the RUTF distribution problem has two primary objectives: minimize the total RUTF supply chain cost and minimize the delivery lead time. To determine the impact of supply chain configuration on performance, we need to take into account existing constraints on producers, logistics, country offices, and warehouse locations. Production constraints involve the cost and capacity of each production location, which is further complicated by the fact that UNICEF is not each facility's only customer and the Horn of Africa is not the only region facing nutritional crises. Logistics constraints include the lead time and cost for each mode of transportation (sea/air) between each potential node in the supply chain, as well as the requirement of expedited transportation during unexpected demand surges. Country Office constraints check that orders for RUTF are released only when funds are available. Warehouse constraints cover the possible location of warehouses and any restrictions on their usage.

The distribution problem described above involves several interrelated decisions to be made simultaneously to achieve multiple objectives. With many potential supply chain configurations to consider, appraising the outcome of changes to the supply chain is a complicated task. Investigating the structure of the supply chain that UNICEF currently uses to plan, procure, produce, and deliver RUTF into the Horn of Africa has revealed a complex network of organizations that must work together to ensure the timely, cost-effective delivery of RUTF into countries plagued with severe acute malnutrition. The uncertain and inconsistent availability of donor funding to purchase RUTF further complicates the challenge of managing this complex supply chain. After analyzing the performance of the current RUTF supply chain, identifying the challenges in the current supply chain, and discussing this analysis with key participants in the RUTF supply chain, we identified the need for a decision support tool that would help UNICEF evaluate alternate configurations of the supply chain, demand profiles, and funding constraints on supply chain performance across multiple objectives. A mathematical model was formulated to aid the development of the decision support tool. The formulation and constraints of the mathematical model are explained in the Appendix. However, the optimization model was not actually used in the decision support. The mathematical model helped us to understand the various constraints, which were then embedded in the simulation based tool. While an optimization-based decision support tool would have been an option to utilize, the complexities of the real scenario in terms of demand uncertainty/spikes, funding uncertainty, and alternatives in transportation modes channeled us toward using a simulation-based performance evaluation approach for the tool.

6 Decision Support Tool

There are many classes of decision support tools. Due to the variety of performance measures that are important to UNICEF, this decision support tool is designed as a "What-If" tool. In other words, this tool will allow the user to gauge performance of a particular supply chain configuration across a variety of different performance measures and see how this performance changes as supply chain design changes are considered. Figure 5 depicts a conceptual design of the key elements of the RUTF supply chain decision support tool. The basic elements of the model are Demand locations, Warehouse locations, and Production locations. In order to make sure that the tool adequately reflected the real setting, we simulated data from the current environment to make sure that the results from the tool were close to the actual performance seen in practice.

6.1 Data Collection

At the time of this project, UNICEF did not have an end-to-end view of the current supply chain. In order to create this, we collected pieces of data from

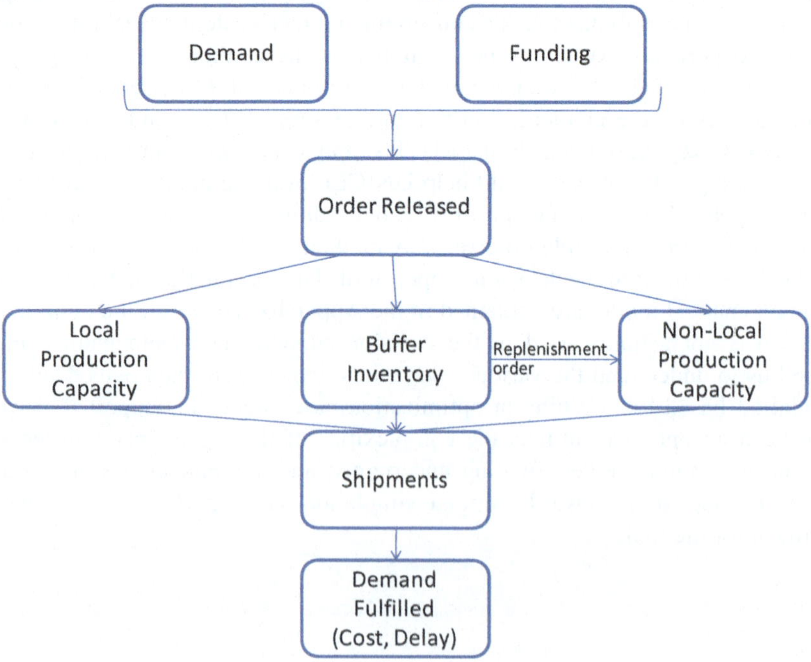

Fig. 5 Conceptual design of supply chain decision support tool

multiple players and combined them to determine baseline performance for the supply chain as currently configured. Due to multiple formats of data storage and reporting among different organizations, we had to collect the same data from different sources to verify timeliness and ensure consistency across the supply chain. We collected monthly expected demand for RUTF in Kenya, Somalia, and Ethiopia from individual Country Offices as well as Supply Division. The demand data exhibited significant variability, which was correlated across countries due to common, weather-related periods of increased malnutrition. We collected inventory data and details on warehouse operations from Country Offices and implementing partners in Kenya and Somalia. Lead-time parameters, for each transportation mode and route pair, were calculated from historic data (where available) and verified by Supply Division and Kuehne+Nagel. Finally, we obtained production capacity from Nutriset, and determined effective capacity (based on the portion of that capacity available to satisfy UNICEF demand in the Horn of Africa), based on input from Supply Division and Nutriset. RUTF purchase prices were based on long-term agreements UNICEF had in place with RUTF suppliers. We also collected qualitative data on key concerns, current performance, and expectations of the current supply chain through surveys and extensive interviews with the stakeholders.

6.2 Data Inputs/Model Outputs

Two key elements of any decision support tool are the data inputs and the model outputs. Data inputs can be further split into (i) items that are necessary inputs to the model, but are unlikely to change as the model is being used to evaluate alternative scenarios, and (ii) those items that will be changed as the model is used, in order to assess the impact of these changes on the performance of the supply chain. The model outputs, in this case, are the indication of the performance of the supply chain. The decision support tool has been designed to assess performance across a variety of factors. See Fig. 6 for a detailed flowchart that describes the logic that the decision support tool uses to convert the data inputs into model outputs. The data inputs for this model can be broken down into several key categories, each of which will be described below.

6.2.1 Demand

Monthly RUTF demands for each of the three demand locations (Kenya, Somalia, Ethiopia) for 2 years are input into the model. These data will be distributed into weekly demand buckets based on a prespecified number of weeks for each month (with the total number of weeks adding to 52). We adopt a weekly demand schedule to coincide with the existing supply chain configuration. In addition to this base level of demand, it will be possible to enter up to two unforecasted surges in demand

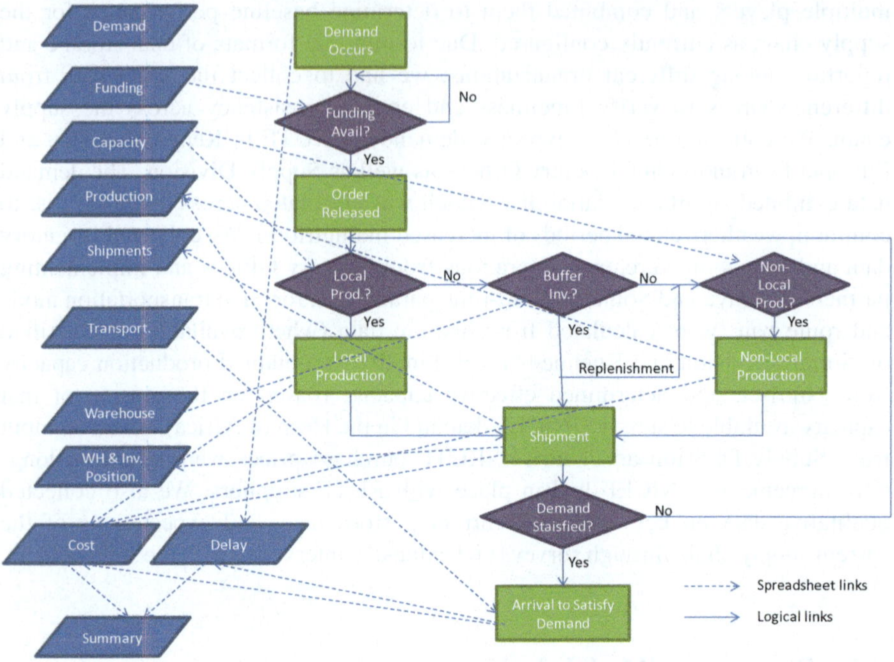

Fig. 6 Flowchart of supply chain decision support tool logic

(to represent a sudden famine, or other emergency) for each country. The demand surges are input as a peak percentage increase in demand, number of weeks to reach peak, length of peak, and number of weeks to come back down from peak. To allow for different treatment protocols across demand location, the amount of RUTF (in kilograms) needed to treat each patient is entered for each demand location. This information is used to convert quantities of RUTF into the number of children that could be treated.

6.2.2 Funding

Monthly funding levels at each demand location for each of the 2 years are input into the model. This funding should represent the money available for purchasing RUTF and will be split into weekly buckets in the same manner as RUTF demand. Demand will be not be converted into an order unless sufficient funding (to cover both purchase price and transportation cost) is available. If funding data are not available, or one wants to calculate the funding that would be required to support a given supply chain configuration and demand schedule, there is a place in the tool to indicate that unlimited funding should be assumed. The model will then calculate the monthly funding levels that are needed to pay for the procurement, transportation, and warehousing of RUTF used in the model. This option allows UNICEF to have a clear understanding of required funding levels to meet anticipated demand.

6.2.3 Production/Capacity

At the time of this project, UNICEF was procuring all of its RUTF from Nutriset. However, to enable UNICEF and partners to evaluate the impact of alternate supply chain configurations, we enhanced the decision support tool to allow up to seven production sites to be designated in the model. These seven production sites were chosen after consulting with UNICEF on the different possibilities for setting up local production facilities. The data for each production site are the week it can begin satisfying demand (assumed to be 1), the total weekly capacity (in metric tons), the purchase price to UNICEF at that site (in $ per metric ton), and the percentage of the site's capacity that is available to satisfy UNICEF demand from the Horn of Africa. This last data element is necessary to control for the fact that the production sites will also be serving non-UNICEF customers (such as MSF) and will be providing RUTF to UNICEF and others for countries outside the Horn of Africa (HOA). As an example, if UNICEF contracted to purchase 40% of a production site's capacity and 20% of the RUTF purchased by UNICEF from this site typically went to HOA, this would imply that 8% (20% of the original 40%) of the facility's capacity is available for UNICEF HOA demand.

The first three production sites are assumed to be local production in each of the three demand locations. Due to the rapid response a local production facility can provide as well as the desire to build local capabilities, any demand from a country will be first met by local production (up to the capacity of the local production facility). The next production sites are France (Nutriset) and up to three additional nonlocal production sites. After the local production site, demand will first be ordered from the primary nonlocal production site (left to user specifications). Any remaining unsatisfied demand will be ordered from the back-up production site, provided it has sufficient capacity available. If all three options (local, primary nonlocal, and back-up nonlocal) do not have sufficient capacity to meet demand, the unsatisfied demand will be carried forward to the following week.

6.2.4 Price Changes

The final set of inputs related to RUTF production allows the model to assess the impact of price changes in up to five raw materials. For each of these raw materials, the percent of the total cost of RUTF (taking into consideration costs of packaging, labor, equipment, etc.) that is comprised by that raw material is entered. A sixth category is used to capture all remaining cost elements. To evaluate the impact of a change in the purchase price of one or more raw materials, the user would enter a new price as a percentage of the baseline price of the material. For example, entering

120% would indicate that the price of the raw material is expected to increase by 20%. The impact of this 20% increase on the overall cost of producing RUTF is calculated (e.g., if the material represented 15% of the cost of RUTF, a 20% increase in the cost of that material would increase the cost of RUTF by 3%), and the cost of producing RUTF at each production location is assumed to be increased by the resulting percentage.

6.2.5 Warehouse

Through surveys and qualitative interviews with UNICEF and its partners, we ascertained possible warehouse locations for storing RUTF. We found that in addition to local country offices, UNCIEF's warehouses at Mombasa and Jebel Ali (Dubai) were viable alternatives, as they already had an existing structure for accommodating other aid supplies like vaccines and retrovirals. Hence, these were included as potential warehouse locations. Additionally, the option for maintaining local buffer inventory is also available for each of the demand locations. Local buffer inventory is assumed to be maintained only if neither of the warehouse locations are being used. In the presence of local buffer inventories, demand is satisfied first from these buffer inventories, with additional demand (and buffer inventory replenishment) coming first from local production, and finally nonlocal production as a last resort.

The cost of maintaining inventory at each warehouse location (measured in $ per metric ton per week) and the cost of moving RUTF in and out of the warehouse (measured in $ per metric ton) are input into the model. Because all weights in the decision support tool are assumed to be net weight of RUTF, the warehouse costs should be appropriately scaled to reflect this assumption. If either of these warehouse sites are used, they will store up to a fixed maximum level of RUTF, and the cost of this initial investment will be displayed as an up-front investment that would need to be made to facilitate holding such a buffer inventory. The model will use at most one warehouse location (i.e., buffer inventory can be stored in either Mombasa or Jebel Ali, but not both). When a warehouse is being used, demand is fulfilled from the warehouse site, and the warehouse inventory is replenished by nonlocal production.

6.2.6 Transportation

A transportation cost ($ per metric ton) and time (weeks) will be input for two alternative transportation modes (assumed to be surface and air) between each production site and warehouse/demand site, and between each warehouse and demand site. The decision support tool allows the user to specify the transportation mode between any pair of locations (i.e., via surface or air). This will allow UNCIEF and its partners to evaluate the cost-benefit analysis of alternative transportation modes, especially in times when surface routes are blocked or inaccessible due to internal conflicts. In addition, the decision support tool also allows the user to specify whether orders placed during times of demand surge (which are interpreted as emergency orders) should be sent using air shipment, regardless of the designated transportation mode between each pair of locations.

6.3 Model Outputs (KPI's)

An important facet of this project was to have an efficient supply chain that would not only minimize overall cost of the supply chain, but also improve the effectiveness of the supply chain. Based on our discussions with UNICEF and its partners, we found that different stakeholders monitored the effectiveness of the supply chain in different ways. For example, Supply Division might be most interested in measuring delay as the average weekly delay across all demand locations, whereas a nutrition officer in the Kenya country office would measure delay as the delay in treatment borne by the children they serve. Hence, we developed a comprehensive set of key performance indicators to be provided as outputs from the model that would enable each of these stakeholders to measure the effectiveness of the supply chain. Specifically, the model outputs are

- *Annual Supply Chain Cost*: The total annual supply chain cost, broken down for each demand location and in aggregate, based on procurement, warehouse, and delivery cost.
- *Landed Cost*: The average total landed cost per metric ton of RUTF, for each country and in aggregate.
- *Buffer Inventory*: The investment needed to create the buffer inventory at any warehouse or demand location.
- *Average Delay*: The average delay measured in weeks, from time of demand until time of delivery at each country's centralized distribution point (Nairobi, Mogadishu, and Addis Ababa), for each country and in aggregate. This measures the responsiveness of the RUTF supply chain.

In addition to the quantitative performance measures that indicate the absolute performance of any indicated supply chain configuration, the decision support tool output also indicates the performance of a given configuration relative to the baseline supply chain configuration. The relative performance is indicated as a quantitative change in each of the key performance indicators (current case – baseline case), and a graphical representation of annual supply chain cost and average delay for both the current case and the baseline case.

7 Analysis of RUTF Supply Chain Configurations

The analysis begins with a supply chain configuration that mimics the current RUTF supply chain: forecasted RUTF demand in each of the three demand locations is satisfied by production at the Nutriset facility in France and a local production facility in Ethiopia, and the RUTF is then transported via surface routes (involving transshipment points) from France into the Horn of Africa. The model is used to perform a baseline assessment of the current supply chain along each of the performance measures. Detailed analysis of several important supply chain configuration options is presented below.

7.1 Prepositioned Buffer Inventory

The current RUTF supply chain operates almost entirely on a build-to-order basis, with funded demand from the country offices triggering the procurement, production, and delivery of RUTF. As discussed earlier, capacity issues at the production site, long physical distances, and multiple transshipment points can all significantly delay the fulfillment of RUTF demand. An alternative is to hold prepositioned, buffer inventories at a warehouse location closer to the countries where RUTF will be needed. Under this configuration, demand will be satisfied from the warehouse's buffer inventory, and the buffer inventory will be replenished by production at a nonlocal production facility. The hope is that the investment in warehouse buffer inventory will significantly reduce the delays inherent in the current supply chain. The reduction in delays does not come without a price, as the buffer inventory at the warehouse location must be originally funded. Beyond this initial funding, the impact on ongoing supply chain costs is not immediately clear, but can be assessed by using the decision support tool.

To assess the complete impact of using warehouse locations closer to the Horn of Africa to maintain buffer inventories, we simulated the performance of the RUTF supply chain with different levels of buffer inventory at each of the two potential warehouse locations: Mombasa and Jebel Ali. Figure 7 displays the impact of varying levels of buffer inventory on the average delay in the RUTF supply chain, as compared to the baseline. For large quantities of buffer inventory, utilizing a prepositioning warehouse in Mombasa induces a greater reduction in delay because of its location already in the HOA. A Jebel Ali warehouse also provides a significant advantage as compared to the baseline, but the need for a lengthier shipment (and customs clearance into all three demand locations) mitigates the benefit to some extent. For both potential warehouse locations, the benefits of prepositioned inventory stabilize at about 500 metric tons (MT). For the demand level assumed in the model, investment in additional buffer inventory beyond 500 MT provides little incremental benefit to the RUTF supply chain. The desired level of buffer inventory will change depending on the magnitude of underlying demand in the supply chain that the buffer inventory is designed to support.

Figure 8 displays the up-front investment needed to maintain a buffer inventory of a given size at either of the warehouse locations. The investment needed to create the buffer inventory is essentially the same at either location. Creating a buffer inventory of 500 MT would require a one-time, up-front investment of approximately \$2,600,000 (\$2.6 MM). Alternatively, creating a buffer inventory of

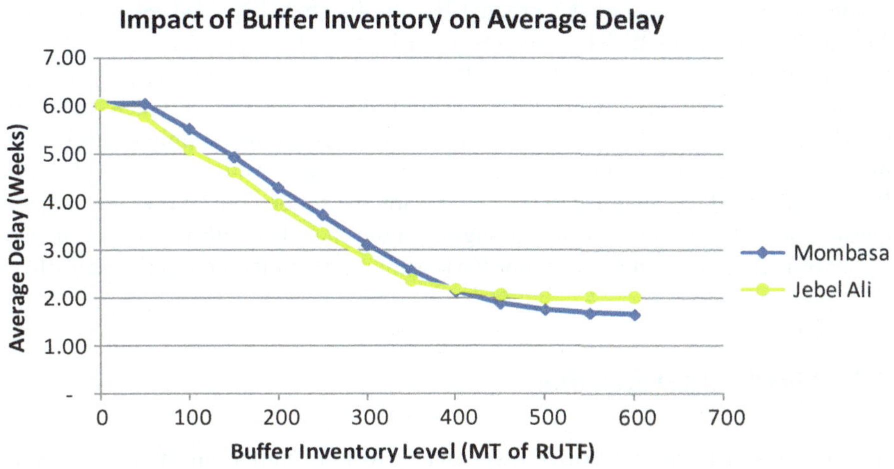

Fig. 7 Impact of buffer inventory on average delay in RUTF supply chain

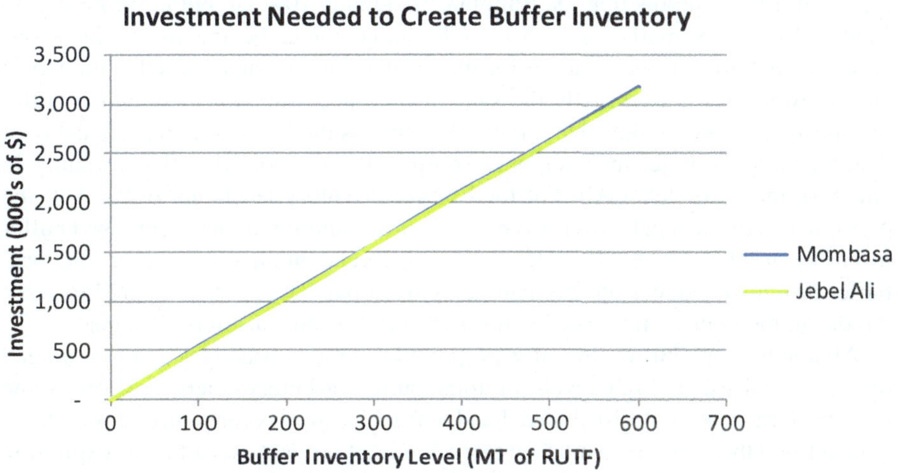

Fig. 8 Investment required to fund buffer inventory

300 MT would only require an investment of $1.6 MM, and Fig. 7 indicates that much of the full benefit of a 500 MT buffer inventory could be achieved with only 300 MT. The investment needed to develop a buffer inventory would be a one-time cost; replenishment of the buffer inventory would be funded with the normal money used by the country office to purchase RUTF. Although the model focuses on the impact on the RUTF supply chain within a given year, the benefits of maintaining the buffer inventory would continue year after year (with no additional investment).

An additional consideration for prepositioned buffer inventories is the added risk that RUTF could be wasted, because the time the product spends in the buffer inventory delays the use of the product beyond its shelf life. The relatively long, 24-month shelf life of RUTF mitigates the risk of product spoilage, but estimating the time RUTF will spend at the warehouse is important. Assuming proper stock rotation procedures (first-expiry-first-out) are followed, the time a typical carton of RUTF spends in the warehouse can be estimated. For the full supply chain benefit that is experienced by a buffer inventory of 500 metric tons, the average carton of RUTF will spend less than 2 months in the warehouse. For a buffer inventory of 300 metric tons, RUTF will only spend slightly more than 1 month in the warehouse. Either of these storage times account for less than 10% of the product's shelf life.

7.2 *Local Buffer Inventory*

Another option regarding buffer inventory is to hold buffer inventory locally in each of the three demand locations, as opposed to one centralized location for the entire Horn of Africa. Given the levels of demand in each location, and considering the local RUTF production in Ethiopia, assigning 10% of buffer inventory to Kenya, 45% to Somalia, and 45% to Ethiopia would be the most efficacious allocation of buffer inventory at the local level. The investment required to fund local buffer inventories is essentially the same as that necessary for a combined buffer inventory of the same total size. Figure 9 compares the impact on average delay of distributed, local buffer inventories as compared to the pooled buffer inventory in either Mombasa or Jebel Ali. For total buffer inventory levels up to 250 MT, the performance of the local buffer inventories is quite similar to that of a pooled buffer inventory in Jebel Ali. As the buffer inventory level continues to increase, the local buffer inventory reduces the average delay by about 1 week as compared to Jebel Ali due to the reduced time needed for transportation and customs clearance.

Although local buffer inventories provide some advantages over a pooled resource, at least at high levels of total buffer inventory, there are also some important drawbacks. A distributed, local buffer inventory is consumed only by local demand, and therefore has a much greater chance of product exceeding its expiration date if demand in a single country is lower than anticipated. Additionally, a buffer inventory that is pooled in a single location for an entire region is able to protect the region from unanticipated surges in demand with a smaller amount of total inventory than a buffer inventory that is maintained independently in each country. Local buffer stocks, by definition, must be maintained in each demand location, thereby increasing the administrative burden associated with maintaining inventory records, procedures, and facilities, as well as exposing the supply chain to additional opportunities for shrinkage and pilferage.

When deciding the location and level of buffer inventories, other factors in addition to the output from the decision support tool must be taken into consideration. The level of funding that UNICEF is able to generate to support the investment

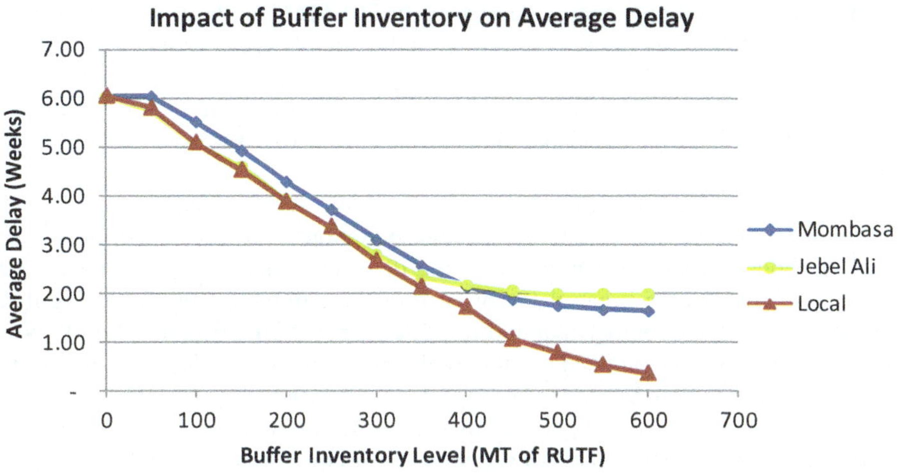

Fig. 9 Impact of local buffer inventory on average delay in RUTF supply chain

in buffer inventories will clearly play a role in the size of the inventory. A buffer inventory is also likely to support demand from countries outside the Horn of Africa, so the location and level of demand from these countries will impact buffer inventory decisions. Legal considerations, such as restrictions in Kenya concerning how long material destined for export can remain in bonded warehouses, will also factor into the final decision regarding warehouse location. By gathering information regarding transportation times and costs for alternative warehouse locations, such as Djibouti, that might be more conducive to the broader needs of UNICEF, the decision support tool can be used to assess the impact of these alternatives on the performance of the RUTF supply chain in the Horn of Africa.

7.3 Alternative Transportation Choices

Due to the long physical distance that RUTF travels in the current supply chain, from its primary manufacturing site in France to important demand locations in the Horn of Africa, choices surrounding the mode of transportation play a significant role in both the time and cost of transporting RUTF. Surface transportation (via a combination of land and sea) is the preferred mode of travel due to the significant cost advantages that surface transportation affords. In times of emergency, however, air transportation is used to rapidly deliver RUTF from the production site into countries that are facing a humanitarian crisis.

Using the model to simulate performance of the supply chain with surface transportation used along all routes, we establish a baseline level of performance along dimensions of cost and responsiveness. Shifting transportation entirely to air, we find an increase in supply chain cost of 46%, or $10.7 MM per year. Focusing solely on transportation costs (as opposed to the entire supply chain costs of procuring, transporting, and warehousing RUTF), moving from surface to air represents a 14-fold increase in cost. Utilizing the more rapid mode of transportation, however, reduces the average delay in the supply chain from 6.1 weeks to 2.0 weeks, a difference of 4.1 weeks.

When we consider the use of warehouses in the supply chain to store buffer inventories, the option exists to use air transportation from the production site to the warehouse, from the warehouse to the demand location, or both. Figure 10 shows the impact on average delay of each of these three options, assuming that the level of buffer inventory required to achieve most of the benefit (300 MT, see previous section) is maintained at either of the two warehouses. Using air shipments on the production-warehouse leg (vs. warehouse-demand) has a greater impact on the responsiveness of the supply chain for the Mombasa warehouse, but has an equivalent impact for the Jebel Ali warehouse. For either warehouse location, using air shipments for the production-warehouse leg adds about twice as much cost to the supply chain as using air shipments for the warehouse-demand leg. When air shipments are used on both legs, we see that the responsiveness of the supply chain is reduced from 6.1 weeks in the baseline (no buffer inventory, surface shipments) to 0.9 weeks when the buffer inventory is maintained in Mombasa and 1.0 weeks when the buffer inventory is maintained in Jebel Ali. Of this reduction in delay, we see that just adding buffer inventory and continuing to use surface shipments accounts for 60% (Mombasa) and 65% (Jebel Ali) of the maximum reduction in delay caused by buffer inventory and air shipments, and the percentages are even larger for a 500 MT buffer inventory. The one-time investment needed to create a 300 MT buffer inventory is also just a fraction of the cost needed for air shipments (17% for Mombasa, 15% for Jebel Ali), and one must remember that the air shipment cost will be an expense that is borne each and every year.

7.4 Availability of Funds

A major factor that impacts the performance of the RUTF supply chain is the availability of funds within each Country Office that are used to purchase RUTF. Even if RUTF is needed to treat children with severe acute malnutrition (demand), an order will not be released in the supply chain unless necessary funding is available. A mismatch frequently exists between the availability of funding and the request for RUTF, resulting in significant additional delays from the time the need for RUTF is identified and the time RUTF is delivered in country.

The baseline case we have examined in this section assumes that funding is always available so that orders can be released to the supply chain at the same time demand is recognized. If the annual budget needed to procure RUTF is not available evenly throughout the year, and is instead backloaded in the third and fourth quarter, significant delays will occur. Figure 11 displays the impact of funding

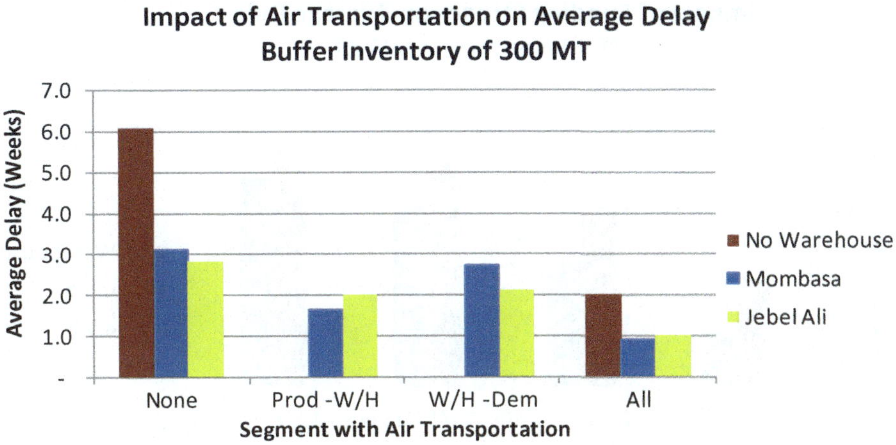

Fig. 10 Impact of air transportation on average delay in RUTF supply chain

disruptions on the responsiveness of the RUTF supply chain. Different funding scenarios, represented as the percent of annual funding available in each quarter (i.e., 25/25/25/25 would represent even distribution of funding across each quarter), are modeled to show their impact on the average delay experienced by the supply chain. This analysis shows that even a moderate slowdown in funding (20/20/20/40) will cause a 66% increase in the length of delays experienced by the supply chain, from 6.1 weeks to 10.1 weeks. A funding schedule that is heavily backloaded (15/15/15/55) will have enormous consequences on the ability of the RUTF supply chain to respond to demand, causing average delays that are over twice (2.3×) the delay experienced in the baseline case.

A delayed funding schedule has little effect on the overall cost of the supply chain. Delayed funding just shifts the production and delivery of RUTF until later in the year, but does not add or remove costs from the supply chain, presuming that the mode of transportation remains the same. If, however, air transportation is used to try to counteract the effects of delayed funding on responsiveness, the cost of operating the supply chain will increase. For a moderate delay in funding (20/20/20/40), switching from surface to air transportation will have a disastrous effect on supply chain performance, unless additional funding can be secured to support the air transportation. Without this additional funding, the eagerness to expedite the transport of RUTF will cause the already limited money to be spent on much more expensive air transportation, resulting in even longer delays as funding becomes increasingly scarce and eventually causing a significant percent of the requests for RUTF to remain unfulfilled due to funding shortfalls. Any benefit from more rapid transportation is outweighed by the decrease in RUTF that can be purchased each month due to higher costs.

Even with the addition of buffer inventories at warehouses in Mombasa or Jebel Ali, delays in funding will have serious consequences on the performance of the

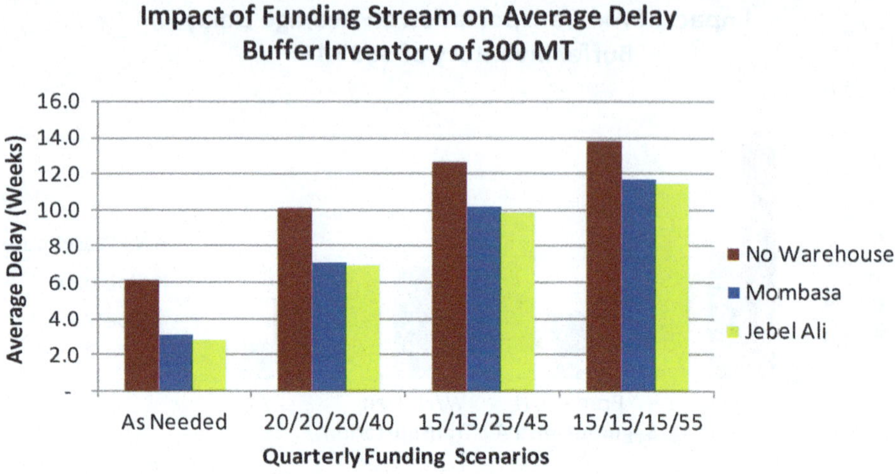

Fig. 11 Impact of funding delays on average delay in RUTF supply chain

RUTF supply chain. As seen in Fig. 11, a moderate delay in funding (20/20/20/40) will completely erode the supply chain benefits provided by maintaining a buffer inventory of 300 MT. In the case of both Mombasa and Jebel Ali, the moderate delay in funding results in a delay in the delivery of RUTF that is at least 15% greater than the baseline performance before the warehouses were added to the supply chain configuration.

Demonstrating the impact of funding levels on the RUTF supply chain can be a powerful tool to use with potential donors. Showing them the benefit of earlier, more consistent funding on the key performance indicators, not just in dollars and delay, but also in the number of children who can be treated more quickly and treated at all, should help underscore the importance of securing funding as early as possible.

7.5 Demand Surges

A contributing factor to the challenge in managing the RUTF supply chain is the fact that demand for RUTF is very difficult to predict. Even if treatment protocols were consistent across implementing partners and countries, the fact that nutrition crises caused by drought, violence, or other famine can occur rapidly can cause demand for RUTF to increase dramatically.

We simulate a demand surge within a given country (demand location) by specifying the intensity (percent increase in demand at peak) and duration (weeks to reach peak demand, weeks at peak demand, weeks to return to baseline demand) of the demand surge. Such an increase in demand will cause an increase in cost, as more RUTF must be procured and more rapid transportation modes may be used,

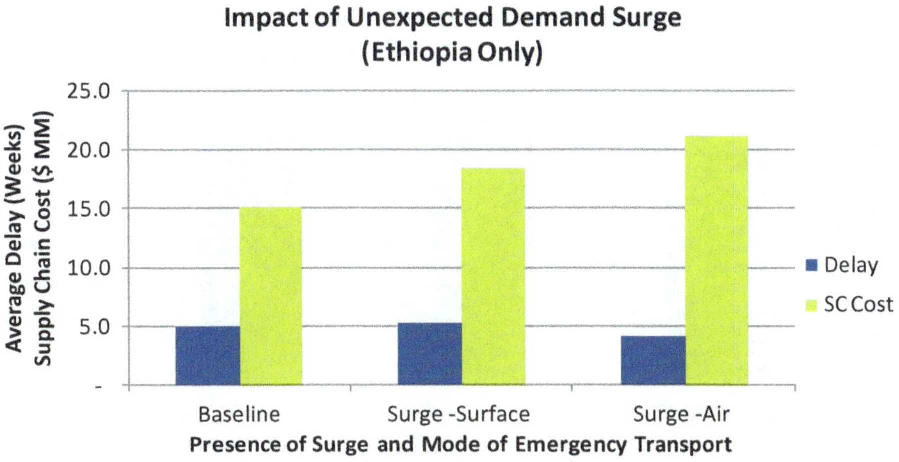

Fig. 12 Impact of unexpected demand surge in Ethiopia on performance of RUTF supply chain for Ethiopia (no buffer inventory)

and may also cause a delay in fulfillment if there is not sufficient production capacity or funding to meet the additional demand.

Figure 12 displays the impact of a surge in demand that affects only one country (Ethiopia), results in demand increasing by 50% over nominal demand, takes 4 weeks to reach peak, remains at peak for 5 weeks, and then takes 4 weeks to return to nominal demand. If surface transportation continues to be used during the nutrition crisis, this surge in demand results in an increase in supply chain cost within the afflicted country (Ethiopia) of 23% and an increase in the average supply chain delay from 5.0 weeks to 5.3 weeks. Because the decision support tool incorporates the significant increase in production capacity that Nutriset is currently implementing, the additional demand from Ethiopia can be accommodated without causing significant congestion at the nonlocal production site that might also impact lead-time performance for countries where demand has not changed (Kenya and Somalia). If air transportation is used to move RUTF from the no-local production site to Ethiopia during the time of crisis, the average supply chain delay for Ethiopia is actually reduced by 0.9 weeks from the baseline case, but the cost to the Ethiopia country office has now increased by 40%, representing an additional $2.7 MM above using surface transportation for shipments during this emergency.

Holding buffer inventory closer to the location of a nutrition crisis should allow the supply chain to respond more quickly and cost-effectively. Figure 13 shows the impact on supply chain responsiveness of the same surge in demand when a 300 MT buffer inventory is maintained in Jebel Ali (the results for Mombasa are similar). As opposed to the case of no buffer inventories, when the emergency causing the demand surge was met with supply chain delays that exceeded 5 weeks, a moderate buffer inventory in Jebel Ali can absorb the surge in demand and still provide response times that average less than 3 weeks for Ethiopia, greatly decreasing the

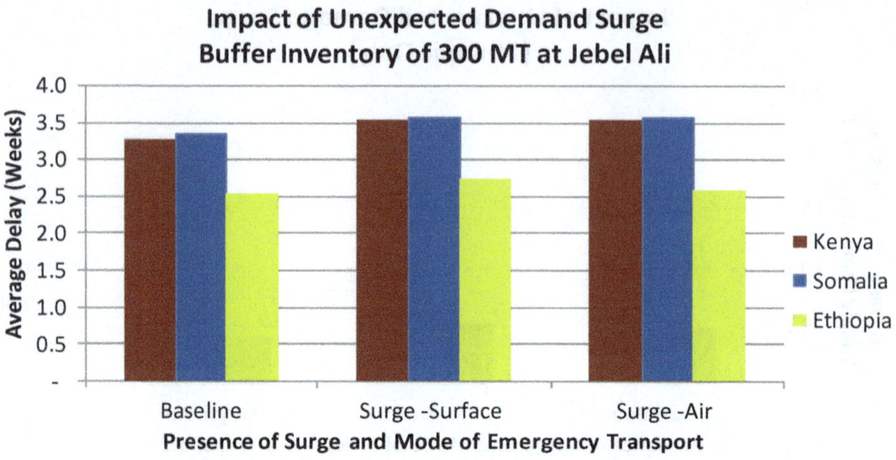

Fig. 13 Impact of unexpected demand surge in Ethiopia on average delay in each country (buffer inventory of 300 MT in Jebel Ali)

likelihood that expensive air transportation will be needed to appropriately respond to the nutrition emergency. Holding a buffer inventory not only makes the baseline supply chain more responsive, but also equips the supply chain to remain adequately responsive in the face of a nutrition crisis.

7.6 Local Production

Due to the long transportation times associated with shipping RUTF via surface routes from the primary production source in France to the Horn of Africa, local production capability can provide an opportunity to create a more responsive supply chain. Many challenges, such as locating raw material sources, ensuring product quality, and obtaining necessary approvals, must be overcome before a new local production source can be added to the supply chain. The decision support tool will allow UNICEF and its supply chain partners to assess the impact that qualifying a local supplier will have on supply chain performance. Since local suppliers will primarily provide products to meet demand within their country, this analysis will likely be especially useful at the Country Office level.

The baseline supply chain model assumes that local production is available in Ethiopia, but not in Kenya or Somalia. Figure 14 displays the impact of adding a local production facility in Kenya with an annual capacity of 3000 MT. In addition to the capacity of the facility, an assumption must be made regarding how much of the capacity will be available to satisfy demand from UNICEF, recognizing that the production facility will most likely also provide RUTF to other organizations. Given the relatively small UNICEF demand for RUTF in Kenya, however, even 20%

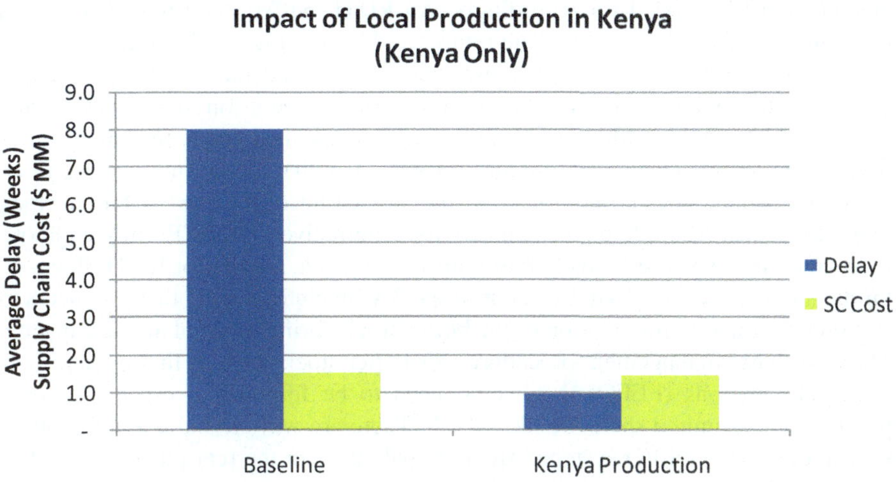

Fig. 14 Impact of local production in Kenya on performance of RUTF supply chain for Kenya

of this facility's capacity will be sufficient to meet all Kenya demand from UNICEF. Adding this facility to the supply chain will reduce the average supply chain delay for Kenya from 8.0 weeks to 1.0 weeks. Furthermore, supply chain costs for Kenya will be reduced by approximately $80,000 per year due to savings in transportation costs. Although adding a local production facility will have a dramatic impact on supply chain performance (especially lead time) for a country like Kenya, which has relatively low demand for RUTF, obtaining similar benefits for countries with higher demand and less production infrastructure will be much more challenging.

7.7 Recommendations

Based on the above analysis, the project team recommended that UNICEF preposition 300 MT buffer stock of RUTF at Jebel Ali (Dubai). This option would have yielded a considerable savings in transportation lead time, helped lessen the impact of capacity constraints at Nutriset, and leveraged existing UNICEF warehouse operations at Jebel Ali.

8 Execution Details

Creating a buffer stock creates some practical challenges. If the buffer stock is only used to support demand in the Horn of Africa, a level of 300–500 MT is recommended. If additional country offices will also utilize the buffer stock, the quantity must be scaled up accordingly. An RUTF buffer stock would require a substantial up-front investment. The return on this investment will come over time in cost savings through reduced transportation costs and increased supply chain efficiency, but funds for the initial purchase will require a long-term view of the return on investment. Although some donors earmark their funds for emergencies only, other donors do set aside monies for strategies that are not in response to an acute emergency, but can help prevent the worsening of a crisis. A buffer stock might be a clear example of such an activity. Alternatively, UNICEF might choose to leverage its own core funds to build this buffer stock. Orders for RUTF fluctuate throughout the year, so UNICEF needs to speak with Nutriset and other producers to schedule production for creation of the buffer stock during times of ample capacity. There are basic management procedures for buffer stock, such as first-expiry, first-out stock rotations (FEFO) that would need to be formalized, especially for a product with a limited shelf life like RUTF. There are ways to build a buffer stock to help encourage FEFO systems: stocking pallets from the rear pushes the oldest cartons to the front for easy pick-up.

Additionally, if total demand could not be met by warehouse stocks, protocols to prioritize the available stock to various country offices need to be in place. The priority system would have to be transparent to all parties to avoid creating new sources of distrust in the supply chain. Products with language-specific instructions would need to be labeled at the buffer stock location, so that the RUTF could be exported to multiple countries. A centralized buffer stock serves as a shared resource that can benefit multiple countries, but this may raise questions about who actually "owns" RUTF before it is assigned to a country. This may be mitigated by delegating buffer stock fundraising and procurement to a central or regional authority within UNICEF. The buffer inventory could be purchased with a one-time allocation of centralized funds, raised by a single UNICEF office. Once the stock is prepositioned, country offices would then place orders to the warehousing facility. These orders would be paid from country office accounts, and ownership over that allotment of RUTF would transfer to the specific country office. As orders are placed and the stock is consumed, new production would be initiated to replenish supply and maintain appropriate buffer stock levels.

9 Conclusions and Future Research

UNICEF has utilized the supply chain analysis carried out in this project to consider prepositioning buffer stock at Jebel Ali (Dubai). However, this is a complicated and time-consuming process as UNICEF tries to iron out several geopolitical issues in this regard. One of the key issues in implementing a prepositioning strategy involves generation of funding up-front to purchase the required level of RUTF. This requires willingness on the part of all agencies and countries involved to collaborate to achieve the best solution for distribution. As a result of utilizing our decision support tool, they have been able to obtain advance funding to preposition inventory for the Western Africa region working with USAID. Furthermore, the decision support tool is also being adopted to demonstrate the impact of varying funding patterns on effectiveness of the supply chain at donor meetings. UNICEF expects the decision support tool to help make a compelling argument to potential donors regarding the importance of early, long-term commitment of financial resources. Finally, our analysis has also prompted UNICEF to actively consider alternate sources of supply for RUTF and push Nutriset to allow for more local production facilities. The net result has been a dramatic increase in the total number of local producers of RUTF. There are more than ten production facilities worldwide as of 2011.

Our research highlights the need to bring to bear learnings from operations management to the field of humanitarian operations in an effective and practical manner. In 2015, the UN member countries reaffirmed their commitment to development goals by pledging to 17 Sustainable Development Goals (SDGs) to be achieved by 2030. While the MDGs were set up to get us "half way" to the goal of ending hunger and poverty (similar proportional goals in other fields), the SDGs are designed to finish the job and aim for a target of "zero hunger and poverty" by 2030.[3] Targeted prepositioning of inventory is one approach to achieving this goal. It can also complement additional localized and focused sustainable development approaches in target countries. Toward this, UNICEF is piloting several supply chain improvement initiatives including establishment of a Nutrition Dashboard (NutriDash) that would help use historical nutrition program information to improve country demand forecasting and diversification of the supplier base by supporting local franchises with technical, production, and supply chain knowledge and expertise.[4] As part of a long-term strategy, UNICEF is also looking to incorporate social, economic, and environmental impact as part of procurement decisions. Each of these initiatives directly impacts the supply chain for humanitarian operations and highlights the need for continued research on effective ways to translate these objectives to practice.

Acknowledgments This project would not have been possible without the support and assistance of many at UNICEF, including members of Supply Division, Programme Division, the ESARO Regional Office, and the Kenya and Somalia Country Offices. Many other partners also provided input for the data analysis and report, including from the Ethiopia Country Office and UNICEF-Brussels. We also greatly appreciate the assistance of UNICEF implementing partners who were instrumental in allowing the project team to visit and understand their on-the-ground operations, and of supply chain partners Nutriset and Kuehne+Nagel in providing insights and input into the report. The Global Nutrition Cluster provided financial support for this research. Research assistants Sara Abdoulayi, Kevin Hwang, and Kevin Martin also provided invaluable support to this project.

[3]https://advocacy.thp.org/2014/08/mdgs-to-sdgs/

[4]https://www.unicef.org/supply/files/Sustainable_Procurement_Information_Note.pdf

Mathematical Formulations

The objective function is to minimize the sum of weekly supply chain costs across the three demand locations, namely, Kenya, Ethiopia, and Somalia (formulation 1 below), and minimize the delay in the delivery of RUTF to the three demand locations (formulation 2 below). The weekly cost (2) consists of production costs at each manufacturing facility (3), pro-rated inventory handling and holding cost from each warehouse location (4), and transportation costs associated with moving RUTF from the production facility to the demand location (5). For each week, the formulation chooses quantities to transport from each of 7 production sites to each of 3 final demand locations (i.e., Kenya, Ethiopia, and Somalia) and each of 2 warehouses (thereby determining production quantities, since product cannot be stored at the production site), quantities to transport from each warehouse to each demand location, and the quantity of each demand location to backlog (note: backlogging occurs only as a last resort, when either lack of capacity or lack of funding prevents demand fulfillment). The key constraints faced by the supply chain are (i) Capacity at each production site (6), (ii) Production release for each demand location based on unfulfilled demand and funding availability (7), (iii) Production at each production site to equal shipments out from that site (8), (iv) Backlogging of any released production for which there is insufficient capacity or funding (9), (v) Warehouse shipments cannot exceed warehouse inventory (10), and (vi) Balance equation for warehouse inventory (11).

An alternative objective function (see Formulation 2) is used with the same constraints to minimize delay in the RUTF supply chain. The average delay for each country is calculated as the average delay in each week's demand, and each country's delay is weighted by the proportion of the total demand represented by that country (12). The delay in each demand is the number of weeks until that week's demand is completely delivered to the country placing the order (13).

(Note: Some of the complexity of the actual formulation has been suppressed for notational simplicity.)

Formulation 1: Cost Minimization

$$\underset{QT_{idt},QT_{ijt},QT_{jdt},QB_{dt}}{\text{Min}} \sum_{t=1}^{52}\sum_{d=1}^{3} C_{dt} \tag{1}$$

where

$$C_{dt} = P_{dt} + W_{dt} + T_{dt} \tag{2}$$

$$P_{dt} = \sum_{i=1}^{7} QM_{idt}CM_i + QB_{dt}M \tag{3}$$

$$W_{dt} = \sum_{j=1}^{2} \left(QI_{jt}CI_j + QH_{jt}CH_j + QO_{jt}CO_j\right)\gamma_{jd} \tag{4}$$

$$T_{dt} = \sum_{i=1}^{7} QT_{idt}CT_{id} + \sum_{j=1}^{2} \left(QT_{ijt}CT_{ij}\gamma_{jd} + QT_{jdt}CT_{jd}\right) \tag{5}$$

Subject to the constraints:

$$\sum_{d=1}^{3} QM_{idt} \leq K_i, \forall t \tag{6}$$

$$PR_{dt} = \text{Min}\left(\left(\sum_{k=1}^{t} N_{dk} - \sum_{k=1}^{t-1}\sum_{i=1}^{7} QM_{idk}\right), \left(\sum_{k=1}^{t} B_{dk} - \sum_{k=1}^{t-1} C_{dk}\right)\Big/\tilde{C}_d\right), \forall d, t \tag{7}$$

$$\sum_{d=1}^{3} QT_{idt} + \sum_{j=1}^{2} QT_{ijt} = \sum_{d=1}^{3} QM_{idt}, \forall i, t \tag{8}$$

$$\sum_{i=1}^{7} QM_{idt} + QB_{dt} = PR_{dt}, \forall d, t \tag{9}$$

$$\sum_{d=1}^{3} QT_{jdt} \leq QH_{jt}, \forall j, t \tag{10}$$

$$QH_{jt} = QH_{jt-1} + \sum_{i=1}^{7} QT_{ijt'} - \sum_{d=1}^{3} QT_{jdt} \tag{11}$$

For each pair of supply chain nodes, t' represents the week a shipment must leave to arrive at week t.

Formulation 2: Delay Minimization

$$\underset{QT_{idt}, QT_{ijt}, QT_{jdt}, QB_{dt}}{\text{Min}} \sum_{d=1}^{3} \left[\left(\sum_{t=1}^{52} N_{dt} \Big/ \sum_{d=1}^{3}\sum_{t=1}^{52} N_{dt}\right) \frac{\sum_{t=1}^{52}(X_{dt} - t)}{52}\right] \tag{12}$$

where

$$X_{dt} = \min_{m} \; such \; that \sum_{k=1}^{m} QA_{dk} - \sum_{k=1}^{t} N_{dk} \geq 0 \tag{13}$$

$$QA_{dt} = \sum_{i=1}^{7} QT_{i d t'} + \sum_{j=1}^{2} QT_{j d t'} \tag{14}$$

Mathematical Notation

C_{dt}	Total supply chain cost for demand location d in week t
P_{dt}	Production cost for demand location d in week t
W_{dt}	Warehouse cost for demand location d in week t
T_{dt}	Transportation cost for demand location d in week t
QM_{idt}	Quantity manufactured at production site i for demand location d in week t
CM_i	Manufacturing cost (per MT) at production site i
QI_{jt}	Quantity arriving at warehouse j in week t
CI_j	Cost (per MT) to move RUTF into warehouse j
QH_{jt}	Quantity held at warehouse j in week t
CH_j	Cost (per MT) to hold RUTF into warehouse j
QO_{jt}	Quantity leaving warehouse j in week t
CO_j	Cost (per MT) to move RUTF out of warehouse j
QT_{idt}	Quantity transported from production site i to demand location d in week t
CT_{id}	Cost (per MT) to move RUTF from production site i to demand location d
γ_{jd}	Estimated proportion of warehouse j activity performed for demand location d
K_i	Production capacity at production location i
PR_{dt}	Production release quantity from demand location d in week t
N_{dt}	Demand for RUTF from demand location d in week t
B_{dt}	Budget for procuring RUTF at demand location d in week t
$\tilde{C}_d$	Approximate total cost (per MT) for filling demand at location d
QB_{dt}	Quantity backlogged at demand location d in week t
M	Large number, used as cost of backlogging, so only capacity limitations will prevent production
X_{dt}	Week that demand from location d in week t is completely fulfilled
QA_{dt}	Quantity arriving at demand location d in week t
t'	Week that material arriving in week t is originally shipped

Use of RUTF in Treatment of Severe Acute Malnutrition

RUTF are portable, shelf-stable, single-serve foods that are rich in proteins, carbohydrates, vitamins, and minerals. Children 6 to 59 months of age who meet clinical guidelines for severe acute malnourishment (SAM) without additional complications are given RUTF to eat at home directly from the packet. Depending on a child's weight, a protocol details how many packets of RUTF will be needed per day to treat the malnourished child (Valid International, 2006). A caretaker is typically given one or 2 week's worth of RUTF to take home, and is asked to bring all empty packets back during the next follow-up appointment.

Plumpy'Nut® is an oil-based paste of peanuts, sugar, milk powder, vitamins, and minerals. It is packaged in foil sachets weighing 92 grams, each containing 500 kilocalories, which are then packed into cartons weighing 13.8 kilograms each.

References

Apte A (2009) Humanitarian logistics: a new field of research and action. Found Trends Technol, Inform Oper Manag 3(1):1–100

Balcik B, Beamon B (2008) Facility location in humanitarian relief. Int J Log Res Appl 11(2): 101–121

Beamon BM, Kotleba SA (2006b) Inventory management support systems for emergency humanitarian relief operations in South Sudan. Int J Logist Manag 17(2):187–212

Duran S, Gutierrez M, Keskinocak P (2011) Pre-positioning of emergency items for CARE international. Interfaces 41(3):223–227

Enserink M (2008) The peanut butter debate. Science Magazine 32:36–38

Green L, Kolesar PJ (2004) Improving emergency responsiveness with management science. Manag Sci 50(8):1001–1014

Oloruntoba R, Gray R (2006) Humanitarian aid: an agile supply chain? Supply Chain Manag 11(2):115–120

Ozdamar L, Ekinci E, Kucukyazici B (2004) Emergency logistics planning in natural disasters. Ann Oper Res 129(1–4):217–245

Sodhi MS, Tang CS (2014) Buttressing supply chains against floods in Asia for humanitarian relief and economic recovery. Prod Oper Manag 23(6):938–950

Thomas AS, Kopczak LR (2005) From logistics to supply chain management: the path forward in the humanitarian sector. White paper from Fritz Institute

Thomas AS (2007) Humanitarian logistics: Enabling disaster response. Retrieved 25 Jan 2012. http://www.fritzinstitute.org/PDFs/WhitePaper/EnablingDisasterResponse.pdf

UNICEF Somalia Country Office 2008 *Annual Report* 2008

Valid International (2006) Community-Based Therapeutic Care (CTC): A Field Manual. Oxford, England. Available at: http://www.fantaproject.org/ctc/manual2006.shtml

Van Wassenhove LN (2006) Humanitarian aid logistics: supply chain management in high gear. J Oper Res Soc 57(5):475–489

Disability Inclusion in Operations

Sriram Narayanan, Edward Terris, and Dustin Cole

Abstract In recent times, there has been a substantial interest in the issue of employing individuals with disabilities in the workforce. For example, The Economist (2012) labeled the employment of workers with disabilities in the workforce the "new green." The importance given to disability inclusion has been growing in several spheres, including the issue coming into focus in the United Nations Sustainable Development Goals. Specifically, reducing inequality in employment is a key goal of the United Nations in Goals 8 and 10 (United Nations 2015). Disability inclusion is also an important hot-button issue for corporations with underemployment proliferating among individuals with disabilities. For example, the Disability Equality Index (DEI), a benchmarking tool for disability inclusion, has observed a 32% annual increase in organizational participation across industries in four consecutive years, including Fortune 1000 companies (Kubik 2018). This gains increased relevance when considering that 12.6% of the American population has some form of disability. Furthermore, this population also suffers from chronic unemployment despite recent trends. Specifically, the underemployment of individuals with disabilities is more than twice that of individuals without disabilities (Accenture 2018), with only 35% of workers with disabilities having some form of full-time employment (Gaudiano and Hunt 2017). Clearly, more needs to be done. In this chapter, we detail the following with the aim of promoting greater awareness related to improvement of employment of individuals with disabilities in corporate environment. We first focus on the different rationale that organizations use to employ individuals with disabilities. Next, we introduce the different types of organizations that employ individuals with

S. Narayanan (✉) · D. Cole
Department of Supply Chain Management, The Eli Broad Graduate School of Management, Michigan State University, East Lansing, MI, USA
e-mail: narayanan@broad.msu.edu; coledust@broad.msu.edu

E. Terris
Department of Supply Chain Management, Fixed-Term Faculty, Michigan State University, Lansing, MI, USA
e-mail: terrised@msu.edu

J. M. Swaminathan, V. Deshpande (eds.), *Responsible Business Operations*, Springer Series in Supply Chain Management 10,
https://doi.org/10.1007/978-3-030-51957-5_6

disabilities, and their general mission. Finally, we discuss challenges and strategies that can facilitate superior productivity, and inclusion, when employing individuals with disabilities. The specific aim here is to put individual ability first. An important caveat in our discussions is that we focus on firm-level issues, not economy-level issues, consistent with interests of the operations management community. Furthermore, inclusion is also becoming an important topic in our contexts as seen by recent publications in journals such as Production and Operations Management (Kalkanci et al. 2019). Finally, while our attention is at the firm level, individual-level aspects also are important in these settings.

Keywords Employee disability · Social enterprise manufacturing · Responsible operations · Inclusive operations · Ability-centric operations

1 Introduction

In recent times, there has been a substantial interest in the issue of employing individuals with disabilities in the workforce. For example, The Economist (2012) labeled the workers with disabilities in the workforce the "new green." The importance given to disability inclusion has been growing in several spheres, including the issue coming to focus in the United Nations Sustainable Development Goals. Specifically, reducing inequality in employment is a key goal of the United Nations in Goals 8 and 10 (United Nations 2015). Disability inclusion is also an important hot-button issue for corporations with underemployment proliferating among individuals with disabilities. For example, the Disability Equality Index (DEI), a benchmarking tool for disability inclusion, has observed a 32% annual increase in organizational participation across industries in four consecutive years, including Fortune 1000 companies (Kubik 2018). This gains increased relevance when considering that 12.6% of the American population had some form of disability.[1] Furthermore, this population also suffers from chronic unemployment despite recent trends. Specifically, the underemployment of individuals with disabilities is more than twice that of individuals without disabilities (Accenture 2018), with only 35% of workers with disabilities having some form of full-time employment (Gaudiano and Hunt 2017). Clearly, more needs to be done. In this chapter, we detail the following with the aim of promoting greater awareness related to improvement of employment of individuals with disabilities in corporate environment. We first focus on the different rationale that organizations use to employ individuals with disabilities. Next, we introduce the different types of organizations that employ individuals with disabilities, and their general mission. Finally, we discuss challenges and strategies that can facilitate superior productivity, and inclusion, when employing individuals with disabilities. The specific aim here

[1] Source: http://disabilitystatistics.org

is to put individual ability first. An important caveat in our discussions is that we focus on firm-level issues, not economy-level issues, consistent with interests of the operations management community. Furthermore, inclusion is also becoming an important topic in our contexts as seen by recent publications in journals such as Production and Operations Management (Kalkanci et al. 2019). Finally, while our attention is at the firm level, individual-level aspects also are important in these settings.

2 Rationale for Employing Individuals with Disabilities

Organizations have several reasons for employing individuals with disabilities. Many organizations may choose to become inclusive due to the social goodwill inclusiveness creates. Beyond the social good dimension, there can be clear business/economic rationale for employing individuals with disabilities and promote inclusiveness. These reasons may include labor market situations and financial incentives.

2.1 Pursuit of Social Good

The pursuit of social good may engender workforce loyalty, community well-being, reduced turnover, and higher motivation levels. An example is Walgreens. Walgreens pioneered the idea of employing workers with disabilities in their warehouses (Kaletta et al. 2012). Kaletta, Binks, and Robinson (2012, p. 62) note that the firm aims to "*create an integrated work environment in which employees with and without disabilities would work side by side*" with no pay, or productivity, distinction. Similarly, other firms such as Microsoft have successfully built a disability hiring program for people on the autism spectrum. Bank of America has started a support services team including 300 employees with intellectual disabilities (Accenture 2018). These efforts also complement the push by organizations such as the United Nations that are prioritizing the employment of individuals with disabilities. The United Nations 2030 Sustainable Development Goals call out seeking full employment for, among others, persons with disabilities (United Nations 2015). Some nations in Europe (e.g., Spain) have already instituted various quota systems to improve the employment opportunities of persons with disabilities (Shima et al. 2008). The deputy chief of the United Nations (Ms. Amina Mohammed) even declared that "*It is up to us – leaders from government, business, civil society, organizations of persons with disabilities, international organizations and others – to turn this situation around*" when referring to disability inclusion.[2]

[2]https://news.un.org/en/story/2019/12/1053001

2.2 Labor Market Reasons

One of the earliest, if not the earliest, document published in the United States on workers with disabilities was *A Scheme for Finding Employment for Disabled Soldiers and Sailors* (Rothband 1917). This short book was written during the throes of World War I, a conflict that left innumerable men permanently disabled. This meant finding meaningful employment for an excess of labor that did not fit into traditional worker norms. Fast forward a few decades, International Business Machines (IBM) hires Michael Supa, a man blind from birth, during World War II, to create a training program for workers with disabilities (IBM 2019). This time not due to an excess of workers with disabilities, but instead due to severe labor shortages of workers during the war. Workers with disabilities were a readily available source to fill the worker shortages experienced at the time. In more recent times, the historically low unemployment rates among workers in the United States are forcing firms to pay attention to individuals with disabilities. Unemployment rates in the United States are a historically low 3.5% (Bureau of Labor and Statistics 2019a). Further, the demand for and the number of workers entering the labor force are expected entering the labor force are expected to both grow at a pace of 0.5% per year over the coming decade (Bureau of Labor and Statistics 2019b). This results in additional incentives for firms to hire individuals with disabilities, particularly when labor participation rate for workers with disabilities is an extremely low 20.8% compared to nondisabled worker labor participation rates of 68.4% (Bureau of Labor and Statistics 2019c, d). In developing countries, this situation is even more dire with the United Nations estimating anywhere between 80% and 90% of individuals with disabilities are unemployed.[3] Clearly, workers with disabilities are an important missed opportunity within the labor force. On the opposite end of the spectrum in some more developed economies, there are countries such as Spain where commercial firms are mandated, by law, that if the organization has an "*average of 50 or more employees in the last 12 months are required to hire at least 2% of workers with disabilities (with an equal to or higher than 33% degree disability).*"[4] Finally, in developed economies, aging is an important issues that is linked to disability in the workforce. Specifically, the United Nations estimates that more than 46 percent of people aged 60 years and over have disabilities. With the global trend in workforce aging, organizations need to be ready to face the challenge of inclusion in a substantive manner.

[3]https://www.un.org/development/desa/disabilities/resources/factsheet-on-persons-with-disabilities/disability-and-employment.html

[4]https://private.disabilityin.org/global/spain/

2.3 *Financial Incentives*

Organizations can reap financial benefits of employing individuals with disabilities. These incentives come in two forms: institutional support and consumer support. Support from institutions may involve support from governmental or other institutions that support employing workers with disabilities (Lalive et al. 2015). For example, government financial incentives in the form of tax credits and reimbursements exist for accommodating workers with disabilities (IRS.gov 2019). These tax credits provide direct financial support to organizations which employ workers with disabilities. Indirect support is forthcoming in the form of additional business opportunities. For example, the US Ability One Commission facilitates and acts as a conduit for exclusive contract opportunities to community rehabilitation organizations that employ a 75% or more workers with qualifying disabilities that would not be available otherwise (US Ability One Commission 2019).

On the consumer side, financial incentives of employing workers with disabilities can come in the form of commercial advantages. Organizations gain the goodwill that can come from an organization outwardly showing they care about the local community and employing workers who may not be able to find employment elsewhere. However, there are also advantages that can come in the form of serving niche markets. Persons with disabilities, like everyone else, patronize businesses. Service organizations can find a unique advantage in being able to provide services to persons with disabilities by persons with disabilities. A person with a similar disability will better understand the patron's needs and can improve the service experience (Houtenville and Kalargyrou 2012). Finally, there are niche firms that exclusively sell products made by individuals with disabilities. These include, for example, John's Crazy Socks, a company that employs individuals with disabilities to make socks with a focus on spreading awareness around the issue of autism.[5]

3 Types of Organizations Employing Workers with Disabilities

There are several types of organizations that primarily focus on employing individuals with disabilities. At one end are organizations which focus on providing services to individuals with disabilities – sometimes referred to as sheltered workshops in Europe and the United States. The aim of these workshops is to exclusively serve individuals with disabilities (Hoffman 2013). Their goal is to serve individuals with disabilities with the aim of transitioning the workers to an open market. In 2014, sheltered workshops employed 136,000 adults in the United States alone (Cooney 2016). While sheltered workshops are designed to either provide long-term

[5]https://johnscrazysocks.com/collections/autism-awareness-socks

employment to persons with disabilities or help them in transitioning to long-term employment elsewhere in commercial organizations (Hoffman 2013, pg 151), there has been pressure in Europe and the United States for sheltered workshops to integrate workers with disabilities into the broader labor market (Mallender et al. 2015; Hoffman 2013). In the United States, sheltered workshops have been criticized for not accomplishing their objectives of inclusion (Hoffman 2013). The argument is that much of the goals of these organizations can be accomplished by commercial enterprises. Sheltered workshops are increasingly transitioning into social enterprises that focus on providing individuals with services in addition to focusing on a particular mission. The terminology used in these contexts is *work integration social enterprise* (WISE).[6] WISE firms have immense pressures to improve their financial performance, while competing with commercial enterprises, to support the costs of their workforce independently (Battilana et al. 2015). Further, there is a strong need to balance the needs for operational efficiency with the social mission (Narayanan and Terris 2020). A WISE is different from a traditional social enterprise in the sense that these organizations focus on improving employment prospects for individuals that otherwise may not easily find employment in the open market. In contrast, a social enterprise may focus on other social mission, which may include workforce integration as well.

Examples of social enterprises abound. One such organization based out of Detroit is called the Empowerment Plan – an organization that was founded to help homeless individuals living in cold weather places such as Detroit. Empowerment Plan focuses on employing individuals from shelters in Detroit who find it difficult to find traditional jobs to manufacture coats that can turn into sleeping bags for homeless people (Source: www.empowermentplan.org/about). In the process, the firm also provides substantial support services to the employees to help them achieve financial stability and integrating them into the main workforce. The organization has been successful in allowing every individual hired by them to move out of homeless shelters within 6 weeks, as well as ensuring that none of the hired individuals return to homelessness (Empowerment Plan 2019).

Similarly, within Michigan, there is another organization called Peckham, Inc. This organization focuses on integrating a workforce with disabilities into the mainstream. As a nonprofit, community rehabilitation organization Peckham, Inc., provides a wide range of opportunities for persons with disabilities and other barriers to employment. A key stated mission of the firm is to maximize human potential for persons with disabilities and other barriers to employment striving for greater independence and self-sufficiency (source: www.peckham.org). Frequently, WISEs such as Empowerment plan and Peckham, Inc., need the support of community members, and other community organizations, including traditional businesses. In some cases, such organizations may not be able to generate sufficient revenue from their operations and may need outside support. While our examples are focused in the Michigan Area, such organizations exist countrywide.

[6] http://www.inworkproject.eu/toolbox/index.php/glossary-resources/glossary/work-integration-social-enterprise

Increasingly commercial organizations are increasingly focused on employing individuals with disabilities – both voluntarily and involuntarily. Microsoft and Walgreens – cited earlier – focus on employing individuals with disabilities, typically in a diverse set of roles. Walgreens has found success partnering with local agencies and developing programs specifically aimed at developing workers with disabilities. This program has proven especially successful in its warehouse and distribution portions of the business (Walgreens 2019). Similarly, Microsoft has made concerted efforts to both hire and support workers with disabilities. Reaching beyond its own workforce, Microsoft hosts an annual "Hackathon" aimed at attempting to address problems, including empowering persons with disabilities, through technology. Two projects that have won the annual "Hackathon" include creating a means to control a wheelchair with one's eyes and a learning tool for persons with dyslexia (Lay-Flurrie 2018). While these are only two prominent examples, there are organizations like IBM, Proctor & Gamble, and Cisco Systems among many more that have found success integrating persons with disabilities into their workforce voluntarily. If we look at less voluntary, but successful integration of workers with disabilities, there are regulations in place in many European countries that mandate employment of individuals with disabilities and use quota systems (Shima et al. 2008; Mallender et al. 2015).

4 Challenges and Benefits of Employing Workers with Disabilities

We now detail the challenges of employing individuals with disabilities. The challenges of employing individuals with disabilities are primarily that of the firm's culture and processes. By culture, we mean the collective will and paradigms that the organization functions with, and by processes, we mean the internal processes the firm follows to facilitate inclusion and put abilities-first. Both are inextricably intertwined by accommodations that are necessitated by the employment of individuals with disabilities. Cultural challenges start with the perception of the disabled workforce and its consequent needs,[7] as well as management of the workforce with disabilities on a day-to-day basis in terms of working with colleagues, discussion of disabilities in the workplace, and potential challenges with discrimination lawsuits.[8] A study in the UK conducted by Dixon et al. (2018) found that only about 20% of individuals noted that there was categorically no discrimination, or hardly any discrimination of individuals with disabilities. Furthermore, the study identified a substantial perception gap (11%) between individuals with disabilities feeling there was "a lot" of discrimination as opposed to nondisabled individuals feeling there

[7] https://www.in.gov/spd/files/Myth.pdf

[8] https://www.disabilityrightsuk.org/sites/default/files/pdf/DIsability%20and%20Employment%20V7.pdf

was "a lot" of discrimination. These perception differences are a cornerstone to potential disparities in corporate culture that may treat workers with disabilities and those without differently.

Such differential treatment is likely due to difficulties that employing individuals with disabilities within the organization entails. Studies in human resource management have suggested that there is substantial variability in how people with disabilities handle workplace situations, and how coworkers consequently respond (Shore et al. 2009, p. 121). Further, within a team, perceptions of fairness among coworkers (Colella 2001), and the exchanges between supervisor and subordinate(s) are also important to consider (Colella et al. 1998). In a case study within an automotive facility, Zanoni (2011) documents challenges with work allocation depending on the type of individuals with varying physical prowess, in the context of a flexible allocation of tasks to employees. Of interest is the quest for worker flexibility within a standardized manufacturing process that focuses on reduction of cycle time. This need for improved process times was a key impediment to appropriately matching tasks to individual skills – an important component in the context of employing individuals with disabilities. When an individual's physical and mental limitations were considered, challenges of allocation fairness and supervisor treatment became salient. These examples show how processes within the organization and the culture of the overall organization in the context of task allocation are deeply intertwined. Cases as in Zanoni (2011) may be all too common in several firms that have standardized operational processes. This standardized system, when pitted against the individualized attention needed for employees, is often challenging given accommodation needs for individual workers in the case of disabilities. Naturally, these are likely to create productivity variations. Indeed, Schur et al. (2005, p. 12) note a report from a consulting company Manpower that focused on effective practices for accommodating workers with disabilities:

> The company's investment in individualized training, job skills assessment, and career development was critical to the company's success in hiring and retaining workers with disabilities and in employees' success in attaining their employment goals . . . [This] suggested a corporate culture emphasizing that every individual has job skills and aptitudes, every job can be broken down into essential tasks, and every individual can attain employment if his or her skills are developed to match essential tasks (Blanck and Schartz 2001).

Of interest in this context is the foresight by Henry Ford who noted in Ford and Crowther (1922, p. 87-88), in the context of the Ford Factory that

> We are too ready to assume without investigation that the full possession of faculties is a condition requisite to the best performance of all jobs. To discover just what was the real situation, I had all of the different jobs in the factory classified to the kind of machine and work–whether the physical labour involved was light, medium, or heavy; ....and the description of the strain upon the worker. It turned out ... that there were then 7,882 different jobs in the factory. Of these, 949 were classified as heavy work requiring strong, able-bodied, and practically physically perfect men; 3,338 required men of ordinary physical development and strength. The remaining 3,595 jobs were disclosed as requiring no physical exertion and could be performed by the slightest, weakest sort of men. In fact, most of them could be satisfactorily filled by women or older children. The lightest jobs

> were again classified to discover how many of them required the use of full faculties, and we found that 670 could be filled by legless men, 2,637 by one-legged men, 2 by armless men, 715 by one-armed men, and 10 by blind men. Therefore, out of 7,882 kinds of jobs, 4,034—although some of them required strength—did not require full physical capacity. That is, developed industry can provide wage work for a higher average of standard men than are ordinarily included in any normal community. If the jobs in any one industry or, say, any one factory, were analyzed as ours have been analyzed, the proportion might be very different, yet I am quite sure that if work is sufficiently subdivided to the point of highest economy—there will be no dearth of places in which the physically incapacitated can do a man's job and get a man's wage.

In general, understanding these task level challenges requires additional work and substantial investments in time and energy by firms. Internal changes may include preparing the organization for reasonable accommodations and, importantly, developing an inventory of a person's ability to match with the nature of the task so that accommodations become less visible and are not salient in the work context. Another key element is that allocation flexibility is not focused on cross-training efforts, but rather based on the job-specific attributes. In practice, variability in ability of individuals and its impact on task performance can manifest itself both at the individual and group levels. At the individual level, variability manifests in challenges, or even inability, in performing certain tasks in a work setting, putting additional stress on task-ability matching. At the group level, task interdependency means that one individual can affect how the entire group performs, requiring an understanding of the interrelationships between tasks and abilities. Group dynamics mean accounting for the variations in ability, which individuals bring to the table, and how they can be aligned or paired with other individuals. Thus, team settings can introduce additional complexities in managing the flow of tasks and the overall dynamics of employee-task interactions, creating additional variability. Some studies suggest that in team settings, it is likely that disabilities may become invisible in accommodating variability in skill sets across employees (Miralles et al. 2007). Recent research the context of apparel factories suggests that a diversity of disabilities potentially benefits a line (Narayanan and Terris 2020) – though understanding microinteractions requires additional research.

Beyond the role of culture-process interactions, there are several other challenges that are explored in the literature but are unclear in terms of their implications. These include absenteeism where research is less than conclusive. For example, while there is some research that finds workers with disabilities are absent from work more often than nondisabled workers (Garcia-Serrano and Malo 2014), that finding does require some additional consideration as to what absences entail. While workers with disabilities do take more unexcused absences, or sick days, they also take fewer excused absences, or vacation days (Hernandez and McDonald 2010). The specific claim of workers with disabilities taking more time away from work than nondisabled workers is not necessarily an accurate one and is dependent on what employers are more concerned with. If total time away from work is the greatest concern, workers with disabilities are relatively equivalent to nondisabled workers, though those days away from work do tend to lean toward being unplanned.

While there can be operational challenges in employing workers with disabilities, there can also be operational benefits. Specifically, workers with disabilities have been found to have lower turnover rates than nondisabled workers (Adams-Shollenberger and Mitchell 1996). Having workers stay in the job longer can provide tangible benefits to an organization. Less turnover means less time spent training replacement workers as well as reducing the loss of skill and knowledge that leaves with the worker. While it may be an indirect benefit, it could be substantial for organizations struggling with turnover, as well as emphasizing benefits that can come from less a less traditional workforce. In addition, employing workers with disabilities can come with tax incentives (IRS.gov 2019). In addition, other benefits of diversity within the organization include higher creativity. Finally, as stated before, social good that organizations create is an important benefit in these contexts that organizations cannot overlook. As businesses pursue sustainability as a key goal, providing opportunities to individuals with disabilities can reduce the societal costs of operations. Overall, the set of costs and benefits that come with accommodating workers with disabilities paints a complex picture that requires several different standpoints to be considered. It requires organizations to carefully understand the diverse implications of employing individuals with disabilities holistically. Studies have noted that fears around cost of accommodations have largely subsided in recent times (Cimera 2000). As organizations learn to better accommodate workers with disabilities, such costs can go down further. Others have also found that costs of accommodation are minimal (Hernandez and McDonald 2010, p. 15). We believe that what is lacking is a clear knowledge-base articulated to reduce the cognitive overload within organizations that facilitates this effort. Beyond costs of accommodations, a holistic model that considers the overall costs must consider all of the different benefits and perspectives. These include developing a better understanding of firm-specific preparedness, societal awareness and benefits, other governmental benefits, and benefits firms accrue from the consumer's perspective (Clark et al. 1998). For example, Cook and Burke (2002) study somewhat similar attributes on cost outcomes for community rehabilitation organizations. Such perspectives need to be thought through for commercial entities as well. We now discuss the operational strategies for integrating workers with disabilities within firms.

5 Strategies for Inclusion and Abilities: First Approach

Organizations that employ individuals with disabilities can follow several core ideas that are proposed in this chapter. We propose that organizations create *inclusionscapes* (Narayanan et al. 2019). *Inclusionscapes* refer collectively to inclusion friendly *workspaces* and *workplaces*. Inclusion friendly workspaces adhere to principles of universal design. Universal Design, a term coined by Ronald L. Mace, a fellow of the American Institute of Architects, established seven key principles in the design of workplaces. These include pursuing the following rules: (a) equitable use, (b) flexibility in use, (c) simple and intuitive use, (d) perceptible information, (e) tolerance and error, (f) low physical effort, and (g) size and space for approach and use. For more information, we refer a reader to www.universaldesign.ie.[9] For example, the overall factory at Peckham, Inc., has been designed with these ideas in mind. Many of the core ideas and principles of universal design at the operational design of processes are embedded in the notion of lean management – an issue we will be discussing. Inclusion friendly *workplaces* focus on the collective social environment that makes workers with disabilities comfortable. These include the company culture, policies, and practices. We first focus on ideas related to processes to make the workspace more inclusion friendly through the use of lean management principles.

5.1 Lean Management and Inclusion Workspace

Our experience suggests that concepts of lean management are key to successful operations when employing workers with disabilities. Specifically, bringing in the "lean thinking" as defined by Womack and Jones (2003). Given that variability is a challenge in managing these operations, lean principles can help in managing variability and improve flow (Shah and Ward 2003). This starts by designing the overall processes better and to accommodating the individual by respecting their judgment and ability.

Specifically, firms can focus on strategies to manage variability in tasks and skillsets that workers with disabilities bring. First, organizations can lean into the advantages of diversity of disabilities in the workforce by leveraging diversity in task design (Narayanan and Terris 2020). The greater the number of different types of task within the repertoire of the organization, the better they can accommodate individual abilities given the flexibility in assigning workers to tasks. In doing so, it is likely that cross-training (defined as having individuals using different abilities to fill roles across different tasks) may not work well in these settings. Rather, cross-tasking (where individuals abilities are matched to tasks that require the same abilities) is likely to work better. For example, in apparel sewing, it may be possible to move an individual across steps that may not necessarily be contiguous. It is likely that cross-tasking can be more valuable in contexts where individuals with disabilities are employed. Since cross-training requires individuals to undertake multiple types of tasks, in the presence of accommodations, cross-training can become more challenging to manage. Thus, having a clear overview of task portfolios and skill portfolios becomes an important aspect of overall process design.

Furthermore, when executing the task, it is important for the organization to empower the employee and cocreate the process of task execution. These gel with

[9] http://universaldesign.ie/What-is-Universal-Design/The-7-Principles/

the notion of putting faith in the judgment of people and "respect" for individuals performing the job. In this context, the overall task execution needs to be explored at the collective intersection of process design, task design, and technologies (Narayanan et al. 2019). Performing this requires effective infrastructure that allows organizations to match jobs to specific physical or cognitive skills, and even understand the task level physical and cognitive demand for the jobs present within the firm. A specific framework that one can use here is to associate the barrier to work, the consequent work restriction, and a broad repertoire of conditions that can directly relate to these elements. Specifically, a key element of this infrastructure is a comprehensive database of skill inventory necessary to accomplish specific jobs that the firm will undertake. Such inventory taking can facilitate identification of abilities. These may also facilitate better matching of job with skills. In addition to this, a key element of matching in these contexts is to build awareness of technologies that aid in mitigating skill variability. For example, an individual with blindness may be able to take the help of counters, and sensors, to accurately count the number of apparel units that are packaged (Narayanan et al. 2019). Within sewing, there are other technologies where foot pedals are replaced by a mouth-operated machine, or adaptive scissors that require less effort to cut (Source: www.abledata.com). These aspects of technology are useful to integrate when mitigating and managing variability in task performance times. In general, considering these attributes can aid the organization in better aligning the tasks to the abilities of the individual and manage the variability of individual skills to maximize opportunities.

Another key aspect of managing variability, and improving flow, in settings with employees with disabilities is the need to re-engineer processes frequently, making them dynamic (Narayanan et al. 2019). Re-engineered production processes can allow for work to be designed specifically for the workers on the line, rather than the other way around. Re-engineering processes frequently may require careful attention to how a new employee (with different abilities) can be assigned to the process, and the potential changes necessary in matching skills, technologies, and abilities. While this does not change the overall value stream, this introduces the idea of how individuals are embedded in the overall value stream of the process and workflow can be redesigned as necessary around individual abilities. These concepts are also at the core of continuous improvement efforts for the processes within the organization. This is not to say that every workflow must be in a constant state of re-design; however, there is a reasonable balance that organization must strike when managing the workflow to suit the employee's abilities.

Other ideas of Lean are useful in this context. For example, Jidoka – or automation with human touch – is useful. Frequently, this can translate into well-designed poka-yokes. These poka-yokes typically are simple solutions that are designed to improve workforce safety. For example, in Peckham, Inc., there is an in-house automation group that focuses on creating solutions that can help in designing and thinking about solutions that are not available out of the factory. One such contraption allowed an individual with no eyesight to effectively locate and cut extraneous threads in a garment and execute stitches on a sewing machine with the help of a simple guide. The guide prevented the individual's fingers from getting caught, while performing the job, and, importantly, acted as a guide to help perform the job better as well. These simple contraptions helped create an accident-free environment where individuals could perform a task that otherwise would be unthinkable under normal situations.

We believe that 5S (sort, set in order, shine, standardize, sustain) is extremely useful in these contexts. The visual management philosophy inculcated by the pursuit of 5S philosophy makes the workplace easier to understand. These relate to the immediate stations where work is being performed but also design of the entire factory environment. For example, simple clear job instructions are not only useful for workers with learning disabilities, but also useful for the broader workforce. In that sense, organizing principles that can be followed for a workforce that has disabilities can benefit the broader workforce that does not have any disabilities.[10] Thus, superior organizing and visual management take the entire firm to a higher level when they serve workers with disabilities and help the broader population.

5.2 *Creating Inclusion Friendly Workplace*

A key element of inclusion friendly workplace is the creation of culture within the firm that is supportive of workers with disabilities. As Schur et al. (2005, p. 16) note, senior leadership of a firm "*sets a tone of inclusion and helps change or reinforce corporate norms and managerial/employee behaviors to improve treatment and opportunities for employees with disabilities.*" Effective workplace culture in the context of inclusion needs to develop processes that make employees feel that that the system is designed to be fair to them and treats them respectfully (Colella et al. 1998). The issue of fairness comes from the perspective that processes not only need to be seen as fair to them by individuals, but their accommodations need to be seen as fair by others (Colella 2001), particularly when full information about why accommodations are provided may be lacking. In that sense, accommodations provided to specific individuals need to adhere to standards of fairness not only for specific individuals, but also need to be seen as fair to other individuals.

Overall, careful management of perceptions of accommodations within the firm is necessary. Strategies such as awareness campaigns or affinity groups that encourage employees with disabilities to be more participative and interactive in order to build a healthy acceptance and respect for accommodations among employees may be useful (Schur et al. 2005). Matching employees with disabilities to leaders with disabilities may be another strategy to improve their affinity toward the workers. Research Suggests suggests that supervisors with disabilities perform better particularly when the number of employees with disabilities in the team is increasing (Cole et al. 2020). Furthermore, incentive structures designed to

[10]The first author thanks Prof. Charles Corbett for bringing up this point during a discussion.

promote teamwork in these contexts may matter more than incentive structure that tend to boost individuals. These team-based incentive structures may motivate individuals to focus on collective well-being. For example, apparel production in Peckham, Inc., follows a progressive bundling system that focuses on providing target achievement bonus to employees. In general, employee interactions and social needs must be designed into the organizational fabric. Effective design can be anchored on organizational justice dimensions. In this regard, three specific justice dimensions are critical. These relate to (a) distributive justice, (b) procedural justice, and (c) interactional justice (Colquitt et al. 2001; Cohen-Charash and Spector 2001). Studies in the past have focused on examining the implications for organizational justice measures on outcomes such as job satisfaction. Distributive justice focuses on fairness of outcomes relative to individual effort. In the context of employing workers with disabilities, this may depend on the degree to which accommodations to other individuals with disabilities (and non-accommodations to those with no disabilities) are provided as well, since employees also may compare their efforts relative to other individuals (Colella et al. 2004; Colella 2001). In addition, an individual may believe that a worker with a disability is being accommodated in such a way that increases the workload of the individual, but no additional compensation is being provided to the individual for their increased workload. Procedural justice refers to the perceived fairness of processes that are used to determine the outcomes. For example, providing accommodations may produce grievances among employees related to accommodation provided to others (Zanoni 2011; Colella 2001). These grievances need to be resolved with due process, one that is not ad-hoc. Such a process is likely to provide voice to the employee. Finally, interactional justice focuses on how individuals are treated in the organization (Cohen-Charash and Spector 2001). Here the focus should not just be on complying with the legal requirements of the ADA, but a genuine concern that stems from setting up appropriate corporate culture. For example, in describing challenges faced by workers with disabilities, a study by Kaye et al. (2011 p. 535) found that respondents suggested solutions that included increase in "respect" for individuals with disabilities in the corporate culture, and cited that organizations lacked the preparation to onboard individuals with disabilities. Summarizing their findings, Kaye et al. (2011, p. 535) note the following:

> Organizations providing ADA and disability training to managers, supervisors, and human resources personnel need to expand their focus to emphasize not only legal requirements but also problem-solving strategies, information resources, and concrete solutions to accommodation and disability issues. A greater emphasis needs to be placed on communicating to employers that people with disabilities can be effective, productive, and reliable employees; one approach would be to feature employed people with diverse disabilities as trainers or as participants in the training. Advice to employers should also include guidance on procedures they could implement to improve the accommodation process and ensure a more hospitable workplace for employees with disabilities.

Clearly, this summary provides an overarching theme that the three justice dimensions in the context of employing individuals with disabilities are deeply intertwined. In addition to providing effective processes and culture within the organization for ensuring fairness, and creating the right culture, effective inclusion friendly workplace needs an organization that is well integrated within, and with outside agencies.

5.3 Internal Integration of Departments Within the Firm

Effective internal integration of human resources, operations, and vocational rehabilitation groups within firms is critical when employing workers with disabilities (See Fig. 1).

In general, while human resources is responsible for recruiting individuals, assessing the fit of an individual to the job, and placing them on the job, the vocational rehabilitation group in a firm has the key responsibility of deciding on accommodations and ongoing performance of the employee. Finally, operations is where the individual is embedded and undertakes day-to-day tasks. In some companies, the vocational rehabilitation supports operations depending on the employee's specific needs. When each of these groups operate in their silos, the everyday needs of the employees become subservient to the goals of the firm. Furthermore, operations designs processes with minimal consideration of skills and

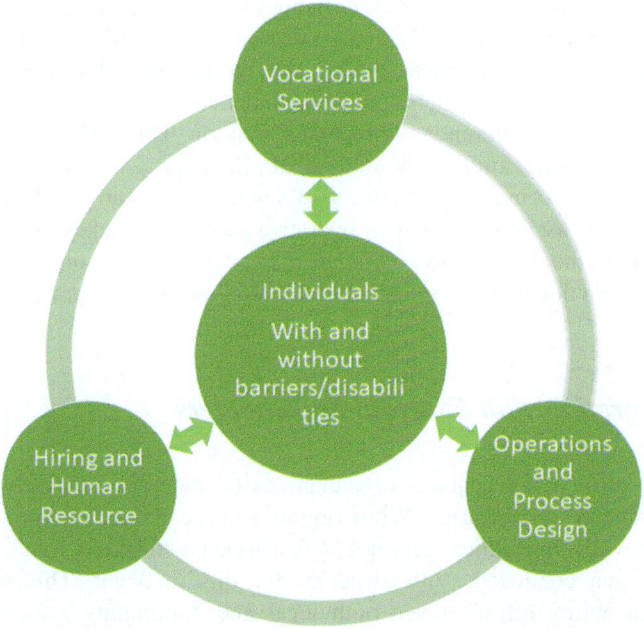

Fig. 1 Stakeholders in building an inclusive ability-first environment. (Reproduced with permission from Supply Chain Management Review – Narayanan et al. 2019)

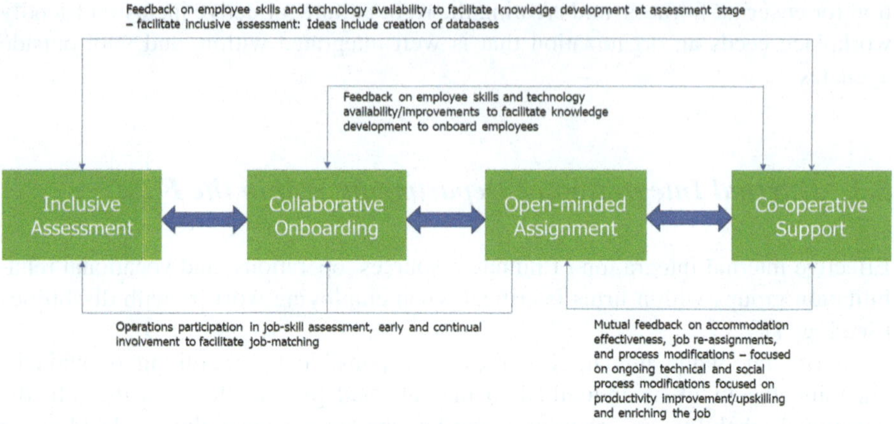

Fig. 2 Feedback loop for interdependencies in human-centric supply chain. (Reproduced with permission from Supply Chain Management Review – Narayanan et al. 2019)

abilities of employees and recruiting is designed to fit existing processes. Rather, processes are designed to maximize efficiencies. In contrast, when considering workers with disabilities, effective integration of operations, human resources, and vocational rehabilitation allows the organization to put abilities at the core of the entire process. The benefits of such collaborations may include consideration of potential process automation tools, active and concurrent participation of operations in employee skill-fit assessment during the recruitment phase, and the active engagement of vocational rehabilitation to understand the accommodation needs of the individual with reference to processes early on. This early identification can facilitate effective utilization of the individual. The approach is presented in Fig. 1. Specifically, Fig. 2 focuses on inclusive assessment, collaborative onboarding, open-minded employee assignment, and co-operative support as the key process pillars of the integration among operations, human resources, and vocational rehabilitation groups. Pursuing this requires a fundamental mindset change among firms.

5.4 *Integration with External Stakeholders*

The pursuit of inclusion requires organizations to integrate externally with stakeholders outside the organization. While organizations can internally provide support for workers with disabilities, this needs to happen within the framework of the community that creates the infrastructure for this to occur. This is especially unique to disability efforts, since both local and community governments play an active role in this effort. For example, within Michigan, organizations such as the Michigan Rehabilitation Services (a state-run organization) focus on providing support for businesses in Michigan with a view to fostering employment of disabled individuals, and run a talent acquisition portal. There are other not-for-profit organizations that focus on such efforts in each state as well. These efforts at the community level are invaluable for organizations to integrate into not only for access to work talent with disabilities, but also critical knowledge that may be available from outside sources. In addition to these organizations, networking with local transportation organizations and health organizations to provide support can be critical in facilitating individuals with disabilities the opportunity within the workforce. These include what we call mobility inclusion, health inclusion, and financial inclusion. Effective community or alternative partnerships to facilitate these within the workforce can help individuals with disabilities to better participate in everyday work.

Mobility Inclusion Supporting the mobility of all people, regardless of ability, is arguably one of the most important urban planning issues facing public- and private-sector professionals. According to estimates, nearly 16 million Americans use wheelchairs, canes, crutches, or walkers.[11] In addition, those that have vision impairments, hearing impairments, or serious cognitive impairments have challenges in mobility. While urban planners can think about mobility for the population, firms can focus on providing mobility services partnering with external stakeholders. For example, ensuring that bus lines are accessible for those who cannot afford cars, or are not mobile, helps provide a means of transportation for those persons to be able to access employment (O'Connor 2010). Peckham, Inc., knowing that 1500 of its employees depended on the bus line, worked with the transit authority in Lansing, Michigan, to add additional bus routes to their facility in order to make bus usage more feasible for its workers with mobility challenges. Planning bus routes in order to make these locations accessible can make a considerable difference for persons with disabilities. Bus routes can also be a means of improving affordable housing for workers. Overall, such collaborations improve ability especially of workers with disabilities, while benefiting those without disabilities, to move around.

Financial Inclusion Previous literature has identified poverty and chronic illness go hand in hand (Braithwaite and Mont 2009). Disability is noted to be a fundamental cause, as well as a consequence of income poverty (Fremstad 2009). Whittle et al. (2017), in their qualitative study, find that participants with disabilities frequently experience poverty. This was attributed to chronic delays in receiving cash assistance and having paycheck cut-offs for many individuals. In everyday work environments, these challenges are likely to be manifested in poor engagement and motivation. As firms continue to pursue an agenda of inclusion for individuals with disabilities, policies that facilitate financial support is a key aspect of worker engagement. Not only are such issues due to financial access, but the level of financial literacy among employees with disabilities. Mittapalli et al. (2009, p. 4) define financial literacy as consisting of (a) financial knowledge (ability to manipulate

[11] https://www.planning.org/planning/2018/feb/inclusivemobility/

money and deal with everyday financial matters), (b) financial socialization (ability to acquire values, attitudes, norms, and information that contribute to one's financial knowledge and skills), (c) financial skills (the ability to apply financial knowledge across a range of contexts), and (d) financial behavior (the ability to appreciate wider impact of financial decision on one's circumstances). Collectively, we refer to programs that ensure employees financial well-being, through a combination of financial incentives for employees and financial literacy, as financial inclusion. Peckham, Inc., for example, offers programs for financial literacy to its employees to educate them on financial security. However, not all the financial incentives need to be monetary. For example, Peckham Housing Corporation partners with several agencies such as the House of Ruth, Capital Gardens Apartments, and Independence Square Apartments to offer subsidized housing for eligible employees.[12] These programs, along with financial literacy programs, go a long way in promoting employee's well-being and success. Importantly, these programs and partnerships are also likely a serious signal to employees that the firm means for its inclusion effort to be successful.

Health Inclusion Finally, individuals with disabilities also face substantial lack of access to healthcare (Okoro et al. 2018). This appeared to be particularly true among older adults who have unmet-healthcare needs (Okoro et al. 2018). Further, higher level of medical needs also put undue financial strain on individuals with disability, particularly among older adults (Okoro et al. 2018). From a firm's standpoint, it is important to not only facilitate access to quality healthcare, but also organize education about appropriate self-care and incentivize employees to pursue healthy behaviors. Peckham, Inc., not only pursues financial training but also incentivizes employees with raises to keep their health in check, for example, to induce them to continue being healthy. Clearly, employee health, absenteeism, and productivity are intrinsically lined.

6 Conclusion

To conclude, inclusion and putting abilities first among employees within a firm is a difficult task. Firms need to pay careful attention to the processes and systems within the organization not only within the context of the organization but also the broader ecosystem of organizations. Within the supply chain and operations communities, we believe that the research in this stream is only starting. For example, Kalkanci et al. (2019) have provided an approach to study inclusive innovations that promote community engagement in business models. Our focus here has been primarily on integrating employees with disabilities in mainstream workforce. As demonstrated by the write-up, this not only requires thought at the process level, but has several

[12]https://www.peckham.org/Human Services/Residential-Services.aspx

layers of processes that the firm needs to tackle. Overall, we have endeavored to provide a thought framework to facilitate this process in this chapter.

References

Accenture (2018) Getting to equal: the disability inclusion advantage. https://www.accenture.com/_acnmedia/PDF-89/Accenture-Disability-Inclusion-Research-Report.pdf. Accessed on 11/10/2019

Adams-Shollenberger G, Mitchell T (1996) A comparison of janitorial workers with mental retardation and their non-disabled peers on retention and absenteeism. J Rehabil 62(3):56–60

Battilana J, Sengul M, Pache AC, Model J (2015) Harnessing productive tensions in hybrid organizations: the case of work integration social enterprises. Acad Manag J 58:1658–1685

Braithwaite J, Mont D (2009) Disability and poverty: a survey of World Bank poverty assessments and implications. Alternatives 3(3):219–232

Cimera RE (2000) The cost-efficiency of supported employment programs: a literature review. Journal of Vocational Rehabilitation 14(1):51–61

Clark RE, Xie H, Becker DR, Drake RE (1998) Benefits and costs of supported employment from three perspectives. J Behav Health Serv Res 25(1):22–34

Cohen-Charash Y, Spector PE (2001) The role of justice in organizations: a meta-analysis. Organ Behav Hum Decis Process 86(2):278–321

Cook JA, Burke J (2002) Public policy and employment of people with disabilities: exploring new paradigms. Behav Sci Law 20(6):541–557

Cole D, Narayanan S, Vickery S (2020) Does leader disability status improve performance outcomes for workers with a disability? An empirical study in the apparel industry. Working Paper, Michigan State University

Colella A, DeNisi A, Varma A (1998) The impact of ratee's disability on performance judgments and choice as partner: the role of disability-job fit stereotypes and interdependence of rewards. J Appl Psychol 83(1):102–111

Colella A, Paetzold R, Belliveau MA (2004) Factors affecting coworkers procedural justice inferences of the workplace accommodations of employees with disabilities. Pers Psychol 57:1–23

Colella A (2001) Coworker distributive fairness judgments of the workplace accommodation of employees with disabilities. Acad Manag Rev 26(1):100–116

Colquitt JA, Conlon DE, Wesson MJ, Porter CO, Ng KY (2001) Justice at the millennium: a meta-analytic review of 25 years of organizational justice research. J Appl Psychol 86(3):425–445

Cooney K (2016, December) Work integration social enterprises in the United States: operating at the nexus of public policy, markets, and community. In Nonprofit policy forum, De Gruyter 7(4):435–460

Dixon S, Smith C, Touchet A (2018) The disability perception gap policy report. Scope. Retrieved online 12–31-19 from https://www.scope.org.uk/scope/media/files/campaigns/disability-perception-gap-report.pdf

The Economist (2012) The new green; disabilities and business. Retrieved online 12–31-19 from https://link-gale-com-proxy2-cl-msu-edu-proxy1-cl-msu-edu.proxy2.cl.msu.edu/apps/doc/A301745698/ITOF?u=msu_main&sid=ITOF&xid=b76ed4b1

Empowerment Plan (2019) Accessed online 12-22-2019 from https://www.empowermentplan.org/about and https://www.empowermentplan.org/the-program

Ford H, Crowther S (1922) My life and work. Doubleday, Page, New York

Fremstad S (2009) Half in ten: why taking disability into account is essential to reducing income poverty and expanding economic inclusion (No. 2009–30). Center for Economic and Policy Research (CEPR)

Gaudiano P, Hunt E (2017) 10 tips for unlocking the talent and potential of employees with disabilities. Forbes (September 09, 2017). Accessed from https://bit.ly/31xJjmu
Garcia-Serrano C, Malo M (2014) How disability affects absenteeism: an empirical analysis for six European countries. Int Labour Rev 153(3):455–471
Hernandez B, McDonald K (2010) Exploring the costs and benefits of workers with disabilities. J Rehabil 76(3):15–23
Hoffman LC (2013) An employment opportunity or a discrimination dilemma: sheltered workshops and the employment of the disabled. U Pa JL & Soc Change 16:151–179
Houtenville A, Kalargyrou V (2012) People with disabilities: employers' perspectives on recruitment practices, strategies, and challenges in leisure and hospitality. Cornell Hosp Q 53(1):40–52
IBM (2019) The accessible workforce. Accessed online 12-22-2019 from https://www.ibm.com/ibm/history/ibm100/us/en/icons/accessibleworkforce/impacts/
Kaletta JP, Binks DJ, Robinson R (2012) Creating an inclusive workplace: integrating employees with disabilities into a distribution center environment. Prof Saf 57(6):62–71
Kalkanci B, Rahmani M, Toktay LB (2019) The role of inclusive innovation in promoting social sustainability. Prod Oper Manag 28(12):2960–2982
Kaye HS, Jans LH, Jones EC (2011) Why don't employers hire and retain workers with disabilities? J Occup Rehabil 21(4):526–536
Kubik E (2018) 126 major businesses rated best places to work for disability inclusion. https://www.aapd.com/press-releases/ 126-major-businesses-rated-best-places-to-work-for-disability-inclusion/. Accessed on 11/10/2019
Lalive R, Wuellrich J, Zweiumuller J (2015) Do financial incentives affect firms' demand for disabled workers? J Eur Econ Assoc 11(1):25–58
Lay-Flurrie J (2018) The ability hacks: The story of two hackathon teams embracing the transformative power of technology. Accessed online 12-22-2019 from https://blogs.microsoft.com/on-the-issues/2018/07/23/the-ability-hacks-the-story-of-two-hackathon-teams-embracing-the-transformative-power-of-technology/
Mallender J, Liger Q, Tierney R, Beresford D, Eager J, Speckesser S, Nafilyan V (2015) Reasonable accommodation and sheltered workshops for people with disabilities: costs and returns of investments. European Parliament Policy Department. Accessed May 21, 2020). https://www.europarl.europa.eu/RegData/etudes/STUD/2015/536295/IPOL_STU(2015)536295_EN.pdf
Miralles C, Garcia-Sabater J, Andres C, Cardos M (2007) Advantages of assembly lines in sheltered work centers for disabled. A case study. Int J Prod Econ 110:187–197
Mittapalli KM, Belson SI, Ahmadi H (2009) Financial literacy for youth with disabilities. Social Dynamics. Access Document, Gaithersburg, MD. https://www.dol.gov/sites/dolgov/files/odep/research/financialeducationyouthdisabilitiesliteraturereview.pdf
Narayanan S, Terris E (2020) Inclusive manufacturing: the impact of disability diversity on productivity in a work integration social Enterprise. Manufacturing & Service Operations Management, Forthcoming
Narayanan S, Terris E, Arjun S (2019) Abilities-first: Steps to create a human- centric, inclusive supply chain. Supply Chain Management Review (November/December) 34–41.
O'Connor L (2010) Creating transportation connections. Accessed online 12-23-2019 from https://www.secondwavemedia.com/capitalgains/features/transit0409.aspx
Okoro CA, Hollis ND, Cyrus AC, Griffin-Blake S (2018) Prevalence of disabilities and health care access by disability status and type among adults—United States, 2016. Morb Mortal Wkly Rep 67(32):882–887
Rothband H (1917) A scheme for finding employment for disabled soldiers & sailors. Cornell University Press, Ithaca
Schur L, Kruse D, Blanck P (2005) Corporate culture and the employment of persons with disabilities. Behav Sci Law 23(1):3–20
Shah R, Ward P (2003) Lean manufacturing: context, practice bundles, and performance. J Oper Manag 21(2):129–149

Shima I, Zolyomi E, Zaidi A (2008) The labour market situation of people with disabilities in EU25. Policy Brief 1

Shore LM, Chung-Herrera BG, Dean MA, Ehrhart KH, Jung DI, Randel AE, Singh G (2009) Diversity in organizations: where are we now and where are we going? Hum Resour Manag Rev 19(2):117–133

United Nations (2015) Transforming our world: the 2030 agenda for sustainable development. Retrieved 12-8-2019 from https://sustainabledevelopment.un.org/post2015/transformingourworld

United States Ability One Commission (2019) AbilityOne program. Retrieved 12-22-2019 from https://abilityone.gov/

United States Bureau of Labor and Statistics (2019a) A look at the future of the U.S. labor force to 2060. Retrieved 12-22-2019 from https://www.bls.gov/spotlight/2016/a-look-at-the-future-of-the-us-labor-force-to-2060/pdf/a-look-at-the-future-of-the-us-labor-force-to-2060.pdf

United States Bureau of Labor and Statistics (2019b) Persons with a disability: labor force characteristics – 2018. Retrieved 12-22-2019 from https://www.bls.gov/news.release/pdf/disabl.pdf

United States Bureau of Labor and Statistics (2019c) Employment projections 2018–2029. Retrieved 12-22-2019 from https://www.bls.gov/news.release/ecopro.nr0.htm

United States Bureau of Labor and Statistics (2019d) The Employment Situation – November 2019. Retrieved 12-22-2019 from https://www.bls.gov/news.release/pdf/empsit.pdf

United States Internal Revenue Service (2019) Tax benefits for businesses who have employees with disabilities. Retrieved 12-4-2019 from https://www.irs.gov/businesses/small-businesses-self-employed/tax-benefits-for-businesses-who-have-employees-with-disabilities

Walgreens (2019) Walgreens earns best place to work in 2019 disability equality index. Accesses 12-22-2019 from https://news.walgreens.com/press-releases/general-news/walgreens-earns-best-place-to-work-in-2019-disability-equality-index.htm

Whittle HJ, Palar K, Ranadive NA, Turan JM, Kushel M, Weiser SD (2017) "The land of the sick and the land of the healthy": disability, bureaucracy, and stigma among people living with poverty and chronic illness in the United States. Soc Sci Med 190:181–189

Womack JP, Jones DT (2003) Lean thinking: banish waste and create wealth in your corporation. Simon and Schuster

Zanoni P (2011) Diversity in the lean automobile factory: doing class through gender, disability and age. Organizations 18(1):105–127

Socially Responsible Co-Product Design

Yen-Ting Lin, Haoying Sun, and Shouqiang Wang

Abstract As consumers become increasingly concerned about the environmental impact of their consumption, co-production technology that manufactures products of different qualities from a common source of raw material has emerged as a viable option to reduce natural resource consumption. Specifically, co-production technology allows a manufacturer to introduce a new co-product using raw material that would otherwise be discarded because of its inferior quality relative to conventional quality standards. In this chapter, we examine whether and how a manufacturer should leverage co-production technology to design its product offerings. We show that introducing co-products can both enhance a manufacturer's profitability and curb resource consumption. In particular, when the co-product is introduced, greener demand in general results in lower resource consumption and waste. However, an exception may arise when the raw material is costly, forcing the manufacturer to underproduce and leave some demand unfulfilled. Finally, we also discuss other business strategies to reduce material usage and waste from a product life cycle perspective.

Keywords Co-production · Sustainable operations · Pricing · Product line design · Environmentally conscious consumers

Y.-T. Lin (✉)
School of Business, University of San Diego, San Diego, CA, USA
e-mail: linyt@sandiego.edu

H. Sun
Gatton College of Business and Economics, University of Kentucky, Lexington, KY, USA
e-mail: Haoying.Sun@uky.edu

S. Wang
Naveen Jindal School of Management, University of Texas at Dallas, Richardson, TX, USA
e-mail: Shouqiang.Wang@utdallas.edu

J. M. Swaminathan, V. Deshpande (eds.), *Responsible Business Operations*,
Springer Series in Supply Chain Management 10,
https://doi.org/10.1007/978-3-030-51957-5_7

1 Introduction

Accelerated depletion of scarce natural resources has attracted unprecedented public attention in recent years. Consumers become increasingly "green" and wary of the environmental impacts resulted from their consumptions. According to a survey conducted by the global business solution provider CGS in 2019, nearly 70% of the US respondents deemed sustainability to be a "somewhat important" issue, and 47% of the respondents would pay at least 25% more for a sustainable product (CGS 2019). In response, a growing number of companies introduce so-called green or eco-friendly products that are designed to reduce their harm to the environment either during the manufacturing process or at the consumption point.

Resource conservation and waste reduction are widely regarded as two important sustainability measures. Products made of material that would otherwise be discarded due to inferior quality compared to the conventional standard offer a great opportunity to improve these two sustainability measures. Such practice emerges in industries where raw material is purchased or acquired in bulk with exogenous variation in quality. Traditionally, a manufacturer would use the material with quality meeting the conventional standard to make a *traditional* product and discard the material with subpar quality. A manufacturer now may use these would-be discarded materials to make a *co-product*, as referred to in the operations literature, catering to the emerging green consumers who value the product's resource saving. The name "co-product" reveals a salient feature in this type of production: both the traditional product and the co-products are manufactured out of the same process and sold in the same market. Since the raw material for those co-products is oftentimes discarded before due to cosmetic imperfection rather than functional issues, purchasing such co-products can signify a consumer's support for waste reduction.

First studied around the late 1980s and early 1990s (Bitran and Leong 1992; Bitran and Gilbert 1994), the notion of co-production refers to a production process where multiple products of different quality levels are simultaneously produced. The semiconductor and petroleum industries represent the classic examples of co-production processes with the following three features: First, one production run produces multiple products at once. For example, after crude oil goes through refineries, petroleum products with different grades, such as gasoline, jet fuel, and diesel fuel, are produced simultaneously. Second, these multiple products have the same basic functionality but differ in one quality dimension. For example, a wafer semiconductor plant can produce multiple memory chips, but some chips have larger storage capacity than others due to natural variation in the process. Third, the proportion of high- versus low-quality products is dictated by an exogenously specified distribution function. That is, for a given co-production technology, the firm cannot influence the natural quality distribution of the co-products.

In a uni-product manufacturing process where one product is produced at a time (or multiple products are made without sharing a common source of raw material), the production quantity, as well as the raw material quantity for each product, can be determined independently of each other. In a co-production setting, however, this is not the case because the output quantity of each quality grade in a production run is now interdependent. Consequently, matching the production output of each quality grade to their respective demand is much more challenging. This challenge is usually alleviated by "downward substitution" where a co-product of higher quality is used to satisfy the demand for a co-product of lower quality. For example, gasoline with octane rating 93 can satisfy the demand from luxury cars whose engine requires this type of gasoline as well as demand from regular cars that require lower octane levels of 89 or 87.

Consequently, early work in co-production focuses on the optimal allocation of co-products such as how to leverage inventory decisions to downward substitute the low-quality co-products with higher-quality co-products (Bitran and Gilbert 1994). Subsequent works also explore the pricing decisions for co-products and the optimal number of co-products to offer, which is often referred to as product "bins" (Tomlin and Wang 2008). More recently, scholars further examine the interaction between the supply chain structure and these decisions (Lu et al. 2019). Nevertheless, companies who conduct co-production rarely note the environmental value of this practice. Similarly, the research community on the co-production also largely ignored the environmental consequence of this practice.

Taylor Guitars, a premier acoustic guitar manufacturer, headquartered in El Cajon, CA, is perhaps the first company that introduces co-products with an explicit resource conservation flare. Ebony wood has been the primary raw material for fretboard (a.k.a. fingerboard), which sits at the top of the guitar's neck. The uniformly black color is ebony's signature trademark, making it the conventional choice for many musical instruments. As a less known fact, only one out of ten ebony trees is pure black, while most ebony trees are actually "streaked" with natural, continuous variability of tan-colored swirls. The streak level of the wood can only be discerned through eyeballing after being harvested.[1]

Traditionally, guitar makers use only pure black, "streak-less" ebony and simply discard all the aesthetically inferior streaked ebony wood. After years of such extravagant logging practice and wasteful production method, ebony species become scarce and are prohibited from harvesting in many parts of the world, leaving Cameroon in Africa the only remaining legal source for high-quality ebony woods.

Consumers' growing awareness of environmental sustainability has invigorated a zero-waste movement in other markets. In the grocery industry, for example, up to 20% of fruit and vegetables are discarded merely due to cosmetic imperfections (Godoy 2016). To fight against food waste, Intermarche, the third largest supermarket in French, decided to sell these imperfect fruits at a 30% discount in its "inglorious fruits and vegetables" campaign in 2014. The campaign gained a host of admirers and spread quickly within the industry. In 2016, Walmart piloted sales of weather-dented apples at a discount in 300 stores in Florida under the brand "I'm

[1] "Vertical Integration for Corporate Social and Environmental Responsibility at Taylor Guitars" in this book offers a case study on Taylor Guitar's sustainable ebony sourcing practice.

Perfect." In a similar effort to combat food waste, the US supermarket giant Kroger Co. also plans to introduce Pickuliar Picks in 2019 to sell imperfect but perfectly delicious produce that used to be discarded due to unappealing appearance (Driscoll 2018).

In 2011, Taylor Guitars acquired the largest ebony mill in Cameroon. Owning the wood mill allows the company to learn the wasteful harvesting practice for the first time. In response, Taylor Guitars started paying loggers an equal rate for all harvested ebony, whether streaked or streak-less. In 2014, Taylor Guitars introduced guitars made of streaked ebony along with those made of traditional pure black ebony. To educate the market about the dire situation of ebony, the company also promotes the story of ebony through its magazines and reseller training, convincing guitar buyers that variations in wood color, often perceived as flaws, are actually signs of sustainably harvested ebony.

Given that co-products are made by material with inferior quality, sometimes co-products require additional processes and treatments to bring their quality up to standard. For example, cellphone remanufacturers such as ReCellular Inc. purchase end-of-use products (called *cores*) from brokers, such as Gazelle and NextWorth, in bulk and remanufacture them to functional products. Since the cores are unsorted with huge quality variations, this remanufacturing process is the same as the co-production process we described before. The cost of this restoration process highly depends on the quality of the cores. A lower-quality core requires more materials and labor and hence more cost to be remanufactured (Mutha et al. 2016).

Introducing co-products may offer a novel approach for businesses to achieve a win-win outcome in terms of both the profitability for the private industry (because of the improved resource utilization and the resulting cost savings) and the environmental benefits for the society. However, companies face several challenges in this new opportunity:

(1) **Should a company introduce a co-product at all?** Sometimes co-products require additional processing costs to bring their quality up to standards. Furthermore, the sustainable feature of the co-product is not valued by every consumer. So it is unclear whether the demand for the co-product and the potential cost savings on the raw material justify the introduction of co-products.
(2) **What are the pricing strategy and quality choice for the co-product?** If a manufacturer determines to embrace this business opportunity, how should it price the co-product? Should a manufacturer charge a premium to the co-product to leverage green consumers' willingness to pay for a product's sustainability feature? Apparently, doing so will sweeten the co-product's profit margin but it may hurt the sales. Also, given that raw material varies in quality, what is the ideal quality level for the co-product?
(3) **Will the introduction of a co-product necessarily lead to a better environmental outcome?** Reduced material usage and waste (e.g., fewer ebony trees being cut) are the top claimed sustainability benefits for the co-products. How-

ever, does a co-product always achieve these claimed benefits? Furthermore, companies frequently enhance consumers' green awareness through social media or public education. How will that affect the manufacturer's profitability? Does having a greener consumer population translate into a better sustainable outcome, such as lesser resource waste or usage?

To answer these questions, we study a manufacturer's optimal product pricing and co-product quality strategies in a model that captures the following key practical features: (1) exogenous variation in material quality, (2) heterogeneity of consumers in that some (but not necessarily all) of them are *green* and willing to pay an additional premium to reward products' sustainability, and (3) co-products may incur additional processing cost. Through the lens of technology management, we are particularly interested in the effects of *resource availability*, which adversely affects the firm's acquisition cost, and *co-production efficiency*, which can be manifested in the co-product's additional unit production cost. Specifically, the material cost is measured by the unit acquisition cost for the raw material; also, a higher additional production cost for the co-product indicates lower co-production efficiency. Our study generates the following key insights.

(1) **When to introduce a co-product?** We find that a manufacturer should introduce a co-product only when the co-product's co-production efficiency is high and the raw material cost is not overly high. As illustrated in Fig. 1, resource availability and co-production efficiency provide the firm with complementary incentives to introduce a co-product. That is, a firm tends to introduce a co-product as the co-production technology enables a more efficient manufacturing process or as the natural resource becomes increasingly difficult to acquire.
(2) **The firm's positioning strategy for the co-product.** Our results show the co-product should always be priced lower than the traditional product. Furthermore, the manufacturer should either adopt a *regular* or a *premium* pricing strategy. Specifically, the regular price forfeits the additional environmental premium that the green consumer is willing to pay for the co-product and effectively positions the co-product as a *low-end* product that appeals to both the green and traditional consumers. The manufacturer should adopt the regular pricing strategy when the co-production efficiency is high and the resource availability is sufficiently, but not overly high (i.e., the LF region in Fig. 1). Otherwise, the manufacturer should adopt a *premium* pricing strategy to extract the co-product's additional environmental premium from the green consumer, effectively positioning the co-product as a *green* product that appeals only to the green consumer but no longer to the traditional consumer (i.e., the GF and GP regions in Fig. 1).
(3) **Impact of material cost and co-production efficiency on the co-product's quality and pricing strategies.** In general, the manufacturer should react to any increase in material cost or additional processing cost by utilizing lower-quality material to make the co-product, resulting in lower usage and waste of the

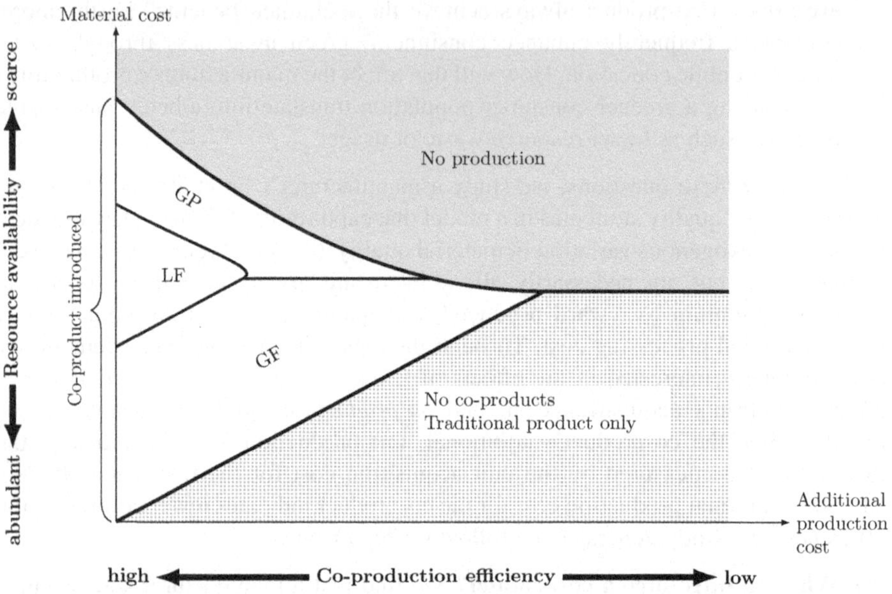

Fig. 1 How does the firm's manufacturing technology drives its product line strategy?

raw material. However, exceptions may arise when the co-product's positioning switches from a low-end product to a green product.

(4) **Demand fulfillment strategy.** We find that a *strategic abandonment* strategy where the manufacture voluntarily forgoes some traditional (non-green) consumer demand can be optimal for the firm. In this case, the manufacture adopts a premium pricing strategy and acquires just enough material to fulfill green consumers' demand using the green co-product, but not enough to produce sufficient traditional products to fulfill traditional consumers' demand. Strategic abandonment is the best strategy only when the material cost is too high for the firm to remain profitable without introducing a co-product. In all other cases, the firm should fulfill the entire market's demand. Figure 1 illustrates the firm's optimal product positioning and demand fulfillment strategy.

(5) **Resource usage and waste.** When the material cost is not overly high so that the firm makes a profit even without introducing the co-product, introducing a co-product always reduces the firm's material usage and waste. That is, the introduction of a co-product indeed yields positive environmental impacts. However, given that a co-product is introduced, does "greener" demand always ameliorate the firm's environmental impacts? Not necessarily! We find that having more green consumers will raise the firm's material usage and waste under the strategic abandonment strategy.

2 Model

Our model considers a manufacturer (the firm) who acquires the raw material (e.g., wood) for its products. We normalize the units so that each product requires one unit of the raw material. The firm acquires Q units of the raw material at a per-unit cost c. The raw material is characterized by a single physical attribute (e.g., the color purity of the wood) that represents its quality. The quality is measured by a parameter $q \in [0, 1]$, with a higher value of q representing higher material quality. The quality spectrum of the acquired material follows a uniform distribution. In other words, the portion of material with quality lower or equal to any q is also q.

Consumers evaluate the final products based on material quality. We say a product is of quality q if the product is made of raw material with quality in $[q, q']$ for some $q' > q$. In other words, the product quality is determined by the minimum material quality that goes into that product. For musical instruments and many other products, the industries have established a conventional standard for product quality, which we refer to as the *traditional quality* and denote as $q_t \in (0, 1)$. For instance, only the ebony wood with color purity above a certain level qualifies for making the guitar fretboards. The status quo production process only uses raw materials with quality in $[q_t, 1]$ to make the *traditional products* but discards any material with quality level below q_t. In our base model, the traditional quality q_t is an exogenous parameter.

Nowadays, some consumers become "green" in the sense that they not only value the product quality as it brings consumption utility but also value the environmental benefit (e.g., resource conservation) embedded in the product. In response, the firm can introduce a *co-product* made of material quality in $[q_o, q_t]$ for some q_o lower than the traditional quality q_t.[2] Additional production procedures may be needed to process raw material of quality below q_t (e.g., restoration cost of the recycled "cores" that are collected in bulk form the end-of-use mobile phones). Without loss of generality, we normalize the traditional product's unit production cost to zero and denote $k \geq 0$ as the co-product's unit production cost. Note that the production cost is the cost that the firm has to incur in addition to the material cost. For any given co-product's quality q_o and material quantity Q, the quantities of the traditional and co-products are, respectively, given by

$$Q_t := Q(1 - q_t) \text{ and } Q_o := Q(q_t - q_o). \tag{1}$$

As such, the manufacturing process represented here is a co-production technology: the quantities of the traditional and co-products are simultaneously determined by material quantity Q through their quality levels, q_t and q_o, as well as the exogenous distribution of material quality.

[2]While both the traditional product and the product of quality q_o are sometimes referred to as co-products according to the literature, we hereafter reserve the term *co-product* to refer to the latter.

On the demand side, without loss of generality, we normalize the total market size to one and denote $n \in [0, 1]$ as the fraction of green consumers. We refer to the remaining $1 - n$ fraction of consumers as the traditional consumers. Green consumers value a product's potential resource conservation, while traditional consumers do not. Specifically, both traditional and green consumers are willing to pay $v_u q$ for the consumption value of a product with quality q. Green consumers differ from the traditional consumers and are willing to pay an additional environmental premium $v_e\,(q_t - q)$ for the product's resource conservation relative to the traditional product. Here, $v_e \in (0, v_u)$ represents the green consumers' marginal willingness to pay for resource conservation, and the quality differential $q_t - q$ measures the product's resource conservation: for each unit of raw material, a product of quality $q \leq q_t$ can salvage $q_t - q$ units of raw material that would otherwise be discarded without introducing the product of quality q. Thus, in our setup, the traditional product does not generate this additional environmental premium, and only the co-product does. The assumption $v_e < v_u$ suggests that a product's usage value is still the primary consideration while its value on resource conservation is secondary. For expositional simplicity, we normalize $v_u = 1$ and abbreviate v_e as $v < 1$. Table 1 below summarizes the utility functions for the two consumer segments purchasing the two products. The default utility of purchasing nothing is normalized to zero.

Table 1 Consumer utility functions

	Traditional product (q_t, p_t)	Co-product (q_o, p_o)
Traditional consumers	$q_t - p_t$	$q_o - p_o$
Green consumers	$q_t - p_t$	$q_o + v(q_t - q_o) - p_o$

For exogenously given traditional product's quality q_t, the profit-maximizing firm needs to decide the material quantity Q, the co-product's quality q_o, as well as both traditional and co-products' prices, which we denote as p_t and p_o, respectively.

3 Firm's Optimal Strategy

In this section, we first formulate the firm's problem in Sect. 3.1 and then solve for its optimal product line strategy in Sect. 3.2.

3.1 Firm's Problem Formulation

In this section, we will characterize the firm's revenue and then formulate the firm's product line design problem into an optimization problem. We begin our analysis from the firm's retail price decision for the products.

First, Table 1 shows that all of the consumers value the traditional product at $q_t - p_t$ and a consumer's default utility of not purchasing at all is zero. Therefore, $p_t = q_t$ is the highest price a consumer would be willing to pay for the traditional product, implying $p_t = q_t$ being the firm's optimal retail price for the traditional product.

On the other hand, following the same analysis, we show that there are two candidates for the optimal co-product price: a *regular price* $p_o = q_o$ and a *premium price* $p_o = q_o + v(q_t - q_o)$. At the regular price, the firm only extracts the co-product's consumption value and forfeits the opportunity to exploit the environmental value embedded in the co-product. Thus, the regular price essentially acts to position the co-product as a *low-end* product (relative to the traditional product as a high-end product) that fully extracts the traditional consumer's surplus but leaves a positive surplus to the green consumer from purchasing the co-product. At the premium price, the firm extracts both consumption and environmental value embedded in the co-product and hence positions the co-product as a *green* product. However, at the premium price, the co-product is priced so high that traditional consumers will never consider buying it (due to negative utility). In particular, under both pricing strategies, a traditional (resp. green) consumer prefers a traditional product (resp. co-product) over the other product.

The analysis for the firm's pricing strategy allows us to derive the firm's profit for any given co-product quality q_o, green consumer size n, and product supply Q_o and Q_t. In deriving the firm's revenue, we need to consider possibilities that a consumer may consider purchasing his or her second choice when the most preferred product is not available. This complication is illustrated through the following example.

Suppose 20% of consumers are green (i.e., $n = 0.2$) and only raw material in the top 10% quality spectrum is qualified for making a traditional product (i.e., $q_t = 0.9$), which is then priced at $p_t^* = q_t = 0.9$. The per-unit material cost is $c = 0.2$ and it costs $k = 0.1$ to make a co-product. Let us say that the firm acquires one unit of raw material (i.e., $Q = 1$) and uses raw material with quality in $[0.5, 0.9]$ to make a co-product (i.e., $q_o = 0.5$), which is priced at $p_o = q_o = 0.5$. In this case, the firm makes $Q_t = Q(1 - q_t) = 0.1$ and $Q_o = Q(q_t - q_o) = 0.4$ units of traditional and co-products, respectively. We note that the traditional product's supply is lower than the traditional consumers' demand (i.e., $Q_t < 1 - n = 0.8$) whereas the co-product's supply exceeds the green consumers' demand (i.e., $Q_o > n = 0.2$). Thus, the firm's profit can be calculated as follows:

$$\text{profit} = \underbrace{q_t Q_t}_{\substack{\text{sales of traditional}\\ \text{products to traditional}\\ \text{consumers}}} + \underbrace{q_o n}_{\substack{\text{sales of co-products to}\\ \text{green consumers}}} + \underbrace{q_0 \min\{1 - n - Q_t, Q_o - n\}}_{\substack{\text{sales of co-products to}\\ \text{traditional consumers}}} - \underbrace{(cQ + kQ_o)}_{\substack{\text{material and}\\ \text{co-production costs}}},$$

where the third term is the revenue generated by selling the co-product's excess supply to the traditional consumers who are not fulfilled by the traditional product. In this example, the traditional product's supply is insufficient to fulfill the entire traditional consumer segment, and hence some traditional consumers end up buying their next preferred product (i.e., the co-product). The opposite, where some green consumers end up buying the traditional products, may also arise depending on the firm's production strategy.

In general, there are four possible revenue sources for the firm (each consumer demand can be fulfilled by each of the two products). Specifically, let R_i^j represent the firm's revenue from selling product $i \in \{t, o\}$ to consumer segment $j \in \{T, G\}$, where superscripts T and G indicate the traditional and green consumer segments, respectively. The explicit expressions for R_i^j are available in the Appendix. Then we can formulate the firm's product line design as follows:

$$\Pi^* = \max_{q_o, p_o, Q} \quad R_t^T + R_o^G + R_o^T + R_t^G - cQ - kQ_o \qquad (P)$$
$$\text{subject to } \; 0 \leq q_o \leq q_t, \; p_o \in \{q_o, q_o + v(q_t - q_o)\}, \text{ and } Q \geq 0.$$

3.2 *Firm's Optimal Product Line Strategy*

As alluded to above, the firm can position the co-product either as a green product, which can only be used to fulfill the green consumers, or as a low-end product, which can fulfill the demand from both traditional and green consumers. When the supply of the traditional product and the co-product exactly matches the demand from traditional and green consumers, respectively, the market is fully covered, in which case the co-product obviously should be positioned as a green product to extract the additional WTP from green consumers, leading to what we refer to as the *Green co-product, Full coverage* (GF) strategy.

However, since the supply of the two products is regulated through the co-production technology and may not exactly match the demand from the two segments, the firm thus may need to fulfill the demand with both products. When the co-product is positioned as a green product but cannot meet the entire green demand, the firm may cover the entire market by letting some green consumers purchase the traditional product, again leading to the GF strategy. Likewise, when the co-product is positioned as a low-end product and its supply exceeds the green demand, the firm may cover the entire market by letting some traditional consumers purchase the co-product, leading to what we refer to as the *Low-end co-product, Full coverage* (LF) strategy. Is it possible for the firm to only cover the market partially (i.e., leave some consumers unfulfilled)? If so, how should the co-product be positioned? Our first result below answers these two questions.

Proposition 1 *The firm enters the market if and only if*

$$c \leq \bar{c}(k, q_t, v) := \max_{q_o \in [0, q_t]} (1 - q_t)q_t + (q_t - q_o)[q_o + v(q_t - q_o) - k], \quad (2)$$

in which case the firm's optimal product line strategy must be one of the following three:

Green co-product, Full coverage (GF): $q_o \geq \frac{q_t - n}{1-n}$, $p_o = q_o + v(q_t - q_o)$ *and* $Q = \frac{1}{1-q_o}$. *All traditional consumers purchase a traditional product. If the first inequality strictly holds, some green consumers purchase a co-product, and the rest of the green consumers purchase a traditional product; otherwise, all green consumers purchase a co-product.*

Green co-product, Partial coverage (GP): $q_o < \frac{q_t - n}{1-n}$, $p_o = q_o + v(q_t - q_o)$ *and* $Q = \frac{n}{q_t - q_o}$. *All green consumers purchase a co-product. Some traditional consumers purchase a traditional product, and the rest of the traditional consumers are left unfulfilled.*

Low-end co-product, Full coverage (LF): $q_o \leq \frac{q_t - n}{1-n}$, $p_o = q_o$ *and* $Q = \frac{1}{1-q_o}$. *All green consumers purchase a co-product. Some traditional consumers purchase a traditional product, and the rest of the traditional consumers purchase a co-product.*

Proposition 1 shows the possibility of leaving some traditional consumers unfulfilled by positioning the co-product as a green product (i.e., the GP strategy) but rules out the possibility of partially covering the market by positioning the co-product as a low-end product (i.e., the LP strategy). Intuitively, positioning the co-product as a green product allows the firm to charge the environmental price premium for the co-product but precludes the traditional consumers from purchasing it. Thus, the firm can sacrifice the co-product's sales quantity for the additional marginal revenue brought about by the green co-product, resulting in the GP strategy. However, it is never wise for the firm to give up the sales quantity and the additional price premium of the co-product simultaneously. In other words, the firm can always improve its profit by deviating from the LP strategy to LF or GP strategy.

Proposition 1 allows us to reformulate the firm's problem in (P) as three subproblems that correspond to the three product line strategies therein. Notably, each subproblem has only the co-product's quality q_o as its single decision variable. The firm's optimal strategy will then be determined by the one among these three strategies that yield the highest profit. As our key result, the following proposition characterizes the firm's optimal strategy in terms of the co-production technology's cost parameters.

Proposition 2 *There exist a threshold* $c^* = c^*(q_t, v, n)$ *independent of* k *and four thresholds* $k_i = k_i(c, q_t, v, n)$ $(i = 1, \ldots, 4)$ *such that the firm's optimal product line strategy is represented in the* (c, k)*-space as Fig. 2.*

Proposition 2 shows that the cost characteristics of the firm's co-production technology determine up to five qualitatively different optimal strategies in designing and pricing its co-product, which result in different fulfillment outcomes. Intuitively

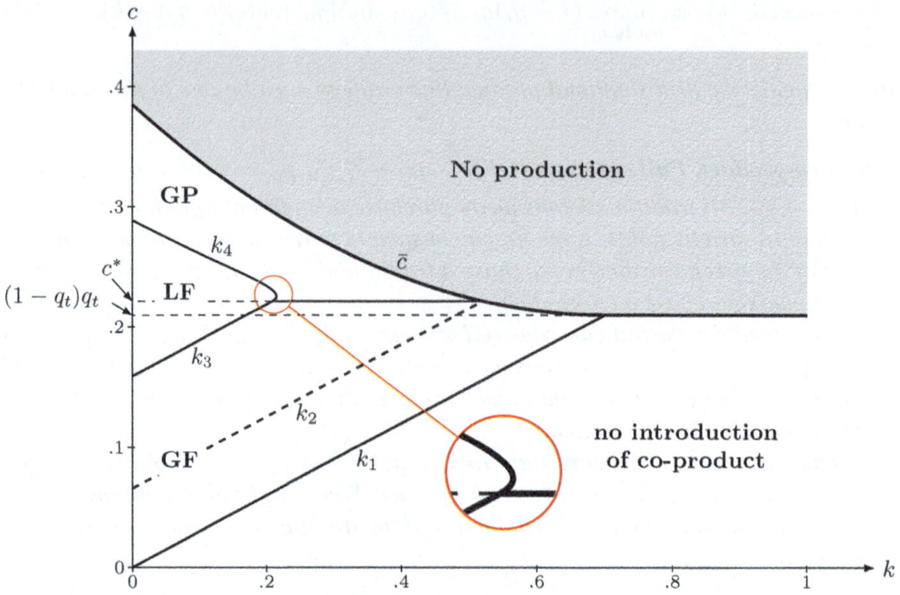

Fig. 2 The firm's optimal product line strategy ($v = 0.3$, $n = 0.3$, $q_t = 0.7$)

speaking, the unit material cost c is recouped by adopting the co-production technology and drives up material utilization by lowering the co-product's quality, while the marginal co-production cost k discourages the introduction of the co-product and brings the co-product's quality closer to that of the traditional product. To provide a holistic view of the interplay between these two forces, Fig. 2 maps the firm's strategies onto the (k, c)-space.

Figure 2 provides several insights into our key research questions. First, Fig. 2 shows that the firm should do so only when the marginal co-production cost k is low and the raw material cost c is not overly high (i.e., GP, LF, and GF regions). As long as the material cost is not prohibitively high so that the firm cannot profitably enter the market at all, the firm is more likely to benefit from introducing a co-product as the material cost escalates. On the other hand, the co-production cost k disincentivizes the introduction of the co-product. The co-production cost is likely to drop over time, whereas the increased resource scarcity such as the depletion of wood resources is likely to escalate material costs. Therefore, our analysis anticipates that these market forces will lead to a growing interest in introducing co-products.

Figure 2 also shows the impact of the material and co-production costs on the firm's co-product pricing strategy. While green consumers are willing to pay a premium for the co-product's environmental benefit (i.e., resource conservation), forfeiting that premium and choosing a regular pricing strategy can be the firm's profit-maximizing strategy. As Fig. 2 shows, using a regular pricing strategy would be the firm's profit-maximizing strategy only when the material cost c is intermediate and the co-production cost k is relatively low (i.e., LF strategy). That is, the co-product's positioning strategy is not necessarily monotone in the material cost.

Furthermore, Fig. 2 shows that the firm fulfills the entire market demand only when the material cost is not overly high (i.e., LF and GF strategies). When the material cost is sufficiently high, the firm may choose the GP strategy that does not fulfill all of the demand. Specifically, under the GP strategy, the firm adopts a premium pricing strategy, and it produces just enough co-product to fulfill green consumers' demand. However, the firm's material quantity under the GP strategy does not warrant sufficient traditional products to fulfill all traditional consumer demand. In other words, the firm intentionally unfulfills some, but not all, of the traditional consumer demand despite their willingness to purchase one. This phenomenon was referred to strategic abandonment by Lin et al. (2019) in a similar model. Strategic abandonment happens only under the GP strategy, and it is the firm's optimal product line design strategy when the material cost is sufficiently high as Fig. 2 shows. In that case, additional material is needed to fulfill the unmet demand. In doing so, the firm would be able to recoup the cost of the additional material only through the sale of traditional products. There will be no demand for the co-product made by these additional materials since the premium priced co-product is overly expensive for traditional consumers. However, the material cost is so high that the firm can only justify the cost of each material by selling both the traditional product and co-product made by the material, making strategic abandonment a more profitable strategy.

More intriguingly, we find that the GP strategy (and hence strategic abandonment) occurs in the cost parameter region, where the firm would not operate if the co-product is not introduced or green consumers are absent from the market. This observation is formalized below.

Corollary 1 *When GP is the firm's optimal strategy, the firm would not profitably enter the market by offering only the traditional product (i.e.,* $q_o = q_t$*).*

In other words, strategic abandonment is never the firm's best strategy when it can make a profit without introducing a co-product. Strategic abandonment is the firm's best strategy only when the material cost is so high that introducing a co-product is the only means to stay profitable. This result is also illustrated in Fig. 2. Specifically, we can show that the firm makes a profit without introducing a co-product when $c < (1 - q_t)q_t$, which stays below the minimum material cost c^* above which the GP strategy can be the optimal strategy.

4 Environmental Implications

Companies constantly campaign for the environmental benefits represented by their products. For example, Taylor Guitars educates customers on why buying a guitar with streaked ebony can help conserve ebony through magazines such as Inside Supply Management and Wood & Steel. On the company's website, its co-founder, Bob Taylor, tells on a youtube video the true state of ebony to raise buyers' awareness of the scarcity of ebony (Taylor Guitars 2018). Walmart also discusses on its official blog the positive environmental impact of reducing food waste via selling the slightly blemished or oddly shaped fruit and vegetables.[3] These marketing efforts have raised consumers' environmental consciousness or simply consumers' *greenness*. Can such corporate environmentalism indeed help resource conservation? We aim to answer this question in this section.

Our model captures consumers' greenness in two dimensions: the size of the green demand segment n and the marginal WTP for resource conservation v, which we will hereafter refer to as the *volume* and *intensity* of the greenness in the market. In particular, firms can expand the size of green consumers and hence increase the volume of greenness through advertisement, while educating existing green consumers can strengthen their WTP for environmental value embedded in the co-product and hence enhance the intensity of greenness. Meanwhile, the firm's environmental performance can be measured by three metrics: (1) resource consumption as measured by Q^*;[4] (2) resource utilization as measured by $U^* := 1 - q_o^*$; and (3) resource waste as measured by $W^* := Q^* q_o^*$. In Table 2, we analyze the impact of the consumers' greenness on these environmental performance metrics as well as the firm's optimal profit Π^*.

Table 2 shows that enlarging the volume of greenness and enhancing its intensity may not be strategic substitutes in reducing resource consumption and waste. Specifically, as the green consumers become more willing to pay for resource conservation (i.e., higher v), the firm's three environmental performance metrics never deteriorate (i.e., resource consumption Q^* goes down, resource utilization U^* goes up, and resource waste W^* goes down). However, having a larger size of green consumers (i.e., higher n) does not necessarily yield the same effect as one might intuitively expect. In particular, when the firm's optimal strategy becomes GP (whereby strategic abandonment happens), having more green consumers in fact leads to higher resource consumption (Q^*) and higher resource waste (W^*). Indeed,

Table 2 Effects of market "greenness" on the firm's environmental performance and profitability

	As volume n increases				As intensity v increases			
Strategy	Q^*	U^*	W^*	Π^*	Q^*	U^*	W^*	Π^*
No co-product	–	–	–	–	–	–	–	–
GF	↓	↑	↓	↑	↓	↑	↓	↑
LF	–	–	–	–	–	–	–	–
GP	(↑)	–	(↑)	↑	↓	↑	↓	↑

Notation: ↑ = non-decreasing ↓ = non-increasing – = invariant

[3]http://blog.walmart.com/sustainability/20160719/one-perfect-solution-for-saving-ugly-apples

[4]While the firm uses only a portion of the acquired material, Q^* units of the raw materials have to be harvested from nature.

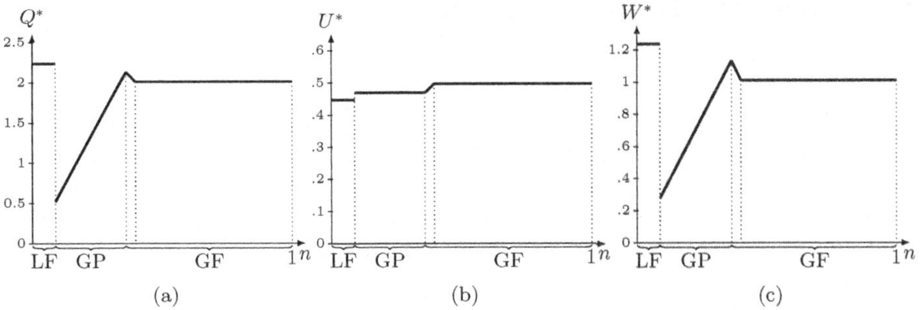

Fig. 3 The effect of greenness volume (n) on the firm's environmental performance ($c = 0.23$, $k = 0.4$, $v = 0.3$, $q_t = 0.7$). (**a**) Consumption Q^*. (**b**) Utilization U^*. (**c**) Waste W^*

when the firm strategically abandons some traditional consumers, the raw material quantity is driven by the size of the green segment, which exactly matches the supply of green products, i.e., $Q^* = \frac{n}{q_t^* - q_o^*}$. In contrast, the firm acquires $Q^* = 1/(1 - q_o^*)$ units of raw material under other strategies so that every consumer purchases a product.

Table 2 also shows that having *more* green consumers (higher n) or enhancing their WTP for resource conservation (higher v) can improve the firm's profitability. In particular, under the GP strategy, the firm's profit always increases as n or v gets higher. In other words, when strategic abandonment turns out to be the firm's optimal strategy, having a greener consumer population always raises the firm's profitability. This result, together with Corollary 1, yields an important insight: when introducing the green co-product is necessary to ensure the firm's profitable entry to the market, the firm's efforts to expand the green market may backfire, resulting in higher consumption and waste of natural resources.

Figure 3 illustrates the *global* impact of having higher green volume (i.e., larger n) on the firm's environmental performance. Notably, the resource consumption (Q^*) and utilization (U^*) can *simultaneously* increase as more consumers become green, a phenomenon also known as the "Jevons paradox" (Alcott 2005; Hertwich 2005). For the specific numerical example in Fig. 3, when the volume of greenness n increases from 0.2 to 0.8, both resource consumption (Q^*) and utilization (U^*) increase (from 1.18 to 2.01 and from 46.9% to 49.7%, respectively) because the firm switches its optimal strategy from abandoning some traditional consumers (corresponding to the GP strategy) to fulfilling the entire market (corresponding to the GF strategy). Moreover, the resource waste also goes up (from 0.62 to 1.01), because the increase of consumption outpaces that of utilization.

5 Endogenous Traditional Product's Quality

In this subsection, we consider the scenario in which the traditional product's quality standard q_t is not rigid or the firm has the power to influence it. As a result, the firm chooses the quality for both products q_t and q_o, their prices p_t and p_o, as well as the raw material quantity Q. In this case, the firm's problem (P) includes an additional decision variable q_t and becomes analytically more involving. Proposition B.1 in the appendix summarizes the complete characterization of the firm's optimal product line decision for this case.

We find that the qualitative nature of our key results in the base model continues to hold. In particular, the firm's optimal strategy again can be categorized into four types, No Co-product, GF, GP, and LF, and the firm should only position the co-product as a low-end product for an intermediate value of the material cost. The effects of the unit material cost c and additional green production cost k on the firm's product line strategy also remain qualitatively the same. In terms of the firm's environmental performance, having a larger volume of green consumers (i.e., larger n) still results in higher resource consumption under the GP strategy.

Nuanced in the setting with endogenized traditional product quality are the impacts of c and k on the optimal q_t^*, which we examine in Table 3 and Fig. 4.

Table 3 Effects of costs (c, k) on the optimal product qualities

	Monotonicity in c		Monotonicity in k	
Optimal strategy	q_t^*	q_o^*	q_t^*	q_o^*
No co-product	↓	↓	–	–
GF	↓ or ↑	↓	↓	↑
GP	↑	↓	–	–
GF = GP	↓	↓	–	–
LF	↓	↓	↓	↑

Notation: ↑ = increasing ↓ = decreasing – = invariant

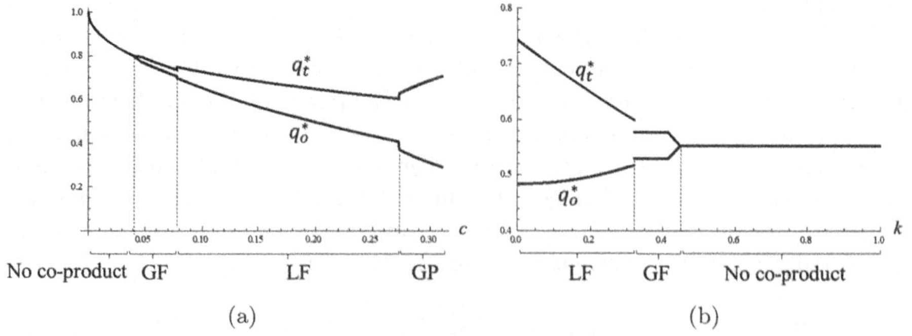

Fig. 4 The firm's optimal product qualities q_t^* and q_o^* when the traditional product's quality is endogenized ($v = 0.4$ and $n = 0.1$). (**a**) The effect of c (with $k = 0.2$). (**b**) The effect of k (with $c = 0.2$)

Table 3 demonstrates the *local* effects of the cost structure on the optimal qualities of both products under each strategy, while Fig. 4 illustrates their global effects. Most notably, when the firm's optimal strategy switches from LF to GP as the material cost c increases, the traditional product's optimal quality q_t^* changes from piecewise decrease to piecewise increase in c. As elaborated earlier, the GP strategy dominates the LF strategy when the material cost c becomes sufficiently high. Since positioning the co-product as a green product trades off the co-product's sales quantity for its higher price, the firm would increase the traditional product's quality q_t^*, when adjustable, to maximize the revenue appropriated from the traditional consumers. In contrast, when c is relatively low and the LF strategy is enacted, the firm can utilize less material and hence reduce the total cost by lowering both products' quality.

While the traditional product's quality q_t^* may be increasing or decreasing in c, the co-product's quality q_o^* always decreases in c under all strategies, because this enables the firm to utilize more expensive raw material. Moreover, the *length* of the firm's product line, $q_t^* - q_o^*$, is always increasing in c, as illustrated in Fig. 4a. As first noted by Chen et al. (2013), this phenomenon counters the result in a unit production setting. However, in their study, the highest product quality nonetheless remains constant. Namely, their result is equivalent to the descending monotonicity of the lowest product quality in c. We establish this result *with the highest product quality* q_t^* *decreasing in* c *even in the presence of additional green production cost* k. Besides, Fig. 4b demonstrates the intuitive yet opposite effect of k on the length of the optimal product line: the length of the product line shrinks as the green production becomes less efficient (i.e., k gets higher).

6 Conclusion

Introducing co-products can achieve environmental benefits (i.e., reducing resource consumption) and enhance firms' profitability. Essentially, such environmental benefit is achieved through higher material utilization, which in turn lowers product costs as well as raw material consumption. Nevertheless, there is a small caveat: when the co-product is positioned as a "green" product that charges consumers a price premium for the product's environmental benefits and when the raw material is quite costly to acquire, having more green consumers may inadvertently elevate raw material consumption.

In addition to introducing co-products, the operations and supply chain management literature also identifies other approaches to conserve natural resources. For example, Li et al. (2019) examine whether a firm should sell or scrap its Not Quite Perfect Products (NQPP), such as memory chips that fail to meet quality specifications.[5] By focusing on the context where NQPP is offered only to a low-end market that is not served by the perfect product, they show that sometimes the firm should scrap the NPQQ at a cost to avoid losing pricing control in the markets. In some cases, a firm can also implement By-Product Synergy (BPS) to reduce its environmental impact. Lee and Tongarlak (2017) define BPS as "a form of joint production that uses the waste stream from one (primary) process as a useful input into another (secondary) process." For example, wastewater/heat from a chemical production plant can be used to cool/heat the plant; cow manure can be used for fertilizer production. Essentially, by feeding waste from a process as an input to produce a different by-product, BPS reduces the virgin raw material required to produce the by-product. However, Lee (2012) cautions that sometimes a firm may overproduce its primary product in an attempt to obtain more waste for the by-product. In that case, BPS may adversely raise raw material consumption.

From a product life cycle perspective, co-production, NPQQ, and BPS represent business strategies at the beginning of the cycle. Recycle, reuse, and remanufacturing, on the other hand, improve sustainability at the end of the product life cycle. Specifically, recycling operations extract useful raw material from used products. Paper recycling is perhaps one of the most celebrated recycling examples. In fact, about 2/3 of the papers are recycled in the USA in recent years according to "sustainable business."[6] A report by the University of Southern Illinois shows that every ton of recycled paper represents "17 trees, 380 gallons of oil, 4,000 kilowatts of energy, 7,000 gallons of water."[7] Electronic waste (e-waste), by contrast, sits on recycling's other end of the popularity spectrum, with an estimated recycling rate of merely 15–20%. In fact, electronic waste contains many valuable components. For example, it is estimated that more than 20,000 lbs of copper, 20 lbs of palladium, 550 lbs of silver, and 50 lbs of gold can be recovered from one million cell phones, according to EPA.

While the environmental benefit of e-waste recycling is obvious, designing an efficient reverse supply chain poses some major challenges. For example, how to efficiently collect end-of-life products? Who should be responsible for collecting items from consumers? Who should finance the recycling operations? E-waste is the fastest-growing stream of waste. Unfortunately, the complex recycling process, variation in item qualities, and fluctuation in commodity prices all make the e-waste recycling profit razor thin or even negative. Consequently, many countries and states, including the European Union, Japan, and China, establish e-waste take-back legislation to mandate recycling responsibility on producers. Atasu and Van Wassenhove (2012), for example, offer a comprehensive review of the imple-

[5]Co-products in the semiconductor wafer production are considered NQPPs. However, a NQPP does not necessarily be a co-product. It could be a slightly defective product from the unit production.

[6]https://www.thebalancesmb.com/paper-recycling-facts-figures-and-information-sources-2877868

[7]https://www.usi.edu/recycle/paper-recycling-facts/

mentation of take-back legislation. They identify six stakeholders in this recycling process: manufacturers, consumers, recyclers, collectors, municipal cities, and the environment. Atasu et al. (2013) investigate the impact of two widely adopted e-waste take-back legislation, tax model and rate model, on various stakeholders. In a tax model, a government collects either a disposal fee (when used items are collected) or an advanced recycling fee (when a new item is purchased). In a rate model, a government specifies a target recycling rate for the producers. They find that oftentimes stakeholders possess inconsistent preferences over these two models, potentially contributing to the inconsistent adoption between them in practice.

While voluntary recycling is less common, many producers voluntarily remanufacture or reuse end-of-life products, essentially replacing or upgrading their components and selling them back to consumers again. Remanufacturing/reuse programs are gaining popularity due to the increased consumer awareness and desire to reduce virgin material consumption as well as their new profit opportunity. For example, Xerox designs and produces copy machines such that it remanufactures and reuses almost 100% of them. Remanufacturing and reuse have received much scholarly attention in the past decade (see Atasu et al. (2008) for a comprehensive review in this area). Much of the research in remanufacturing focuses on operational issues including determining the optimal material acquisition quantities given that the amount of returned products is uncertain (Galbreth and Blackburn 2010), sorting returned products for different remanufactured products (Galbreth and Blackburn 2006), pricing strategies for new and remanufactured products (Akan et al. 2013), and the impact when a firm allows the third party to remanufacture its products (Mutha et al. 2016).

While the environmental benefit and resource savings from remanufacturing seem to be straightforward, Galbreth et al. (2013) find in some circumstances, it may unexpectedly elevate the consumption of virgin material. Specifically, as technology advances and new versions of products are introduced, once a producer collects used or returned products, it can replace the worn-out components and remanufacture them to their original product specifications, or it can upgrade components in the returned products to make them as good as the latest new products. In this context, Galbreth et al. (2013) find that remanufacturing raises the consumption of virgin material for mature products with little innovations over time. In contrast, remanufacturing generally lowers the consumption of virgin material for products with a rapid rate of innovation.

In addition to reducing virgin material consumption at the beginning of the product life cycle (co-products, NPQO, and by-products) or at the end of it (remanufacturing and recycling), product consumption phase also offers an opportunity to reduce consumption of raw materials. Such opportunity can be exemplified by a tire retreading company that switched from selling retreaded tires to providing tire management services to its clients such as trucking companies (Yadav et al. 2003). Before the switch, the tire retreading company encourages tire consumption at its clients since its revenue grows from selling more tires. This relationship, however, was reversed after the change of business model: using more retreaded tires at its clients now means higher cost to the tire company. As a result, the company better managed its tire retreading and maintenance schedules to reduce the tire needs of its clients. However, as a company switches from selling goods to offering service management to its clients, as in the previous example for the tire retreading company, new challenges also arise. For example, Corbett and DeCroix (2001) pointed out that "the goals of maximizing joint profits and minimizing consumption are generally not aligned." In other words, as companies change their business models from direct selling to service provision, they may face the dilemma between corporate social responsibility and pursuit of profitability.

Appendix A: Formulation for Firm's Revenue

In Sect. 3, we introduce R_i^j as the firm's revenue from selling product $i \in t, o$ to consumer segment $j \in T, G$. The explicit expression for R_i^j is derived in Lin et al.'s (2019) which is also given in the following table (Table 4).

Appendix B: Proofs and Additional Results

Proof of Proposition 1. The proposition follows directly from Lin et al.'s (2019) Lemma 2 by specializing the material quality distribution to the uniform distribution. □

Proof of Proposition 2. Under the GF strategy, the firm's problem (P) reduces to

$$\Pi_1(c,k,q_t,v,n) := \max_{q_o \in \left[\frac{(q_t-n)^+}{1-n}, q_t\right]} \frac{1-q_t}{1-q_o} q_t + \frac{q_t-q_o}{1-q_o}\left[q_o + v(q_t-q_o)\right] - \frac{c}{1-q_o} - k\frac{q_t-q_o}{1-q_o}. \tag{GF}$$

Under the GP strategy, the firm's problem (P) reduces to

Table 4 Firm's revenue sources

Consumers	Purchase	Revenue
	Traditional product	$R_t^T := q_t \min\{1-n, Q_t\}$
Traditional	Co-product	$R_o^T := p_o \min\left\{(1-n-Q_t)^+, (Q_o-n)^+\right\} \mathbb{K}[p_o = q_o]$
	Traditional product	$R_t^G := q_t \min\left\{(n-Q_o)^+, (Q_t-(1-n))^+\right\}$
Green	Co-product	$R_o^G := p_o \min\{n, Q_o\}$

$$\Pi_2(c,k,q_t,v,n) := \max_{q_o \in \left[0, \frac{q_t-n}{1-n}\right]} \frac{n}{q_t-q_o}(1-q_t)q_t + n\left[q_o + v(q_t-q_o) - k\right] - \frac{cn}{q_t-q_o}. \tag{GP}$$

Under the LF strategy, the firm's problem (P) reduces to

$$\Pi_3(c,k,q_t,v,n) := \max_{q_o \in \left[0, \frac{q_t-n}{1-n}\right]} \frac{1-q_t}{1-q_o}q_t + \frac{q_t-q_o}{1-q_o}q_o - \frac{c}{1-q_o} - k\frac{q_t-q_o}{1-q_o}. \tag{LF}$$

The three subproblems, (GF), (GP), and (LF), are of a single decision variable q_o. The solution to the subproblem that yields the highest profit determines the optimal solution to the firm's problem (P). Define

$$k_1 := c/(1-q_t), \quad k_2 := \frac{c}{1-q_t} - \frac{1-v}{1-q_t}\left\{\left[1 - \frac{(q_t-n)^+}{1-n}\right]^2 - (1-q_t)^2\right\},$$

$$k_3 := \frac{c}{1-q_t} - \left[\left(\frac{1+\sqrt{v}n}{1-n}\right)^2 - 1\right](1-q_t),$$

$$k_4 := \begin{cases} 1 - \frac{2(1-q_t)}{(1-n)^2} + \frac{1-q_t+n[(1-v)q_t+c/q_t]}{1-n} - \frac{2(1-q_t)}{1-n}\sqrt{\frac{q_t-n}{(1-q_t)(1-n)}\left(\frac{c}{(1-q_t)q_t} - \frac{1-vn}{1-n}\right) + \frac{vn^2}{(1-n)^2}}, & \text{if } c \geq q_t - vq_t^2, \\ 1 - \frac{(1+n^2)(1-q_t)}{(1-n)^2} + \frac{2n\sqrt{1-v}\sqrt{c-(1-q_t)q_t}}{1-n} - \frac{2(1-q_t)}{1-n}\sqrt{\left(\frac{\sqrt{c-(1-q_t)q_t}}{1-q_t} - \frac{n\sqrt{1-v}}{1-n}\right)^2 + \frac{vn^2}{(1-n)^2}}, & \text{if } c \leq q_t - vq_t^2, \end{cases}$$

$$c^* := (1-q_t)q_t + (1-v)\frac{n^2}{(1-n)^2}(1-q_t)^2, \quad \text{and}$$

$$\bar{c}(k,q_t,v) := \begin{cases} (1-q_t)q_t, & \text{if } k \geq q_t, \\ (1-q_t)q_t + \frac{(q_t-k)^2}{4(1-v)}, & \text{if } q_t \geq k \geq (2v-1)q_t, \\ [1-(1-v)q_t - k]\,q_t, & \text{if } k \leq (2v-1)q_t. \end{cases}$$

where k_3, k_4, and c^* are only defined for $q_t \geq n$.

It can be shown that *ceteris paribus*, (i) the threshold $\bar{c} = \bar{c}(k,q_t,v)$ in (2) is decreasing in k; (ii) the threshold $c^* = c^*(q_t,v,n)$ is independent of k; (iii) k_1, k_2, and k_3 are linearly increasing in c; (iv) $\bar{c}\,(k_2(c^*,q_t,v,n),q_t,v) = c^*$ if $n \leq q_t$; (v) k_4 is nonlinearly increasing first and then decreasing in $c \geq c^*$; (iv) $k_1 > k_2 > k_3 \geq k_4$ with $k_3 = k_4$ if and only if $c = c^*$; and (vi) the optimal solution (q_o^*, p_o^*, Q^*) to the firm's problem (P) is given by Table 5, where $\Gamma_1 := \max\left\{n, \frac{2(1-v)n}{1+(1-2v)n}\right\} \leq \Gamma_2 := 1 - \left(\frac{1-n}{\sqrt{1-(1-v)n^2}+\sqrt{v}n}\right)^2$. □

Proof of Table 2. The monotonicity of the three environmental performance metrics follows from direct examination of the expressions for the optimal q_o^* and Q^* obtained in Table 5. □

Proposition B.1 (Firm's optimal decisions for endogenous q_t) *When the firm endogenizes its choice of q_t, there exist threshold values c_1, c_2, c_3, and c_4 such that the firm earns positive profit if $c \leq c_4$. In that case, the firm sets the price $p_t^* = q_t^*$ for the traditional product; the firm's optimal quality decisions q_t^* and q_o^*, optimal price for the co-product p_o^*, and optimal material quantity Q^* are given in Table 6.*

Table 5 The firm's optimal decision (q_o^*, p_o^*, Q^*)

Dominant subproblem	Conditions	q_o^*	p_o^*	Q^*
No co-product (GF)	$c \le \bar{c},\ k \ge k_1$	q_t	q_t	$\frac{1}{1-q_t}$
(GF)	$c \le \bar{c},\ k_1 \ge k \ge k_2$	$\left(1 - \sqrt{(1-q_t)^2 + \frac{c-k(1-q_t)}{1-v}}\right)^+$	$q_o^* + v(q_t - q_o^*)$	$\frac{1}{1-q_o^*}$
(GP)	$q_t \ge \Gamma_1,\ c^* \le c \le \bar{c},\ k \ge k_4$	$\left(q_t - \sqrt{\frac{c-(1-q_t)q_t}{1-v}}\right)^+$	$q_o^* + v(q_t - q_o^*)$	$\frac{n}{q_t-q_o^*}$
(GF) = (GP)	$q_t \ge \Gamma_1,\ c \le c^*,\ k_2 \ge k \ge k_3$	$(q_t - n)/(1-n)$	$q_o^* + v(q_t - q_o^*)$	$\frac{1}{1-q_o^*}$
(LF)	$q_t \ge \Gamma_2,\ c \le c^*,\ k \le k_3$	$1 - \sqrt{(1-q_t)^2 + c - k(1-q_t)}$	q_o^*	$\frac{1}{1-q_o^*}$
	$q_t \ge \Gamma_2,\ c \ge c^*,\ k \le k_4$			

Table 6 The firm's optimal decisions when q_t is endogenized

Optimal strategy	Region in (k, c)-space	q_t^*	q_o^*	p_o^*	Q^*
No co-product	$c \leq \min\{k^2, c_4\}$	$1 - \sqrt{c}$	$1 - \sqrt{c}$	q_t	$\frac{1}{1-q_t^*}$
GF	$k^2 \leq c \leq \min\{c_1, c_4\}, v < \frac{3}{4}$	$1 + \frac{2v-1}{2(1-v)}\Delta_1 - \frac{k}{2(1-v)}$	$1 - \Delta_1$	$q_o^* + v(q_t - q_o^*)$	$\frac{1}{1-q_o^*}$
GP	$c_2 \leq c \leq c_4, k < \frac{1-2n(1-v)}{2-n}$	$\frac{1}{2}(1 + \Delta_2)$	$\frac{1}{2}(1 - \Delta_2)$	$q_o^* + v(q_t - q_o^*)$	$\frac{n}{q_t^* - q_o^*}$
GF = GP	$c_1 \leq c \leq \min\{c_5, c_6\}, k < \frac{1-2n(1-v)}{2-n}$	$1 - (1-n)\sqrt{\frac{c}{\Delta_3}}$	$1 - \sqrt{\frac{c}{\Delta_3}}$	$q_o^* + v(q_t - q_o^*)$	$\frac{1}{1-q_o^*}$
LF	$c_5 \leq c \leq c_7$	$1 - \frac{k}{2} - \Delta_4$	$1 - 2\Delta_4$	q_o^*	$\frac{1}{1-q_o^*}$

$\Delta_1 = \sqrt{\frac{4c(1-v)-k^2}{3-4v}}$, $\Delta_2 = \sqrt{\frac{4c-1}{3-4v}}$, $\Delta_3 = 1 - n + n^2(1-v)$, $\Delta_4 = \sqrt{\frac{4c-k^2}{12}}$

$c_1 = \frac{k^2\Delta_3}{(1-2n(1-v))^2}$, $c_2 = \min\{c_6, c_7\}$, $c_3 = \min\{c_5, c_6\}$, $c_5 = \frac{k^2(1-5n+n^2(9+2v)-4n^3(2-v)+4n^4(1-v)+2(1-2n)n\sqrt{3\Delta_3 v})}{(1-4n+4n^2(1-v))^2}$

$$c_4 = \begin{cases} \frac{1-k+k^2-v}{3-4v} & \text{if } k \leq \frac{1}{2} \text{ and } v < \frac{3}{4} \\ v - k & \text{if } v \geq \max\{\frac{3}{4}, k(k+1)\}, \\ \frac{1}{4} & \text{otherwise} \end{cases} \quad c_6 = \begin{cases} \frac{\Delta_3}{(2-n)^2} & \text{if } v < \frac{3}{4} \\ \frac{2(1-(1-n)\sqrt{\Delta_3})-3n+n^2(2-v)}{n^2} & \text{otherwise} \end{cases}$$

c_7 is the relevant root of

$$\sqrt{4c-1}(\sqrt{3(4c-k^2)}-2+k)(3-4v)$$
$$+n(\sqrt{4c-1}(1-2k)(3-4v)-(4c-1)(3-4v)^{3/2})=0. \quad (3)$$

References

Akan M, Ata B, Savaşkan-Ebert RC (2013) Dynamic pricing of remanufacturable products under demand substitution: a product life cycle model. Ann Oper Res 211(1):1–25

Alcott B (2005) Jevons' paradox. Ecol Econ 54(1):9–21

Atasu A, Van Wassenhove LN (2012) An operations perspective on product take-back legislation for e-waste: theory, practice, and research needs. Prod Oper Manag 21(3):407–422

Atasu A, Guide VDR, Van Wassenhove LN (2008) Product reuse economics in closed-loop supply chain research. Prod Oper Manag 17(5):483–496

Atasu A, Özdemir Ö, Van Wassenhove LN (2013) Stakeholder perspectives on e-waste take-back legislation. Prod Oper Manag 22(2):382–396

Bitran GR, Gilbert SM (1994) Co-production processes with random yields in the semiconductor industry. Oper Res 42(3):476–491

Bitran GR, Leong TY (1992) Deterministic approximations to co-production problems with service constraints and random yields. Manag Sci 38(5):724–742

CGS (2019) CGS survey reveals sustainability is driving demand and customer loyalty. https://www.cgsinc.com/sites/default/files/media/resources/pdf/CGS_2019_Retail_Sustainability_infographic.pdf. Retrieved 26 June 2019

Chen Y-J, Tomlin B, Wang Y (2013) Coproduct technologies: product line design and process innovation. Manag Sci 59(12):2772–2789

Corbett CJ, DeCroix GA (2001) Shared-savings contracts for indirect materials in supply chains: channel profits and environmental impacts. Manag Sci 47(7):881–893

Driscoll K (2018) Kroger's fruit, vegetables will look ugly next year: here's why. https://www.daytondailynews.com/business/kroger-fruit-vegetables-will-look-ugly-next-year-here-why/WxKTDiLGDGY46lG3uotT7J/. Retrieved 26 June 2019

Galbreth MR, Blackburn JD (2006) Optimal acquisition and sorting policies for remanufacturing. Prod Oper Manag 15(3):384–392

Galbreth MR, Blackburn JD (2010) Optimal acquisition quantities in remanufacturing with condition uncertainty. Prod Oper Manag 19(1):61–69

Galbreth MR, Boyacı T, Verter V (2013) Product reuse in innovative industries. Prod Oper Manag 22(4):1011–1033

Godoy M (2016) Wal-Mart, America's largest grocer, is now selling ugly fruit and vegetables. https://www.npr.org/. Retrieved 30 June 2019

Hertwich EG (2005) Consumption and the rebound effect: an industrial ecology perspective. J Indus Ecol 9(1–2):85–98

Lee D (2012) Turning waste into by-product. Manuf Serv Oper Manag 14(1):115–127

Lee D, Tongarlak MH (2017) Converting retail food waste into by-product. Eur J Oper Res 257(3):944–956

Li R, Xia Y, Yue X (2019) Scrap or sell: the decision on production yield loss. Prod Oper Manag 28(6):1486–1502

Lin Y-T, Sun H, Wang S (2019) Designing sustainable products under co-production technology. Working paper

Lu T, Chen YJ, Tomlin B, Wang Y (2019) Selling co-products through a distributor: the impact on product line design. Prod Oper Manag 28(4):1010–1032

Mutha A, Bansal S, Guide VDR (2016) Managing demand uncertainty through core acquisition in remanufacturing. Prod Oper Manag 25(8):1449–1464
Taylor Guitars (2018) The ebony project. https://www.taylorguitars.com/ebonyproject
Tomlin B, Wang Y (2008) Pricing and operational recourse in coproduction systems. Manag Sci 54(3):522–537
Yadav P, Miller DM, Schmidt CP, Drake R (2003) McGriff treading company implements service contracts with shared savings. Interfaces 33(6):18–29

Vertical Integration for Corporate Social and Environmental Responsibility at Taylor Guitars

Adem Orsdemir, Vinayak Deshpande, and Daniel Lin

Abstract Following the acquisition of an ebony mill in Cameroon, Taylor Guitars implemented a series of social and environmental responsibility (CSER) initiatives in ebony sourcing. The company also supplies the responsibly sourced ebony to its competitors through horizontal sourcing. Inspired by their example, we study vertical integration as an alternative strategy for CSER in sourcing. In this case, firm can vertically integrate with its supplier to ensure responsible practices in the supply chain. In a competitive setting, an exposed CSER violation in one supply chain may increase the competing supply chain's demand (positive externalities) because of product substitution or decrease the competing supply chain's demand (negative externalities) because of public's heightened suspicion about the entire industry's social and environmental practices. Furthermore, NGOs' scrutiny and reporting policies may influence the chance of a violation exposure, as well as demand externalities created by the violation exposure. We examine horizontal sourcing as a potential strategy for mitigating the impact of a CSER externality caused by a competing supply chain. When horizontal sourcing is infeasible, we find that higher violation exposure externalities induce better CSER, but overly intensive violation scrutiny alongside strongly negative externalities may backfire and discourage CSER. By contrast, when horizontal sourcing is feasible, intensive violation scrutiny induces CSER, but strongly positive externalities may impair industry-wide CSER.

A. Orsdemir (✉)
School of Business, University of California Riverside, Riverside, CA, USA
e-mail: adem.orsdemir@ucr.edu

V. Deshpande
Kenan-Flagler Business School, University of North Carolina at Chapel Hill, Chapel Hill, NC, USA
e-mail: vinayak_deshpande@kenan-flagler.unc.edu

D. Lin
School of Business, University of San Diego, San Diego, CA, USA
e-mail: linyt@sandiego.edu

J. M. Swaminathan, V. Deshpande (eds.), *Responsible Business Operations*, Springer Series in Supply Chain Management 10,
https://doi.org/10.1007/978-3-030-51957-5_8

These findings have important implications for firms interested in ensuring CSER in their supply chain, as well as for NGOs' violation scrutiny and reporting policies.

Keywords Taylor Guitars · Responsible sourcing · Social and environmental resposibility · Non-governmental organization · Demand externalities

1 Introduction

Corporate social responsibility violations have come under high scrutiny in recent years. This is largely driven by consumers' growing awareness on their consumption's impact on societies and environment (Landrum 2017). They expect companies to go beyond providing products and services; they expect companies to also ensure corporate social and environmental responsibility (CSER) in their supply chains. This instinct has gained traction especially after several high-profile CSER violations.

In the 1990s, Nike became the poster child of CSER violations. Since then Nike has frequently appeared in news as the perpetrator of several CSER violations, as recently as 2017 (Sergran 2017), despite each time assuring public of rectifying the social responsibility violations.

Nike is hardly the only one that is accused of CSER violations. The $2.4 trillion apparel industry has been accused a host of CSER violations including, but not limited to, slave labor, child labor, sweatshop conditions, and low wages. The Rana Plaza incident in 2013 likely marks the nadir of the garment industry. Rana Plaza, a multistory factory building in Bangladesh housing garment factories, collapsed and killed more than 1,000 garment workers, making it one of the deadliest industrial disasters. Investigations uncovered that despite clear evidence the building had been a safety hazard, the factories had continued to operate, resulting in this tragedy (Yardley 2013). The factories in Rana Plaza were contract manufacturers for well-known European and American brands, including Benetton, Bonmarche, the Children's Place, Mango, Primark, and Walmart. After the incident, these brands faced widespread protests and criticism (Greenhouse 2013). In response to the intense scrutiny, these firms signed a 5-year legally binding agreement to improve the working conditions in Bangladesh, known as Accord.[1] However, to this day CSER violations stay rampant in the garment industry (Chua 2016). Tackling the CSER violations is not easy due to the complexity of global supply chains as pointed out by Human Rights Watch: "While complex global supply chains can offer important opportunities for economic and social development, they often present serious human rights risks that many companies have failed to mitigate and respond to effectively (Human Rights Watch 2016)."

[1] https://bangladeshaccord.org/

Complexity of supply chains makes it difficult to ensure suppliers' CSER. Auditing is popular among the limited tools to that end. However, auditing can be ineffective. Brand inspector can at best visit their suppliers periodically but for a short duration, making it difficult to monitor the suppliers' behavior in between audits (Human Rights Watch 2017). In addition, suppliers use sophisticated strategies to evade buyers' audits. They use fake accounting book, showroom factories dedicated for audit visits, and unauthorized subcontracting. These strategies add challenges to detect CSER violations.

These challenges necessitate a more structural and thorough transformations in supply chains. Taylor Guitars, a California based high-end guitar manufacturer, is leading the way for transforming its supply chain to ensure CSER. In 2014 Taylor Guitars received the Award for Corporate Excellence (ACE) for its sustainability efforts in the ebony trade and transformative work in the lives of its many employees at its ebony mill, Crelicam, in Cameroon. How does Taylor Guitars achieve its excellence? The following case study discusses their strategy to ensure CSER in their supply chain.

2 Case Study on Taylor Guitars

Building guitars has always been Bob Taylor's passion. In 1972, at the age of 18, he began working at a guitar making shop named American Dream. In 1974, when the owner decided to sell the company, Bob Taylor and Kurt Listug, another employee at the company, bought American Dream and changed the name to Taylor Guitars. In the next 40 years, the El Cajon, California, based company has evolved into the largest acoustic guitar maker in the USA with a thousand employees and over $100 million in annual sales. Taylor Guitars focuses on premium acoustic guitars with a price point around three to four thousand dollars for its most popular models. To this day, Bob and Kurt remain the co-owners of the company. Taylor Guitars is recognized for its tone and playability, attracting many celebrated musicians, including Paul McCartney, Neil Young, Taylor Swift, and Jason Mraz, to own Taylor Guitars.

2.1 The Guitars Industry

The guitar industry enjoyed a healthy 1.4% annual growth from 2012 to 2017 (Maxwell 2018). In the USA, nearly 1.5 million acoustic guitars were sold in 2018, generating $1.4 billion in revenue (Statista 2019). Taylor Guitars faces competition from makers such as Martin and Gibson (filed bankruptcy in 2018) with more than a hundred years of history. While their guitars are often very traditional in appearance, Taylor Guitars pioneered many innovations in the guitar industry. For example, Taylor Guitars is the first American acoustic guitar manufacturer to use computer numerically controlled (CNC) milling machines for production. It is also the first in the industry to introduce computer-controlled milling, laser-cutting, and robotic finish spraying and buffing.

2.2 Guitar Manufacturing

The guitar making process begins with wood procurement. Once woods are shipped to the factory, they first stay in an acclimation room for weeks to a few months. Since woods come from different parts of the world, this step ensures that the moisture content of the living, breathing piece of wood stays at their ideal level of 4–6% before it is ready for the next stage. After acclimation, wood pieces go to one of the two parallel processes that manufacture guitar body and neck.

In the guitar body process, woods are cut to make the guitar tops, backs, and sides. From there the guitar tops and backs enter into a detailed bracing process, while the guitar sides are bent from flat wood pieces to the curved sides. Then the top, back, and side are glued to form a guitar's body. The body is then hand routed before adding the decorative binding and edges to it.

In the neck process, traditionally a neck was carved out of one large piece of wood; so much wood scrap was generated in this process. Taylor Guitars innovated a new process by first gluing two pieces of wood to form the overall shape of the neck, followed by finishing the detail with CNC machines. Then the fretboard is glued to the top of the neck and then the frets are inserted. This buildup process generates much less wood scrap than the traditional carve-out process.

Finally the finished guitar body meets the neck. Traditionally, the neck would be glued onto the guitar body. However, this eliminates the possibility to replace the neck should any quality problem arise. Instead, Taylor Guitars invented a bolt-on neck system that enables easy neck replacement and allows for proper adjustment of the guitar pieces.

2.3 Wood Sourcing and the Lacey Act

Acoustic guitars are made of wood. The wood also uniquely determines a guitar's sound and tone. No two pieces of wood, even of the same species, sound exactly the same. Besides the tonal application of wood, they also serve a visual appeal. Different woods have different grain patterns, color variegation, and other visual aesthetics that set them apart and make them unique. A single guitar is made up of multiple types of woods: for example, mahogany, sapele, and maple for the neck, ebony for the fretboard, spruce for the top, and a variation of sapele, mahogany, maple, Indian rosewood, and ebony for the body.

Taylor Guitars sources wood from all over the world. Unfortunately, an estimated 20–40% of global wood production is logged illegally, resulting in $10 to $15 billion in annual untaxed and unregulated funds according to the World Bank (UNECE/FAO 2007). In the USA, the Lacey Act was passed in 1900 to ban the illegal trade of animals and plants. It covers wildlife and plants protected by State law and the Convention on International Trade in Endangered Species of Wild Fauna and Flora (CITES). In 2008, the Lacey Act was amended to also cover products made from illegally logged woods. That means responsible sourcing is now mandatory. Simply trusting on suppliers' promise is no longer enough; companies need to actively understand their supply chains.

Violation to the Lacey Act is triggered when a plant is harvested illegally and traded. In those cases, whether a company exercises "due care" to prevent violation greatly affects the level of penalty. Penalties are much less severe if a company who unknowingly violates the prohibition demonstrates efforts to prevent such illegal activities in its supply chain.

Obtaining third-party sustainable forestry certifications is a common practice to demonstrate due care. For example, in the wood industry, both the Forest Stewardship Council (FSC) and the Programme for the Endorsement of Forest Certification (PEFC) are non-profit organizations that offer chain-of-custody certifications for sustainable sourcing. The LegalHarvest Verification Program by SCS Global Services also helps companies demonstrate compliance to the Lacey Act. All of these certifications involve external third-party audits. While certifications are not required by the Lacey Act nor do they exempt a company from penalties, violation is less likely to happen with these audits.

In addition to certifications, Rainforest Alliance offers customized services to help businesses analyze their supply chain and develop solutions to assess and manage their sourcing risks. Their SmartSource program also provides businesses with a framework to demonstrate due care under the Lacey Act.

The Lacey Act gained much publicity with two high-profile violations. The first violation came from the Nashville-based Gibson Guitar Corporation ("Gibson") in 2009 and 2011 (Ghianni 2012). In those cases, a supplier illegally sourced ebony from Madagascar. Making things worse, Gibson knowingly ignored red flags for the supplier's illegal sourcing. The violations led to a penalty of $300,000 on Gibson. The Lacey Act made headlines again in 2015 when Lumber Liquidators, the largest hardwood flooring retailer in the USA, paid $13.2 million in penalty for importing illegally harvested timber (Kaldjian and Barber 2015).

The law prompted Taylor Guitars to conduct a full risk assessment of their wood suppliers. Ebony emerged as the number one item in their list of risky items due to its importance and scarcity in legal supply.

2.4 Ebony

Every Taylor Guitars has an ebony fingerboard. Ebony's aesthetic beauty and hardness have made it one of the most desirable woods among stringed musical instrument makers. As players' fingers are constantly rubbing and pressing frets on fingerboards, ebony wood's hardness makes it a perfect material to keep the frets in place. Aesthetically its dark color suits it for the fingerboards on guitars and violin as well as piano keys. Its high density also allows it to be finish-sanded to a very smooth surface that is comfortable to touch.

Nevertheless, legally sourced ebony is scarce. Ebony grows predominantly in Africa and India. The African strains tend to be the best for musical instruments. However, ebony has become a threatened species due to years of poor harvesting practice. Although there are other countries that sell ebony (Gabon and Democratic Republic of Congo are major sources), political turmoil has made their legal supply very scarce. As a result, Cameroon has become a primary supplier of ebony for the musical instrument industry under the Lacey Act.

2.5 Vertical Integration and New Opportunities

Taylor Guitars has sourced ebony from Cameroon for over 30 years. In 2011, an opportunity came up when the owner of Crelicam, the Cameroon-based largest ebony mill in Africa, decided to sell the business and retire. In order to secure the legal supply of ebony, Taylor Guitars partnered with Madinter Trade, S.L., a Spain-based wood distributor, to purchase Crelicam. The acquisition has made Taylor Guitars a vertically integrated company.

The acquisition unveiled wood logging practice and new opportunities to Taylor Guitars. First, they realized that it was an enormous amount of work to deliver the wood. In Cameroon, Crelicam is permitted to harvest ebony in specific regions of the country designated in volumes renewed each year by the Cameroonian government. The villagers who have lived in these areas for generations are contracted by Crelicam to assist in the harvesting process. Ebony trees close to the roads had been harvested, so the villagers have to hike several miles in the jungle on foot to find one tree. The working condition is primitive. The villagers cut trees into logs on site with machetes and take them back with people, usually in extremely hot and humid weather.

After owning Crelicam, Bob Taylor also realized that most ebony is not purely black as most people thought. In fact, only 10% of the trees are solely black; the majority of ebony wood actually contains color streaks. However, the villagers had been only bringing back ebony wood that is solely black. This is because western wood buyers were only interested in black ebony. With the low demand on the streaked ebony, Crelicam previously only paid a fourth of the black ebony price for ebony with colors.

The price discrepancy does not justify the work, so if there are streaks of colors, the wood would be discarded on site. In other words, on average nine ebony trees were cut down for nothing before they find one tree to carry back. So 90% of the streaked ebony trees have the identical physical properties as the black ones, but they were discarded simply due to aesthetic preferences. Furthermore, ebony trees are so dense that cutting down the tree is the only way to discern its color.

The harvesting practice was wasteful and unsustainable, but this also leads to a new business opportunity: Bob Taylor decided to use all the trees cut, black or streaked, for guitars. The company also decided to pay the same price for all ebony trees, black and streaked alike. Now, there is ten times the amount of ebony available. Taylor Guitars introduced streaked ebony to their flagship model, the 800 series. The company advocated through media and its magazines to guitar buyers the true state of ebony. Many guitar buyers see the color streaks as a unique feature as well as a symbol of their support to the company's sustainability efforts on ebony.

2.6 Challenges in Vertical Integration

Managing a new company in a drastically different culture comes with many challenges. First, the tension between Crelicam employees and the management was tense. The employment rate was low in the country, and many employees relied on their income to support their entire family, even extended families. Many employers in Cameroon leverage the employees' financial need, hiring many of them undocumented and compensating them below the legal minimum wage. The employees at Crelicam worried that this type of exploitation would be present with the new management.

The business practice in Cameroon is quite different too. Cameroon operates on a cash-based economy, and suppliers are accustomed to be paid in cash prior to delivering the product or service. Also, the lack of a credit system means that the new Crelicam owner had little information to determine a supplier's credibility. As a result, several contracted wood loggers disappeared without delivering the product.

2.7 Supplying to Competitors

As the largest (legal) Cameroon ebony supplier, Crelicam also supplied ebony to other guitar makers. Consequently, when Taylor Guitars acquired Crelicam, many makers concerned that Crelicam would leverage its market power to create price disadvantage for them. They also concerned the risk of unavailability when ebony becomes scarcer. As a result, some guitar makers diversified their supply base to reduce their reliance on Crelicam. Some makers even left or started looking for alternative materials.

Amid other makers' concerns, Crelicam decided to maintain similar ebony prices and charge the same price to all guitar makers. With illegal logging still rampant in other places, changing ebony price may motivate buyers turning to illegal sources. Given that the musical instrument industry accounts for a significant portion of ebony demand, Crelicam hoped that maintaining a similar ebony price will prevent buyers from acquiring the wood illegally.

Taylor Guitars also leveraged its access to ebony to change how ebony is used. The company started the change in the guitar industry from both buyers and makers. On the demand side, Taylor Guitars actively promoted to guitar buyers the fact that most ebony trees come with color patterns through magazine, social media, and news. On the supply side to wood buyers, Crelicam enforced all of the orders to contain some streaked ebony.

Taylor Guitars also explored additional avenues to reduce ebony waste and promote ebony sustainability. For example, it launched an ebony plantation project in Cameroon. In 2018, the company launched a website called The Ebony Project to document their efforts to preserve and replant ebony in Cameroon.[2] Taylor Guitars has developed a kitchen products company called Stella Falone to use ebony that cannot be used for musical instruments, thereby using as much of the waste wood as possible.

3 Model

To investigate how Taylor Guitar's vertical integration strategy impacts CSER outcome, we build a model with two competing firms. These firms sell products to their respective shares in the same market. Each firm purchases a component that is necessary for the production of the end product from its own supplier at an exogenous wholesale price w. We normalize the supplier's cost of processing a component into a final product to zero. We refer to the buying firms as buyers. Initially, both of the supply chains are disintegrated. We use subscript A and B to denote the two supply chains and their members. Each buyer can sell Q units of products to its own market at an exogenous retail price p.

One of the key observations we made in guitar industry is that buyers cannot verify whether suppliers are in compliance with CSER codes or not. The buyer can only ensure full compliance by obtaining the full control of the supplier through vertical integration and then deciding to maintain CSER. $\sigma \in (0, 1)$ denotes the probability that a CSER violation will be exposed at each supplier[3] and that the exposure probabilities for the two suppliers are independent (correlated exposure probabilities are investigated in Sect. 6). This single parameter captures the CSER risks embedded in this industry's current common practices. All parties are risk-neutral.

If a violation is exposed at one supplier, its buyer's demand would drop to $(1 + \alpha)Q$. Here, $\alpha \in (-1, 0)$ and it captures a violation's direct negative demand impact. In addition, the CSER violation exposure may positively or negatively impact the

[2]https://www.taylorguitars.com/ebonyproject/

[3]There are two sources of uncertainty contributing to a violation exposure: whether a supplier violates CSER codes and whether the violation is exposed. The parameter σ captures the combined effect.

competing firm's demand. The competing firm's demand becomes $(1+\beta)Q$, where $\beta \in (\alpha, -\alpha)$ models the possible negative or positive externalities of a CSER violation exposure. $|\beta| < |\alpha|$ because a violation exposure's direct impact should be stronger than its indirect impact, i.e., externality. Finally, if violations are exposed at both suppliers, we assume both supply chains' demands drop to $(1+\alpha)Q$.

Two modeling assumptions merit further discussion. First, we assume the demand changes in the macro level after a CSER violation exposure without modeling the consumer behavior in the micro level. We do so because the exact market dynamics behind the demand impact is not our focus. A descriptive model is simple yet general enough for us to study our problem. Similar descriptive models can be found in literature (Boyaci and Gallego 2004; Kraft et al. 2013a,b); in particular, Fang and Cho (2015) adopt a very similar setup to capture CSER violation externalities. Second, we assume the retail price p is fixed—a setting also used in Boyaci and Gallego (2004) and Huang et al. (2016), among others. In practice, firms may adjust their retail prices to account for a violation exposure's demand impact. However, even with endogenous retail price, the firms' revenue changes will qualitatively be similar to the demand changes in our model. Thus, we expect that our structural results should continue to hold.

Among the two buyers, we assume that only buyer A can vertically integrate with its supplier. This assumption is consistent with what we observe in the guitar industry. Taylor Guitars had the first and only (as of December 2013) vertically integrated supply chain in the musical instrument industry (Arnseth 2013). Taylor Guitars was able to vertically integrate because of its many years of experience sourcing ebony from Cameroon. Buyer A incurs a fixed cost f to vertically integrate with supplier A and ensure CSER. After vertical integration the cost of obtaining the component increases to c_r where $c_r > w$. The increased cost is due to the investments made to achieve CSER. For instance, Taylor Guitars had great difficulties navigating the legal system in Cameroon while obtaining required permits; they also expanded power grid and doubled worker salaries (White 2012).

Consistent with the case of Taylor Guitars, an integrated firm A has the *option* to ensure CSER, which increases the component sourcing cost to c_r. The increased sourcing cost reflects the necessary investments and efforts to rectify irresponsible practices, which often improve the local residents' livelihood. In Taylor Guitars' case, they overcame great difficulties navigating a highly complex legal system to obtain all required permits, expanded power grid, and doubled worker salaries (White 2012). In exchange, firm A eliminates its own violation exposure risk ($\sigma = 0$). However, even in this case, firm A may still be indirectly affected by an exposed violation at supplier B. This is because consumers may not be aware of a firm's CSER efforts and furthermore may not trust a firm's CSER claims if a violation at a similar supplier has just been exposed. On the other hand, if the integrated firm A decides to maintain conventional practices (the status quo), the violation exposure risk and the demand impact remain unchanged. The possibility of vertical integration without ensuring CSER in the model allows us to disentangle CSER from other drivers of vertical integration. We further assume $c_r > w$ to capture the reality that suppliers in developing economies often depend on very

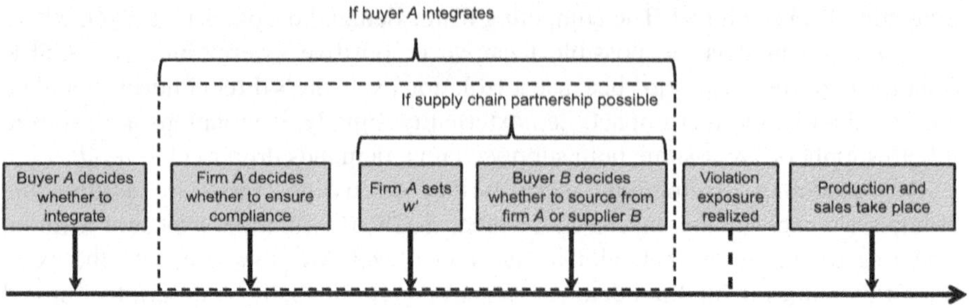

Fig. 1 Sequence of events in the model

thin margins, and it is economically infeasible to ensure CSER and improve worker conditions by themselves.

Note that one of the fundamental differences in Orsdemir et al. (2019) and this model is that Orsdemir et al. (2019) merge vertical integration and social responsibility decisions into one by assuming if buyer A vertically integrates, it also ensures compliance. On the other hand, we assume that these are two separate decisions. As a result, firm A can vertically integrate but maintain conventional practices in our model.

Finally, an integrated firm A (conventional or responsible) may supply components to buyer B through horizontal sourcing at an endogenous wholesale price w'. In this case, we assume that buyer B can choose to source components from either supplier B or firm A, but not both. If firm A ensures CSER in sourcing and supplies buyer B, the violation exposure risks at both supply chains are eliminated. However, if firm A maintains conventional practices and also supplies buyer B, a CSER violation exposure at firm A will reduce both firms' demands to $(1+\alpha)Q$ because both of the firms receive the supplies from where the violation is exposed. We first study the model without horizontal sourcing in Sect. 4 and then with horizontal sourcing option in Sect. 5. We, then, compare these two cases.

The sequence of events is presented in Fig. 1. First, buyer A decides whether to vertically integrate with supplier A or not. If so, it then decides whether to ensure CSER or maintain conventional practices. Next, if horizontal sourcing is an option, a vertically integrated firm A sets wholesale price w' for buyer B, who decides whether to source from firm A or supplier B. A violation may be exposed at suppliers maintaining conventional practices. Unless firm A is vertically integrated and ensures CSER, each supplier has independent probability σ to be exposed of a violation, which leads to the direct and indirect demand impact as described earlier (the case with correlated violation exposure risks is investigated in Sect. 6). Finally, the firms purchase components and make products to satisfy the demands. Table 1 summarizes all parameters and decision variables.

Table 1 Parameters and decision variables

Symbol	Definition
$p > 0$	Retail price
$w > 0$	Component wholesale price from a supplier
$w' > 0$	Component wholesale price through horizontal sourcing
$c_r > w$	Unit cost of responsibly sourced components
$f > 0$	Fixed cost of vertical integration
$Q > 0$	Current market size of each firm
$\alpha \in (-1, 0)$	Direct impact of an exposed violation
$\beta \in (\alpha, -\alpha)$	Indirect impact (externalities) of an exposed violation
$\sigma \in (0, 1)$	Probability of a violation exposure

4 Analysis Without Horizontal Sourcing

We first analyze the model assuming horizontal sourcing is infeasible (i.e., an integrated firm A cannot supply buyer B). In practice, horizontal sourcing is not commonplace for the following reasons. First, if the component supplied is specifically customized to one firm's product, it will not be feasible for other firm to use the same component. Second, there may be a fierce competition between the two firms which may make horizontal sourcing infeasible due to internal reasons we do not model here.

Our goal is to understand the following strategic decisions of buyer A: whether to integrate with supplier A and, if integrated, whether to ensure CSER. We use I and D to, respectively, denote buyer A's decision to integrate with supplier A or stay disintegrated and R and C to, respectively, denote buyer A's decision to ensure CSER (only if integrated) or maintain conventional practices. Therefore, buyer A has three possible strategies—(D, C), (I, C), and (I, R). Let π_X^i denote buyer i's expected profit when buyer A follows strategy X. Below are the expressions of the expected profits (recall that σ is a supplier's violation exposure probability):

$$\pi_{IC}^A = pQ[\sigma^2(1+\alpha) + \sigma(1-\sigma)(1+\alpha) + (1-\sigma)\sigma(1+\beta) + (1-\sigma)^2] - f,$$

$$\pi_{IR}^A = (p - c_r)Q[\sigma(1+\beta) + (1-\sigma)] - f,$$

$$\begin{aligned}\pi_{DC}^A = \pi_{DC}^B = \pi_{IC}^B = (p-w)Q[&\sigma^2(1+\alpha) + \sigma(1-\sigma)(1+\alpha) \\ &+ (1-\sigma)\sigma(1+\beta) + (1-\sigma)^2],\end{aligned}$$

$$\pi_{IR}^B = (p-w)Q[\sigma(1+\alpha) + (1-\sigma)].$$

We assume a sufficiently small fixed cost f such that (D, C) does not dominate (I, C) and (I, R). We also assume a sufficiently small cost of responsibly sourced component: $c_r < \frac{-\alpha p}{2(\alpha+2)}$ (recall that $-1 < \alpha < 0$) such that conventional sourcing does not dominate responsible sourcing. These assumptions rule out

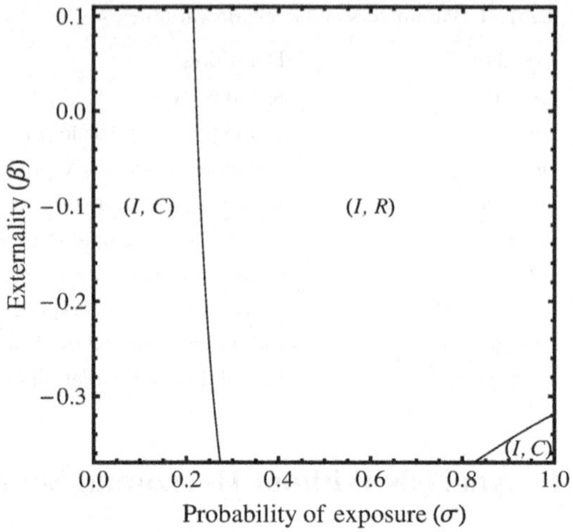

Fig. 2 Buyer A's optimal strategy with zero fixed cost, no horizontal sourcing with $p = 3$, $w = 1/8$, $c_r = 1/4$, $Q = 1$, $\alpha = -3/8$, $f = 0$

uninteresting cases and they are also satisfied in Taylor Guitars' case. For simplicity of presentation, we first solve the problem without fixed cost ($f = 0$), in which case buyer A will always integrate with supplier A, and later investigate the effect of positive fixed costs. The following proposition characterizes the structure of the optimal strategy, and Fig. 2 visualizes the optimal strategy.

PROPOSITION 1 *Assume* $f = 0$ *and no horizontal sourcing. There exist thresholds* $\underline{\sigma}^R$ *and* $\overline{\sigma}^R$ *such that:*

1. *When* $\beta < \frac{\alpha p + c_r}{p - c_r}$, *we have* $0 < \underline{\sigma}^R < \overline{\sigma}^R < 1$. *In this case, if* $\sigma \in (\underline{\sigma}^R, \overline{\sigma}^R)$, *buyer A's optimal strategy is* (I, R); *otherwise its optimal strategy is* (I, C).
2. *When* $\beta \geq \frac{\alpha p + c_r}{p - c_r}$, *we have* $0 < \underline{\sigma}^R < 1$, *but* $\overline{\sigma}^R < 0$ *or* > 1. *In this case, if* $\sigma > \underline{\sigma}^R$, *buyer A's optimal strategy is* (I, R); *otherwise its optimal strategy is* (I, C).

We first explain buyer A's optimal strategy. Since fixed cost $f = 0$, buyer A always integrates with supplier A. The integrated firm A then decides whether to ensure CSER (R) or maintain conventional practices (C). If the violation exposure probability σ is sufficiently low, not surprisingly firm A maintains the conventional practices, reflecting the basic trade-off between avoiding one's own violation exposures and reducing sourcing costs. What is surprising, however, is high probabilities of violation exposure can also incentivize firm A to maintain conventional practices rather than to ensure CSER. This happens when externalities are strongly negative. Even though an integrated firm A can eliminate its own violations by ensuring CSER, the negative externalities due to supplier B's violation exposure can still impact its demand. Therefore, when externalities are strongly negative and exposure probabilities are high, firm A's own CSER efforts become futile as its demand is likely to be negatively impacted by an exposed violation at the other firm. Thus firm A is better off maintaining conventional practices and not incurring an additional cost to ensure CSER.

The above observations have important managerial implications for NGOs who can alter the violation exposure probabilities by adjusting the resources allocated to scrutinizing firms: it is easy to assume that more intensive scrutiny is more likely to "scare" firms into ensuring CSER in sourcing (Baron et al. 2011; Greenhouse 2013). Yet, our analysis suggests that when externalities are strongly negative, NGOs' increased scrutiny may backfire and drive firms *away* from CSER.

Furthermore, Fig. 2 also shows that the (I, R) region expands as the externalities become more positive. The following proposition formalizes this observation (which holds for $f > 0$ as well).

PROPOSITION 2 *Suppose that horizontal sourcing is infeasible, then the range of probabilities of exposure* σ *where buyer* A*'s optimal strategy is* (I, R) *expands as externality* β *increases.*

Similarly, NGOs can influence the violation externalities through how they expose and report the violations: an exposè that broadly blames the entire industry or a region would create negative externalities. Alternatively, an exposè that is more specific about directly involved firms while exonerating uninvolved firms can create positive externalities. Proposition 2 suggests that increasing externalities is more likely to induce CSER when horizontal sourcing is not feasible. (Interestingly, we show that if horizontal sourcing is feasible, this is no longer the case; see Sect. 5.)

Note that in Orsdemir et al. (2019) (I, C) region does not exist because of the assumption that integration is synonyms with ensuring compliance. Yet, the insights in terms of probability of exposure and externalities are similar to our model.

Next we investigate the impact of the fixed cost for integration. With the fixed cost, a direct consequence is that buyer A no longer always integrates with supplier A. This intuition is confirmed by Fig. 3, generated with the same parameters as in Fig. 2 except f.[4] More specifically, in Fig. 3a, b, as the fixed cost grows larger, the (D, C) region—indicating that buyer A stays disintegrated—gradually invades the (I, C) and (I, R) regions. As f keeps increases, eventually, as Fig. 3c shows, the (D, C) region becomes much larger, and the (I, C) region disappears. However, in all three examples, buyer A's CSER behaviors remain structurally unchanged from our earlier discussion. Therefore, introducing fixed cost of integration does not alter our main insights.

We finally investigate how violation exposure probabilites impact the firms' profits. Counter to common intuition, we find that having a higher violation exposure probability may actually increase profitability of buyer B, who sources from a conventional supplier and is prone to violation exposures.

[4]Full analytical characterization with $f > 0$ is available from the authors upon request.

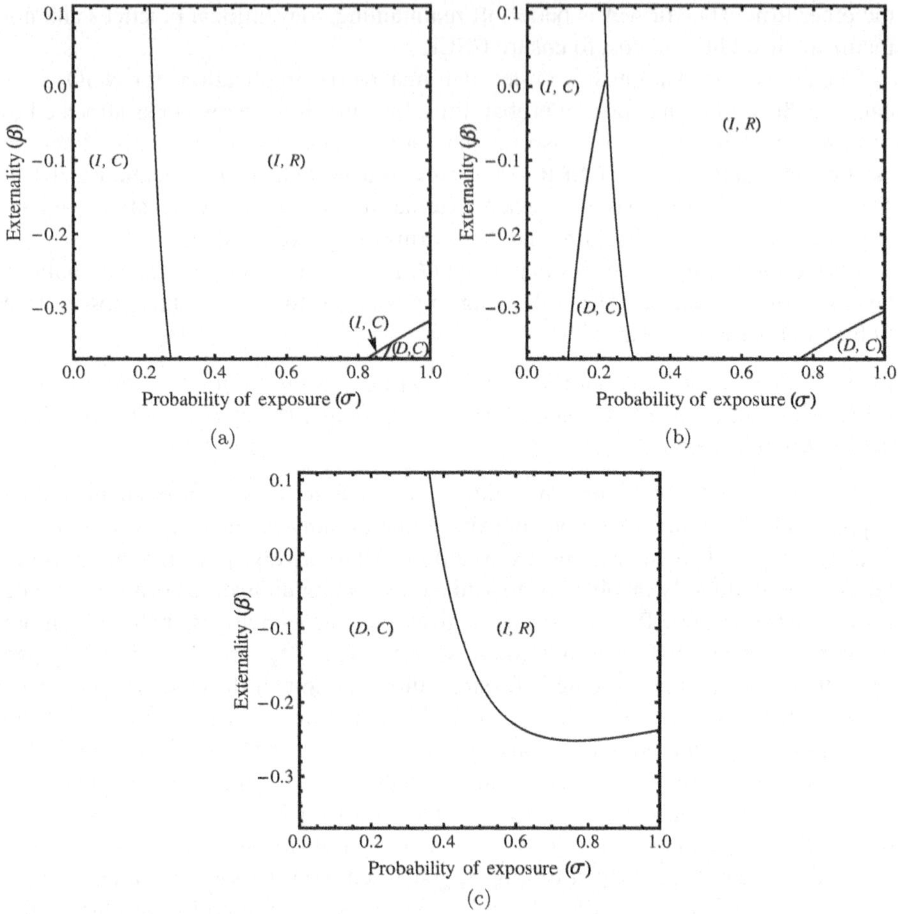

Fig. 3 Buyer A's optimal strategy with fixed cost: (**a**) $f = 0.079$, (**b**) $f = 0.12$, (**c**) $f = 0.3$, no horizontal sourcing

PROPOSITION 3 *Assume $\beta < 0$ and $\underline{\hat{\sigma}}^R - \Delta_1 < \sigma \leq \underline{\hat{\sigma}}^R$ so that the optimal strategy is either (D, C) or (I, C). Then, an increase of σ by $\tau \in (\underline{\tau}^c, \overline{\tau}_c)$ shifts the optimal strategy to (I, R) and increases buyer B's profit.*

The exact thresholds and the proof can be found in the Appendix. Here, with negative exposure externalities, buyer B benefits from an increased probability of a violation exposure because it drives firm A to ensuring CSER and hence preventing buyer B from any negative externalities.

In sum, without horizontal sourcing, our analyses suggest that violation externalities significantly alter buyer A's behavior. In general, buyer A is more likely to ensure CSER through vertical integration with higher externalities. But when externalities are strongly negative, overly intensive scrutiny may backfire and drive the firm away from CSER. These findings have significant managerial implications for NGOs who can strategically influence the externalities and violation exposure probabilities to induce CSER in sourcing.

5 Analysis with Horizontal Sourcing

We now analyze the model with horizontal sourcing. To identify the horizontal sourcing equilibrium, we use subscripts S and N on (I, C) and (I, R) to denote whether or not buyer B sources from the integrated firm A through horizontal sourcing. Recall that firm A sets w' to sell components to buyer B. As in Sect. 4, we first provide the analytical characterization assuming zero integration fixed cost (i.e., $f = 0$) and then graphically illustrate the impact of the fixed cost. Using backward induction, we solve the four-stage (integration, CSER, pricing, procurement) sequential game (as shown in Fig. 1). The following proposition characterizes the equilibrium.

PROPOSITION 4 *Assume $f = 0$ and that horizontal sourcing is feasible. There exist thresholds $0 < \underline{\beta} < \overline{\beta} < 1$, $\underline{\sigma}^R$ as defined in Proposition 1 and $0 < \sigma_1 < \sigma_2 < \sigma_3 < \sigma_4 < 1$ for the β ranges stated below, such that:*

1. *When $\beta \le \underline{\beta}$, for $\sigma \in (0, \sigma_1]$, the equilibrium is $(I, C)_S$, and for $\sigma \in (\sigma_1, 1)$ it is $(I, R)_S$.*
2. *When $\underline{\beta} < \beta \le \overline{\beta}$, for $\sigma \in (0, \sigma_2]$, the equilibrium is $(I, C)_S$, for $\sigma \in (\sigma_2, \sigma_3]$ it is $(I, C)_N$, and for $\sigma \in (\sigma_3, 1)$ it is $(I, R)_S$.*
3. *When $\overline{\beta} < \beta \le \frac{-\alpha(p-w)+w-c_r}{p-c_r}$, for $\sigma \in (0, \sigma_2]$, the equilibrium is $(I, C)_S$, for $\sigma \in (\sigma_2, \underline{\sigma}^R]$ it is $(I, C)_N$, for $\sigma \in (\underline{\sigma}^R, \sigma_4]$ it is $(I, R)_N$, and for $\sigma \in (\sigma_4, 1)$ it is $(I, R)_S$.*
4. *When $\frac{-\alpha(p-w)+w-c_r}{p-c_r} < \beta$, for $\sigma \in (0, \sigma_2]$, the equilibrium is $(I, C)_S$, for $\sigma \in (\sigma_2, \underline{\sigma}^R]$ it is $(I, C)_N$, and for $\sigma \in (\underline{\sigma}^R, 1)$ it is $(I, R)_N$.*

The equilibrium horizontal sourcing wholesale prices are $w' = \frac{\beta p(\sigma-1)\sigma+\sigma w(\beta+\alpha)+\beta\sigma^2(-w)+w}{\alpha\sigma+1}$ when firm A maintains conventional practices (in equilibrium $(I, C)_S$) and $w' = w - \alpha\sigma(p - w)$ when firm A ensures CSER (in equilibrium $(I, R)_S$).

Figure 4 demonstrates the equilibria using the same parameters in Fig. 2.

In terms of probability of exposure, Fig. 4 shows that higher violation exposure probabilities encourage firm A to ensure CSER. This is opposite to Proposition 1 and Fig. 2 (the case without horizontal sourcing), where higher exposure probabilities may discourage firm A from ensuring CSER. As explained previously, without horizontal sourcing, high probability of exposure combined with strong negative externality may nullify firm A's CSER efforts, thereby discouraging firm A from ensuring CSER. When horizontal sourcing is feasible, however, such negative externalities can be eliminated through horizontal sourcing. As a result, more

Fig. 4 Firms' equilibrium strategy with zero fixed cost, with horizontal sourcing

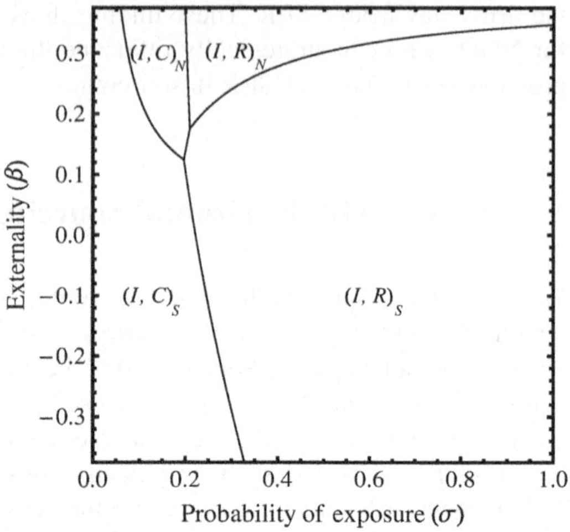

intense scrutiny always encourages CSER. Additionally, as probability of exposure increases, the equilibrium region may shift from $(I, R)_N$ to $(I, R)_S$, indicating higher probability of exposure can incentivize firm A to share responsible supply with buyer B. This is welcoming news since it makes the entire industry compliant. This happens because as the probability of exposure increases, buyer B becomes more willing to pay a premium for responsible supply, incentivizing firm A to share it.

Next, we study the impact of externalities. Figure 4 shows that when not strongly positive, higher externalities make the $(I, R)_S$ region expand against the $(I, C)_S$ region. This is characterized in the following proposition.

PROPOSITION 5 *When horizontal sourcing is feasible, the range of violation exposure probabilities σ where $(I, R)_S$ is the equilibrium grows as externality β increases, if and only if $\alpha < \beta \leq \frac{4\alpha^2 w(2p-w)(2c_r-p)}{(p-w)(4c_r-w)(4c_r+4\alpha p-(2\alpha+1)w)}$, or $\frac{4\alpha^2 w(2p-w)(2c_r-p)}{(p-w)(4c_r-w)(4c_r+4\alpha p-(2\alpha+1)w)} < \beta \leq \underline{\beta}$ and $f < \bar{f}$.*

However, when strongly positive, higher externalities discourage *industry-wide* CSER: Proposition 5 and Fig. 4 demonstrate that as externalities increase, equilibrium may switch from $(I, R)_S$ to $(I, R)_N$. This once again is opposite of what we discussed in Proposition 2 and Fig. 2 and yet intuitive in this setting: due to positive externalities, firm A benefits from buyer B's violation exposures, and thus it inhibits buyer B from sourcing responsibly. Note that this issue is nonexistent without horizontal sourcing. Therefore, interestingly, while horizontal sourcing improves the effectiveness of scrutiny, it diminishes the effectiveness of positive externalities. Therefore, NGOs should account for the feasibility of horizontal sourcing in an industry when choosing their scrutiny and reporting policies to avoid unintended consequences.

To compare our results with Orsdemir et al. (2019), we note that in their work $(I, C)_N$ and $(I, C)_S$ regions do not exist. In $(I, C)_S$ region firm A shares its supply with buyer B without ensuring compliance. Therefore, the existence of $(I, C)_S$ region in our model indicates that horizontal sourcing may arise solely because of economic factors other than the impact of violation exposures, a result cannot be observed in Orsdemir et al. (2019).

Finally, we investigate the impact of fixed cost of integration.[5] Below we illustrate an example in Fig. 5 (generated with the same parameters as in Figs. 2 and 4 except f). Similar to Fig. 3, we find that as f increases, the (D, C) region gradually invades the (I, C) and (I, R) regions, until in (c) with a very high fixed cost where the (D, C) region grows much larger.

We once again note that the CSER behaviors remain structurally identical to our earlier discussion. Therefore, introducing fixed cost of integration does not alter our main insights.

In sum, when horizontal sourcing is available, intensified scrutiny always encourages firms to become more responsible, while strongly positive externalities may discourage firms' socially responsible behavior. These insights are direct contrast to the case where horizontal sourcing is not available; in that case higher externalities help with CSER compliance, while intensive scrutiny may backfire.

In the next proposition, we study the impact of probability of exposure on the firms' profits. Interestingly, we show that both firms may benefit from a higher probability of exposure.

PROPOSITION 6 *Assume* $\beta < 0$ *and* $\sigma_1 - \Delta_2 < \sigma \le \sigma_1$ *so that the equilibrium is* $(I, C)_S$. *Then, an increase of* σ *by* $\tau \in [\underline{\tau}^r, \overline{\tau}_r]$ *shifts the equilibrium to* $(I, R)_S$ *and increases both firm A and buyer B's profits.*

In the case described in Proposition 6, the industry transforms from fully conventional sourcing to fully responsible sourcing, making the case a win-win-win situation.

Finally, we compare the CSER outcomes of with and without horizontal sourcing to understand the value of horizontal sourcing in ensuring CSER. We find that, with positive externalities, horizontal sourcing strictly improves industry-wide CSER:

PROPOSITION 7 *When* $\beta > 0$, $(I, R) \subseteq \{(I, R)_N \bigcup (I, R)_S)\}$.

Moreover, Figs. 2 and 4 show that the entire industry can be compliant for a large parameter region due to horizontal sourcing. In other words, horizontal sourcing improves industry-wide CSER.

[5]The full analysis is available from the authors.

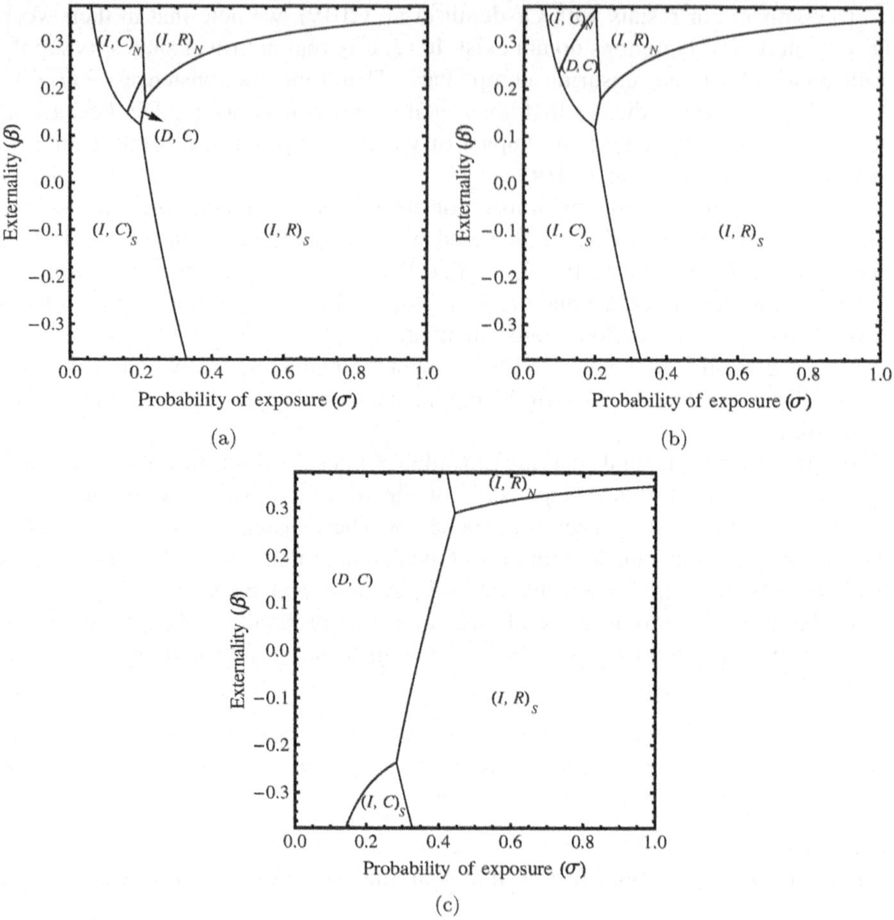

Fig. 5 Firms' equilibrium strategy with fixed cost: (**a**) $f = 0.120$, (**b**) $f = 0.123$, (**c**) $f = 0.5$, with horizontal sourcing

6 Correlated Exposure Probabilities

So far we assumed that exposure probabilities are independent for the two suppliers. In practice, they may be positively or negatively correlated. For instance, NGOs may intensify their scrutiny on suppliers following a violation exposure, leading to a positive correlation. Alternatively, following a supplier's violation exposure, other suppliers may proactively rectify and/or conceal malpractices, leading to a negative correlation. We now conduct numerical studies to examine the impact of correlations on the equilibrium outcome and the resulting social responsibility performance. Essentially, we find the main insights in Sects. 4 and 5 are robust under correlated exposure probabilities. The study also provides additional insights on how violation exposure risk correlations impact firms' CSER behaviors.

Specifically, we denote the joint probabilities of four possible cases by q_{00}, q_{01}, q_{10}, and q_{11}, where 1 represents a violation exposure and 0 represents no exposure, at suppliers A and B. For example, q_{10} represents the probability of a violation exposure at supplier A but not at supplier B. We define $(q_{00}, q_{01}, q_{10}, q_{11}) = (r\sigma(1-\sigma)+(1-\sigma)^2, (1-r)\sigma(1-\sigma), (1-r)\sigma(1-\sigma), r(1-\sigma)\sigma+\sigma^2)$ for $r \geq 0$ and $(q_{00}, q_{01}, q_{10}, q_{11}) = (r\sigma^2+(1-\sigma)^2, \sigma-(r+1)\sigma^2, \sigma-(r+1)\sigma^2, (r+1)\sigma^2)$ for $r < 0$, where $r \in [-1, 1]$ is a proxy for correlation. When $r = 0$, this setup reduces to the independent violation risk case; when $r = 1$, violation exposures occur to either both suppliers A and B or none of them ($q_{01} = q_{10} = 0$), indicating perfect positive correlation; when $r = -1$, violaion exposure always occurs to only one of the suppliers ($q_{11} = 0$), indicating perfect negative correlation.

We use the same parameters $p = 3$, $w = 1/8$, $c_r = 1/4$, $Q = 1$, as in all previous figures. We test α values from -0.9 to -0.1, r values from -0.9 to 0.9, and various f values, finding consistent results. Below we present numerical examples with $f = 0$, $\alpha = -3/8$, and selected values of r, so that they are comparable to Figs. 2 and 4 (they are also generated with $f = 0$ and $\alpha = -3/8$). Positive fixed costs do not lead to structurally different behaviors.

Figure 6 demonstrates buyer A's optimal strategies when horizontal sourcing is not available. In the figure, (a) and (b) have positive correlations, and (c) and (d) have negative correlations. Note that (a) and (b) are structurally similar to Fig. 2, thus confirming that our main insights in the base model in Sect. 4 are robust when probability of exposures is positively correlated. However, there is a difference in (c) and (d) when compared to Fig. 2: the (I, C) region in the lower-right corner of Fig. 2 disappears. Notice that Fig. 5c and d only considers $\sigma \lesssim 0.54$ instead of the entire range of exposure probabilities ($0 \leq \sigma \leq 1$). This is because the firms' exposure probabilities *cannot* be negatively correlated when they are overly high. To see that, suppose the marginal probability of exposure for both suppliers A and B is 0.9; then they will almost always be exposed simultaneously. Therefore, their violation exposure risks are strongly positively correlated. In other words, when marginal exposure probabilities are very high, they would entail a positive correlation. Therefore, Fig. 6c and d are not completely comparable to Fig. 2; but they are structurally similar to Fig. 2 when they are comparable ($\sigma \lesssim 0.54$).

We now investigate how our insights pertaining to CSER outcome change when exposure risks are correlated. Figure 6 shows that with positive externalities, the (I, R) region grows with correlation (algebraically speaking); on the other hand, with negative externalities, the (I, R) region shrinks with correlation. The intuition is as follows. When firm A maintains conventional practices, a higher correlation means that it is less likely that only one of the suppliers is exposed of a violation. Consequently, a conventional firm A is less likely to experience spillovers from its competitor. As a result, with positive (negative) externalities, a higher correlation makes conventional practices less (more) attractive, resulting in a larger (smaller) (I, R) region.

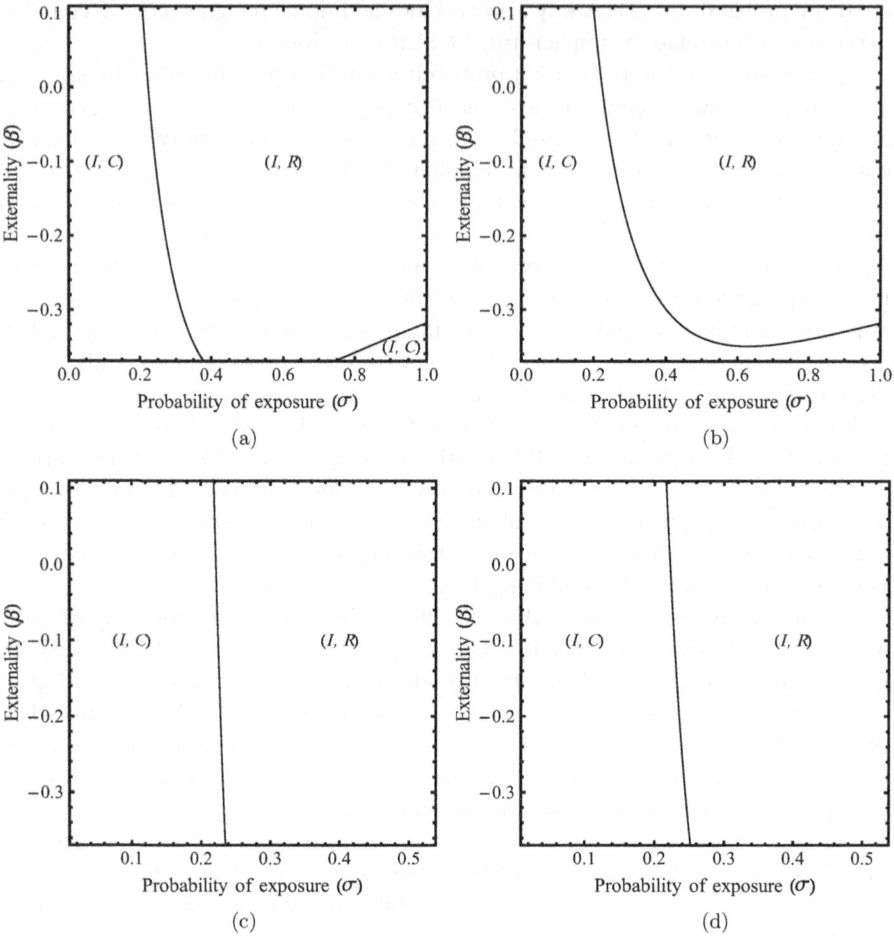

Fig. 6 Buyer A's optimal strategy with correlated violation exposure probabilities, no horizontal sourcing. (**a**) $r = 0.2$. (**b**) $r = 0.4$. (**c**) $r = -0.4$. (**d**) $r = -0.2$

This result has managerial implications for NGOs on how to choose their scrutiny policies. NGOs can influence violation exposure correlations to some extent. For example, when a violation is exposed, NGOs can direct their resources on the involved supplier to further investigate, a strategy that would lead to negative correlations, or allocate more resources to other suppliers, a strategy that leads to positive correlations. Our results shows that whether the externalities are positive or negative in the relevant industry is important in determining a policy. In particular, NGOs should try to create positive (negative) correlations with positive (negative) externalities.

Next we investigate the impact of violation exposure correlations when horizontal sourcing is feasible. Figure 7 presents examples with the same parameters as

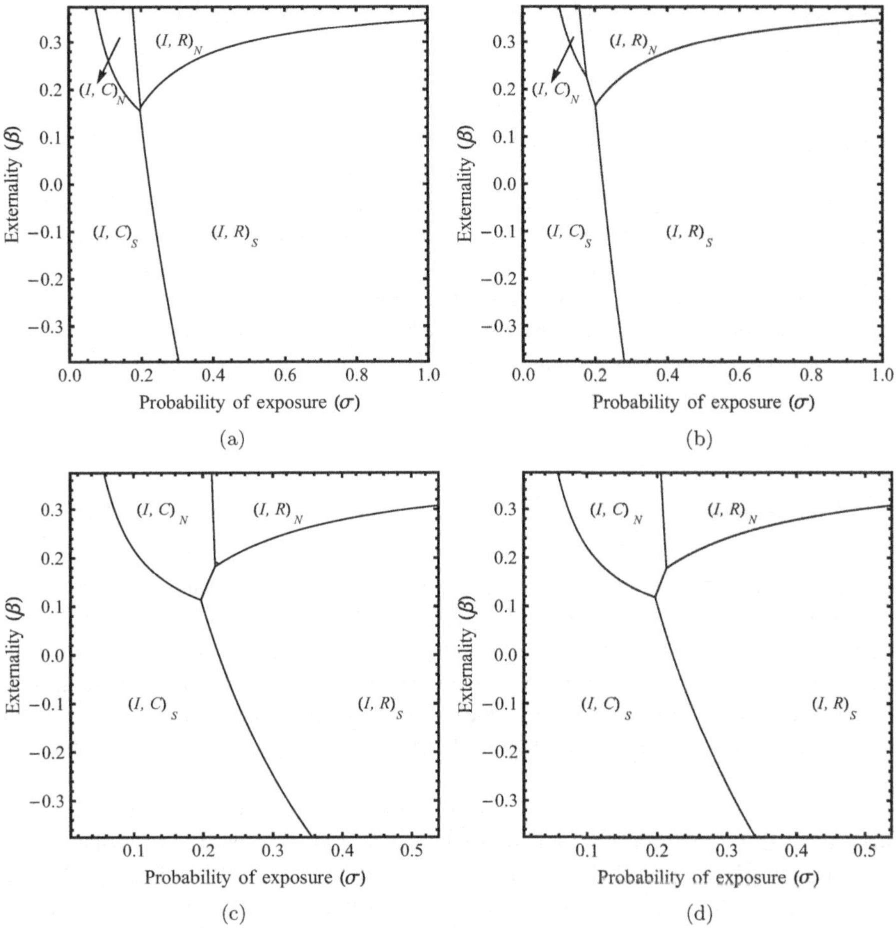

Fig. 7 Firms' equilibrium strategies with correlated violation exposure probabilities, with horizontal sourcing. (**a**) $r = 0.2$. (**b**) $r = 0.4$. (**c**) $r = -0.4$. (**d**) $r = -0.2$

in Fig. 6 allowing horizontal sourcing. Surprisingly, we discover that with positive (negative) externalities, the $(I, R)_S$ region shrinks (grows) against the $(I, C)_S$ region when the correlation increases, which is *opposite* to our observation about Fig. 6. The explanation is as follows. When firm A ensures CSER, or when firm A supplies buyer B through horizontal sourcing, the violation exposure correlation becomes meaningless. The correlation only affects the equilibrium strategies by affecting how much buyer B is willing to pay firm A for conventional supply. With positive (negative) externalities, a higher correlation makes buyer B's own supplier less (more) attractive; thus buyer B is willing to pay more (less) for firm A's conventional supply. This makes firm A's conventional supply more (less) attractive, and thus the $(I, C)_S$ region grows (shrinks). The fact that firms' CSER behaviors with respect to violation exposure correlations are exactly opposite with and without horizontal sourcing echoes the contrast between Propositions 1–2 and Propositions 4–5. This once again highlights the importance of NGOs' conscious awareness of whether horizontal sourcing is feasible in the relevant industries when choosing their scrutiny and reporting policies.

We finally note that our results for horizontal sourcing case differ from Orsdemir et al. (2019). In their paper, no horizontal sourcing and horizontal sourcing lead to qualitatively similar results, while in our paper they do not. Their results primarily apply to the industries where vertical integration is mainly driven by CSER since in their paper integration always leads to social responsibility. Our paper, on the other hand, allows vertical integration to be mainly driven by incentives to capture the supplier's margin since integration without ensuring responsibility can be an equilibrium outcome.

7 Conclusion

In many cases, vertical integration can be the only viable strategy for ensuring compliance at the suppliers. Inspired by Taylor Guitars story, we study the factors that incentivize firms to vertically integrate to ensure compliance at their suppliers. To do so, we build two different models: in one, we assume that vertically integrated firm uses its own supply for only itself (no horizontal sourcing case), while in the other, we allow vertically integrated firm to sell to its competitor (horizontal sourcing case).

In no horizontal sourcing case, NGOs' pressure can backfire and scare the firm away from becoming responsible when potential impacts due to violations in its competitor's supply chain are strongly negative. On the other hand, if NGOs actively promote and name the responsible firms, it would encourage vertical integration and becoming responsible. These results are somewhat reversed when horizontal sourcing is feasible. In this case, NGOs' pressure always encourages becoming responsible. Yet, actively promoting the responsible firms may backfire because it may discourage the responsible firm from sharing the responsibly sourced components with its competitor, leaving the competitor prone to CSER violations.

Taylor Guitars achieves ethical sourcing through vertical integration. However, this is a capital-intensive strategy and it is not always feasible. In addition to vertical integration, the operations and supply chain management literature also identifies several common strategies to enhance ethical and sustainable sourcing:

(1) Auditing: Auditing suppliers is the most direct way to ensure suppliers' compliance. However, auditing is resource consuming. Sometimes two buyers who share a common supplier may end up not auditing the common supplier at all due to the hope that the supplier would be audited by the other buyer (Chen et al. 2020). Forming industry-wide auditing coalition can avoid such inefficiency. For example, in the pharmaceutical industry, Pfizer and GSK

formed the Pharmaceutical Supply Chain Initiative (PSCI) to jointly audit their suppliers (PSCI 2018). Furthermore, buyers' increased auditing efforts may backfire, motivating suppliers to hide information during audits or act to deceive auditors (Plambeck and Taylor 2016). This is more likely to happen when the supplier's violation penalty or sustainable efforts are low. In those situations, instead of having more frequent or intense auditing, increasing violation penalty or squeezing the supplier's margin will be more effective in motivating the supplier's sustainable efforts. Bribery is another common challenges in regions with lax law enforcement. For example, many Chinese factories with substandard factory conditions passed the audits through bribing auditors (Watch 2009). Under such bribery risks, a buying firm's procurement policy should deny any payment to a supplier who fails to pass the audit (Chen et al. 2019).

(2) Contract design: Buyers can achieve ethical/sustainable sourcing through procurement contract design. When violation by unethical suppliers is difficult or impossible to detect through product inspection (e.g., wood product), Chen and Lee (2017) show that buyers should deter unethical suppliers by requiring potential suppliers to pay for certifications to demonstrate sustainable or ethical sourcing (e.g., Starbucks' C.A.F.E. program). If a buyer can audit its supplier, then the buyer can implement a contingency payment contract where the buyer withholds a portion of the payment that is subject to forfeiture if violation is found through audits.

(3) Supplier development: Buyers may invest on suppliers to help them enhance their sustainability. For example, Starbucks plans to invest $50 million by 2020 to provide financing to coffee farmers, aiming to support agronomy, restoration, and infrastructure improvement (Market Watch 2015). However, a buyer usually does not have much visibility into its suppliers' true level of sustainability. Auditing offers a snapshot into a supplier's sustainable practice and hence the level of supports the supplier needs to enhance sustainability performance. Based on the observed information (albeit subject to potential manipulation as mentioned earlier), a buyer should invest more if the supplier's sustainable practice is poor (Kraft et al. 2019). A buyer's investment on supplier development is typically more worthwhile for a buyer when the violation penalty or the third-party auditing cost efficiency is high (Chen et al. 2019). For example, blockchain technology has the potential to improve tracking and tracing efficiency of timbers in the supply chain (Radocchia 2018), making a buyer's investment on supplier development more worthwhile.

8 Appendix

We provide the sketch of proofs below. Full proofs are available upon request from the authors.

Proof of Proposition 1 First of all, because $f = 0$, firm A is always better off with vertical integration. Therefore, we need to compare firm A's profits for two equilibria: (I, C) and (I, R). This proves the result. $\overline{\sigma}^R$ and $\underline{\sigma}^R$ can be found by finding the σ values where profits under two equilibria are equal to each other. □

Proof of Proposition 2 To prove this proposition, we need to show that as β increases, the cutoff σ values (σs as defined in the proof of Proposition 1) that define the (I, R) region increase or decrease in a way to expand the (I, R) region. In other words, the following must hold: (1) $\mathrm{d}\underline{\sigma}^R/\mathrm{d}\beta < 0$; (2) $\mathrm{d}\overline{\sigma}^R/\mathrm{d}\beta > 0$ whenever $\overline{\sigma}^R \in (0, 1)$; (3) $\mathrm{d}\sigma_r^1/\mathrm{d}\beta < 0$ whenever $\sigma_r^1 \in (0, 1)$; and (4) $\mathrm{d}\sigma_r^2/\mathrm{d}\beta >$ whenever $\sigma_r^2 \in (0, 1)$. These can be shown utilizing implicit function theorem. □

Proof of Proposition 3 This can be shown by using proof by construction approach. We first look how firm B's profit behaves as a function of σ and construct the conditions that ensure that firm B's profit may increase with increasing σ. $\mathrm{d}\pi^B_{(I,C)}/\mathrm{d}\sigma = \mathrm{d}\pi^B_{(D,C)}/\mathrm{d}\sigma = Q\alpha(p - w) < 0$, $\mathrm{d}\pi^B_{(I,R)}/\mathrm{d}\sigma = Q(p - w)(\alpha - 2\beta\sigma + \beta) < 0$, and also $\pi^B_{(I,R)} - \pi^B_{(I,C)} = \pi^B_{(I,R)} - \pi^B_{(D,C)} = \beta Q(\sigma - 1)\sigma(p - w) > 0$ when $\beta < 0$. Thus, π^B jumps upward when firm A switches from strategy (I, C) to (I, R) or from (D, C) to (I, R). Define $\hat{\sigma}^R$ as the threshold σ at which firm A switches from strategy (I, C) to (I, R) or from (D, C) to (I, R). Thus,

$$\hat{\sigma}^R = \begin{cases} \underline{\sigma}^R & \text{if optimal strategy switches from (I,C) to (I,R)} \\ \sigma_r^1 & \text{if optimal strategy switches from (D,C) to (I,R)} \end{cases}$$

where $\underline{\sigma}^R$ and σ_r^1 refer to the thresholds at which firm A's optimal strategy changes. $\underline{\sigma}^R$ is defined in Proposition 1. σ_r^1 is the threshold where $\pi^A_{(D,C)} = \pi^A_{(I,R)}$. Δ_1 is such that $\pi^B_S(\hat{\sigma}^R - \Delta_1) = \pi^B_{(I,R)}(\hat{\sigma}^R)$ for all $S \in \{(I, C), (D, C)\}$. Define $\underline{\tau}^c = \hat{\sigma}^R - \sigma$ and $\overline{\tau}_c$ in the following way: $\pi_S(\sigma) = \pi_{(I,R)}(\sigma + \overline{\tau}_c)$ for all $S \in \{(I, C), (D, C)\}$. To see the existence of Δ_1 and $\overline{\tau}_c$, note that $\pi_S(\sigma = 0) = \pi^B_{(I,R)}(\sigma = 0)$ and $\pi^B_S(\sigma = 1) = \pi^B_{(I,R)}(\sigma = 1)$ for all $S \in \{(I, C), (D, C)\}$. Since at $\sigma = \hat{\sigma}^R$ the profit jump upward, firm B's profit would increase with increasing σ so long as $\tau \in (\underline{\tau}^c, \overline{\tau}_c)$. □

Proof of Proposition 4 Buyer B would purchase from firm A if and only if $\pi^B_{i_N} \leq \pi^B_{i_S}$ where $i \in \{(I, C), (I, R)\}$. Thus firm A would offer a price to buyer B that would make buyer B indifferent to sourcing from firm A or from supplier B. Solving for this, we will provide w'. Plugging this w' to firm A's profit function, the rest of the proposition can be shown by comparing firm A's profits under different equilibrium strategies similar to Proposition 1. The thresholds in the proposition will naturally emerge during these comparisons. □

Proof of Proposition 5 Define σ_j^i's as the boundaries between equilibrium region i and j. Then, we need to show the following to prove the proposition:

1. $\mathrm{d}\sigma^{(I,R)_S}_{(I,C)_S}/\mathrm{d}\beta < 0$, whenever $(I, C)_S$ and $(I, R)_S$ have a shared boundary.

2. $d\sigma^{(I,R)_S}_{(I,C)_N} / d\beta > 0$, whenever $(I, C)_N$ and $(I, R)_S$ have a shared boundary.
3. $d\sigma^{(I,R)_S}_{(D,C)} / d\beta > 0$, whenever (D, C) and $(I, R)_S$ have a shared boundary.
4. $d\sigma^{(I,R)_S}_{(I,R)_N} / d\beta > 0$, whenever $(I, C)_N$ and $(I, R)_S$ have a shared boundary.

These can be shown by utilizing the implicit function theorem. □

Proof of Proposition 6 When $\beta < 0$, $d\pi^A_{(I,C)_S}/d\sigma < 0$, $d\pi^A_{(I,R)_S}/d\sigma > 0$, $d\pi^B_{(I,C)_S}/d\sigma < 0$, and $d\pi^B_{(I,R)_S}/d\sigma < 0$. Furthermore, $\pi^B_{(I,R)_S} - \pi^B_{(I,C)_S} = \beta Q(\sigma - 1)\sigma(p - w) > 0$. Thus, buyer B's profit jumps up at σ_1 when the equilibrium changes from $(I, C)_S$ to $(I, R)_S$. Let σ_A such that $\pi^B_{(I,C)_S}(\sigma_A) = \pi^B_{(I,R)_S}(\sigma_1)$ and $\sigma_A \in (0, \sigma_1)$; σ' such that $\pi^B_{(I,C)_S}(\sigma_1) = \pi^B_{(I,R)_S}(\sigma')$ and $\sigma' \in (\sigma_1, 1)$; and σ_B such that $\pi^A_{(I,C)_S}(\sigma_B) = \pi^B_{(I,R)_S}(\sigma')$ and $\sigma_B \in (0, \sigma_1)$ if it exists. Otherwise, $\sigma_B = 0$. Furthermore, let $\zeta(\sigma) = (\pi^A_{(I,R)_S})^{-1}(\pi^A_{(I,C)_S}(\sigma))$ for $\sigma \in (\max(\sigma_A, \sigma_B), \sigma_1]$ and $\nu(\sigma) = (\pi^B_{(I,R)_S})^{-1}(\pi^B_{(I,C)_S}(\sigma))$ for $\sigma \in (\max(\sigma_A, \sigma_B), \sigma_1]$, where $()^{-1}$ represents the inverse of profit functions. It is easy to verify that these inverses are well defined for the given σ range. Note that $d\zeta/d\sigma < 0$ and $d\nu/d\sigma > 0$. Furthermore, $\sigma' = \nu(\sigma_1) > \zeta(\sigma_1) = \sigma_1$. Thus, if $\nu(\max(\sigma_A, \sigma_B)) < \zeta(\max(\sigma_A, \sigma_B))$, there exists a $\sigma_X \in (\max(\sigma_A, \sigma_B), \sigma_1)$ such that $\nu(\sigma_X) = \zeta(\sigma_X)$. Otherwise, let $\sigma_X = \max(\sigma_A, \sigma_B)$. Define $\underline{\tau}^r = \zeta(\sigma) - \sigma$ and $\overline{\tau}_r = \nu(\sigma) - \sigma$ for $\sigma \in (\sigma_X, \sigma_1)$. Furthermore, $\sigma_X = \sigma_1 - \Delta_2$. Then the result follows. □

Proof of Proposition 7 We essentially need to prove that the responsible region with horizontal sourcing includes the responsible region without horizontal sourcing. The proof is omitted for brevity. □

References

Arnseth L (2013) The music of true sustainability. Inside Supply Manag 9:18–31

Baron D, Harjoto M, Jo H (2011) The economics and politics of corporate social performance. Bus Polit 13(2):1–46

Boyaci T, Gallego G (2004) Supply chain coordination in a market with customer service competition. Prod Oper Manag 13(1):3–22

Chen L, Lee HL (2017) Sourcing under supplier responsibility risk: the effects of certification, audit, and contingency payment. Manag Sci 63(9):2795–2812

Chen J, Qi A, Dawande M (2020) Supplier centrality and auditing priority in socially responsible supply chains. Manuf Serv Oper Manag. Forthcoming

Chen L, Yao S, Zhu K (2019) Responsible sourcing under supplier-auditor collusion. Working paper

Chen S, Zhang Q, Zhou YP (2019) Impact of supply chain transparency on sustainability under NGO scrutiny. Prod Oper Manag 28(12):3002–3022

Chua JM (2016) Human rights in supply chains. https://www.hrw.org/. Retrieved 16 June 2019

Fang X, Cho S (2015) Cooperative approaches to managing suppliers: joint auditing and information sharing. Available at SSRN 2686018

Ghianni T (2012) Gibson Guitar settles probe into illegal wood imports. https://www.reuters.com. Retrieved 1 Nov 2016

Greenhouse S (2013) Retailers are pressed on safety at factories. www.nytimes.com. Retrieved 1 May 2015
Huang L, Song J, Swinney R (2016) Managing social responsibility in multi-tier supply chains. Available at SSRN 2837332
Human Rights Watch (2016) Why is it so hard for clothing manufacturers to pay a living wage? https://www.hrw.org/. Retrieved 16 June 2019
Human Rights Watch (2017) Follow the thread: the need for supply chain transparency in the garment and footwear industry. https://www.hrw.org/. Retrieved 16 June 2019
Kaldjian E, Barber CV (2015) $13 million fine for Lumber Liquidators shows U.S. Lacey Act's clout. https://www.wri.org. Retrieved 1 Nov 2016
Kraft T, Erhun F, Carlson RC, Rafinejad D (2013a) Replacement decisions for potentially hazardous substances. Prod Oper Manag 22(4):958–975
Kraft T, Zheng Y, Erhun F (2013b) The NGO's dilemma: how to influence firms to replace a potentially hazardous substance. Manuf Serv Oper Manag 15(4):649–669
Kraft T, Leon V, Zheng YK (2019, forthcoming) Motivating supplier social responsibility under incomplete visibility. Manuf Serv Oper Manag Forthcoming
Landrum S (2017) Millennials driving brands to practice socially responsible marketing. https://www.forbes.com/. Retrieved 16 June 2019
Market Watch (2015) Starbucks more than doubles global farmer loan commitment to $50 million by 2020. https://www.marketwatch.com/. Retrieved 26 June 2019
Maxwell J (2018) Guitar industry is growing, study finds. https://www.guitarworld.com/. Retrieved 16 June 2019
Orsdemir A, Hu B, Deshpande V (2019) Ensuring corporate social and environmental responsibility through vertical integration and horizontal sourcing. Manuf Serv Oper Manag 21(2):417–434
Plambeck EL, Taylor TA (2016) Supplier evasion of a buyer's audit: implications for motivating supplier social and environmental responsibility. Manuf Serv Oper Manag 18(2):184–197
PSCI (2018) PSCI inaugural annual report 2017/2018. https://pscinitiative.org/resource?resource=330. Retrieved 25 June 2019
Radocchia S (2018) How deforestation and timber issues can be battled with blockchain. https://www.forbes.com/. Retrieved 25 June 2019
Sergran J (2017) Escalating sweatshop protests keep nike sweating. https://www.fastcompany.com/. Retrieved 16 June 2019
Statista (2019) Unit sales of acoustic guitars in the U.S. 2005–2018. https://www.statista.com/. Retrieved 16 June 2019
UNECE/FAO (2007) Forest products annual market review, 2006–2007. http://www.unece.org/. Retrieved 1 Nov 2016
Watch, China Labor (2009) Corrupt audits damage worker rights: a case analysis of corruption in Bureau Veritas factory audits. http://www.chinalaborwatch.org/upfile/2009_12_9/2009bvcorruption1209.pdf. Retrieved 25 June 2019
White R (2012) Taylor Guitars buys ebony mill, pitches sustainable wood. www.latimes.com. Retrieved 1 May 2015
Yardley J (2013) Report on deadly factory collapse in Bangladesh finds widespread blame. https://www.nytimes.com/. Retrieved 16 June 2019

Environmental Sustainability Trade-Offs in a Product's Supply Chain

Mahsa Boroushaki, Mark Ferguson, and Tava Lennon Olsen

Abstract Nowadays, businesses are showing increasing interest toward the concept of sustainability as a process of maintaining a balanced environment, in which the resource exploitation, direction of investments, technological development, and institutional change are all in balance and enable meeting human needs in current and future generations. Sustainability is generally defined through the three interrelated pillars of environment, economic, and social responsibility.

Keywords Supply chain management · Sustainability · Life cycle assessment · Trade-Offs · Eco-efficiency

1 Introduction

Nowadays, businesses are showing increasing interest toward the concept of sustainability as a process of maintaining a balanced environment, in which the resource exploitation, direction of investments, technological development, and institutional change are all in balance and enable meeting human needs in current and future generations. Sustainability is generally defined through the three interrelated pillars of environment, economic, and social responsibility.

Generally, demographic patterns, economic, and industrial activities such as the burning of fossil fuels, deforestation, and vehicle emissions lead to the rapid rise in atmospheric CO_2 and other greenhouse gas (GHG) emissions that cannot be absorbed by the earth's natural processes. As a result, the imbalance of GHGs in the environment causes many problems including climate change and global warming, ozone depletion, ocean acidifications, eutrophication, etc. While it does not receive

M. Boroushaki · T. L. Olsen (✉)
University of Auckland Business School, Auckland, New Zealand
e-mail: t.olsen@auckland.ac.nz

M. Ferguson
Darla Moore School of Business, University of South Carolina, Columbia, SC, USA

J. M. Swaminathan, V. Deshpande (eds.), *Responsible Business Operations*, Springer Series in Supply Chain Management 10,
https://doi.org/10.1007/978-3-030-51957-5_9

as much attention as GHG emissions, freshwater scarcity is another environmental problem that often presents more immediate consequences for many affected communities and has been identified among the highest global systematic risks (WEF 2014). Water scarcity is a top public concern in the face of increasing water demands, mainly due to population growth, and its outcomes on required energy and food production. Questions often arise, however, when a choice improves one sustainability measure at the expense of another.

One of the main challenges related to sustainable business studies is that it is a broad discipline with many interlinking issues and trade-offs. Even if we limit ourselves to the environment, it is still difficult to characterize a truly sustainable system. Eventually, the more sustainable system is the one that best balances the trade-offs between sustainability measures. Avocado, a fruit of a tree native to Latin America and the Caribbean, provides a good example of this type of environmental sustainability trade-off.

Avocado is cultivated in many countries with tropical climates across Asia, New Zealand, Africa, and Latin America, as well as in California and Florida in the United States. The United States is the biggest importer of avocados in the world and Mexico is the world's leading avocado producer.[1] There are many environmental concerns about avocado production and consumption in the United States due to drastic water restrictions in California. Avocado production requires a lot of water, to begin with, but in dry regions, such as Chile and California, farming avocado needs even more water, which might intensify the water scarcity in those regions (Mekonnen and Hoekstra 2010a). Most of the water usage in California is for agriculture, and avocados are one of their big water sinks (Mekonnen and Hoekstra 2010b). In Mexico, a region identified by the UN as being under physical water scarcity,[2] avocado production has become a critical environmental issue as well. Beyond the displacement of forests and the effects on water retention, the high use of agricultural chemicals, large volumes of wood needed for packing, and using trucks for transportation are factors that have negative effects on the area's environment.[3] On the other hand, New Zealand is a country with little fresh water scarcity that is planning to grow its avocado industry. In particular, the NZ Avocado Go Global program[4] aims to further develop this industry into a competitive, high-value, sustainable industry. Due to its geographical location relative to its main export destinations and long-distance distributions aka "food miles," however, exporting avocados from NZ has attracted some negative attention due to the GHG emissions required for transport.

In the cases such as avocado production and transportation, results based on a standalone indicator (carbon footprint or water footprint) can be misleading

[1]www.usaid-acceso.org, Market survey #19, December 2014.

[2]https://www.un.org/waterforlifedecade/scarcity.shtml

[3]www.nypost.com/2016/08/10/your-avocado-obsession-is-mexicos-deforestation-problem/

[4]https://www.mpi.govt.nz/funding-and-programmes/primary-growth-partnership/primary-growthpartnership-programmes/new-Zealand-avocados-go-global/

because, due to the severe water scarcity in many countries around the world, usually, a "good global warming potential (GWP) performance" can be in contradiction to a "good water performance" (Stoessel et al. 2012). There is often a trade-off between the relatively low carbon footprint of local production and consumption and the induced water stress; therefore, we cannot generalize localization benefits to all crop types, all countries with different environmental circumstances, and all product types.

Recently, researchers, by studying the same apple cultivation in different European regions, found that producing the same crop in different locations may have completely different requirements, and consequently very different environmental impacts (Mouron et al. 2012). Thus, it is worthwhile to investigate to what extent, production location, and long-distance transportation can affect climate change, energy, and water usage. For example, which part of the product life cycle (production, processing, transportation, and consumption) has the most contribution to climate change, energy usage, water usage, and other impact categories? Do different types of production and processing methods offer environmental advantages? Finally, yet importantly, how does one measure the environmental trade-off of longer-distance shipments of more environmentally friendly production systems?

Another important issue that makes the sustainability studies more challenging is that the majority of the burden on our environment and natural resources is indirect, as businesses are becoming more tightly integrated globally, risks and opportunities related to the upstream or downstream activities within the supply chain will increasingly affect their own operations as well. Thus, methods introduced to measure the environmental impacts of business operations are taking the entire supply chain or life-cycle perspective into account.

In recent years, within the field of supply chain management (SCM), an increasing community is paying attention to sustainable supply chains. Traditionally, supply chain management (SCM) has been defined as the management of physical, logistical, and financial interorganizational flows in order to add value and achieve customer satisfaction (Mentzer et al. 2001; Stock and Boyer 2009). SCM has mainly focused on economic and financial business performance, deals with lowering costs, ensuring on-time delivery, and shrinking transportation times to allow better response to business challenges. However, the increasing environmental costs of these networks and growing consumer pressure for green products has led many organizations to look at supply chain sustainability as a new measure of profitability and competitiveness. Currently, the main approach enabling a comprehensive assessment of a product's environmental sustainability throughout the product's supply chain is a Life-Cycle Assessment (LCA). Therefore, in the next section, we discuss the LCA method from an operations management perspective.

2 Life-Cycle Assessment from an Operations Management Perspective

Intrinsically measuring something can stimulate finding ways for improvement. The ability of a firm to measure and reduce its environmental impacts starts with looking closely through its entire supply chain operations. Furthermore, measuring the environmental impact of these operations is not straightforward. Usually, a product goes through numerous industrial and transportation activities, and its environmental impact is closely interlinked to economic risks and opportunities of these activities carried out by various companies within the supply chain. The operation management community usually evaluate the time/cost-effectiveness of operations and express performance in monetary terms, which is challenging for environmental impact assessment, although there might be some cases in which environmental enhancements are not necessarily worth pursuing from an economic perspective. Therefore, it is worthwhile to look at environmental impact measurement tools from an operations management perspective to be able to have a more precise measurement of both economic and environmental factors of products or processes.

Life-cycle assessment is a comprehensive and prevalent tool for assessing and benchmarking the environmental impacts of different systems. The idea of a life-cycle assessment basically tries to assess the environmental burdens of a product or service, back to the raw materials and down to waste removal (Klöpffer 1997). The life-cycle assessment methodology was defined by ISO 14040:2006 as "the compilation and evaluation of the inputs, outputs, and the potential environmental impacts of a product system throughout its lifecycle" (ISO 2006). Major developments have occurred since 1990, resulting in an international standard, and implementation by various guidelines that improve the maturity and robustness of the life-cycle assessment method (Finnveden et al. 2009; Saunders et al. 2009). Today's LCA framework and principals are commonly accepted based on the series of technical reports issued by the ISO 14040 series.

Businesses may engage in LCA studies to appropriately design their products, comply with regulations and various emissions trading schemes, voluntarily disclose their sustainability practices, apply for eco-labels, or identify opportunities for cost saving. Moreover, stakeholders such as customers, governments, and NGOs impose pressure on firms in order to disclose more information about their products and processes, individually or through trade associations (Blass and Corbett 2018). According to (ISO 2006), a life-cycle assessment study consists of four phases (Fig. 1), which we describe next.

Phase 1: Goal and Scope Definition

An LCA study should include the reason (goal) for conducting the study and a scope that identifies the system boundaries and level of detail. In this stage, one should identify all the materials, activities, and processes that contribute to each stage of the chosen product's life cycle and a representative functional unit on which the

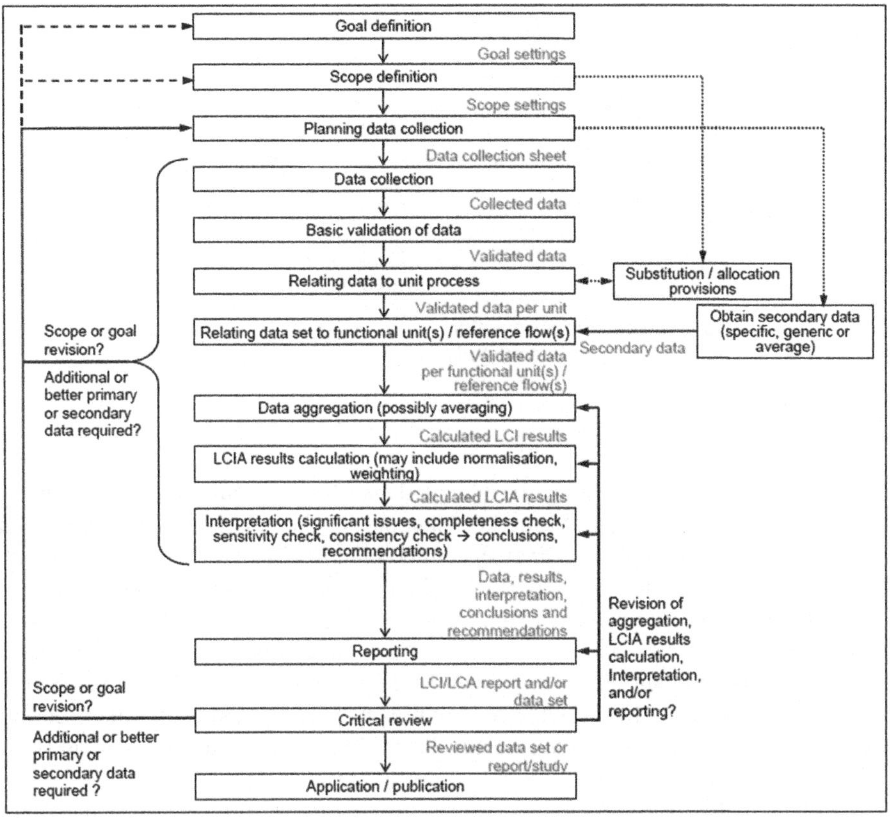

Fig. 1 Details of an iterative approach to LCA. (From ISO 14044:2006)

environmental impacts will be based. Major types of system boundaries include those between the technical system and the environment (see Fig. 2), significant and insignificant processes, and technological systems and other systems. In some cases, time and geographical limits have also been mentioned as system boundaries. Some studies considered emissions during 100 years while others considered infinite time horizon until all materials from the system are emitted (Finnveden et al. 2009).

Most of the time, boundaries between the system and the environment are explicit; however, in some cases such as agriculture, system boundaries must be defined clearly, particularly for emissions to water waste systems or landfills (ISO 2006). Cradle-to-gate and cradle-to-market are the two most frequently used system boundaries in the LCA of agricultural systems (Cerutti et al. 2014). In the cradle-to-gate category, the focus is on environmental impacts of the production phase, including upstream processes up to the farm gate. For example, the nursery is one of the main upstream processes in crop production, where orchard seedlings are produced, and grafted plants are delivered to the orchards. The environmental

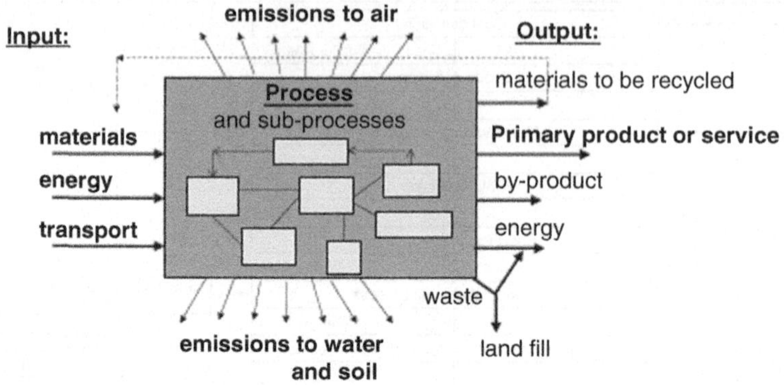

Fig. 2 The basic structure of a system in LCA (Vogtlander 2012)

impact during this stage should be included in LCA, although a lack of data is a big challenge. The cradle-to-market category further includes the distribution and commercialization phase. Other system boundaries are cradle-to-retailer, which includes processing and transportation to the distribution center, and cradle-to-use that contains consumers' environmental impacts as well. It is difficult to define the system boundaries between significant and insignificant processes because identifying insignificant data is unknown at the beginning of the study. Generally, researchers consider all accessible data within their study and refine them during the iterative processes of inventory analysis and life-cycle impact assessment (Leif et al. 1995).

Fundamentally, an LCA is anchored in a quantitative description of the function(s) provided by the analyzed system and the outcome of the study is represented in the environmental impact per functional unit. There are various debates regarding what exactly constitutes the functional unit. Firstly, the associated impacts per functional unit of a business operation may vary over time due to changes in the decision-making process or the competitive context of businesses. Secondly, evaluating the environmental impacts of the same system using different functional units may lead to quite different scenarios. For instance, in a crop production context, high-yield crop cultivars have a significantly better environmental performance using a mass-based functional unit; however, it cannot account for crop quality that affects the targeted market (e.g. the local fresh market, industrial processing, or exporting to international markets). On the other hand, low-yield crop cultivars are favored by a land-use-based functional unit (Cerutti et al. 2013).

In the context of operations and supply chain management, the outcome of a study is expressed in performance (such as profit, cost, inventory level, etc.) per unit time within the economically driven system boundaries. For example, in a newsvendor model, the company has to determine production quantities for next season's sale; thus, the performance of the production decision is evaluated per season (per unit time), rather than per product. If we integrate LCA to the newsvendor problem to evaluate the environmental impacts of the product, functional units based on volume or weight will not differentiate products, which will be sold at full price versus products, which might be sold at a lower price (overproduced units), resulting in all units being allocated equal environmental impacts. Economic system boundaries comprise elements that contribute to overall profit or costs; therefore, life-cycle stages that are relevant from an environmental perspective might be neglected (such as raw material extraction or end-user consumption).

Meanwhile, LCA results would lead to different scenarios if impacts were allocated based on the functional unit such as "product unit sold at full price" that will treat the overproduced units as by-products[5] and their impacts allocated differently. This example illustrates that the impacts of a product can vary substantially depending on the functional unit and system boundary (Blass and Corbett 2018). Accordingly, both environmentally and economically significant life-cycle stages should be included in the study to facilitate greater consistency of LCA within supply chain management studies (Blass and Corbett 2018).

Phase 2: Life-Cycle Inventory Analysis

Life-cycle Inventory (LCI) is the data collection portion of LCA. This stage is an iterative process and includes data collection and calculation procedures to quantify related inputs and outputs of a product system. Unit processes are the smallest component in the LCI analysis and often considered a black box. Therefore, for each unit process in the LCA study, one should determine the size of inflows and outflows and collect data accordingly.

Typically, LCA studies assume that technologies are linear and simply by multiplication, one can scale the data of a unit process. However, in supply chain processes, there are various sources of nonlinearity such as congestion, production in batches, the bullwhip effect, etc. (Blass and Corbett 2018). The linear assumption of the system creates some challenges when trying to quantify the upstream production process (or downstream disposal process) with multifunctional processes.

To address the first issue related to substantially large systems, the impact of some very distant upstream processes may be negligible and can be ignored. Therefore, instead of measuring the processes directly, one can estimate the missing processes or estimate the error when a cut off is made.

The second issue can be stated as an example: a manufacturing company produces a product and sells it to different markets. Assume that the manufacturer compiles a list of inputs in order to calculate an entire supply chain LCI of its product. One part of this LCI is associated with producing a product to be sold to the local market, and the remainder is associated with selling product to other businesses. The latter part forms an input to other businesses' LCI, were they to prepare one. If added up, LCIs would double-count (multiple-count) supply chain impacts. Furthermore, a product sold to other businesses could be used to produce

[5]By-products are products, which can be used directly in other product systems (e.g., wood chips from saw mills can directly be used in chipboard, saw dust can be applied in MDF plates).

items that, directly or indirectly, are purchased as inputs by the manufacturer. Thus, double-counting would even occur within the manufacturer's own LCI (Lenzen 2008).

Typically, a product supply chain consists of various companies from suppliers and manufacturers to distributors and retailers. Companies can collaboratively invest in reducing the environmental impact of the product through its supply chain even by modifying the product's appearance (e.g., dimension or form), or by changing product features (e.g., strength, storage requirements, or durability). Additionally, companies can affect others' impacts through coordination and information sharing. For example, sharing demand information might result in lower GHG emissions by reducing the need for fast transportation due to smoother suppliers' operations. On the other hand, LCA may not recognize that each company in the supply chain will act according to their incentives and interests, whereas, SCM, with the aid of models from economics and game theory, tries to recognize the incentives' effects on firms' decisions and profit. Incorporating incentives in the LCA studies can implicitly change decisions. For instance, as discussed in the previous paragraph, to understand the fair physical breakdown of impacts between firms in the supply chain, it is essential to avoid double-counting in LCI, but the double-counting phenomena will be challenging when impact allocation has economic consequences. Many environmental impacts are the result of processes that are influenced cooperatively by two or more parties; thus, all parties should have the right incentives to put effort and reduce the environmental impacts of those processes. Caro et al. (2013) showed that, in some contexts, double-counting would be desirable in the supply chain that provides the right incentive for firms to achieve the socially optimal investments derived from the joint effort and cost to reduce their emissions.

Phase 3: Life-Cycle Impact Assessment

In this phase, the potential environmental impacts of the intended system should be evaluated and understood through associating inventory data with particular environmental impact categories and related indicators. Impact categories illustrate environmental issues of concern so that the results of the LCI analysis may be assigned. In addition, the life-cycle impact assessment will also provide the required information for the next stage (interpretation phase).

Life-cycle impact assessment (LCIA) interprets the results of the inventory assessment in order to provide additional information for a better understanding of their environmental significance (ISO 2006). The ISO standard on the life-cycle assessment involves different steps for impact assessment. The first step, which is called classification, involves identifying environmental impact categories relevant to the study and assigning emissions from the data inventory to these categories according to the ability of substances to contribute to these environmental problems. The following six impact categories are considered as the most important (midpoint level):

- Acidification Potential (AP)
- Eutrophication Potential (EP)

- Global Warming Potential (GWP)
- Ozone Depletion Potential (ODP)
- Photochemical Ozone Creation Potential (POCP)
- Primary Energy Use

Each impact category contains a causal chain (e.g., the earth absorbs energy from the sun and radiates part of the energy toward the atmosphere and warms it, so the emission of GHGs is changing the radiation balance toward the earth, which leads to changing the climate; this will affect the ecosystem and human activities). In order to model an impact indicator, we need to choose a certain level of the causal chain. There are two main approaches in the LCA for doing so: focus on the front-end (midpoint approach) or focus on the back-end (end-point approach).

In the second step, according to the environmental mechanism, the impact of emissions is modeled quantitatively as an impact score, which for each substance expresses its potential contribution within the impact category. For instance, kg of CO_2-equivalents for GHGs contribute to the "Climate Change" impact category. Thus, the characterization factor of CO_2 for climate change is 1, while the characterization factor of methane is more than 20, reflecting its higher climate change impact. Some impact assessment guidebooks such as "IMPACT2002+", "ReCiPe", and "ILCD" contain a set of recommended impact categories with a category indicator and set of characterization factors.

Normalization as an optional step (step three) in LCIA is applied for better interpretation of the relative magnitude of impact scores in comparison with some reference information. In this step, the characterized results of each impact category are divided by a selected reference value in order to bring all the results to the same scale. Finally, weighting environmental impact categories will reflect their relative importance in the study (ISO 2006).

Based on the ISO standard, the first two steps of classification and characterization are mandatory steps, while the normalization and weighting steps are optional. These optional steps are important, especially when decision-makers are confronted with trade-off situations (Finnveden et al. 2009).

Phase 4: Life-Cycle Interpretation
In this phase, all findings from the inventory analysis and the impact assessment are integrated to provide a consistent result and recommendations for decision-makers that are aligned with the goal and scope of the study. Two important factors that often make the life-cycle interpretation more complicated are uncertainty and variability. Typically, variability originates from real-world intrinsic variations, while uncertainty is caused by a lack of data, incorrect measurements, and various model assumptions. If LCA outcomes are to be used in decision-making, the result of the study should be robust with clear quality.

In the current LCA structure, some aspects such as spatial (variability across locations) and temporal characteristics (inventory data of several years) of processes under study cannot be modeled. Additionally, choices of the functional unit, allocation procedures during LCI, and the assumption of linear technologies add more uncertainty to LCA studies. Therefore, the LCA outcomes should be evaluated based on decision uncertainty as well as the functional unit chosen for the study.

3 Toward an Integrated Carbon and Water Footprint

Recently, based on the classical methods of LCA, there is a trend toward new approaches as a lifecycle-based assessment focusing on the subset of impact categories (such as carbon footprint and water footprint methods). In that case, the researcher would have to justify why certain impact categories are not considered.

According to ISO 14040:2006, the carbon footprint of products is "the system to calculate the category indicator of the targeted product for the global warming potential or climate change in life cycle assessment" (Galli et al. 2011). Fundamentally, carbon footprint originated from LCA; consequently, the use of a functional unit, the LCI data assumptions, limitations, and LCIA methods will directly affect the reliability of the carbon footprint results. For example, quantifying the carbon footprint of agricultural products entails a large database with data on the amount of energy consumption, fertilizers used, plant protection products for each activity, as well as the annual production yield and energy use for transportation.

Accordingly, the international standard for water footprinting (ISO 14046) defines the Water Footprint (WF) as "metric(s) that quantifies the potential environmental impacts related to water." In this approach, water use consequences integrate with LCA impact categories similar to the climate change impact category, which uses carbon footprint to represent the midpoint category in quantitative LCA modeling. Researchers who consider water use as a midpoint impact category compare physical resource availability with the demand to evaluate the potential environmental impacts of water consumption. This formulation indicates the severity of water consumption compared to the available water amount. An important issue in water use assessment of products and/or services is the lack of data sources on water consumption and a commonly agreed impact assessment method. Due to the absence of water inventories, the WF community tries to make use of LCA databases and software tools (like ecoinvent and GaBi), although the geographical and quality-related information content of these databases is limited. Furthermore, the validity and reliability of the available data are debatable because it is not clear whether all relevant water flows, particularly those from the background system, are included (Berger and Finkbeiner 2010).

Additionally, in the context of WF assessment, pure inventory-based WF can be misleading because, as mentioned earlier, in areas with water shortage, a low WF can be of more environmental significance than a large WF in areas where water is abundant. The place where the involved processes in the life cycle take place is critical, since water scarcity is local. Therefore, from a supply chain management perspective, locating facilities (or growing crops) in regions with water shortage may bring water-intense processes that expose water risk to those regions and lead to future financial losses.

Generally, interests toward global warming overshadow other environmental concerns. This focus on GHG emissions in SCM incurs the risk of concealing impacts of other categories, which are not behaving in the same way as GHG emissions (e.g., the carbon and water trade-off that was discussed earlier in the avocado example). Accordingly, studies in the sustainable supply chains area should be careful that policies that minimize one impact category might not be preferred for others.

Carbon and water footprint assessments have fundamental similarities and differences. For example, both approaches quantitatively assess the sustainability impact; various scopes can be applied to both, from in-house processes to across entire value chains and life cycles, and both can be approached at varying levels of data analysis, from high-level hotspots to precise accounting standards. However, the water footprint measures the volume of blue, green, and gray[6] water footprints and has a geographic and temporal specificity that must be analyzed within the local context. It is important to know where and when water has been consumed, in addition to how much. On the other hand, the carbon footprint is inherently location independent, since all GHG emissions will affect the global atmosphere in the same way.

Simultaneous carbon and water footprint within LCA provides a higher level of insights into main environmental issues than using either indicator separately. It enables our understanding of potential trade-offs or synergies between these intimately linked issues in sustainability. Table 1 shows the characteristics of the carbon and water footprints according to Galli et al. (2011).

It is broadly recognized that environmental issues pose potential risks to businesses due to changing stakeholders' attitude, evolving product markets, higher price of energy and raw material, supply chain interruptions, etc. We can typically categorize environmental risks as a threefold problem of risk related to core business operations, risks related to the value chain, and risks related to the broader supply and demand networks. It is important to note that risks related to environmental issues should be categorized appropriately because the impacts can be both local and global.

Risk 1: Risks Related to Core Operations

Climate change might have direct effects on the physical structures of the business. Factors such as weather extremes and water issues bring significant business risks due to the rising problem of reliability of water supply, requiring design and/or location changes, physical damage to industrial assets, lowering efficiency of production processes, raising the cost of operations and maintenance activities, or the products' quality. Some industries, such as agriculture, fisheries, and forestry, are particularly exposed to physical risks of climate change due to floods, hurricanes, droughts, or rising sea levels.

[6]Blue water refers to ground (surface) water consumption, green water represents the evaporation (transpiration) of rainwater, and graywater is the polluted water.

Table 1 Carbon footprint and water footprint characteristics

	Carbon footprint	Water footprint
What do they measure?	The total amount of direct and indirect GHG emissions over the product or service lifespan.	The human appropriation of the volume of freshwater demanded by human consumption. It intends to illustrate the hidden links among human consumption, water use, and global trade.
What are their databases and sources?	Statistical data on national economic accounts and international trade (OECD, UN, etc.). Environmental accounts data on GHG emissions (GTAP, IEA, etc.). National economic accounts (input-output tables, supply, and use).	Data on population (World Bank and FAO). Total renewable water resources and water withdrawals (FAO), and data on arable lands (FAO). International trade data on agricultural and industrial products. Local data on different parameters (e.g. climate, cropping patterns, soil, water quality, pesticides, and fertilizers rates).
What are their units of measures?	If we only measure CO_2 (Kg CO_2), if measurement includes other GHGs (Kg CO_2-e). No conversion to an area unit.	Water volume per unit of time (usually m3/yr.) for the water footprint of processes. M3/ton or liter/kg for the water footprint of products.
What do they cover?	Carbon footprint is a multidimensional indicator that can be applied to products, processes, companies, and governments. Documents all direct and indirect GHGs emissions due to the use of resources and products. Measures the "demand" side in terms of the amount of GHGs emitted. It has a consumption-based point of view and thus considers a trade.	A geographically explicit and multidimensional indicator that can be calculated for products, organizations, economic sectors, and up to countries. Documents both the direct and indirect use of natural capital as a source (demand on blue and green waters) and as a sink (gray water to dilute pollution). Measures the "demand" side only, in terms of freshwater consumed.

(continued)

Table 1 (continued)

	Carbon footprint	Water footprint
How useful are they?	Provides an alternative angle for international policy on climate change. Provides a better understanding of countries' responsibility and could simplify international cooperation and partnerships. Identifies alternatives for GHG mitigation, e.g., change in consumption patterns. Helps to analyze the impacts of using alternative energies. Helps to design an International price for GHG emissions. Can help to design global policies aiming at implementing the convergence principles. Can be benchmarked against 2050 targets for total global GHG emissions.	Offers a new and global dimension to the concept of water management. Provides a better understanding of nation dependency on foreign water resources. Provides river basin info to which scarce water resources are allocated to low-value export crops. Helps to identify alternatives for reducing water stress, e.g., change in consumption patterns. Helps to analyze the impacts of using different energy sources. Offers companies a way to monitor their dependences on scarce water resources along with their supply chain. Can help to design global policies aiming at implementing the convergence principles.
What are their strengths?	Enables us to assess comprehensively the human contribution to GHG emissions. Consistent with economic and environmental accounting standards. Consistent emissions data are available for the majority of countries.	Illustrates the spatial distribution of a country's water demand. Develops traditional water withdrawal measures (including green and gray waters). Visualizes the link between local consumption and global appropriation of freshwater. Integrates water use and pollution over the production chain.
What are their weaknesses?	There is a need for additional impact assessment models to analyze the impact of climate change at the national and subnational context. Efforts needed to set up and update a system of MRIO tables and related environmental extensions. There is no specific "carbon footprint threshold," though a 'sustainability threshold' for global warming has been agreed.	It relies on local data that are hard to collect or are frequently unavailable. It suffers from possible truncation errors. Despite the significance uncertainty, no uncertainty studies are available. Calculating gray water heavily relies on assumptions and estimations. Characterization factors of water stress are not included. Implications of blue water and green water use are different and difficult to communicate.

Another area of environmental risks is associated with rules and regulations, aiming to decrease GHGs by granting allowances to companies in order to control the amount of specified GHG emissions. In this method, companies should buy additional allowances if they emit more than what is allotted to them. Moreover, there is a risk of a lawsuit for companies such as tobacco, pharmaceutical, and oil and coal companies who generate a significant amount of GHG emissions in their operations. Ultimately, the company's brand will be threatened by negative perceptions of public opinion because of producing products or providing services that have a negative effect on the environment. Besides the high attention to carbon footprint and waste reduction in the operations and supply chain management area, water-related issues need to be included in decision models as well. Many stakeholders from government to different types of businesses will be impacted by water scarcity, and, usually, there is a high level of correspondence in their interests toward reducing shared water scarcity risks; as a result, it is fruitful to recognize common incentives that stimulate stakeholders toward reducing water scarcity risks and risks related to GHG emissions collaboratively. It is essential to generate tailored climate-risk profiles and strategies to mitigate the risk.

Risk 2: Risk Related to the Value Chain
Climate change may also influence the quality or quantity of inputs into production systems, or the demand for products. Climate will affect required natural resources for agricultural and forestry as well as demands for things like cooling during the hot summer months.

Water-related problems are a global issue that needs local solutions. For instance, a below-average precipitation of several consecutive years threatens the production yield, from an agricultural point of view. In a business context, the risks associated with water include sudden stream-flow interruption during peak operation time. From a government perspective, risks include the increasing costs of accessing water and its implications on energy costs and economic growth.

Risk 3: The Broader Supply and Demand Network
Risks related to environmental issues as well as poor water management due to short-term thinking or lack of knowledge threaten all public and/or private utilities, infrastructure, and services, which support business operations, production systems, and supply chains. An obvious effect of climate change would be damaging transport infrastructure and consequently slow flow of inputs (supplies) and outputs such as the high cost of procurements and repairs. However, adapting to these severe effects is not under the direct control of the businesses and may require a high level of collaboration with utilities and government to ensure adaptive actions are feasible.

3.1 Water-Related Risk Response Strategies

According to Larson et al. (2012) and Orr et al. (2009), there are various types of risk response strategies associated with water scarcity. Some of these strategies, such as derivatives/hedging, insurance, and water-trade schemes, enable businesses to help protect themselves against changing costs, the harm from reduced water supplies, or the disruption of supply chains but do not necessarily protect economic productivity. For instance, a cloth manufacturer may need to be protected against a poor cotton crop yield or against higher water prices in a drier than the standard growing season (i.e., purchase yield/revenue-based insurance). Nevertheless, weather derivatives cannot overcome long-term financial losses when extreme events interrupt business opportunities or profit. Further, they do not address the fundamental issue related to water availability and, therefore, economic productivity. We need mechanisms to enhance overall supply in a watershed or aquifer to be able to address sustainable water resources not only for local communities and nature but also for the companies.

Another water management paradigm that tries to incorporate financial and availability considerations is the buying or trading of water rights, which is mainly a mechanism to find, develop, or reallocate a new or existing source of water supply. The main purpose of this mechanism is to enhance water allocation efficiency by setting up a market price for water among competing consumers (Larson et al. 2012). There are various types of water trades. For instance, in the water access entitlement trades, the seller can transfer or lease all or part of his water access rights to the buyer. In the water allocation trades, the seller transfers all or part of his annual water allocation to the buyer for a determined period.

Often water allocation has not been done efficiently between different sectors (e.g. agriculture, municipality, and industry) because they are not equally productive in water usage. Hence, improving the water allocation mechanisms can not only have a significant economic impact but can also incentivize water users to enhance their productivity because of the opportunity to make a profit from selling or leasing their unused annual water allocations (Larson et al. 2012).

Despite various benefits, the above-mentioned water-trade mechanisms will not consider the environmental effects of the change in the timing and location of the water use and will not protect against water risks. Moreover, they are not practical in the national or international level because the transportation of a high volume of water is cost-prohibitive. Thus, there is a need to focus on decreasing demand for water in each sector.

In this regard, water recycling and reuse projects have greater importance. Proactive water stewardship programs are increasingly receiving attention by corporations to enhance their water use practices in their operations. As an example, Coca-Cola improves its water efficiency by reducing or removing water use in its manufacturing processes by investing in new technologies and operating procedures that replace or reduce water use in their operations. Coca-Cola also has two goals concerning wastewater management. The first is to replenish water used in their global sales volume back to communities and nature through water projects outside their manufacturing plant boundaries. The second goal is to return the water used to make beverages back to communities and nature after appropriately treating it. This means that Coca-Cola fully treats 173 billion liters of water and returns it directly to the system.[7]

Although, approaches such as reduce, reuse, and recycle will generally decrease the water demand and, as a result, the water-related risks, they will not ensure that water supply will meet demand. Therefore, companies will need to look beyond their own operations to ensure the sustainability of their water supply. Activities that can be implemented by individual companies to improve the availability of overall water supply in a watershed or aquifer can be related to the supply chain operations water usage or activities to enhance water sources in general. For example, Coca-Cola has commenced projects that support communities and nature to replenish the water used in its beverages. These projects are directed at conservation practices, community water availability as well as water quantity and quality restoration and enhancement (Larson et al. 2012).

4 The Challenge of Environmental Trade-Offs

While profitability often remains the primary goal of most firms, they also attempt to decrease their products' and operations' environmental impacts so as to mitigate their associated risks and to retain the quality of the environment due to increasing awareness of sustainability issues. But environmental quality improvements do not come for free and will not necessarily reduce the firm's cost or increase its demand. In other words, in practice, win-win solutions often seem to be quite difficult to achieve. Questions such as "how much do we have to spend in order to improve environmental quality?" or "what are the trade-offs between the environmental impacts and their associated costs?" should be assessed carefully.

Eco-efficiency analysis is a tool that is based on Pareto optimality for examining the best solution for sustainability in a micro (firms) and macro (society) level, which primarily represents an empirical relation between environmental impact and operations' environmental cost or value. Eco-efficiency can be matched against normative considerations to figure out what the trade-off between the economy and the environment should be if the firm is subject to a certain level of environmental quality. An eco-efficiency approach can assist to evaluate trade-offs and to identify cases in which environmental quality improvements are not necessarily worth pursuing (Huppes and Ishikawa 2005). This method represents results based on economic returns and environmental impacts to demonstrate the strengths and weaknesses of a particular product or process. Consequently, the entire life cycle

[7]https://www.coca-colacompany.com/stories/treating-and-recycling-wastewater

of products and processes should be evaluated while all alternatives are assessed based on the same functional units or customer benefits.

The eco-efficiency has been defined as a ratio between environmental impact (described in Sect. 4.1), to be reduced, and economic value of production (described in Sect. 4.2), to be increased (Huppes and Ishikawa 2007). As a result, four main types of eco-efficiency can be applied, the ratio of the economic value of production to environmental impact, which is environmental productivity and its inverse, which is the environmental intensity of production; both ratios refer to the production realm. In addition, instead of maximizing the production value and minimizing the environmental impacts, the focus can be shifted to the reduction of environmental improvements' costs. In this case, the variables are defined in the opposite way, which demonstrates environmental improvement cost and its inverse, environmental cost-effectiveness (Huppes and Ishikawa 2007).

4.1 Environmental Impact Scores

With regard to the environmental impacts, the main subject in eco-efficiency analysis is which environmental effects need to be specified and how to aggregate them to a single environmental score. The eco-efficiency method is based on the ISO 14045:2012 and ISO 2006a, b (ISO 14040, 14,044) for life-cycle assessments and accomplishes optional phases as well as the water footprint standard (ISO 14046). Typically, the eco-efficiency method considers the seven most important impact categories as energy usage, emissions (to air, water, or land), resource usage, toxicity potential, land use, water use, and risk potential (Finkbeiner 2016). Based on the LCA approach, after defining the study's goal, scope, and system boundary, the process of data collection or life-cycle inventory analysis should be done. It is followed by an impact assessment, which includes classification and characterization of all data inventory as mandatory steps, and normalization and weighting that will facilitate clear understanding and comparison between alternatives.

In normalization, the cumulative life-cycle inventory data or scores in each impact category are normalized relative to the alternative that has the highest impact in that area. The relative value of 1 is assigned to the alternative with the highest impact, and accordingly, other alternatives will receive values less than 1. Figure 3 demonstrates where a certain alternative performs better than others and where it has less desirable results; thus, the trade-offs between different alternatives are clearly visible. This graph is called an environmental fingerprint, which illustrates the impacts of different indicators in a comparison system of different alternatives (Finkbeiner 2016).

However, to clearly understand the environmental strengths or weaknesses of a particular alternative in comparison with other options, we need to prioritize impact categories. Therefore, an additional weighting process will enable us to combine normalized impact scores into a single score. The intention is to consider all relevant

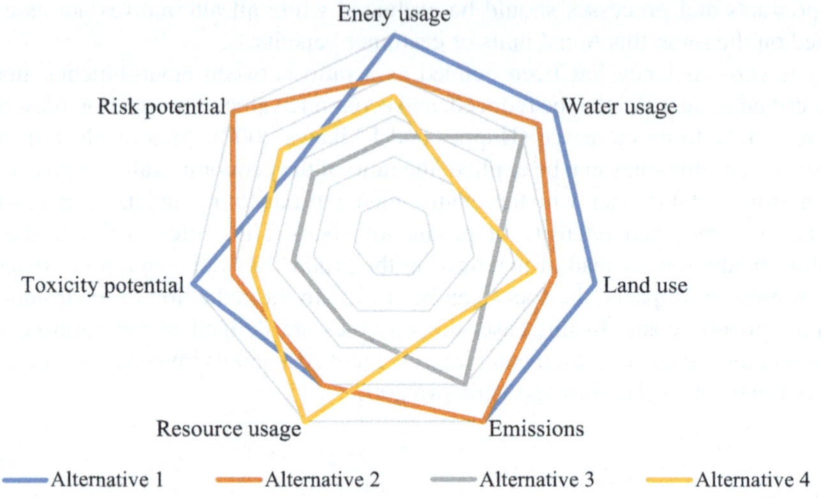

Fig. 3 The environmental fingerprint adapted from (Finkbeiner 2016)

environmental impacts and aggregate their effects based on scientific relevance factors and societal factors in a way that leads to a broadly acceptable single-score result. These factors might be unique for each study and depend on the region the study is implemented.

To determine the normalized environmental factors among impact categories, the outcome of classification and characterization phases of the life-cycle impact assessment is divided by the total environmental impact in the region (usually data can be found in publically available statistical databases). These factors can reflect the level to which the emissions in the specific study (or other impact categories) contribute to the total emissions in a given geographic region.

Concurrently, the societal weighting factors reflect the values, views, and preferences of society on the importance of each environmental impacts. For instance, the environmental preferences of citizens in the society can be aggregated into a social welfare judgment or public policy outcomes can be used as the basis for the aggregated views (Huppes and Ishikawa 2005). These factors are derived from the results of interviews and polling to measure the willingness-to-pay for more environmentally friendly products or services. Another approach to evaluate the society weighting factors is to assess their preferences from the actual choices such as hedonic pricing. The housing market price is a most common example of the hedonic pricing, where the building price is determined by the property characteristics (e.g., size, condition), as well as its environmental characteristics (e.g., the level of air and water pollution).

According to Finkbeiner (2016), the overall environmental score of action can be calculated by taking the geometric mean of the normalized environmental factors and societal weighting factors.

4.2 Economic Score

In the eco-efficiency analysis, economic data needs to be calculated and summarized by using the usual business or national economic models. Two main approaches, which enabled value and cost aggregation, are cost-benefit analysis (CBA) and life-cycle costing (LCC).

Regarding the cost and value concept, several empirical issues must be resolved. For example, the problem of changing market values over time and uncertainty related to expected future prices, as well as the cost/value dependencies to system boundary, functional unit, and considered alternatives. Moreover, costs should account for initial and future costs (or benefits) of the products in addition to the associated costs of environmental impacts as well as the time value of money.

4.3 Eco-efficiency Analysis

An eco-efficiency of a product or process compared to other alternatives can be shown on a graph with environmental scores on the horizontal axis and economic values on the vertical axis (Fig. 4). Huppes and Ishikawa (2005) introduced three basic options for applying eco-efficiency at a micro level. First, incremental eco-efficiency (E/E_{INCR}), which determines the effects of the total value of an alternative and its associated environmental impacts. Second, win-win eco-efficiency (E/E_{WIN_WIN}), which is a comparison between a reference situation and each alternative, and finally, a pairwise eco-efficiency ($E/E_{PAIRWISE}$), which is a comparison between different alternatives. Pairwise eco-efficiency is applied to eliminate dominated alternatives, which are those located within the concave envelope created by the most attractive options.

Figure 4 denotes the dotted curve as the efficient frontier as well as the eco-inefficient area below the curve. In this graph, the current situation (H) located in an inefficient area and by moving to the efficient frontier (Pareto-optimal situation), eco-efficiency can improve. It is the decision maker's choice on which improvement path is more desirable.

The comparative assessment of adjoining alternatives on the optimum frontier may be transformed into a marginal analysis, which indicates the trade-off between different options. It is called *marginal eco-efficiency* for trade-offs at the optimum frontier (Huppes and Ishikawa 2005). Obviously, the optimum alternative will be determined by the decision maker's point of view and the relative weights they assign to environmental and economic value.

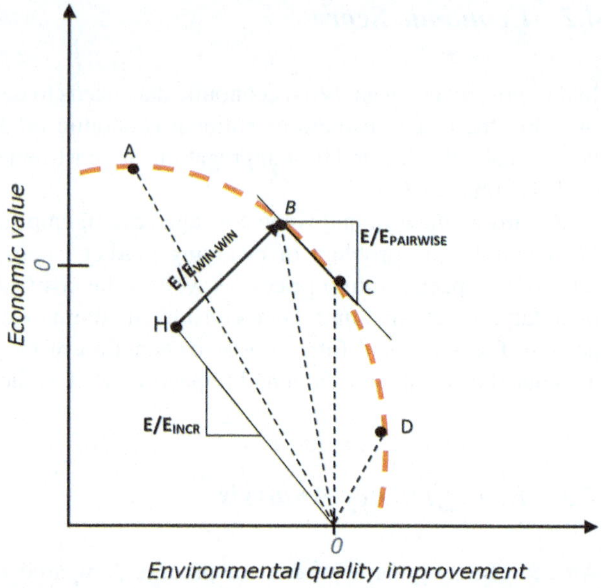

Fig. 4 Eco-efficiency of alternatives A to D- H represents a reference situation. (Adapted from Huppes and Ishikawa (2005))

5 Conclusion

Traditionally, business decisions have been driven by maximizing profitability, minimizing cost, or achieving customer satisfaction. As sustainability goals have been added to companies' business objectives, interest has grown on mitigating the social and environmental impact of products and operations. There are many similarities and differences between the LCA and the SCM viewpoints, which create opportunities for integrating these two fields of studies. For example, in the view of life-cycle thinking, a large share of the world's overall emissions associated with transportation can be mitigated by choosing a different mode of transport or changing routing or loading of the vehicles in the network. Inventory policies of a company significantly influence these logistics choices; for example, choosing a slower transportation mode with lower carbon emission would require increasing the inventory in the supply network, which illustrates that potential trade-offs should be identified and resolved. In addition, transportation environmental performance is strongly determined by the network design, which refers to the location of the factory, packaging centers, distribution centers, or other transport hubs. Apart from logistics choices, inventory policies and facility location, reverse logistics, and closed-loop supply chains are streams of research that directly relate to specific decisions on end-of-life management, such as reuse and recycling and their associated environmental impacts. Hopefully, the closer integration of LCA and SCM will help in better understanding the true environmental impacts of operational decisions.

Moreover, investigating the true environmental impacts of operations is challenging because sustainability factors, such as energy consumption, GHG emissions, water consumption, etc., are interlinked issues and addressing any of them separately will not indicate the true environmental impacts of an action. Consequently, it is necessary to respond to the sustainability challenges in a holistic manner. Recently, many publications consider climate-change-related issues; some of them refer to the risks related to water scarcity or unsustainable energy supplies. They have tried to offer guidance and introduced tools to inspire sustainability debates between stakeholders. But, what is lacking is a united approach to comprehensively assess what has often been regarded as a very diverse issue. For instance, water supply reliability with regard to water scarcity is an emerging challenge of this century. Intrinsically water risks are a local issue, which threatens public health as well as business operations. They require specific strategies related to the area, industry, company, and plant while considering the trade-offs with other interlinked environmental impact categories.

As mentioned, sustainability is accompanied by trade-offs and needs to be more closely integrated within business decisions. To effectively manage these trade-offs, a holistic evaluation of sustainability measures is needed. The detailed in-depth life-cycle-based approaches and different types of footprinting methods, as well as the aggregated results, are the output of environmental sustainability evaluation methods, which efficiently supports decision-making processes. Covering different dimensions including economic, ecologic, and social factors provides a comprehensive overview of positive and/or negative impacts along the whole supply chain. Ultimately, a fully agreed environmental aggregation method will never be reached nor will there be an agreement on the details of establishing economic scores. Therefore, quantification of frameworks, such as eco-efficiency, is the key tool for realizing the environmental consequences of different alternatives.

References

Berger M, Finkbeiner M (2010) Water footprinting: how to address water use in life cycle assessment? Sustainability 2(4):919–944

Blass V, Corbett CJ (2018) Same supply chain, different models: integrating perspectives from life cycle assessment and supply chain management. J Ind Ecol 22(1):18–30

Caro F et al (2013) Double counting in supply chain carbon footprinting. Manuf Serv Oper Manag 15(4):545–558

Cerutti AKB, Donno S, Beccaro D, Bounous GL, Giancarlo (2013) Environmental sustainability of traditional foods: the case of ancient apple cultivars in Northern Italy assessed by multifunctional LCA. J Clean Prod 52:245–252

Cerutti AK et al (2014) Life cycle assessment application in the fruit sector: state of the art and recommendations for environmental declarations of fruit products. J Clean Prod 73:125–135

Finkbeiner M (2016) Special types of life cycle assessment. Springer, Dordrecht

Finnveden G et al (2009) Recent developments in life cycle assessment. J Environ Manag 91(1): 1–21

Galli A et al (2011) Integrating ecological, carbon and water footprint: defining the footprint family and its application in tracking human pressure on the planet. Open-EU, One Planet Economy Network: Godalming

Huppes G, Ishikawa M (2005) A framework for quantified eco-efficiency analysis. J Ind Ecol 9(4):25–41

Huppes G, Ishikawa M (2007) Quantified eco-efficiency. Springer, Dordrecht

ISO (2006) Environmental management – life cycle assessment – principles and framework, in ISO 14040:2006. International Organisation for Standardization

Klöpffer W (1997) Life cycle assessment. Environ Sci Pollut Res 4(4):223–228

Larson WM et al (2012) Mitigating corporate water risk: financial market tools and supply management strategies. Water Alter 5(3):582

Leif CKH, Virtanen Y, Juntilla V, Rønning A, Ekvall T, Finnveden G (1995) *Nordic guidelines on life-cycle assessment*. Nordic Council of Ministers, Copenhagen K

Lenzen M (2008) Double-counting in life cycle calculations. J Ind Ecol 12(4):583–599

Mekonnen MM, Hoekstra AY (2010a) The green, blue and grey water footprint of farm animals and animal products. Value of water research report series no 48 Published by Copernicus Publications on behalf of the European Geosciences Union. UNESCO-IHE Institute for Water Education, The Netherlands

Mekonnen MM, Hoekstra AY (2010b) The green, blue and grey water footprint of crops and derived crop products. Copernicus Publications on behalf of the European Geosciences Union

Mentzer JT et al (2001) Defining supply chain management. J Bus Logist 22(2):1–25

Mouron P et al (2012) Sustainability assessment of crop protection systems: sustainOS methodology and its application for apple orchards. Agric Syst 113:1–15

Orr S, Cartwright A, Tickner D (2009) Understanding water risks: a primer on the consequences of water scarcity for government and business. Understanding water risks: a primer on the consequences of water scarcity for government and business, World Wildlife Fund (WWF): Washington

Saunders CM, Barber A, Sorensen L (2009) Food miles, carbon footprinting and their potential impact on trade. This is paper presented at AARES 53rd annual conference at Cairns 10th to 13th Febuary 2009.

Stock RJ, Boyer SL (2009) Developing a consensus definition of supply chain management: a qualitative study. Int J Phys Distrib Logist Manag 39(8):690–711

Stoessel FJ, Pfister R, Hellweg S, Stefanie (2012) Lifecycle inventory and carbon and water footprint of fruits and vegetables: application to a Swiss retailer. Environ Sci Technol 46(6):3253–3262

Vogtlander J (2012) Lca: a practical guide for students, designers and business managers. VSSD Science and Technology, Delft

WEF (2014) Global risks. 2014: world economic forum. World Economic Forum, Geneva

Renewable Energy Sourcing

Vishal V. Agrawal and Şafak Yücel

Abstract An effective way to reduce carbon emissions is to increase sourcing of renewable electricity. Traditionally, while the majority of the renewable electricity is sourced by utility firms in the USA, consumers are also increasingly sourcing renewable electricity by investing in rooftop solar panels. An emerging trend is corporate sourcing of renewable energy: Several corporations, including Apple, Google, IKEA, and Walmart, have committed to source 100% of their electricity from renewable sources by 2050. In this chapter, we survey the extant academic literature on sourcing of renewable energy by utility firms and consumers. We also discuss the advantages and disadvantages of different mechanisms used by corporations to source renewable energy.

Keywords Sustainable operations · Energy-related operations · Sourcing

1 Introduction

In the USA, approximately one third of carbon emissions are due to electricity generation (Environmental Protection Agency 2019). One way to reduce these emissions is to source more electricity from renewable energy sources, such as wind and solar energy, that generate electricity without carbon emissions. In the USA, the majority of the renewable energy was sourced by utility firms, which procured 63% of wind and 60% of solar energy generated in 2018 (DOE 2019, p. 23 and EIA 2019), while the rest was sourced by consumers and corporations: Residential consumers have installed more than two million solar panels (SEIA 2019), and several corporations have committed to source 100% of their electricity from renewable sources by 2050 (RE100 2019b). For example, in 2018, both Apple

V. V. Agrawal · Ş. Yücel (✉)
McDonough School of Business, Georgetown University, Washington, DC, USA
e-mail: vishal.agrawal@georgetown.edu; safak.yucel@georgetown.edu

J. M. Swaminathan, V. Deshpande (eds.), *Responsible Business Operations*,
Springer Series in Supply Chain Management 10,
https://doi.org/10.1007/978-3-030-51957-5_10

and Google have fulfilled this commitment, and Google has sourced more renewable electricity than any other non-utility firm (Apple 2019, p. 5 and Google 2019, p. 25).

In this chapter, we discuss sourcing of renewable energy from the perspective of utility firms, consumers, and corporations. The academic literature has mainly focused on procurement of renewable energy by utility firms and consumers, motivated by potential savings in electricity procurement costs and utility bills, respectively. We first review this literature on utility firms in Sect. 2, which studies a utility firm's investments and procurement from wholesale electricity markets. This stream of research has also identified how renewable and conventional sources can be integrated in an electricity grid, using mechanisms such as economic curtailment and energy storage. We then survey the academic literature on sourcing of renewable energy by consumers (e.g., through rooftop solar panels) in Sect. 3. This literature studies the timing of investments of consumers under varying investment cost and electricity prices, innovative business models that can facilitate these investments, and the effects of these investments on utility firms.

We also discuss corporate sourcing of renewable energy, which has received limited attention in the academic literature. Although the primary reason for corporations to source renewable electricity is to meet targets for corporate social responsibility and to mitigate climate change (RE100 2019a, p. 13 and Bird et al. 2017, p. 3), renewable energy can also be economically beneficial. This requires a thorough understanding of the mechanisms through which a corporation can choose to source renewable energy. Accordingly, in Sect. 4, we shall discuss the advantages and disadvantages of the following popular mechanisms: unbundled energy certificates, green pricing and tariff programs, power purchase agreements, and ownership.

2 Renewable Energy Sourcing by Utility Firms

A utility firm sources renewable and conventional electricity from its own investments or from a wholesale electricity market. Such sourcing decisions are similar to those in a supply chain (see the discussion in Wu and Ouyang 2015). There are two key factors that a firm needs to consider in practice. First, renewable sources, such as wind and solar energy, present supply-side uncertainty (or intermittency) because their generation is dependent on weather conditions. Second, conventional sources have varying levels of operational flexibility, i.e., how quickly the generation level of a source can be changed. For example, nuclear power plants are inflexible, but natural gas-fired power plants are flexible (Kök et al. 2019). Taking these into account, a utility firm needs to determine how much renewable and conventional energy to source with the objective of minimizing its cost.

For a monopolistic utility firm's investments, Aflaki and Netessine (2017) show that the firm needs to carefully account for the intermittency of renewable energy in forming its optimal capacity portfolio in renewable and conventional sources. Kök et al. (2018) identify how electricity pricing policies affect the investment decisions of a utility firm by changing the daily electricity demand pattern.[1] Kök et al. (2019) investigate the interaction between renewable and conventional energy sources in a utility firm's capacity portfolio by explicitly considering operational flexibility of conventional sources. They show that a renewable source is substituted by an inflexible, conventional source (e.g., nuclear energy) whose output cannot be adjusted quickly. Accordingly, a subsidy for an inflexible source leads to a lower renewable energy investment. In contrast, a renewable source is complemented by a flexible, conventional source (e.g., a natural gas-fired power plant). Webb et al. (2019a) characterize a utility firm's optimal investments when the firm can also invest in a combined heat and power plant, which generates electricity and uses the by-product heat for space, water, and process heating. These papers contribute to the literature by characterizing how a monopolistic utility firm should source energy jointly from conventional and renewable sources.

Another way to source electricity for a utility firm is to procure it from a wholesale electricity market. In such markets, each power plant submits its supply offer to a market operator, where the offer specifies how much electricity a plant commits to generate at different prices. The market operator also collects demand offers and matches the supply commitments with the demand at the equilibrium price (see Birge et al. 2017; Derinkuyu et al. 2019). Al-Gwaiz et al. (2016) show that the existence of inflexible power plants lessens the competition in the wholesale market, leading to higher prices. Accordingly, curtailing renewable sources can intensify the competition by making these sources more flexible. Using a Cournot competition framework, Peura and Bunn (2018) show that electricity prices can be higher due to intermittency of renewable sources even though these sources have a very low generation cost. Sunar and Birge (2019) investigate reliability implications of an undersupply penalty which is charged to renewable sources if they generate less electricity than their commitment. Contrary to the conventional wisdom that a higher undersupply penalty should increase the reliability, Sunar and Birge (2019) show that it can reduce reliability by incentivizing renewable sources to increase their generation commitment. Taken together, these papers identify remedies in coping with the negative effects of supply-side uncertainty from renewable sources. They suggest that market operators can adopt various strategies, such as implementing economic curtailment or lowering the undersupply penalty.

One significant challenge for a utility firm is to integrate renewable and conventional sources (see Parker et al. 2019 for a review). Wu and Kapuscinski (2013) show that if renewable sources are curtailed when their generation is sufficiently high, the cost of intermittency to a utility firm may be lower. Peura and Bunn (2015) analyze how increased volatility in electricity markets, due to supply-side uncertainty from renewable sources, affects pricing decisions of flexible power plants. Qi et al. (2015) and Zhou et al. (2019) show that energy storage can alleviate the intermittency problem of renewable energy. Kouvelis et al. (2019) characterize

[1]See Ata et al. (2018) for an empirical analysis on how consumers respond to different pricing policies by changing their electricity consumption throughout a day.

the optimal dispatch decisions of a utility firm with renewable and conventional sources where the conventional source is servicized by its manufacturer through a long-term contract. Overall, this literature highlights the importance of using flexible power plants and energy storage in integrating renewable and conventional sources to facilitate sourcing of renewable energy.

In order to increase sourcing of renewable energy by utility firms, governments have enacted various policies, including carbon tax (Caro et al. 2013; Drake 2018) and subsidies (Kök et al. 2018, 2019). Aflaki and Netessine (2017) and Kök et al. (2018) show that carbon tax may backfire by leading to lower renewable energy investments due to intermittency. One policy that has not received much attention in the literature is renewable portfolio standards that mandate a utility firm to procure a certain fraction of its electricity from renewable sources. In the USA, 29 states have enacted such standards, for example, California requires its utilities to source 60% of their electricity from renewables by 2030 (Barbose 2019). Drake and York (2019) find empirical evidence that renewable portfolio standards are effective in reducing sourcing of electricity from coal power plants. An interesting open research question is to analytically investigate how such policies should be designed by state regulators and how they affect sourcing decisions of utility firms.

3 Renewable Energy Sourcing by Consumers

In the USA, more than two million residential electricity consumers source renewable energy from their rooftop solar panels (SEIA 2019). A key decision for a consumer is to determine when to invest in the panels in order to minimize its electricity cost. This is a complex decision: First, investment cost and electricity price are not only uncertain but may also change over time, which creates an option value of waiting to invest. Second, the government offers various subsidies, such as the feed-in-tariff policy which provides a guaranteed price for each unit of electricity generated or the tax-rebate policy which reduces the initial investment cost. Moreover, 38 US states mandate utility firms to offer net metering policy under which a utility firm has to compensate consumers with retail electricity price for each unit of electricity generated by their panels. These policies are widely debated in practice and are subject to change, further complicating consumers' adoption decisions. Taking this rich context into account, several papers study these investments by considering investment timing decisions of consumers, innovative business models that facilitated these investments, and the effects of these investments on utility firms. We next review these streams of literature.

Hu et al. (2015) show that a consumer's decision to source renewable energy becomes more accurate as the consumer has more granular data on its electricity consumption and potential for generation. Using a real options framework to consider the uncertainty in the electricity demand of a consumer, Angelus (2019) characterizes optimal investment timing of the consumer in a renewable source. For an industrial consumer, Wang et al. (2019) identify the optimal investment level in a combined heat and power generator that produces electricity on-site and recycles the by-product heat for industrial processes. They show that it may be suboptimal to follow the common practice of choosing the capacity of the generator to match the facility's heat demand. Given adoption decisions of consumers, several papers study how the government should design subsidies. Alizamir et al. (2016) characterize the optimal feed-in-tariff policy when the investment cost decreases due to learning by doing. Goodarzi et al. (2019) show that the optimal feed-in tariff decreases as the competition between solar panel manufacturers intensifies. Babich et al. (2019) investigate a government's choice of implementing either a feed-in-tariff or a tax-rebate policy to manage investment timing decisions of consumers so as to maximize the benefit of a subsidy policy. They find that the government should prefer the feed-in-tariff policy if the price variability is high, but it should prefer the tax-rebate policy if the cost variability is high. The main contribution of this stream is to identify consumers' investment decisions in renewable energy sources under cost and price dynamics as well as subsidies. This allows for analyzing how the optimal subsidies should be set.

Renewable energy sourcing by consumers is facilitated by innovative business models offered by solar power companies, such as Vivint Solar and Sunrun. In addition to the traditional sales model, these companies offer non-ownership business models, such as leasing and power purchase agreements (see Sect. 4.3), under which they install panels at a consumer site with no upfront cost to the consumer and only sell the electricity generated by panels.[2] Guajardo (2018) empirically finds that the generation from non-residential solar panels is higher under non-ownership models as compared to that under sales. This is attributed to better design of solar panels (e.g., the direction that panels face) by the solar power company under non-ownership models. Agrawal et al. (2019b) investigate economic and environmental implications of changes in subsidies and restrictions on non-ownership business models by endogenizing a solar power company's business model decisions. Contrary to conventional wisdom, they show that a higher investment subsidy may lead to a lower adoption of solar panels and restricting a solar power company from offering leasing can increase the adoption of solar panels.

By sourcing their own electricity from renewable sources, such as solar panels, consumers demand less electricity from their utility firms (The Washington Post 2015). Consequently, utility firms lobby against such investments (The New York Times 2017), and they particularly criticize the net metering policy which compensates consumers with retail electricity price for each unit of electricity generated by their panels. Singh and Scheller-Wolf (2018) identify the socially optimal compensation scheme for consumers with rooftop solar panels. Sunar and

[2]There is also a growing literature in sustainable operations (Girotra and Netessine 2013; Agrawal et al. 2019a) that studies economic and environmental implications of non-ownership business models, such as leasing (Agrawal et al. 2012, 2018) and servicizing (Agrawal and Bellos 2016a,b, and Bellos et al. 2017).

Swaminathan (2019) show that adoption of solar panels may actually be beneficial for a utility firm because as customers generate their own electricity, the utility firm needs to procure less electricity from the wholesale electricity market, which reduces the firm's procurement cost. An open question in this stream of research is considering a consumer's joint investments in rooftop solar panels and energy storage, such as Tesla's Powerwall. Although several papers have studied utility-scale storage operations (c.f., Zhou et al. 2016 and Kapuscinski et al. 2019), it remains as an open question to study how the existence of small-scale home batteries would affect utility firms as well as sourcing of renewable energy by consumers.

4 Renewable Energy Sourcing by Corporations

Several corporations, including Apple, Google, IKEA, and Walmart, have committed to source 100% of their electricity from renewable energy by 2050 (RE100 2019b). In 2018, both Apple and Google have fulfilled this commitment, and Google has sourced more renewable electricity than any other non-utility firm (Apple 2019, p. 5 and Google 2019, p. 25). The primary reason for corporations to source renewable electricity is to meet targets for corporate social responsibility and to mitigate climate change (RE100 2019a, p. 13 and Bird et al. 2017, p. 3). Renewable energy can also be economically beneficial for corporations. For example, in the USA, among all energy sources, wind energy has the lowest levelized cost, which accounts for investment and generation costs over the lifetime of a power plant (EIA 2018, p. 7). In addition to the cost advantage, renewable sources can provide a hedge against fluctuations in the retail electricity price, diversifying the sourcing portfolio of a corporation for electricity (Bird et al. 2017, p. 3).

Renewable energy sourcing by corporations has received little attention in the literature. One notable exception is Mohseni-Taheri et al. (2018) which analyze how different mechanisms of sourcing can be used by a corporation to minimize its cost of achieving a target of renewable energy procurement level as a percentage of the corporation's demand. To better understand economic implications of corporate sourcing of renewable energy, it is imperative to analyze advantages and disadvantages of various mechanisms through which a corporation can source renewable electricity. We next discuss these mechanisms.

4.1 Unbundled Energy Certificate

A unique feature of the electricity grid is that an electron cannot be traced back to the power plant where it is generated. That is, from a consumer's perspective, it is not possible to distinguish how much of its consumption physically comes from a renewable or a conventional source (Roberts 2017). This enables the operator of a renewable source to unbundle the physical electricity and its greenness rights and sell these rights as unbundled energy certificates to a corporation. The corporation can then match its conventional energy use with the purchased certificates so as to source renewable electricity on an accounting basis (and not necessarily on a physical basis). The revenue obtained by the operator of the renewable source from these certificates increases economic value of the renewable energy investment and facilitates additional investments in the future.

Unbundled energy certificates are the primary mechanism for corporate sourcing of renewable energy, accounting for 43% of the renewable electricity sourced by corporations in 2018 (RE100 2019a, p. 8). One example is solar renewable energy certificates (SRECs) that can be bought and sold in online marketplaces, such as SRECtrade.com or SRECmarketplace.com. The main advantage of these certificates is that they do not require a long-term commitment from corporations. That is, each year, a corporation can simply buy as many certificates as it needs to cover its conventional energy use, provided that there are available certificates. Moreover, by buying certificates from already existing renewable energy investments, a corporation does not undertake a new investment's performance risk, i.e., the possibility that the investment does not generate as much electricity as expected. Finally, a renewable source requires a high upfront investment cost, and the corporation can avoid this cost by using unbundled energy certificates.

Sourcing renewable energy through unbundled energy certificates has received significant criticism in practice (McConnell 2017), and similar concerns are raised for carbon offsets—counterparts of renewable energy certificates for carbon emissions (see Gino and Toffel 2014).[3] There are three major concerns: additionality, credibility, and double counting. Additionality refers to the principle that an energy certificate should directly result in a specific new investment which would not have happened otherwise. That is, a corporation can only claim that its purchase of certificates is additional if the corporation can link its purchase to the construction of a new renewable energy project. Given that certificates are purchased from an existing project, it is difficult to argue that certificates are always additional. Credibility refers to the requirement that the renewable energy project needs to actually generate sufficient electricity to back the certificates that it claims to have. Finally, double counting refers to the possibility that same certificates can be sold to and claimed by multiple entities.

Given these challenges of unbundled energy certificates, Apple perceives them as the last resort for sourcing renewable electricity, and it follows three principles for coping with these challenges (Apple 2019, p. 11):

- Local displacement: Apple aims to displace its facilities' conventional energy use with renewable sources in the same electricity grid that its facilities operate.
- Materiality: Apple ensures that its involvement is the primary reason for a new renewable energy project to be built.

[3]Also see Gao and Souza (2019) for an analysis of how a firm should complement carbon offsets with its own investments for reducing carbon emissions.

- Accountability: Apple partners with a third-party registration system to measure and track the amount of renewable energy it sources.

Local displacement and materiality principles jointly ensure that any purchased certificates achieve additionality in the same geographical region where Apple consumes electricity. In addition, the accountability principle avoids credibility and double counting issues.

4.2 Green Pricing and Tariff Programs

Utility firms have introduced innovative programs, such as green pricing and tariffs, to facilitate sourcing of renewable electricity for their customers.[4] Under a green pricing program, a utility firm charges a price premium to its customers in order to support renewable energy investments. Under a green tariff, a utility firm signs a long-term contract (e.g., 20 years) with an investor of a renewable energy project on behalf of one of its customers, and the customer purchases electricity from the project at a pre-determined price.

Green pricing and tariff programs accounted for 31% of corporate sourcing of renewable energy in 2018 (RE100 2019a, p. 8). Compared to a green tariff, sourcing under a green pricing program is more flexible for a corporation because it does not need a long-term commitment, but it is subject to the additionality concern, similar to an unbundled energy certificate (see Sect. 4.1). On the other hand, a green tariff program ensures additionality because the renewable energy project would not occur without the funding secured from a utility firm (and backed by a corporation). From a corporation's perspective, green pricing is always an additional cost to its energy expenses, similar to an unbundled energy certificate. On the other hand, with its pre-determined, long-term price, a green tariff can potentially yield cost savings as the retail price for electricity increases over time. Finally, given the intermediary role of a utility firm under both green pricing and tariff programs, credibility and double counting concerns of unbundled energy certificates do not necessarily apply to these programs.

4.3 Power Purchase Agreement (PPA)

A power purchase agreement (PPA) is a long-term contract (e.g., 20 years) that a corporation signs with a renewable energy producer to buy electricity at a fixed

[4]For other innovative business models in the energy context, see Webb et al. (2019b) and Agrawal and Yücel (2020) for demand response, see He et al. (2019) and Wu et al. (2019) for electric vehicles, and see Aflaki et al. (2013), Ding et al. (2017), and Nguyen et al. (2018) for energy efficiency.

price.[5] In essence, through a PPA, a corporation eliminates the utility firm's intermediary role in a green tariff program (see Sect. 4.2). In 2018, PPAs accounted for 19% of corporate sourcing of renewable energy (RE100 2019a, p. 8). Corporations sign PPAs for renewable energy projects that are located either in their own facilities (referred to as on-site PPAs, e.g., rooftop of a Walmart store) or elsewhere (referred to as off-site PPAs, e.g., a wind farm built for a Google data center).

The key benefit of a PPA from a corporation's perspective is that the corporation is not exposed to the performance risk of a project. This is because the corporation only pays the investor of the renewable energy project for each unit of the electricity generated by the project. Although on-site PPAs are subject to the physical limits of available space (e.g., rooftop area for solar panels), off-site PPAs offer virtually unlimited supply to a corporation in order to source renewable electricity. Another important advantage of PPAs is that they do not require high upfront capital investment from a corporation. Finally, a PPA can provide a hedge against increases in retail electricity prices.

The main disadvantage of an on-site PPA is that certain states do not allow them. As explained by Agrawal et al. (2019b), utility firms argue that PPAs violate their monopoly rights because through PPAs, a renewable energy developer directly sells electricity to a utility's consumer. Nevertheless, corporations can sign off-site PPAs for projects located in states without restrictions on PPAs. Another disadvantage of on-site PPAs is that they are difficult to implement on a large scale due to space limitations and/or if a corporate location is leased. Both of these reasons are quoted by Walmart as primary obstacles for its renewable energy sourcing strategy, which depends mainly on on-site PPAs (Walmart 2014). Walmart further notes that it relies on on-site PPAs because this ensures additionality and avoids credibility and double counting issues of energy certificates or green pricing programs.

The main disadvantage of an off-site PPA is that it can expose a corporation to a basis risk by providing an imperfect hedge. Consider Google's primary method of procuring renewable energy for its data centers—a fixed-floating swap—where Google signs an off-site PPA with a renewable energy project (see Google 2016). Google purchases electricity and renewable energy certificates from the project at a fixed price. It then sells the electricity in a wholesale market at the project's location for floating market prices. If the floating market price is greater than the fixed PPA price, Google earns a profit; otherwise, it incurs a loss. For its energy consumption, Google purchases electricity from its utility firm at the location of its data center at a regulated retail price and uses the certificates to cover its consumption. This fixed-floating swap exposes Google to the basis risk because the wholesale price in the project's location may not be perfectly correlated with the regulated retail price in the data center's location. To reduce this risk, Google ensures that both the renewable energy project and the data center are located in the same wholesale market region so that the wholesale and retail prices are correlated. Off-site PPAs

[5] PPAs are also used by utility firms (Wu and Babich 2012) and residential consumers (Agrawal et al. 2019b).

pose additional risks, including counterparty risk, power consumption risk, and accounting risk. For a discussion of these issues, see Brasher and Opadiran (2016), Baker and McKenzie (2018), and Bartlett (2019).

4.4 Ownership

The most traditional approach to sourcing renewable electricity for a corporation is to invest in its own renewable energy project, such as rooftop solar panels. In 2018, direct ownership accounted for a mere 4% of corporate sourcing of renewable energy (RE100 2019a, p. 8). Similar to PPAs, corporations can own renewable energy projects located either on-site or off-site, where off-site projects are not subject to space limitations (see Sect. 4.3).

The main advantage of ownership is that a corporation can exert direct control on the renewable energy project and internalize all of the cost savings by eliminating any intermediaries. Ownership also ensures additionality and eliminates any credibility and double counting issues (see Sect. 4.1). Due to these advantages, ownership is the preferred method of sourcing renewable electricity for IKEA which invested 2.5 billion euros in on- and off-site renewable energy projects over the last decade (IKEA 2019). The disadvantages of ownership include the high upfront capital cost of a renewable energy project and the maintenance and service requirements of the project. Moreover, ownership of an off-site renewable energy project exposes a corporation to the basis risk, as in the case of an off-site PPA (see Sect. 4.3).

5 Conclusion

An effective way to reduce carbon emissions is to increase sourcing of renewable energy by utility firms, consumers, and corporations. Although there is a growing literature on utility firms and consumers, sourcing of renewable energy by corporations has received little attention to date. In this chapter, we first review the literature on utility firms' and consumers' sourcing of renewable energy. We then discuss how a corporation can source renewable energy using different mechanisms so as to better understand their economic implications. We summarize the advantages and disadvantages of these mechanisms in Table 1.

We also identify several directions that merit further research. For sourcing of renewable energy by utility firms, an open research question is to investigate how renewable portfolio standards (which mandate utility firms to procure a certain fraction of their electricity sales from renewable sources) should be designed by state regulators and how they affect sourcing decisions. Another open question is to study how the emergence of small-scale home batteries would affect sourcing of renewable energy from rooftop solar panels by consumers. Finally, corporate sourcing of renewable energy can be a fruitful research direction: Given the

Table 1 Mechanisms of sourcing renewable energy by corporations

Mechanism		Advantages	Disadvantages
Unbundled energy certificates		No long-term commitment Avoids performance risk Avoids capital cost Simple to implement	Lack of additionality Lack of credibility Double counting Can only be an extra cost
Green pricing		No long-term commitment Avoids performance risk Avoids capital cost	Lack of additionality Can only be an extra cost
Green tariff		Additionality Avoids performance risk Potential cost savings over time	Long-term commitment
Power purchase agreement	On-site	Avoids performance risk Moderate cost savings Additionality	Limited by physical constraints Not allowed in certain states Long-term commitment
	Off-site	Virtually unlimited capacity Avoids performance risk Moderate cost savings Additionality	Basis risk Long-term commitment
Ownership	On-site	No regulatory constraint Direct control High cost savings Additionality	Limited by physical constraints Long-term commitment High upfront cost Performance risk Maintenance requirement
	Off-site	Virtually unlimited capacity Direct control High cost savings Additionality	Basis risk Long-term commitment High upfront cost Performance risk Maintenance requirement

structural differences between different mechanisms as summarized in Table 1, what would be the optimal sourcing strategy for a corporation?

References

Aflaki S, Kleindorfer P, de Miera Polvorinos VS (2013) Finding and implementing energy efficiency projects in industrial facilities. Prod Oper Manag 22(3):503–517

Aflaki S, Netessine S (2017) Strategic investment in renewable energy sources: the effect of supply intermittency. Manuf Serv Oper Manag 19(3):489–507

Agrawal V, Atasu A, Ülkü S (2018) Leasing, modularity, and the circular economy. Working paper, Georgetown University

Agrawal V, Atasu A, Van Wassenhove L (2019a) OM forum—new opportunities for operations management research in sustainability. Manuf Serv Oper Manag 21(1):1–12

Agrawal V, Bellos I (2016a) The potential of servicizing as a green business model. Manag Sci 63(5):1545–1562

Agrawal V, Bellos I (2016b) Servicizing in supply chains and environmental implications. In: Atasu A (ed) Environmentally responsible supply chains, vol 3. Springer, 109–124

Agrawal V, Ferguson M, Toktay B, Thomas V (2012) Is leasing greener than selling? Manag Sci 58(3):523–533

Agrawal V, Toktay B, Yücel Ş (2019b) Non-ownership business models for solar energy. Working paper, Georgetown University

Agrawal V, Yücel Ş (2020) Design of electricity demand-response programs. Working paper, Georgetown University

Al-Gwaiz M, Chao X, Wu O (2016) Understanding how generation flexibility and renewable energy affect power market competition. Manuf Serv Oper Manag 19(1):114–131

Alizamir S, de Véricourt F, Sun P (2016) Efficient feed-in-tariff policies for renewable energy technologies. Oper Res 64(1):52–66

Angelus A (2019) Distributed renewable power generation and implications for capacity investment and electricity prices. Working paper, Texas A&M University

Apple (2019) Environmental responsibility report. Last Accessed 22 Dec 2019. https://perma.cc/XXQ9-XNB5

Ata B, Duran A, İşlegen Ö (2018) An analysis of time-based pricing in electricity supply chains. Working paper, University of Chicago

Babich V, Lobel R, Yücel Ş (2019) Promoting solar panel investments: feed-in-tariff versus tax-rebate policies. Manuf Serv Oper Manag Forthcoming

Baker and McKenzie (2018) The rise of corporate PPAs 2.0. Last Accessed 23 Dec 2019. https://perma.cc/E8L5-2S96

Barbose G (2019) U.S. renewables portfolio standards. 2019 Annual Status Update. Lawrence Berkeley National Laboratory. Last Accessed 19 Dec 2019. https://perma.cc/ZC6D-88GZ

Bartlett J (2019) Reducing risk in merchant wind and solar projects through financial hedges. Resources for the future. Last Accessed 23 Dec 2019. https://perma.cc/8TTT-5STK

Bellos I, Ferguson M, Toktay B (2017) The car sharing economy: interaction of business model choice and product line design. Manuf Serv Oper Manag 19(2):185–201

Bird L, Heeter J, O'Shaughnessy E, Speer B, Volpi C, Cook O, Jones T, Taylor M, Ralon P, Nilson E (2017) Policies for enabling corporate sourcing of renewable energy internationally. Last Accessed 21 Dec 2019. https://perma.cc/82SQ-33TE

Birge J, Hortaçsu A, Pavlin M (2017) Inverse optimization for the recovery of market structure from market outcomes: an application to the MISO electricity market. Oper Res 65(4):837–855

Brasher L, Opadiran N (2016) Corporations turn to synthetic PPAs to reduce energy costs, carbon footprints. Last Accessed 22 Dec 2019. https://perma.cc/ZD88-CV6B

Caro F, Corbett C, Tan T, Zuidwijk R (2013) Double counting in supply chain carbon footprinting. Manuf Serv Oper Manag 15(4):545–558

Derinkuyu K, Tanrisever F, Kurt N, Ceyhan G (2019) Optimizing day-ahead electricity market prices: increasing the total surplus for energy exchange Istanbul. Manuf Serv Oper Manag Forthcoming

Ding L, Aflaki S, Kapuscinski R (2017) Performance-based contracts for energy efficiency projects. Working paper, HEC Paris
DOE (2019) Wind technologies market report. Department of Energy (DOE). Last Accessed 23 Dec 2019. https://perma.cc/GGR9-R9SQ
Drake D (2018) Carbon tariffs: effects in settings with technology choice and foreign production cost advantage. Manuf Serv Oper Manag 20(4):667–686
Drake D, York J (2019) Kicking ash: who (or what) is winning the "war on coal"? Working paper, University of Colorado
EIA (2018) Levelized cost and levelized avoided cost of new generation resources in the annual energy outlook (2019) Energy information administration (EIA). Last Accessed 22 Dec 2019. https://perma.cc/63RW-AHKH
EIA (2019) Most U.S. utility-scale solar photovoltaic power plants are 5 megawatts or smaller. Energy information administration (EIA). Last Accessed 23 Dec 2019. https://perma.cc/9QKN-LCBZ
Environmental Protection Agency (2019) Greenhouse gas emissions. Last Accessed 23 Dec 2019. https://perma.cc/HA3E-SFY9
Gao F, Souza G (2019) Carbon offsetting with eco-conscious consumers. Working paper, Indiana University
Gino F, Toffel M (2014) Teaching Note—FIJI water: carbon negative? Harvard Business School Case No. 611–049
Girotra K, Netessine S (2013) OM forum—business model innovation for sustainability. Manuf Serv Oper Manag 15(4):537–544
Goodarzi S, Aflaki S, Masini A (2019) Optimal feed-in tariff policies: the role of technology manufacturers. Prod Oper Manag 28(5):1108–1128
Google (2016) Achieving our 100% renewable energy purchasing goal and going beyond. Last Accessed 21 Dec 2019. https://perma.cc/D6CB-JSR2
Google (2019) Environmental report. Last Accessed 22 Dec 2019. https://perma.cc/YUL4-VVPZ
Guajardo J (2018) Third-party ownership business models and the operational performance of solar energy systems. Manuf Serv Oper Manag 20(4):788–800
He L, Ma G, Qi W, Wang X (2019) Charging electric vehicle sharing fleet. Manuf Serv Oper Manag Forthcoming
Hu S, Souza G, Ferguson M, Wang W (2015) Capacity investment in renewable energy technology with supply intermittency: data granularity matters! Manuf Serv Oper Manag 17(4):480–494
IKEA (2019) Ingka group accelerates investments in renewable energy to exceed 2020 target. Last Accessed 23 Dec 2019. https://perma.cc/JK9Z-8CFS
Kapuscinski R, Wu O, Suresh S (2019) Operations and investment of energy storage in a tree network. Working paper, Indiana University
Kök G, Shang K, Yücel Ş (2018) Impact of electricity pricing policies on renewable energy investments and carbon emissions. Manag Sci 64(1):131–148
Kök G, Shang K, Yücel Ş (2019) Investments in renewable and conventional energy: the role of operational flexibility. Manuf Serv Oper Manag Forthcoming
Kouvelis P, Matsuo H, Xiao Y, Yuan Q (2019) Long-term service agreement in electricity supply chain with renewable energy penetration. Working paper, Washington University in St. Louis
McConnell C (2017) City pledges for "100% renewable energy" are 99% misleading. The wall street journal. Last Accessed 22 Dec 2019. https://perma.cc/UHF8-4ZT3
Mohseni-Taheri D, Nadarajah S, Trivella A (2018) Meeting corporate renewable power targets. Working paper, University of Illinois at Chicago
Nguyen J, Donohue K, Mehrotra M (2018) Closing a supplier's energy efficiency gap through assessment assistance and procurement commitment. Manag Sci 65(1):122–138
Parker G, Tan B, Kazan O (2019) Electric power industry: operational and public policy challenges and opportunities. Prod Oper Manag 28(11):2738–2777
Peura H, Bunn D (2015) Dynamic pricing of peak production. Oper Res 63(6):1262–1279
Peura H, Bunn D (2018) Strategic forward trading and technology. Working paper, Imperial College Business School

Qi W, Liang Y, Shen Z-MJ (2015) Joint planning of energy storage and transmission for wind energy generation. Oper Res 63(6):1280–1293
RE100 (2019a) Annual Report. Last Accessed 22 Dec 2019. https://perma.cc/79LC-5FXA
RE100 (2019b) Member companies. Last Accessed 22 Dec 2019. http://there100.org/companies
Roberts D (2017) No, city pledges to get 100% renewable energy are not misleading. Vox. Last Accessed 22 Dec 2019. https://perma.cc/U6PE-ZYE2
SEIA (2019) United states surpasses 2 million solar installations. Solar energy industries association (SEIA). Last Accessed 19 Dec 2019. https://perma.cc/V4JB-XQMN
Singh S, Scheller-Wolf A (2018) That's not fair: tariff structures for electricity markets with rooftop solar. Working paper, Carnegie Mellon University
Sunar N, Birge J (2019) Strategic commitment to a production schedule with uncertain supply and demand: renewable energy in day-ahead electricity markets. Manag Sci 65(2):714–734
Sunar N, Swaminathan J (2019) Net-metered distributed renewable energy: a peril for utilities? Working paper, University of North Carolina
The New York Times (2017) Rooftop solar dims under pressure from utility lobbyists. Last Accessed 11 Dec 2018. https://perma.cc/7QCU-CAEJ
The Washington Post (2015) Utilities wage campaign against rooftop solar. Last Accessed 11 Dec 2018. https://perma.cc/9PKA-BF5Z
Walmart (2014) Walmart's approach to renewable energy. Last Accessed 21 Dec 2019. https://perma.cc/6N5L-R5MQ
Wang W, Wu O, Souza G (2019) Design and operations of on-site combined heat and power generators under fuel price uncertainty. Working paper, Shanghai University of Finance and Economics
Webb E, Souza G, Wu O (2019a) Utility-owned combined heat and power: improving reliability and lessening environmental impact. Working paper, University of Cincinnati
Webb E, Wu O, Cattani K (2019b) Coordinating energy efficiency and incentive-based demand response. Working paper, University of Cincinnati
Wu O, Babich V (2012) Unit-contingent power purchase agreement and asymmetric information about plant outage. Manuf Serv Oper Manag 14(2):245–261
Wu O, Kapuscinski R (2013) Curtailing intermittent generation in electrical systems. Manuf Serv Oper Manag 15(4):578–595
Wu O, Ouyang Y (2015) Supply chain design and optimization with applications in energy industry. In: Ahmed S, Anjos M, Terlaky T (eds) Advances and trends in optimization with engineering applications. SIAM, pp 457–467
Wu O, Yücel Ş, Zhou Y (2019) Smart charging of electric vehicles. Working paper, Indiana University
Zhou Y, Scheller-Wolf A, Secomandi N, Smith S (2016) Electricity trading and negative prices: storage vs. disposal. Manag Sci 62(3):880–898
Zhou Y, Scheller-Wolf A, Secomandi N, Smith S (2019) Managing wind-based electricity generation in the presence of storage and transmission capacity. Prod Oper Manag 28(4):970–989

Supply Chain Transparency at Goodio Chocolate

Markko Hämäläinen, Tim Kraft, Doug Thomas, and Yanchong Zheng

Abstract This chapter examines the topic of supply chain transparency from both a practice and an academic perspective. The authors' work with Goodio, a Helsinki-based craft chocolate maker, is used as the basis of discussion. To create a transparent supply chain requires a company to both disclose information to consumers and gain visibility into its supply chain. We explore both topics in this chapter. First, regarding the disclosure of information to consumers, we overview an online consumer study the authors conducted with Goodio to test consumers' valuations of transparency. Second, to illustrate the challenges of supply chain visibility, we present examples from practice of innovative methods companies are using to gain visibility into their supply chains. We conclude the chapter by outlining potential future research directions for the topic of supply chain transparency.

Keywords Supply chain transparency · Visibility · Social responsibility · Consumer behaviors · Experiments

---

M. Hämäläinen
Department of Industrial Engineering & Management, Aalto University, Espoo, Finland

T. Kraft (✉)
Poole College of Management, North Carolina State University, Raleigh, NC, USA
e-mail: tckraft@ncsu.edu

D. Thomas
Darden School of Business, University of Virginia, Charlottesville, VA, USA
e-mail: thomasd@darden.virginia.edu

Y. Zheng
Sloan School of Management, Massachusetts Institute of Technology, Cambridge, MA, USA
e-mail: yanchong@mit.edu

J. M. Swaminathan, V. Deshpande (eds.), *Responsible Business Operations*,
Springer Series in Supply Chain Management 10,
https://doi.org/10.1007/978-3-030-51957-5_11

1 Introduction

This chapter is based on the authors' work with Goodio, a Helsinki-based craft chocolate maker that aims to make "the best chocolate in the world" while simultaneously promoting their mission of accelerating positive change in society.[1] To achieve this goal, Goodio is working to create "radical transparency" in their supply chains by establishing new levels of connectivity between its cacao producers in the global South and its consumers in the global North.

Consumers increasingly want to know more about where and how the products they purchase are being made. In practice, to create a transparent supply chain requires a company to not only determine what information to disclose to consumers but also gain visibility into its supply chain (New and Brown 2011). The goal of this chapter is to introduce the operations management community to the topic of supply chain transparency, focusing on the crucial aspects of (i) information disclosure to consumers and (ii) supply chain visibility.

Our discussion is organized as follows. First, we overview Goodio's operations and the challenges it faces in achieving radical transparency. Second, we demonstrate how online studies can be used to gain a better understanding of consumers' valuations of an issue such as supply chain transparency. Specifically, a hypothetical purchase scenario for chocolate is used to investigate how consumers' willingness to buy (WTB) is impacted by topic (e.g., environmental vs. social issues) and message format (e.g., fact-based vs. story-based). Third, we discuss some of the more innovative methods companies are using to gain visibility into their supply chains. Finally, we conclude the chapter by highlighting potential future research directions for the topic of supply chain transparency.

2 The Supply Chain for Chocolate Products

This section discusses Goodio's efforts to increase visibility into its supply chain. A comparison between a traditional chocolate supply chain and Goodio's supply chain is presented. We highlight both the progress Goodio has achieved to date and the challenges that still remain for Goodio.[2]

Founded in 2012, Goodio is a Helsinki-based craft chocolate maker that is committed to social responsibility and purpose over profit. Importantly, Goodio believes that transparency is key to achieving this promise. Goodio sells 13 different flavored dairy-free chocolate bars. In 2016, Goodio achieved over EUR1 million in

[1] https://goodiochocolate.com/

[2] Section 2 is based on the authors' case study with Goodio Chocolate. For further details, please see "Goodio Supply Chain: A Chocolatey Future?" Darden Business Publishing, OM-1613 (2019) by M. Hämäläinen, T. Kraft, D. Thomas, G. Yemen, M.Y. Zhang, and Y. Zheng.

sales with current markets in Finland, Sweden, Norway, Denmark, Germany, the United Kingdom, the United States, and Japan.

2.1 *The Chocolate Supply Chain*

There are three main ingredients for making chocolate: (1) cacao beans or ready-made cacao mass, (2) cacao butter, and (3) sugar. The key ingredient in chocolate is the cacao seeds which are grown on trees in warm climates. There are two cacao bean categories: fine/flavor from Criollo or Trinitario cacao trees and bulk from Forastero trees. Roughly 90% of the world's cacao supply comes from small farmers with approximately 5 to 12 acres of land.[3] More than 40% of cacao is grown in the Côte d'Ivoire.[4]

The cacao beans are encased in pods that farmers harvest from the trees. Farmers traditionally either sell their harvest to small traders who ship the pods to a fermentory or ferment and bag the beans themselves and take them to market to sell. Most cacao beans are either (i) sold through a physical market (e.g., a farmer selling to a small trader who then sells to an exporter) or (ii) sold directly to exporters through farmers' cooperatives. Exporters send the beans to warehouses, where they are graded and loaded on cargo vessels to reach confectionery manufacturers. Once cleaned and inspected, the beans are roasted. Then the husks of the cacao beans are removed and separated from the beans in a process called winnowing. The remaining cacao nibs are either used in the final bean-to-bar chocolate products, or they are processed into cacao mass and used in mass-produced chocolate bar products.

The cacao bean is a commodity; as such, it is vulnerable to large price fluctuations (e.g., weather can have a significant effect on the quantity and quality of crop produced). If the cacao is certified organic or fair trade, a small premium of anywhere from $100 to $200 per ton is added to the price. Fair trade cacao beans are certified based on several requirements that include labor condition standards as well as other social, economic, and environmental standards. For the most part, farmers are unaware of the monetary value of the cacao beans they grow. Indeed, roughly 6% of the total value of chocolate goes to farmers. The average cacao farmer earns only $0.93 per day.[5]

[3]"The Chocolate Industry," International Cocoa Organization, February 8, 2018, https://www.icco.org/about-cocoa/chocolate-industry.html

[4]https://www.forbes.com/sites/eshachhabra/2017/01/12/this-finnish-entrepreneur-wants-food-businesses-to-be-accountable-for-public-health/#37540f1f3f18

[5]"First taste of chocolate in Ivory Coast," YouTube video, 5:55, posted by VPRO Metropolis, Feb. 21, 2014, https://www.youtube.com/watch?v=zEN4hcZutO0 (accessed Nov. 20, 2019).

2.2 Goodio's Supply Chain

Goodio is part of the recent "bean-to-bar" movement in which chocolatiers are taking more ownership of the chocolate-making process, with some brands controlling every stage. Bean-to-bar producers make chocolate from scratch by sourcing the beans, purchasing the beans, and having the beans shipped to their own facilities to dry, roast, and winnow. Traditional chocolate producers may also control their entire supply chain. Mass production means lower costs, often through the use of a lower-quality nib or cacao mass, which makes following the supply chain more difficult. The difference with bean-to-bar is that (i) the transparency in bean-to-bar allows for traceability of the ingredients and (ii) cacao purchases between bean-to-bar producers and farmers are treated as fair trade.

The key ingredient of Goodio's products is the cacao, which is bought from Luis Mancini, a farmer/supplier with whom Goodio has developed a strong working relationship over the years. Mancini, a lawyer by trade, is the son and grandson of cacao farmers in Venezuela. After living in the United Kingdom for several years, Mancini moved back home in 2014 with a mission to give back to the community of cacao farmers who had supported his family. The political situation in Venezuela made things difficult, so Mancini moved to Peru, bought 14 hectares of land with a member of a cooperative, and started a company called CacaoTales – an agrarian cooperative for cacao farmers. The mission is "To give back to the farmers that live in the small communities where our cacao grows, helping them to rediscover their dignity and pride, by directly providing our precious beans to the world's best Chocolatiers." Mancini sources from non-GMO farms in Peru, paying above farm-gate prices to farmers for cacao beans.

Mancini's contract with the farmers commits him to taking delivery of a certain weight and quality of bean for a predetermined price, which is above the average farm-gate price. Because of his relationship with farmers in the region, Mancini is able to pull numerous cacao growers together and store their beans in a single warehouse. This ensures traceability of the beans' origin and quality and protects growers from being underpaid or exploited. As Mancini said, "less than 10% of the [price of a] chocolate bar is the cost of the cacao, 30% is marketing, and 60% is for the ingredients and profit. So for many, many, many years, [chocolatiers have] been exploiting people – farmers. They've been buying products and then never telling them how much is the real cost of what they have."

To produce the 35 tonnes of cacao it needs, Goodio requires approximately 52 farmers. Mancini represents 3 different farm communities in Peru: 1 with 42 farmers (50% female), another with 32 farmers, and a third with 37 farmers. In each community, Mancini has established a fermentation center to take ownership of the cacao. Each batch of beans can be traced back to the farm where it was grown. The fermentation center acts as a cooperative whereby farmers use the tools and knowledge CacaoTales provides to do their own fermenting. From there, the cacao beans are bought by a Cocoanect buying office in Peru and sent to a warehouse in Peru and then a Cocoanect warehouse in Europe, which is where chocolatiers such as Goodio buy beans. By controlling the fermentation process and by creating an environment such that farmers can focus primarily on production, CacaoTales is able to create a consistent-quality product which they can then charge a premium for. From the warehouse in Europe, cacao is shipped to Goodio's factory in Helsinki where it is combined with additional ingredients to make Goodio's chocolate bars.

In addition to cacao beans, Goodio uses coconut palm sugar and coconut flakes that are purchased from farmers in Sri Lanka and different flavor ingredients (e.g., blueberries) that are purchased wild, organic, and raw. As compared to cacao, Goodio has less visibility into where some of these ingredients come from. For example, Goodio purchases the coconut palm sugar from a Foodin warehouse in Jyväskylä, Finland. Foodin is an importer and producer of organic products that pays fair trade premiums to the farmers directly and works with local fair trade organizations on various projects to improve living conditions in villages. However, Goodio is unsure of which processing facility in Sri Lanka Foodin buyers purchase the palm sugar from, and it does not know where the palm sugar is warehoused before reaching Finland.

Working with suppliers to create a transparent supply chain is not always easy for Goodio. For example, Goodio has limited visibility into the process used to make the packaging for one of its products. The supplier that provides the coated foil with the printed Goodio logo and product details declines to identify its source for the foil or to reveal any technical details of the coating process, saying it is a trade secret. This highlights how even a small manufacturer such as Goodio that has only a few products and suppliers can struggle to achieve full visibility into its supply chain.

3 Testing Consumers' Valuations for Supply Chain Transparency

As Goodio works toward its goal of radical transparency, a key question for Goodio is how it should present its greater level of supply chain visibility to consumers. In order to help Goodio address this question, we design and conduct an online study that examines how consumers' valuations for transparency are influenced by the topic presented (e.g., environmental vs. social performance) and the message format (e.g., story-based vs. fact-based). To better understand Goodio's global customer base, we implement the study in both the United States and Finland. Our findings provide insights into how retailers and brands should present sustainability information to consumers (in terms of both content and format) across different cultures.

3.1 Academic Literature

There is a growing interest in empirical and experiment-based research that examines sustainability and transparency related topics. We discuss here some streams of recent works that are relevant for this book chapter and can serve as a starting point for interested researchers to further explore the related areas.

Within the sustainable operations management literature, there is a growing interest in studying how the type and nature of the information presented to individuals affects their perceptions and behavior. For example, Roels and Su (2013) show that the type of comparison information a social planner should present to households regarding their energy consumption (e.g., versus a neighbor's consumption) depends on whether individuals are ahead-seeking or behind-averse. Muthulingam et al. (2013) show that the order in which energy-saving recommendations are shown to small and medium firms significantly affects the adoption rates of the recommendations. More recently, Bansal and Muthulingam (2018) observe from field data that energy efficiency recommendations with precise costs and savings exhibit higher adoption rates than other recommendations. They then use lab experiments to identify credibility as a key mechanism driving this precision effect. Buell et al. (2019) study how transparency into the levels or changes of relative sustainability performance affects consumer choices. They find that revealing the levels (changes) of relative performance is more motivating to consumers when company performance (customer performance) is compared.

Within the literature on consumers' valuations of social responsibility, there is an emerging body of work that investigates the value of companies being transparent to consumers. Researchers have used incentivized experiments in both the laboratory (e.g., Bartling et al. 2015; Pigors and Rockenbach 2016) and the field (e.g., Kimeldorf et al. 2006; Hainmueller et al. 2015; Buell and Kalkanci 2019) to study how the disclosure of information to consumers affects consumers' valuations. For example, Pigors and Rockenbach (2016) study consumers' purchase decisions in a laboratory experiment where the wage of the worker is always known to the manager (who sets the wage), but may or may not be known to the consumers. Similarly, Hainmueller et al. (2015) conduct a field experiment to study consumers' willingness to pay a premium for coffee with a fair trade label. The authors find that (i) sales rise by almost 10% for coffee when it carries a fair trade label as compared to a generic placebo label and (ii) although consumers attach value to ethical sourcing, there is significant heterogeneity in willingness to pay for it. Buell and Kalkanci (2019) employ both lab and field studies to show that transparency into internal responsibility initiatives (e.g., paying a living wage) often outperforms transparency into external initiatives (e.g., charitable donations) in motivating sales. Related to these works, Kraft et al. (2018, 2019a) use lab experiments to test consumers' valuations of a company's social responsibility practices in its upstream supply chain. They examine how consumers' valuations are impacted by aspects such as consumer heterogeneity, reciprocity, and trust. Unlike the other studies within this space, Kraft et al. (2018, 2019a) emphasize how the company's level of supply chain visibility, rather than disclosure to consumers, impacts consumers' valuations.

Researchers have also investigated consumers' valuations of transparency with non-incentivized experiments. For example, Wei et al. (2018) use an online experiment to examine the effect of CSR claims in product packaging on consumers' perceptions. They find that consumer-oriented CSR claims (e.g., GMO-free) are more strongly associated with consumers' health benefit perceptions, whereas employee-oriented CSR claims (e.g., employee welfare) are more strongly linked to consumers' taste perceptions and attitudes toward the company. Lim et al. (2018) use survey and laboratory studies to examine how western and eastern cultures differ in their response to various types of CSR messages. They find that US subjects with dispositional attribution styles have more positive attitudes and supportive intentions toward a company using evidence-based messaging, while Korean subjects with situational attribution styles display more positive attitudes and supportive intentions toward a company using belief-based messaging. Bradu et al. (2014) use a lab experiment to investigate the effectiveness of a traceability label on consumers' willingness to buy (WTB) a chocolate bar. They find that neither the product quality nor the health warning on the product makes a difference in participants' WTB. However, both the organic and the traceability labels produce a significantly higher WTB than the no-label control condition. Kalkanci et al. (2016) use online experiments to compare mandatory versus voluntary disclosure of a company's social and environmental impacts. They find that voluntary disclosure is perceived more positively by consumers.

Our research with Goodio adds to the above literature by using online studies to test how consumers' valuations for transparency are impacted by the topic presented (e.g., environmental vs. social issues), the message format (e.g., story-based vs. fact-based), and the geographical region of the consumers (e.g., the United States vs. Finland).

3.2 Survey Design

Working with Goodio, we design and conduct an online consumer panel study. Online studies can be a valuable tool for gaining insights into potential behavioral effects before implementing changes in practice. In particular, they can provide researchers with the ability to easily scale a project, in terms of both the amount of data and the speed at which it is collected. In our case, online studies allow us to test and explore a large number of treatments to identify which topics and message formats demonstrate the most potential to increase consumers' WTB. Such a large study would not be possible with field and lab experiments which are often less flexible due to, for example, limited access to a retail setting (field experiments) or constrained participant pools (lab experiments). In this regard, online studies can provide a nice starting point for designing future lab and field experiments.

The main part of our study involves a hypothetical purchase scenario where we ask participants to state their willingness to buy (WTB) for a fictitious chocolate, Artisan Cacao. Participants' WTB is measured using a 7-point Likert scale question (1 (very unlikely) to 7 (very likely)).[6] We conduct the study in two of Goodio's primary markets – the United States and Finland.

Our study manipulates information in two dimensions: topic and message format. We consider three different topics: environmental impact (i.e., carbon footprint), internal social responsibility (i.e., fair pricing for farmers), and external social responsibility (i.e., community development with donations). In parallel, we consider two different message formats: story-based (i.e., a quote from the beneficiary) and fact-based (i.e., a statement of fact about the impact).[7] This design yields a 3 $\times$ 2 factorial design with six treatments plus one control condition. We use a between-subject design, i.e., each participant is presented with only one of the seven conditions.

Figure 1 illustrates two example treatments that are shown to the US participants for the topic of fair pricing for farmers. Figure 1a is an example of story-based messaging; and Fig. 1b is an example of fact-based messaging. The control treatment only includes a picture of the chocolate, the price, and the "About the product" texts. Finland participants observe the same pictures, topics, and messaging but with the texts translated into Finnish and the price converted to Euros.

After answering the WTB question, participants answer a series of questions on product perception (e.g., product quality, product cost, and price fairness), company perception (e.g., trust in the company), behavioral mechanisms (e.g., familiarity with sustainability issues), general shopping experiences (e.g., frequency of purchasing chocolates and the extent to which sustainability factors are considered when making purchase decisions), and demographics (e.g., age, gender, income level, and education level).

3.3 Survey Implementation

Given a limited pool of online participants in Finland, we use a multi-step approach to collect our data. The Finland participant pool consists of enough participants to run only four treatments plus the control treatment. Therefore, we first conduct the study in the United States for all seven treatments, with the goal being to identify

[6] We also elicit participants' willingness to pay (WTP) using a scale ranging from \$2 to \$12 for US participants and EUR2 to EUR12 for Finland participants. However, price is not a main focus of our study since Goodio has minimal influence on the prices its retail partners charge. Thus, we do not emphasize our WTP findings here.

[7] We initially also considered a third message format – belief-based (i.e., a statement of values that the company commits to). However, the results from our first wave of data collection showed that belief-based messaging has no effect on participants' WTB for any of the topics studied. Thus, we omit the discussion of this message format.

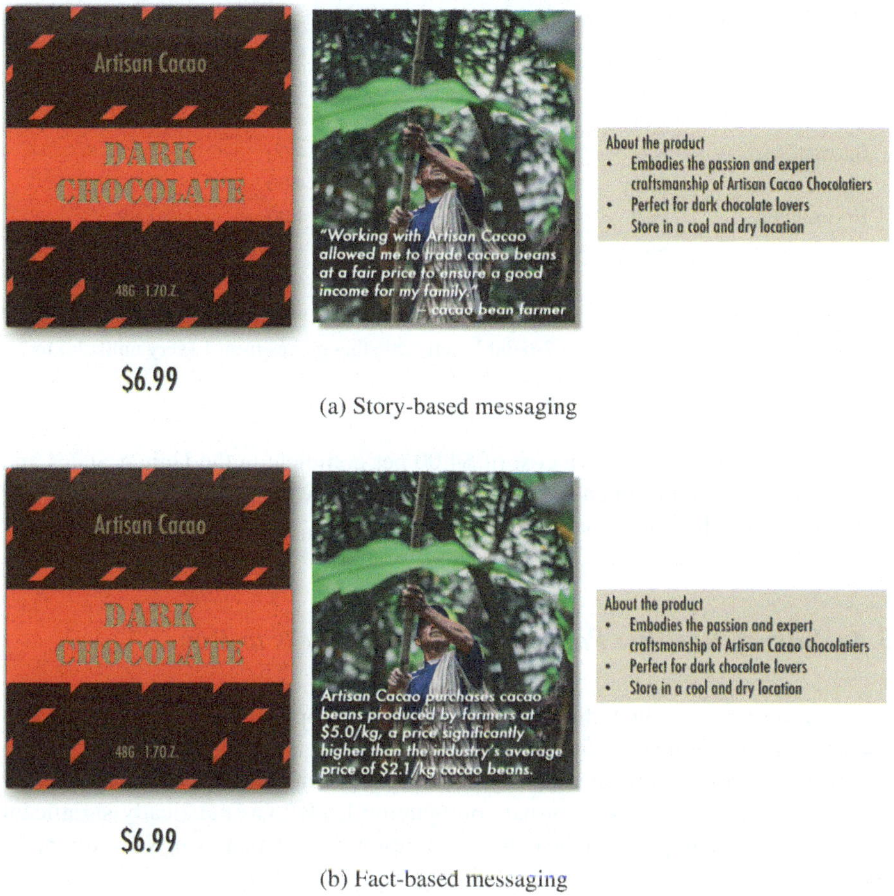

Fig. 1 Example treatments: internal social responsibility (fair pricing for farmers) condition (**a**) Story-based messaging (**b**) Fact-based messaging

the four most promising treatments to run in Finland. For the US study, we target the demographics representative of Goodio's customers: participants of age 25–50, with a target male/female split of 40%/60% and an annual household income of at least $100,000. A total of 1,361 US participants participated in the US study, collecting approximately 90–100 participants for each treatment.

For the Finland study, we had to target a wider demographic to ensure a sufficient number of participants. Specifically, we target participants of age 18–65, with a male/female split of 50%/50% and an annual household income of at least $50,000 (USD). A total of 509 Finland participants participated in this study, with the sample size evenly split among the five treatments.

We worked with a professional survey sampling service provider to conduct the online studies in both countries. The survey took participants on approximately

Table 1 US consumers' willingness to buy

Topic	Message format	Mean	Median	Std dev
External SR	Fact	3.62	4.00	1.99
	Story	3.73	4.00	1.94
Internal SR	Fact	3.80	4.00	1.87
	Story	3.71	4.00	1.92
Environment	Fact	3.38	4.00	1.89
	Story	3.79	4.00	1.82
Control	–	3.28	3.00	1.98
Overall	–	3.62	4.00	1.86

Note: Values above are based on a 7-point Likert scale that ranges from 1 (very unlikely) to 7 (very likely)

12–15 min to complete; with a cost of $4.00 per complete in the United States and $4.40 per complete in Finland. Note that participants were paid for completing our study; however, their decisions were not incentivized.

3.4 *Survey Results: Participants' Willingness to Buy*

To test whether or not including a message (i.e., any topic and any message format) increases US or Finland participants' WTB, we perform an ANOVA test to analyze our aggregate results. For specific comparisons between treatments such as whether a specific topic and message format combination leads to a statistically significant change in WTB compared to the control condition, we use pairwise Wilcoxon rank-sum tests.

Table 1 presents the summary statistics of US consumers' WTB for the three topics and two message formats, as well as the control condition and the overall values. Figure 2 illustrates US consumers' mean WTB for all treatments. When not differentiating message formats, we find that participants' WTB is significantly higher in both the internal (i.e., fair pricing) and external (i.e., community development) social responsibility conditions than in the control condition. In contrast, transparency into the environmental impact does not lead to a significant change in WTB. Differentiating message formats, we observe that this latter nonsignificant result is primarily due to a lack of significant change in WTB (relative to the control condition) when fact-based messaging regarding the company's environmental impact is shown. In all other five treatment conditions, participants' WTB is significantly higher with transparency than without transparency.

Given these results, we conduct the Finland study with four transparency treatments and the control condition. The four treatments involve the internal vs. external social responsibility topics for the story-based vs. fact-based message formats. Table 2 presents the summary statistics of Finland consumers' WTB for the two topics and two message formats, as well as the control condition and the

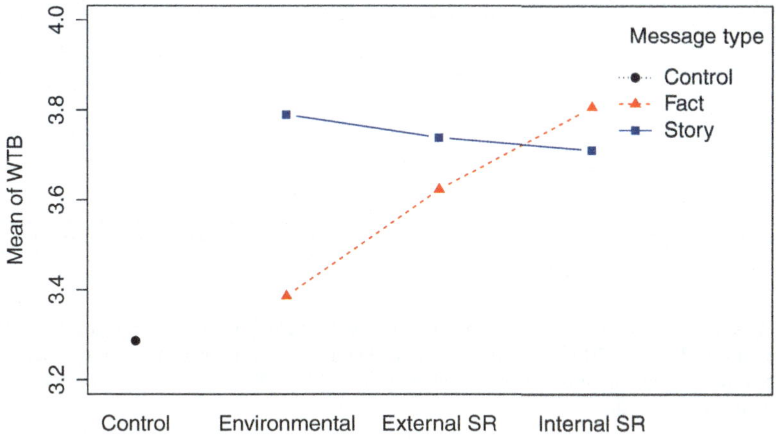

Fig. 2 Mean willingness to buy of US participants by treatment

Table 2 Finland consumers' willingness to buy

Topic	Message format	Mean	Median	Std dev
External SR	Fact	2.87	2.00	1.79
	Story	2.90	3.00	1.49
Internal SR	Fact	3.06	3.00	1.49
	Story	3.32	3.00	1.74
Control	–	2.51	2.00	1.65
Overall	–	2.93	3.00	1.65

Note: Values above are based on a 7-point Likert scale that ranges from 1 (very unlikely) to 7 (very likely)

overall values. Figure 3 presents a comparison of the consumers' WTB across these five conditions between the two countries. We observe that in both countries, the participants' WTB is significantly higher in any of the transparency treatments than in the control condition. This is particularly true for the fair pricing topic. This finding aligns with results from previous studies. For example, Buell and Kalkanci (2019) similarly find that transparency into internal responsibility initiatives (e.g., paying a living wage) often outperforms transparency into external initiatives (e.g., charitable donations) in motivating sales.

The key difference between the two countries resides in the preferred message format. In the United States, the strongest increase in WTB occurs for fair pricing and *fact-based* messaging. Conversely, in Finland, the strongest increase occurs for fair pricing and *story-based* messaging. This is an interesting insight into how Goodio should be communicating with consumers about its social responsibility efforts. Goodio's work to provide cacao farmers with fair pricing is generally well received across all participants. However, Finnish consumers appear to prefer more

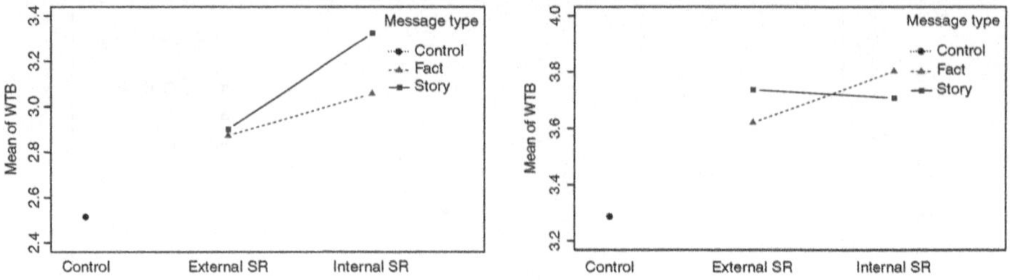

(a) Finland (b) US

Fig. 3 Comparing the effects of transparency on participants' WTB between the United States and Finland (**a**) Finland (**b**) United States. (Note: The Finland version of the survey used a higher price than the US version of the survey. This helps to explain the differences in mean WTB values between the two countries)

personal messaging such as quotes from the farmers, whereas US consumers prefer more detail-oriented messaging such as fact-based results from Goodio's efforts.

The above two findings consistently hold when we dissect our findings further by demographics such as age, education level, gender, and income level. Interestingly, we find a strong gender difference. Specifically, in both countries male participants are highly influenced by the inclusion of transparent messaging, whereas female participants are not. The data shows that male participants' WTB is much lower than female participants' WTB in the *control* condition, and incorporating messaging helps to raise male participants' low WTB for the chocolate without any messaging.

3.5 Survey Results: Perceptions of the Company, Purchase Experience, and Product

To further enhance our understanding of the potential benefits to transparency, we include in the survey additional questions to test how transparency influences participants' perceptions of the company, the purchase experience, and the product. To do so, we take participants' responses to these perception questions as the dependent variable and use similar methods as before to analyze the effects of showing a transparent message on participant perceptions.

We highlight two observations. First, for the United States (either fair pricing or community development topic) and Finland (the fair pricing topic), enhanced transparency always strengthens participants' (i) positive feelings from purchasing the product; (ii) satisfaction toward the company; and (iii) trust in the company. Second, we find almost no benefit to transparency with respect to the perception of the product. That is, including a transparent message about either fair pricing or community development generally does not increase participants' perception of the product's quality or the cost to make the product. In this regard, our findings suggest that any goodwill resulting from transparency into social responsibility practices is primarily related to the actors and actions of doing good but not to the product itself.

4 Improving Supply Chain Visibility: Innovations from Practice

As previously discussed, creating a transparent supply chain requires a company to not only disclose information to consumers but also gain visibility into its supply chain. In practice, many companies do not have extensive visibility into their supply chains. For example, a recent study by The Sustainability Consortium found that 81% of the 1,700 companies surveyed lacked full visibility into the social responsibility practices of their suppliers and 54% had no visibility at all (The Sustainability Consortium 2016). One reason why so many companies lack visibility is that gaining visibility into a supply chain can require a significant investment of time and resources (Doorey 2011). For example, in the United States, public companies spent $709M and 6 million staff hours in their efforts to comply with the 2010 Dodd-Frank regulation which included stipulations requiring public companies to disclose whether or not their products contained conflict minerals (Chasan 2015). Still, 90% of companies who attempted to comply with the regulation admitted after the fact that they remained unsure whether their products were conflict minerals-free.

While well-known brands such as Patagonia, Nike, and H&M are considered leaders with respect to supply chain transparency, many of the more innovative models for gaining visibility into supply chains are occurring within smaller companies. We next discuss some innovative methods companies have used in practice to enhance their visibility into their suppliers' practices.

LaborVoices[8] is a small software company which has developed an innovative way to crowdsource increased transparency using workers in a supply chain and their mobile phones. Specifically, the LaborVoices software allows workers to call or text from their mobile devices at any time to report issues that are occurring in their workplace. LaborVoices then takes this large amount of dynamic data to monitor real-time factory conditions and create rankings and analytics on factories. The company provides the aggregate results to brands and factories on a subscription basis to enable factory improvements, risk mitigation, and improved working conditions. LaborVoices primarily focuses on garment factories in Bangladesh and Turkey. It currently has over 40,000 workers from over 400 factories providing data to its platform.

The second example involves Taylor Guitars, a musical instrument maker who used vertical integration to increase its visibility into its upstream supply chain (Orsdemir et al. 2019). To produce its guitars, Taylor Guitars sources large amounts

[8]https://www.laborvoices.com/

of ebony wood. In the past, it procured its ebony wood from a mill in Cameroon, which sourced its raw wood from numerous suppliers. On a visit to Cameroon to better understand the sourcing process, the owner of Taylor Guitars, Bob Taylor, discovered the mill demonstrated a number of poor labor practices. Furthermore, due to the industry norm to only use pure black ebony wood to make guitars (rather than ebony wood with striped colors), ebony suppliers on average would cut down ten trees to find one tree with the desired pure black color. To fix these issues, Taylor chose to vertically integrate by buying the mill in Cameroon. Taylor Guitars improved the labor standards of the mill and began to accept ebony wood with stripes from suppliers at prices equal to the traditional black wood. In doing so, Taylor Guitars reshaped the industry by changing both instrument makers' and consumers' preferences regarding black wood. Furthermore, Taylor Guitars created a new business for itself by becoming a supplier of ebony wood to its competitors.

Finally, the third example demonstrates how a third party can help to eliminate key barriers to increasing visibility in a supply chain. GreenBlue is an environmental nonprofit dedicated to increasing the transparency of the chemicals and substances used in products and supply chains (Karaer et al. 2017). One significant barrier to creating this transparency is intellectual property. Suppliers are often reluctant to disclose the chemical and material makeup of their products to buyers due to suppliers' fears of revealing commercial secrets and losing their competitive advantage. In order to alleviate this barrier, GreenBlue built a platform called Material IQ (MiQ) for sharing sensitive chemical-toxicity information between upstream suppliers and downstream buyers without divulging intellectual property secrets. Specifically, suppliers submit sample products to SciVera, a GreenBlue partner and third-party chemical safety assessment provider. SciVera then evaluates and scores the chemical makeup and the associated risks of the product. This information is then entered into MiQ. Buyers who subscribe to the platform can view potential hazards of the product, but importantly cannot see enough information to reverse engineer the product, thus protecting suppliers' intellectual property secrets.

5 Conclusion and Future Research Directions

In this chapter, we hope to introduce the operations management community to the topic of supply chain transparency by (i) demonstrating how online studies can be used to examine consumers' valuations of transparency and (ii) highlighting innovations occurring in practice to increase supply chain visibility. From an academic standpoint, this is a rich area for research, particularly because the topic can be studied from the viewpoints of different stakeholders such as companies, regulators, nonprofits, or consumers. We now conclude the chapter by discussing some potential future research directions.

From an empirical perspective, opportunities exist to continue to investigate consumers' valuations of transparency with lab and field experiments, in both retail and service settings. In particular, further insight is needed regarding how consumer heterogeneity impacts consumers' decision-making. Our hope is that the growing body of knowledge on consumers will eventually form the basis for field and lab experiments that examine upstream transparency topics. For example, studies that test how consumers' valuations impact either suppliers' adoption of sustainability practices or disclosure of sustainability information would be interesting. We should note that opportunities also exist to study supply chain visibility topics with secondary data sets (e.g., Caro et al. 2018; Swift et al. 2019). For example, Caro et al. (2018) empirically examine factors that lead suppliers to engage in unauthorized subcontracting. Swift et al. (2019) use data from conflict minerals disclosures and event study methods to analyze differences in operating and market performance between firms with high vs. low supply chain visibility.

From a modeling perspective, there is a growing body of work that examines the intersection between social responsibility and supply chain transparency (e.g., Lewis et al. 2016; Chen and Lee 2017; Chen et al. 2019; Kraft et al. 2019b). However, there are still ample research opportunities within this literature stream. For example, a natural progression for research in this space would be to examine multi-tier supply chains. This is because social responsibility issues often occur in the upper tiers of supply chains; however, firms typically have limited visibility into these tiers. Only recently have OM researchers begun to study social responsibility issues in multi-tier settings with modeling approaches (e.g., Huang et al. 2018; Karaer et al. 2019).

Finally, an emerging issue in practice that deserves further attention in the academic literature is the intersection of supply chain transparency and policy. In the past decade, select regulations have been put into place to increase the transparency in supply chains. For example, in 2011 California enacted the Transparency in Supply Chains Act which requires retailers with sufficiently high sales in California to disclose their efforts to eradicate slavery and human trafficking from their supply chains. In 2010, the US government enacted the Dodd-Frank Act. As part of the act, public companies are required to disclose whether or not their products contain conflict minerals. While it is debatable how effective these laws have been (Chasan 2015; Messinger 2016), the regulations have created challenging problems for firms and have begun to motivate research in the sustainable OM literature (e.g., Cho et al. 2019; Swift et al. 2019; Zhang et al. 2019).

Acknowledgments The authors would like to thank Gerry Yemen (University of Virginia), Meng Yuan Zhang (MIT), and Jingjing Piao (MIT) for their help with this chapter.

References

Bansal S, Muthulingam S (2018) How does precision affect the adoption of energy efficiency practices? Evidence from the field and laboratory data. Working paper, The Pennsylvania State University, State College, PA

Bartling B, Weber R, Yao L (2015) Do markets erode social responsibility? Quarterly Journal of Economics 130(1):219–266

Bradu C, Orquin JL, Thøgersen J (2014) The mediated influence of a traceability label on consumers willingness to buy the labelled product. Journal of Business Ethics 124:283–295

Buell R, Kalkanci B (2019) How transparency into internal and external responsibility initiatives influences consumer choice: Evidence from the field and lab. Working paper, Harvard University, Boston, MA

Buell R, Mariadassou S, Zheng Y (2019) Relative performance transparency: Effects on sustainable choices. Working paper, Harvard University, Boston, MA

Caro F, Lane L, Cuenca ASDT (2018) Can brands claim ignorance? Unauthorized subcontracting in apparel supply chains. Working paper, UCLA Anderson School of Management, Los Angeles, CA

Chasan E (2015) U.S. firms struggle to trace conflict minerals, *The Wall Street Journal*, Aug. 3, available at https://www.wsj.com/articles/u-s-firms-struggle-to-trace-conflict-minerals-1438636575

Chen L, Lee H (2017) Sourcing under supplier responsibility risk: The effects of certification, audit, and contingency payment. Management Science 63(9):2773–3145

Chen S, Zhang Q, Zhou Y (2019) Impact of supply chain transparency on sustainability under NGO scrutiny, forthcoming in Production and Operations Management

Cho S, Fang X, Tayur S, Xu Y (2019) Combating child labor: Incentives and information disclosure in global supply chains. Manufacturing & Service Operations Management 21(3):692–711

Doorey D (2011) The transparent supply chain: From resistance to implementation at Nike and Levi-Strauss. J Bus Ethics 103(4):587–603

Hainmueller J, Hiscox M, Sequeira S (2015) Consumer demand for the Fair Trade label: Evidence from a multi-store field experiment. Review of Economics & Statistics 97(2):242–256

Huang L, Song J, Swinney R (2018) Managing social responsibility in multitier supply chains. Working paper, Duke University, Durham, NC

Kalkanci B, Ang E, Plambeck E (2016) Strategic disclosure of social and environmental impacts in a supply chain. In: Atasu A (ed) Environmentally Responsible Supply Chains, Springer, New York, NY, pp 223–240

Karaer Ö, Kraft T, Khawam J (2017) Buyer and nonprofit levers to improve supplier environmental performance. Production and Operations Management 26(6):1163–1190

Karaer Ö, Kraft T, Yalçın P (2020) Supplier development in a multi-tier supply chain. *IISE Transactions* (formerly *IIE Transactions*) 52(4):464–477

Kimeldorf H, Meyer R, Prasad M, Robinson I (2006) Consumers with a conscience: Will they pay more? Contexts 5(1):24–29

Kraft T, Valdés L, Zheng Y (2018) Supply chain visibility and social responsibility: Investigating consumers' behaviors and motives. Manufacturing & Service Operations Management 20(4):617–636

Kraft T, Valdés L, Zheng Y (2019a) Consumer trust in social responsibility communications: The role of supply chain visibility. Working paper, North Carolina State University, Raleigh, NC

Kraft T, Valdés L, Zheng Y (2019b) Motivating supplier social responsibility under incomplete visibility, forthcoming in Manufacturing & Service Operations Management

Lewis T, Liu F, Song J (2016) A dynamic mechanism for achieving sustainable quality supply. Working paper, Duke University, Durham, NC

Lim RE, Sung YH, Lee WN (2018) Connecting with global consumers through corporate social responsibility initiatives: A cross-cultural investigation of congruence effects of attribution and communication styles. Journal of Business Research 88:11–19

Messinger L (2016) California law aimed at slowing human trafficking and forced labor should do more, report says, *The Guardian*, Jan. 22, available at https://www.theguardian.com/sustainable-business/2016/jan/22/california-anti-slavery-law-development-international-sun-maid-asia-human-trafficking

Muthulingam S, Corbett C, Benartzi S, Oppenheim B (2013) Energy efficiency in small and medium-sized manufacturing firms: Order effects and the adoption of process improvement recommendations. Manuf Serv Oper Manag 15(4):596–615

New S, Brown D (2011) The four challenges of supply chain transparency, *The European Business Review*, July 20, available at http://www.europeanbusinessreview.com/challenges-supply-chain-transparency/

Orsdemir A, Hu B, Deshpande V (2019) Managing opportunistic supplier product adulteration: Deferred payments, inspection, and combined mechanisms. Manufacturing & Service Operations Management 21(2):417–434

Pigors M, Rockenbach B (2016) Consumer social responsibility. Management Science 62(11):3123–3137

Roels G, Su X (2013) Optimal design of social comparison effects: Setting reference groups and reference points. Management Science 60(3):606–627

Swift C, Guide V, Muthulingam S (2019) Does supply chain visibility affect operating performance? evidence from conflict minerals disclosures. Journal of Operations Management 65(5):406–429

The Sustainability Consortium (2016) Greening global supply chains. The sustainability consortium 2016 impact report, available at https://www.sustainabilityconsortium.org/wp-content/themes/enfold-child/assets/pdf/2016-impact-report.pdf

Wei W, Kim G, Miao L, Behnke C, Almanza B (2018) Consumer inferences of corporate social responsibility (CSR) claims on packaged foods. Journal of Business Research 83:186–201

Zhang H, Aydin G, Heese H (2019) Curbing the use of conflict minerals: A supply network perspective. Working paper, Indiana University, Bloomington, IN

Auditing, Inspections, and Testing for Social Responsibility in Supply Networks

Milind Dawande and Anyan Qi

Abstract The operations management literature has investigated the role of auditing, testing, and inspections, in ensuring socially responsible actions by supply chain partners. Specifically, studies have examined the auditing of suppliers for noncompliance of socially responsible practices and the inspection and/or testing of products for social responsibility violations. In this chapter, we examine this stream of literature and summarize its main insights.

Keywords Social responsibility · Supply networks · Auditing · Inspection · Testing

1 Introduction

Supply networks are fast becoming complex and global – driven primarily by the need to make them efficient and economically viable, and maximize customer satisfaction. It is now typical for a firm to have its different entities involved in sourcing, manufacturing, transportation, and distribution activities spread across geographically diverse locations. Further, improved access to cheaper labor markets and efficient production zones, and efforts to mitigate the risk inherent in relying on a single supplier for a component or raw material, have increased both the number of tiers in a supply network and the breadth of each tier. All this, coupled with the increasing awareness and expectations of social and environmental responsibility from external stakeholders, has heightened the challenges firms encounter in ensuring that their supply network partners are compliant or even exceed expectations. The increased complexity has correspondingly generated the need for mechanisms to achieve this important goal. To this end, the operations management literature

M. Dawande (✉) · A. Qi
Naveen Jindal School of Management, The University of Texas at Dallas, Richardson, TX, USA
e-mail: milind@utdallas.edu; axq140430@utdallas.edu

J. M. Swaminathan, V. Deshpande (eds.), *Responsible Business Operations*, Springer Series in Supply Chain Management 10,
https://doi.org/10.1007/978-3-030-51957-5_12

has investigated the role of auditing, testing, and inspections. In this chapter, we examine this stream of literature and summarize its main insights.

We organize the discussion in two sections. In Sect. 2, we discuss studies that analyze the auditing of suppliers for noncompliance of socially responsible practices, e.g., the use of child labor, unsafe working conditions, and excessive environmental pollution. In Sect. 3, we discuss papers that analyze the inspection and/or testing of products for social responsibility violations, e.g., deliberate adulteration of milk and other agricultural products.

2 Auditing Suppliers for Socially Responsible Practices

Section 2.1 discusses the main insights from studies that analyze the auditing of a single supplier by a buyer or a regulator. Section 2.2 examines work in which one or more suppliers are audited in a supply network with more than two players involved.

2.1 Auditing of a Supplier by a Buyer or a Regulator

While buying firms can perform (costly) audits to detect the socially irresponsible behavior of the suppliers, the suppliers may exert (costly) effort to evade buyers' audits instead of exerting (costly) effort to improve their practices. Plambeck and Taylor (2016) study the effectiveness of audits in a supply chain with one buyer and one supplier, under the possibility that the supplier can hide her unsafe practices from the buyer's audit. The authors consider a simultaneous game where the buyer determines his auditing effort and a supplier decides her responsibility effort and hiding effort. The higher the buyer's auditing effort, the higher is the chance of him identifying the supplier's unsafe practice. The higher the supplier's responsibility effort, the more likely it is that her practices are safe. The higher the supplier's hiding effort, the less likely it is for the buyer to identify her unsafe practices. If the supplier's practices turn out to be safe, then both the buyer and the supplier earn their respective profits from selling the product in the market. If the supplier's practices turn out to be unsafe and she fails the audits of the buyer, the buyer does not source from the supplier, and both firms earn zero profit. If the supplier is unsafe but passes the buyer's audits, then both the buyer and the supplier still earn their respective profits from selling the product in the market but incur their respective expected damage costs due to the public identification of the supplier's unsafe practices. The authors show that under a backfire condition, which depends on the relative convexity of the supplier's hiding cost, intuitively appealing actions for the buyer such as increasing the auditing effort could lead to undesired outcomes: the supplier may choose a higher hiding effort to evade the buyer's audits and exert a lower responsibility effort, which reduces the likelihood that the supplier's practices are safe. Thus, given the supplier's evasive behavior, the buyer should be cautious in choosing actions aimed at improving the supplier's social responsibility.

Suppliers in developing countries sometimes employ child labor to reduce production cost. When such practices are exposed in public, the buyers in developed countries who source from these suppliers incur a loss of goodwill. Cho et al. (2018) explore how a buyer can influence a supplier's use of child labor through two levers: the wholesale price and the level of auditing. The authors examine two scenarios, depending on whether the buyer's decision on his auditing level is taken before or after the supplier's choice of labor. Under the *nondisclosure* scenario, the buyer first decides a wholesale price to offer to the supplier. Then, the buyer decides the auditing level, and the supplier simultaneously decides whether to employ child labor. The buyer then audits the supplier according to the chosen level: if the supplier is found using child labor, then she implements corrective actions and incurs the corresponding cost. After auditing, the buyer pays the supplier the wholesale price specified in the first stage, sells the product in the market, and earns the corresponding revenue. Finally, external auditing by a third-party occurs: if the supplier is exposed of the use of child labor, then she loses a portion of the future business with the buyer, and the buyer suffers a loss of goodwill. Under the *disclosure* scenario, the sequence of events is similar to that in the nondisclosure scenario, except that the buyer decides his auditing level *before* the supplier's choice of labor, and the external auditing effort of the third-party is contingent upon the buyer's auditing level. The following strategies to combat child labor are suggested. When the auditing cost is low, it is effective for the buyer to conduct auditing with a low wholesale price. When the auditing cost is high, the buyer should offer a high wholesale price to raise the opportunity cost of the supplier's use of child labor instead of using auditing to deter the use of child labor. Under the disclosure scenario, a hybrid strategy may be more efficient: the buyer should conduct auditing with a medium wholesale price – here, the supplier has an incentive to accept the medium wholesale price and not hire child labor because he is informed that auditing is comprehensive. These strategies illustrate a "strategic substitutes" relationship between the wholesale price premium and the auditing level: if a higher wholesale price is offered, less auditing is needed. The authors also show that information disclosure may not always be effective in combating child labor: the buyer could be better off by offering a low wholesale price and disclosing a low auditing effort, resulting in a higher use of child labor by the supplier. The adverse effect can be mitigated if the buyer can decide the supplier's compensation to the labor force as part of her corrective actions or if the buyer implements a zero tolerance policy under which the business with the supplier is terminated upon the discovery of the use of child labor.

While suppliers in emerging economies may engage in socially irresponsible actions to save production costs, they may differ in intrinsic ethical levels. Chen and Lee (2017) study how to mitigate socially noncompliant behavior in a dyadic supply chain with one buyer and one supplier, through three instruments – supplier certification, process audit, and contingency payment – under heterogeneity in the supplier's (private) intrinsic ethical level. The authors analyze the following setting: A buyer procures a unit of a product from a supplier whose production cost is uncertain and who has a private ethical cost (low or high). The supplier endogenously decides whether or not to engage in noncompliant actions vis-à-vis social responsibility: if he does so, then he saves a portion of his realized production cost; if the noncompliance is discovered in public (with a probability), the supplier incurs a monetary penalty cost and so does the buyer.

- In the base model where none of the three instruments are available, the sequence of events is as follows: the buyer first offers a wholesale price to the supplier, then the supplier's uncertain cost is realized, and the supplier decides whether to engage in socially irresponsible actions, and finally both the buyer and the supplier incur a penalty if any violation is discovered in public.
- In the model where supplier certification is available, the sequence of events is similar to that in the base model, except that the contract offered by the buyer now includes a costly "certification stringency level" besides the wholesale price. The supplier then needs to decide whether to get certified – the high-type ethical supplier always passes certification while the low-type only passes with a probability determined by the stringency level – and then accepts the contract associated with the certification outcome.
- In the model where process audit is available, the sequence of events is similar to that in the base model, with the following differences. The buyer offers a contract with both a (costly) auditing level and a wholesale price; the buyer audits the supplier according to the chosen contractual term after the supplier decides whether or not to engage in a social responsibility violation but before the public discovers the violation (if there is one) – if the audit reveals the violation, then the supplier incurs the cost of implementing corrective actions.
- In the model where contingency payment is available, a fixed auditing level together with a delayed payment term – which is contingent upon the supplier passing the audit – is considered in the contract.

The authors also consider combinations of these different instruments. When none of the three instruments are available, it is shown that the buyer can only offer a pooling contract; this makes it difficult for an ethical supplier to survive in the market. It is also shown that supplier certification, process audit, and contingency payment are effective in lowering the supplier's social responsibility risk. When used alone, supplier certification is the most effective among the three instruments. When used together, these instruments are complementary to each other, meaning that when they are used jointly, there is an additional reduction in the sourcing cost due to a further lowering of the supplier's responsibility risk.

The supplier certification discussed in Chen and Lee (2017) is typically offered by a third-party certifier. Chen et al. (2019b) extend the analysis of the supplier certification instrument by considering the possibility of a low-quality supplier bribing the third-party certifier to pass the supplier certification – this may lead to adverse consequences for the buyer and the certifier if the false certification is identified in public. The authors analyze a buyer's decision to purchase a single unit of product from a supplier. The product's quality follows a uniform distribution a priori; the realized value is the supplier's private information. The buyer sets a minimum quality threshold, and the supplier is certified by a third-party certifier who may or may not be ethical. If the supplier's quality is above the minimum requirement, then the supplier passes the certification, sells the product to the buyer, and earns a fixed payment from the buyer. If the supplier's quality is below the minimum level, then he may still get certified if the certifier is unethical and accepts a side payment from the low-quality supplier. In that case, the supplier sells the product to the buyer and earns the same fixed payment. However, if the false certification is discovered in public, then the certifier incurs a penalty, and the buyer too incurs the cost due to the associated negative externality. The paper reveals the tradeoff faced by the buyer to set the certification level: if the requirement is too high, the supplier is likely to fail the standard and thus may seek to collude with the certifier; if the requirement is too low, the supplier may also seek to collude with the certifier because the required side payment is also lower. It is shown that the equilibrium certification standard can be higher or lower relative to the collusion-free benchmark. Three key factors drive the result: the probability of the certifier being unethical, the certifier's penalty cost if collusion is discovered, and the buyer's externality cost if collusion between the supplier and the certifier is identified. Interestingly, the probability of collusion may increase in the certifier's penalty but strictly decreases in the buyer's externality cost. Thus, it is more effective to control collusion by increasing the buyer's externality cost.

The auditing of firms serves to improve transparency, not just within the supply chain but also externally from the perspective of regulators and investors. Kim (2015) considers the following setting: A firm's production may fail to comply with environmental standards at random times, causing damage to the environment until the factors causing the noncompliance are corrected. To mitigate the negative environmental consequences, a regulator may inspect the firm and impose penalties if noncompliance is detected or the firm may voluntarily disclose noncompliance in exchange for lower penalties. The author investigates whether the regulator should employ a periodic or random inspection policy, given the random nature of the environmental violation and the firm's strategic disclosure behavior, and how the inspection frequency and penalty should be determined. To this end, the author considers an infinite horizon over which a firm's state of production is defined by a two-state continuous-time Markov chain, alternating between the compliance state and the noncompliance state. When the production is on, the firm produces at a constant rate and earns profit continuously; if the production is in the noncompliance state, an environmental cost (that is higher than the profit) is incurred. The regulator's objective is to minimize the total social cost (including the opportunity cost of lost revenue when the production is off, the inspection cost, and the environmental cost) over the long run. The production state information at any time is known to the firm but not to the regulator. To obtain this information, the regulator can incur a fixed cost to perform an *inspection* or let the firm voluntarily disclose the violation; the firm can disclose this information at the beginning of the violation (*early disclosure*) or later (*late disclosure*). At time 0, the regulator announces the (average) time between two consecutive inspections and the penalty levels associated with inspection, early disclosure, and late disclosure. Under random inspections, the time between two successive inspections follows an exponential distribution. Under periodic inspections, the time between two successive inspections is a constant. The firm then accordingly decides if and when to disclose a violation after it occurs. The author derives the subgame perfect equilibrium under the random and periodic inspection policies. Under random inspections, the firm either discloses at the earliest time of violation (full disclosure) or never discloses (nondisclosure). The regulator designs the inspection policy to induce nondisclosure if the maximum penalty allowed is low and full disclosure otherwise. Under periodic inspections, the firm adopts a threshold policy and discloses a violation only if the remaining time till the next inspection is smaller than a threshold; the regulator decides the inspection interval and penalty to induce a preferred threshold. Due to the firm's strategic disclosure behavior, the inspection intensity and penalty can be complements instead of being substitutes. Also, when the regulator cannot charge a high penalty or the fixed cost of inspection is high, periodic inspections can lead to a lower social cost than that under random inspections.

Motivated by a setting similar to that in Kim (2015), Wang et al. (2016) examine how a regulator should design an inspection policy to minimize expected social cost, over the long run. Consider a continuous, infinite time horizon. An environmental hazard (caused by a firm) occurs at a random time following an exponential distribution. The occurrence of the hazard is the firm's private information. The hazard inflicts environmental damage, and the firm may incur a remediation cost to reduce this damage. To detect the hazard, the regulator can either incur a fixed cost to perform an (imperfect) inspection or let the firm voluntarily report the hazard. If the hazard is detected via an inspection, the maximum permissible penalty is imposed. If the hazard is voluntarily reported, the firm addresses it at a specified remediation level and receives a monetary reward. The regulator's policy, announced at time 0, specifies at any time the remediation level and the monetary reward upon disclosure, as well as an inspection policy under which inspections will take place; an inspection could occur at a specified time with a certain probability (impulsive inspection) or during a time interval with probability proportional to the length of the interval (intensive inspection). A discount factor applies to the firm and the regulator. At any given time, the firm decides whether or not to disclose the hazard, if any. The regulator inspects according to the specified probability, and the reward or penalty is realized if the hazard becomes known to the regulator. The paper develops a dynamic mechanism to minimize the regulator's social cost. The optimal policy is shown to have a simple cyclic structure when inspections are perfect. The regulator schedules inspections periodically, and, after each inspection, the mandated remediation level remains constant over time, while the reward decreases until the next inspection. If no hazard is detected at the next inspection, the reward level is reset to a high level, and the cycle repeats. When inspections are imperfect, the optimal policy is qualitatively similar.

Kalkanci and Plambeck (2018) study the consequence of a firm's attention to short-term capital market valuation on its suppliers' social and environmental impact and the effect of regulatory policies such as mandatory disclosures of known information regarding its suppliers. The authors analyze the following setting: A buying firm first observes the realization of its cost to learn a supplier's long-term (negative) impact on the firm and decides whether or not to learn this impact. If the firm chooses not to learn, the supplier's impact is unaffected. Otherwise, it observes the realized value of the impact and decides its (costly) effort aimed at reducing the impact. The firm then decides whether or not to disclose the impact to investors. The firm's learning cost and the cost to reduce the supplier's impact lead to a reduction in its short-term profit. In the long term, the firm incurs a cost corresponding to the supplier's impact. The investors observe the firm's short-term profit and the disclosed impact, if any, of the supplier, and value the firm based on the expected discounted long-term profit. Two interventions are shown to be equivalent in reducing the supplier's impact: aligning the firm's objective with the long-term profit of the firm and mandating disclosure of known information about the supplier. It is also shown that these interventions could backfire and lead to a worsening of the supplier's impact under certain conditions.

2.2 *Auditing in a Supply Network*

Often, multiple firms share a common supplier. In such a scenario, one firm's violation may affect other firms in the same market either positively because of demand spillover or negatively because of the damage in the reputation of the entire market. To manage social responsibility risk, firms may jointly audit the common supplier or share the results of an independent audit with other firms. Fang and Cho (2019) employ cooperative game theory to examine the tradeoff between *joint auditing* and *audit sharing*. The authors consider a supply chain where multiple firms share a common supplier. The sequence of events in the benchmark *individual auditing* case is as follows. The supplier decides her social responsibility effort, and each firm simultaneously decides its individual auditing effort, which corresponds to the probability of detecting the supplier's violation. If the supplier fails a firm's audit, the firm switches to a more expensive but socially responsible backup supplier. If not, the firm sources from the supplier. In either case, the firm earns a profit from the market from selling the product. If the supplier turns out to be socially irresponsible and a violation is identified in public, the firms that source from the supplier incur a loss, whereas those that do not source from the supplier may increase their profit due to demand spillover from the affected firms but may also incur a loss due to the negative externality on the entire market. The sequence of events under *joint auditing* is similar, except that firms that form a coalition jointly conduct the audit, and if any violation is identified, it affects all the firms in the coalition. The sequence of events under *audit sharing* is also similar – while the firms in a coalition still conduct individual audits; if a violation is detected by one firm, all the firms in the coalition switch to the backup supplier. If the negative externality is high, the firms have incentives to cooperate to improve social responsibility. If the positive externality is high, neither approach necessarily improves the supplier's social responsibility. Even if the firms do not form a coalition before conducting individual audits, social responsibility can still be improved under appropriate incentive systems that induce the firms who discover a violation to share the results of their audit.

Motivated by a context similar to that in Fang and Cho (2019), Caro et al. (2018) consider cooperation between two buyers in auditing one supplier using *joint auditing* or *audit sharing*. The paper employs noncooperative game theory to analyze the problem. Consider a supply chain with two firms that share a supplier. Under the *individual auditing* benchmark, the supplier decides her responsibility effort, which is the probability that her practice is compliant, while the two firms simultaneously decide their auditing efforts. If the supplier is compliant, she will pass an audit with probability 1. Otherwise, she fails an audit with a probability proportional to the auditing effort, no transaction occurs between the supplier and the buyer, and the supplier incurs a loss of goodwill. If the supplier passes the audit, the transaction between the buyer and the supplier occurs, but there is a chance that the noncompliance is detected in public; this results in a cost to the buyer and a penalty on the supplier. Under *joint auditing*, both firms agree on an auditing effort and share the auditing cost evenly, and the supplier incurs a penalty twice as much as that under individual auditing. Under *audit sharing*, after the individual audits are conducted, the firms share the outcomes with each other. It is shown that joint auditing results in a higher compliance from the supplier relative to that under individual auditing, a lower profit for the supplier, and a higher profit for the buyer. In addition, when the buyer's damage cost is high, the additional supply chain surplus under joint auditing allows the buyers to make a transfer payment that makes the supplier better off as well. Similar comparison results hold between audit sharing and individual auditing. The results are shown to be robust when the wholesale price is endogenously determined.

Most real-world supply networks consist of firms that procure from multiple suppliers and suppliers who serve multiple firms. This results in suppliers who differ in their *degree centrality*, i.e., the number of firms they supply to. With the auditing of a supplier being time-consuming and expensive, firms with limited resources then face the challenge of deciding which suppliers should be prioritized for auditing. Chen et al. (2019a) investigate whether firms should prioritize the auditing of suppliers with low or high centrality. Consider a representative W-shaped assembly supply network with two (competing) buying firms and three suppliers. Each buyer sources from two suppliers: one independent supplier who uniquely supplies to that buyer and one common supplier who supplies to both the buyers. The sequence of events in the *unilateral auditing* scenario is as follows. Each supplier is endowed with a probability with which her practices are socially responsible. The two buying firms simultaneously decide which one of their two suppliers should be audited and decide their (costly) auditing efforts. If the audited supplier turns out to be socially responsible, then she passes the audit, and no negative consequences occur. If the supplier is socially irresponsible, a firm may detect it via the audit with a probability that is proportional to the auditing effort invested. If the supplier's irresponsible practices are identified via the audit, then the supplier incurs a cost in undertaking corrective actions, and no further negative consequences occur. Otherwise, the supplier's social responsibility violations may be identified (with a probability) in public, which results in damages for both the buyer and the supplier. After the auditing is done and the associated costs and damages, if any, are realized, both the buying firms engage in quantity competition in the downstream market. Under the *joint auditing* scenario, the sequence is similar except that the buying firms jointly decide which two of the three suppliers to audit and the associated audit efforts and then share the auditing cost in a fair manner. The authors show that, under unilateral auditing, while auditing the common supplier is better for the aggregate profit of the buyers, competition drives them away from auditing that supplier. This inefficiency is corrected under joint auditing: the common supplier is always audited. The practice of joint auditing, however, may not necessarily be good for a social planner interested in minimizing the probability of damage from social irresponsibility. The authors identify conditions under which joint auditing improves social welfare.

Zhang et al. (2019) study a buyer's problem of auditing suppliers to ensure social responsibility compliance in a three-tier supply network with one buyer in tier 0, two suppliers in tier 1, and an arbitrary number of suppliers in tier 2. Each supplier may be either compliant or noncompliant with social responsibility standards. If the violation at a supplier is exposed in public, the buyer incurs economic damages. To mitigate such damages, the buyer may audit some of the suppliers at a cost to accurately identify their compliance status prior to production by the suppliers. Specifically, there are two phases in the model. In the *auditing* phase, the buyer decides which suppliers to audit sequentially, and if a supplier is detected to be noncompliant, whether the buyer should incur cost to rectify this supplier's practices or drop the supplier (and its exclusive suppliers, if any) from the supply network. After the auditing phase concludes, in the *production* phase, all the remaining suppliers engage in quantity competition within each tier. The authors show that there exists a unique production phase equilibrium. The authors also identify the buyer's optimal auditing strategy with two sub-phases: the buyer will audit and drop some suppliers, before either auditing and rectifying suppliers or proceeding directly to the production phase.

Firms often disclose the list of their suppliers. Such a disclosure may influence an NGO's perception of a supplier and impact the intensity of the NGO's scrutiny on the supplier. Motivated by this observation, Chen et al. (2019c) consider a buying firm's decision to reveal in public its list of suppliers. The authors consider a game among three players: a buyer, a supplier, and an NGO. There are two types of the supplier: high or low, with the former being more efficient in her compliance effort cost. The buyer first learns the type of the supplier and decides whether or not to reveal the supplier list. Then, the supplier decides her compliance effort, and the NGO simultaneously decides its auditing effort based on the updated belief about the supplier's type. If the supplier is detected as being noncompliant by the NGO, both the buyer and the supplier incur a cost, and the NGO gains utility – both these values depend on whether or not the supplier list is revealed. The analysis characterizes the buyer's optimal revelation strategy and the equilibrium effort levels of the supplier and the NGO. It is shown that revealing the supplier in public can help improve the supplier's responsibility effort and benefit the buyer. The buyer can also use the revelation strategy as a signaling mechanism to influence the NGO's perception of the supplier's compliance, resulting in higher or lower auditing effort in the buyer's favor. Kalkanci and Plambeck (2019) study how a firm can gain by committing to reveal the identities of its suppliers and/or the identity and violation of a terminated supplier, for a setting in which two firms share a common supplier. The paper characterizes the conditions under which the firm should commit to reveal its suppliers and shows that commitment to reveal the blacklist of suppliers with violations can help increase their responsibility efforts. These two commitment mechanisms are shown to be complementary when suppliers are uncertain about their social responsibility violations.

Supply chains are often multitiered in practice. There are documented incidents of tier-2 suppliers being identified of socially irresponsible practices in public and damaging the reputation of tier-1 suppliers and tier-0 buyers. Huang et al. (2017) consider how, in a three-tier supply chain, a tier-0 buyer should manage the responsibility risk of a tier-2 supplier. The authors consider a three-tier supply chain in which the buyer sources from a perfectly responsible tier-1 supplier, who in turn sources from a tier-2 supplier. The tier-2 supplier is subject to social responsibility risk, and the probability of a violation being detected is the detection probability multiplied by the probability of the supplier being socially irresponsible. All supply chain members can exert costly effort to reduce the probability of the tier-2 supplier being socially irresponsible; the efforts of the buyer and tier-1 supplier (which can be considered as their auditing efforts) are substitutes, and the efforts from the tier-2 supplier and those from the buyer and tier-1 suppliers are complements. The buyer, the tier-1 supplier, and the tier-2 supplier sequentially decide their efforts. Then, social irresponsibility risk is realized, and the members decide their orders sequentially. Effectively, if the tier-2 supplier is exposed as being socially irresponsible, all supply chain members are subject to their respective penalty costs. The authors show that the buyer's optimal strategy is one of the following extremes: only the buyer directly invests effort to work with the tier-2 supplier, only the tier-1 supplier invests effort to work with the tier-2 supplier, or neither the buyer nor the tier-1 supplier exerts any effort. It is also shown that strategies such as increased pressure (indicated by a higher detection probability) may backfire and result in a higher chance of responsibility violations.

3 Inspecting or Testing Suppliers' Products for Social Responsibility Violations

Motivated by the industrial incidents such as Mattel's recall of toys and the subsequent intensive inspection of its suppliers, Babich and Tang (2012) investigate the effectiveness of three mechanisms – a deferred payment mechanism, an inspection mechanism, and a combined mechanism (which combines deferred payment and inspection) – to manage a supplier's opportunistic product adulteration in a supply chain consisting of a buyer and a supplier. The authors consider a moral hazard problem faced by the buyer: the supplier has an inherent incentive to adulterate products due to lower production costs and the action of adulteration being unobservable by the buyer. However, if the supplier indeed adulterates and the buyer does not detect the adulteration, then customers discover the adulteration at an exponentially distributed random time, leading to a severe penalty on the buyer. To deter adulteration, three incentive mechanisms are considered. (1) Under the *deferred payment mechanism*, the buyer specifies an upfront payment and defers a second payment to a pre-specified time T contingent upon customers not detecting any adulteration by that time. (2) Under the *inspection mechanism*, the buyer specifies an upfront payment, together with a second payment contingent upon the product passing the buyer's inspection (if any) at time 0. (3) Under the *combined* mechanism, the buyer specifies an upfront payment, a second payment contingent on passing the buyer inspection (if any) at time 0, and a third payment at time T contingent upon customers not detecting any adulteration by that time. Under each of these mechanisms, after the buyer offers the contract, the supplier decides whether or not to engage in adulteration. Under mechanisms (2) and (3), the buyer also decides whether or not to perform a costly inspection to detect adulteration. The authors show that the combined mechanism is redundant, in the sense that either the deferred payment mechanism or the inspection mechanism alone can achieve the same outcome. Thus, the buyer can restrict attention to the simpler mechanisms. The paper then characterizes conditions under which the deferred payment mechanism is preferable to the inspection mechanism.

In a related paper, Rui and Lai (2015) endogenize the buyer's order quantity decision and study the interaction between this decision and the design of quality control mechanisms using either deferred payments and inspections or both. The model in Rui and Lai (2015) is similar to the one in Babich and Tang (2012), with the key difference being that the quantity decision of the buyer is endogenized. A random amount of time is associated with each unit as the discovery time of a defect in that unit; the discovery time of a defect in an order is the minimum of the discovery times over all units in that order. Thus, the larger the order quantity, the sooner will a defect be discovered. The buyer faces a downward sloping demand function. The deferred payment mechanism is similar to the one in Babich and Tang (2012), with the additional decision of the order quantity. The inspection mechanism is also similar, except that the buyer needs to decide the sample size to inspect and incurs an inspection cost that increases linearly in the sample size. The authors show that the optimal deferred payment mechanism may defer the entire payment or a partial amount, depending on the severity of the moral hazard (measured by the extent of the saving in the supplier's cost from adulteration) and the information accumulation rate (the instantaneous growth rate of the probability of detecting a defect). The inspection mechanism is also analyzed. The analysis shows that the deferred payment mechanism is preferred to the inspection mechanism when the market size is small or the profit margin is low. The paper also characterizes necessary conditions under which these two mechanisms are complementary.

While firms often inspect incoming parts from their suppliers for quality control, they may also use other instruments such as directly investing in supplier quality improvement or indirectly incentivizing a supplier's own effort in improving quality via appropriate contracts. Lee and Li (2018) study strategies for a buyer using direct investment, indirect incentives, and inspections, when the buyer's investment effort and the supplier's quality improvement effort act in either a complementary or a substitutable or an additive manner in improving quality. The authors consider a supply chain in which a buyer procures one unit of a product from a supplier. If the product turns out to be defective, the buyer incurs a loss of goodwill; otherwise, the buyer collects a fixed revenue from the market. The buyer and the supplier simultaneously decide their respective investment efforts in improving the probability of the supplier to deliver good-quality products; the cross-derivative of this probability with respect to the two efforts may be positive (complementary), negative (substitutable), or 0 (additive). In addition, the buyer can conduct an internal inspection of the incoming product and can choose to incur a cost to improve the accuracy of the inspection: the higher the accuracy, the more likely it is that a defect is detected. The buyer's payment to the supplier is contingent upon the inspection outcome: the buyer pays the wholesale price if the product passes the inspection and charges a penalty otherwise. When the efforts of the buyer and the supplier are strongly substitutable, the buyer's equilibrium strategy emphasizes direct investment effort; when the efforts are strongly complementary, the buyer's strategy emphasizes inspection; when the efforts are additive, the buyer's strategy emphasizes all three instruments: direct investment, indirect incentives, and inspection.

Quality issues in milk – arising primarily from deliberate adulteration by producers (typically, smallholder farmers) – have been extensively reported in several developing countries. Mu et al. (2014, 2016, 2019) examine incentive issues (for milk producers and individual milk collection stations or milk cooperatives) and operational considerations (in the collection of milk) that conspire to reduce the quality of milk via deliberate adulteration by producers. The authors provide recommendations that are both practical and solve the quality problem with minimal testing.

In the noncooperative setting, the milk supply chain consists of three main players: milk farmers produce milk and sell it to rural milk collection stations (typically independent intermediaries) that mix the milk and sell it to large urban dairies. These dairies then sell processed milk and other milk products to end consumers. Two types of tests by milk stations are common in practice: an *individual test* and a *mixed test*. In an individual test, a station tests the milk supplied by a specific farmer. In a mixed test, the station collects milk samples from many farmers, mixes them, and tests the mixed milk once. The mixed test reveals only the quality of the mixed milk and is not able to distinguish the qualities of the individual portions that were mixed. Milk stations are paid (by large milk dairies) based on the quality of the mixed milk and, therefore, have a natural incentive to sell high-quality milk. However, due to high testing costs and a large number of farmers, it becomes infeasible for a station to test each producer individually. Mixed testing can reduce testing cost for a station significantly, but it might create an incentive for the farmers to free ride, i.e., provide adulterated milk in the hope that other farmers supply high-quality milk. Furthermore, when milk stations compete for supply, testing can play a potentially socially damaging role: stations attract farmers by *lowering* their testing standards. To summarize, inducing farmers to supply high-quality milk with minimal testing – both individual and mixed – is a basic challenge for the stations.

Typically, milk producers are poor farmers with limited ability to transport milk daily over a significant distance. Mu et al. (2014) consider a setting where milk farmers are dedicated to one milk station, and study non-cooperative games between a station and a population of farmers. They examine the impact of several monetary incentives, such as rewarding high-quality farmers, penalizing low-quality farmers, and self-declaration on the quality of milk. One interesting insight is that providing rewards to farmers of high-quality milk can generate perverse incentives. They also examine the "sequence" of testing by analyzing two structures based on the ordering of individual testing and mixed testing of milk: *premixed individual testing* (first test a fraction of farmers individually and then (possibly) perform a mixed test on the remaining farmers) and *post-mixed individual testing* (first test the mixed milk from all farmers and then test a fraction of farmers individually). While premixed individual testing can be socially harmful, a combination of post-mixed individual testing and other incentives achieves a socially beneficial equilibrium outcome, namely that all farmers supply high-quality milk with only one mixed test and no further testing by the station.

Mu et al. (2016) analyzes the impact of competition among milk stations on the equilibrium quality of milk. Because of demand pressures and the relatively unorganized nature of the production sector, the supply of milk is usually not plentiful in many developing countries. Stations, therefore, compete with one another to acquire the milk from farmers. Since the wholesale price of milk (the price paid to the farmers) is often regulated, the major basis for differentiation between stations is testing: stations attract farmers by being more lenient on testing, thus generating an incentive for them to supply adulterated milk. While mixed testing (instead of individual testing) helps in lowering testing costs, it leaves the system vulnerable to opportunism: milk farmers are encouraged to free ride, and milk stations enter a testing war that drives down testing standards. The authors counter free riding by instituting a credible threat of individual testing (but interestingly, not its actual use in equilibrium). Two policies are proposed to address the harmful competition between stations: one involves mixed pricing, and another utilizes a bonus proportional to the testing standard differential between the stations. Both solutions achieve a socially beneficial equilibrium outcome. The analysis provides several insights with policy implications. One such implication that recurs is that the relaxation of a constraint by improving infrastructure does not necessarily have a beneficial effect in a competitive setting. Another example is the cost of testing: under competition, subsidizing the cost of testing could hurt milk quality. Thus, policy interventions to improve outcomes in milk supply chains have to be handled with care or they could do more harm than good.

Using milk cooperatives as an iconic example, Mu et al. (2019) study smallholder agricultural cooperatives from the perspective of a planner who wishes to achieve the simultaneous goals of quantity efficiency (formation of a large, stable cooperative), quality efficiency (production of high-quality output), and minimal testing. Smallholder agricultural cooperatives enable individual farmers to pool their individual outputs for better pricing, storage, marketing, and other such activities needed to bring the commodities to the market. However, such agricultural cooperatives also face several operational challenges. Given the small production amounts from individual members, it becomes necessary for the output from a large number of farmers to be mixed prior to marketing the produce. This generates incentives for producers to free ride on the quality of others. Thus, as the size of a smallholder cooperative increases, an individual farmer's incentive to produce low-quality output also increases. To achieve the virtues of a large-sized cooperative, one could pay in terms of low quality or in terms of costly testing. The authors use cooperative game theory to analyze the following setting: a set of producers (farmers) first form coalitions and then choose their individual qualities. Each coalition mixes the output from all the farmers in that coalition and then sells it to a downstream firm, which then tests the mixed output from each coalition and offers a payment based on the quality and quantity of the mixed output. To achieve the goal of forming a stable smallholder cooperative of a large size that produces high-quality output and yet tests minimally, the authors show that the basic challenge is that of countering an endogenous value function associated with a coalition of producers. This value function emerges from the joint interaction of three forces: (1) an individual producer's payoff-maximizing behavior, (2) the testing policies employed by the cooperative, and (3) the manner in which the value earned by a coalition is shared among the producers (allocation rule). A novel allocation rule – which exploits individual incentives to guide the collective behavior of the producers and thereby the value-function endogeneity – is proposed that achieves the planner's goals in the presence of these forces. Several modifications to this allocation rule are made to address the goals of practicality, namely, the presence of low-income producers, unintended variation in the quality of a producer's output, and the desire to keep the cooperative solvent in the short run.

Economically motivated adulteration has been observed at farms and can either be *preemptive* (adulteration takes place before the quality uncertainty resolves), e.g., when antibiotics are overused, or *reactive* (adulteration takes place after the quality uncertainty resolves), e.g., addition of melamine to milk to increase its perceived protein content. Motivated by this observation, Levi et al. (2020) study the equilibrium adulteration behavior of farms and analyze how quality uncertainty, supply chain dispersion, traceability, and testing sensitivity affect this behavior. The authors consider a manufacturer who procures the total supply chain output (in equal amount) from multiple homogeneous farms. The quality of a unit of the product from each farm is uncertain ex ante and follows a two-point distribution, and the total number of low-quality units of the product from each farm follows a binomial distribution. The sequence of events under preemptive adulteration is as follows. (1) Each farm simultaneously decides the amount of adulterants to add to reduce the probability of low-quality output. (2) Then, the uncertain quality of the output is realized at each farm. (3) The manufacturer purchases from each farm and pays based on the average quality of its output, stores a sample of the output from a subset of farms, and, with a certain testing accuracy, tests the aggregate output from all farms for adulteration. If the aggregate output is tested positive for adulteration, then each of the stored samples is tested, and if a farm is found guilty of engaging in adulteration, a penalty is imposed. Under reactive adulteration, step (3) above remains the same, and the first two steps are revised as follows. (1) The uncertain quality of the output is realized at each farm and is private information of the farm. (2) Each farm simultaneously decides whether or not to adulterate all the realized low-quality units to create (adulterated) high-quality ones. Supply chain dispersion is measured using the total number of farms from which the output is procured from, and traceability with the number of samples stored for testing later if needed. Under perfect testing, one can accurately detect if the residual amount of adulterant exceeds the maximum permissible limit. Under imperfect testing, the detection probability of the adulterant increases linearly in the relative amount of the adulterant in the total output. The authors derive the equilibrium adulteration behavior of the farms under both preemptive and reactive adulteration and show that the risk of adulteration can be affected by supply chain dispersion, traceability, and testing sensitivity. Also, investing in quality by reducing the probability of low-quality output without enhancing testing capability may further increase adulteration risk.

Firms have been observed to test the compliance of competitors' products in order to block the sale of noncompliant competing products. Motivated by this observation, Plambeck and Taylor (2019) study a game among firms that exert effort to comply with a standard and test competitors' products for violations. Consider multiple firms that compete in a fixed-size market. Each firm simultaneously invests a costly compliance effort and produces a fixed quantity of a product, whose probability of compliance is proportional to the compliance effort. Each firm incurs a linear cost for the effort it invests in testing competitors' products and so does a regulator (who can test the products of all the firms) whose effort is a parameter. If a product is noncompliant, it is detected with a probability that increases in the testing effort of the firms and the regulator. A firm is able to bring its product to the market only if it is not detected as being noncompliant; in that case, the market price is derived from a standard consumer utility model. The equilibrium compliance effort and the testing effort are derived. It is shown that testing by the regulator crowds out testing by competitors and can reduce the compliance efforts of the firms. This observation, combined with the fact that firms can test competitors' products at a lower cost, suggests that testing by competitors can improve social welfare. The paper also derives conditions under which competitor testing is more effective to enforce a product standard. The results are robust to endogenous quantity and quality decisions of the firms and consumers' beliefs about the compliance of the products in the market.

4 Concluding Remarks

Globalization and improved societal awareness of responsible and sustainable business practices are motivating firms to pay greater attention to the social and environmental impact of their own operations and policies as well as those of their supply chain partners. To this end, the increasing complexity of supply networks creates both challenges and opportunities for the effective use of informational tools such as auditing, inspections, and testing, in assessing compliance with socially responsible actions. In this chapter, we summarized the main insights from the operations management literature on the auditing of suppliers for socially responsible practices and the inspection or testing of products for harmful ingredients and opportunistic adulteration.

There are a variety of fruitful opportunities in this stream of literature. To provide just one example, a topic that has not received much attention yet is the design of cooperative strategies among stakeholders in different tiers of a supply chain to collectively ensure socially responsible actions across the supply chain. While there has been some recent work that examines cooperation among firms to jointly audit their common suppliers, we believe much more can be done. In a multitier network, suppliers in one tier of the network are buyers in the next (upstream) tier. Thus, the utilities of different players from actions such as auditing, inspections, and testing become interconnected in a complex manner. Consequently, the sharing of costs in a fair manner to incentivize cooperation across tiers becomes challenging. We refer the reader to Lee and Tang (2018) for a discussion of other recent developments and research opportunities in the domain of socially responsible operations.

References

Babich V, Tang CS (2012) Managing opportunistic supplier product adulteration: Deferred payments, inspection, and combined mechanisms. Manuf Serv Oper Manag 14(2):301–314

Caro F, Chintapalli P, Rajaram K, Tang CS (2018) Improving supplier compliance through joint and shared audits with collective penalty. Manuf Serv Oper Manag 20(2):363–380

Chen L, Lee HL (2017) Sourcing under supplier responsibility risk: the effects of certification, audit, and contingency payment. Manag Sci 63(9):2795–2812

Chen J, Qi A, Dawande M (2019a) Supplier centrality and auditing priority in socially responsible supply chains. Manuf Serv Oper Manag Forthcoming

Chen L, Yao S, Zhu K (2019b) Responsible sourcing under supplier-auditor collusion. Manuf Serv Oper Manag Forthcoming

Chen S, Zhang Q, Zhou YP (2019c) Impact of supply chain transparency on sustainability under ngo scrutiny. Production Oper Manag 28(12):3002–3022

Cho SH, Fang X, Tayur SR, Xu Y (2018) Combating child labor: incentives and information transparency in global supply chains. Manuf Serv Oper Manag Forthcoming

Fang X, Cho SH (2019) Cooperative approaches to managing social responsibility in supply chains: joint auditing and information sharing. Manuf Serv Oper Manag Forthcoming

Huang L, Song JSJ, Swinney R (2017) Managing social responsibility in multitier supply chains. Working paper

Kalkanci B, Plambeck EL (2018) Managing supplier social & environmental impacts with voluntary vs. mandatory disclosure to investors. Manag Sci Forthcoming
Kalkanci B, Plambeck EL (2019) Reveal the supplier list? A trade-off in capacity vs. responsibility. Manuf Serv Oper Manag Forthcoming
Kim S (2015) Time to come clean? Disclosure and inspection policies for green production. Oper Res 63(1):1–20
Lee H, Li C (2018) Supplier quality management: investment, inspection, and incentives. Prod Oper Manag 27(2):304–322
Lee HL, Tang CS (2018) Socially and environmentally responsible value chain innovations: new operations management research opportunities. Manag Sci 64(3):983–996
Levi R, Singhvi S, Zheng Y (2020) Economically motivated adulteration in farming supply chains. Manag Sci 66(1):209–226
Mu L, Dawande M, Mookerjee V (2014) Improving the milk supply chain in developing countries: analysis, insights, and recommendations. Prod Oper Manag 23(7):1098–1112
Mu L, Dawande M, Geng X, Mookerjee V (2016) Milking the quality test: improving the milk supply chain under competing collection intermediaries. Manag Sci 62(5):1259–1277
Mu L, Dawande M, Mookerjee V (2019) Shaping the values of a milk cooperative: theoretical and practical considerations. Prod Oper Manag 28(9):2259–2278
Plambeck EL, Taylor TA (2016) Supplier evasion of a buyer's audit: implications for motivating supplier social and environmental responsibility. Manuf Serv Oper Manag 18(2):184–197
Plambeck EL, Taylor TA (2019) Testing by competitors in enforcement of product standards. Manag Sci 65(4):1735–1751
Rui H, Lai G (2015) Sourcing with deferred payment and inspection under supplier product adulteration risk. Prod Oper Manag 24(6):934–946
Wang S, Sun P, de Véricourt F (2016) Inducing environmental disclosures: a dynamic mechanism design approach. Oper Res 64(2):371–389
Zhang H, Aydin G, Parker RP (2019) Social responsibility auditing in supply chain networks. Working paper

Index

J. M. Swaminathan, V. Deshpande (eds.), *Responsible Business Operations*, Springer Series in Supply Chain Management 10,
https://doi.org/10.1007/978-3-030-51957-5

The manufacturer's authorised representative in the EU is Springer Nature Customer Service Centre GmbH, Europaplatz 3, 69115 Heidelberg, Germany. If you have any concerns regarding our products, please contact ProductSafety@springernature.com

Printed and bound by CPI Group (UK) Ltd, Croydon, CR0 4YY
30/09/2026
02225693-0005